American Vistas

1877 to the Present

Seventh Edition

Edited by

LEONARD DINNERSTEIN

and

KENNETH T. JACKSON

New York   Oxford

OXFORD UNIVERSITY PRESS

1995

Oxford University Press

Oxford   New York   Toronto
Delhi   Bombay   Calcutta   Madras   Karachi
Kuala Lumpur   Singapore   Hong Kong   Tokyo
Nairobi   Dar es Salaam   Cape Town
Melbourne   Auckland   Madrid

and associated companies in
Berlin   Ibadan

Published by Oxford University Press, Inc.,
200 Madison Avenue, New York, New York 10016

Oxford is a registered trademark of Oxford University Press

Library of Congress Cataloging-in-Publication Data
American vistas / edited by Leonard Dinnerstein
and Kenneth T. Jackson.—7th ed.
p. cm.   Includes bibliographical references
Contents: [v. 1.] 1607–1877—[v. 2.] 1877 to present.
ISBN 0-19-508783-6 (v. 1)—ISBN 0-19-508784-4 (v. 2)
1. United States—History.   I. Dinnerstein, Leonard.
II. Jackson, Kenneth T.
E178.6.A426   1995
973-dc20   94-7567

9 8 7 6 5 4 3 2 1

Printed in the United States of America
on acid-free paper

AMERICAN VISTAS
1877 to the Present

For Barbara Jackson
and
To the bright, enduring memory of our son,
Kenneth Gordon Jackson III
(1968–1984)

O my son Absalom,
my son, my son Absalom!
would God I had died for thee

2 Samuel 18

PREFACE

It is now more than two decades since we first embarked on our project of bringing together a series of historical essays that combined interest with readability and which could be used in conjunction with a survey text or a wide variety of other books. We have been gratified by the initial reader response as well as the enthusiasm with which our subsequent editions were received. The comments that we have read indicate that there are a large number of instructors who find the combination of traditional and off-beat essays on the American past suitable to their own teaching styles. We are particularly pleased that *American Vistas* has been used by a wide diversity of people in every region of the country as well as in Canada and overseas. It reaffirms our belief that the American past can be both enlightening and instructive to people who are fascinated with the development of societies.

For this revision we have made a searching reexamination of the contents and have kept only those essays we believe have been particularly successful in the past. Letters from users and comments from other colleagues and scholars clearly indicated which pieces were most suitable for college classes. We have tried to follow this advice whenever possible. Many of our selections fit so well into the teaching patterns of a large number of introductory courses that it seemed an injustice to students and teachers alike to eliminate them. On the other hand, more recent scholarship and the changing emphasis of societal and classroom interests have resulted in new selections on the Army's role in the massacre of the Chinese in Wyoming in 1886, Theodore Roosevelt, working women in Baltimore during the Progressive Era, Henry Ford and anti-Semitism, WACs in World War II, Harry Truman, and Sam Walton, founder of Wal-Mart stores.

Several former teaching assistants at the University of Arizona made suggestions about inclusions and incisions. For their valuable insights we would like to thank Allen Broussard, Susan Hill, John Krueckeberg, Renee Obrecht Como, and Phyllis Smith.

Tucson   L. D.
New York   K. T. J.
November, 1993

CONTENTS

AMERICAN VISTAS
1877 to the Present

I

Trouble in Mind: The Bicentennial and the Afro-American Experience

LEON F. LITWACK

● *The Bicentennial of the adoption of the Constitution of the United States was an occasion for great celebration and self-congratulation across the land. Of course, Americans have long had other documents and words of which they could be inordinately proud—the Declaration of Independence, the Gettysburg Address, and the poem on the Statue of Liberty, among them—but nothing could quite match the Constitution. More than anything else, this brief document defines the United States, and it proudly proclaims the principles for which the republic stands: freedom of religion, freedom of assembly, freedom of speech.*

African-Americans, however, do not need to be reminded that the nation's ideals have been easier to proclaim than to realize. For centuries, people of color have endured substandard housing, inferior schools, and discriminatory employment practices, even as they have watched more recent, and white, immigrant groups find opportunities closed to them. Is it surprising then, as Professor Leon F. Litwack of the University of California at Berkeley points out in the following essay, that many African-Americans had mixed feelings during the bicentennial of the Constitution? Is it time, as he suggests, that we honor those who were losers in their own day, but whose struggle for civil rights gave meaning to the words of the Constitution?

When Americans commemorated the one hundredth birthday of the Constitution, in 1887, they staged appropriate celebrations, the most

Leon F. Litwack, "Trouble in Mind: The Bicentennial and the Afro-American Experience," *Journal of American History*, 74 (September 1987), 315–37. Reprinted by permission.

spectacular of them in Philadelphia. Amid a sea of flags and patriotic banners, a Civic and Industrial Procession highlighted American progress over the past century. The planners did not overlook black America. Three floats formed "The Colored People's Display." The first float, labeled 1787, showed a plantation during slavery, featuring a small Negro cabin surrounded by growing cotton. The second float, labeled 1887, displayed a school scene, with sixty-five black pupils at their studies under the direction of four teachers. Symbolic of the progress of the race, banners proclaimed Emancipation, Enfranchisement, Full Political Rights and Privileges, and God Bless 1887. The third float, labeled Industry, depicted blacks at a variety of trades.

This was less than the parade's planners had envisioned. The display had been hastily organized, largely because of the black community's indifference. "Early in my work I appealed to its most distinguished representatives," reported the chief marshal. This was an opportunity, he told them, to assemble "one of the most striking contrastive exhibits of the demonstration," illustrating "the marvelous advance of the race from bondage to freedom, from ignorance to intelligence, from poverty to comfort, with all the blessings coming from political freedom, education, and equality under the law." The response was less than overwhelming. For the float depicting the slave cabin, in fact, the organizers could find no blacks, "even with the offer of a liberal pecuniary reward," willing to appear in the role of slaves.

The indifference of black leaders reflected the indifference of most blacks to the centennial. It was perceived as a white people's affair. The urgent need of blacks in 1887 was not to mythologize the Constitution, but to preserve and protect its most recent amendments. For the vast majority of black people, the six million who resided in the South, the principles proclaimed by the centennial organizers—"political freedom, education, and equality under the law"—had become almost meaningless. Only four years earlier, a northern, Republican-dominated Supreme Court had declared unconstitutional the Civil Rights Act of 1875, leaving to local option what, if any, rights black people might exercise. The apathetic response of most Americans to the decision suggested to a northern editor that "the extravagant expectations...of the war have died out." The decision, in Frederick

Douglass's view, contained the makings of a "black Ireland in America."

For much of the previous century, black leaders had debated the meaning of the Constitution for their people. It had been the genius of the Founding Fathers to sanction, protect, and reinforce the enslavement of black men and women in the same document that promised to "establish justice, insure domestic tranquillity, provide for the common defense, promote the general welfare, and secure the blessings of liberty" to Americans. It had been the genius of the founders to build safeguards for slavery into the Constitution without even mentioning slavery by name. The legitimization of slavery was the price of the new federal union, and the Founding Fathers shared the racial values and attitudes of most Americans, among them the assumption that blacks were culturally and genetically unsuited for democracy. In none of the ratifying conventions did the protection afforded slavery in the Constitution become a major issue.

The Constitution remained for the first seventy-eight years of its life a document protective of racial enslavement and discrimination. When Chief Justice Roger B. Taney declared in 1857 in *Dred Scott v. Sandford* that at the time of the Constitutional Convention blacks "had no rights which the white man was bound to respect," his statement was less a sign of moral callousness than an important historical truth; the decision confirmed both state and federal practices. It required years of agitation and a stalemate in a bloody civil war to bring national leaders to consider extending the Constitution to black Americans. It required the efforts of the enslaved themselves—seeking refuge behind the Union lines, claiming their freedom, enlisting in the federal army, undermining the slavocracy in small and large ways—and the blindness, greed, and self-delusion of the postwar South to bring black Americans within the meaning of the Constitution. It would require still another century of long, bitter, and violent struggle, waged in the streets, the courts, and the jails, often in defiance of law enforcement, before black people could fully realize the constitutional protections granted them one hundred years earlier.

The bicentennial of the Constitution has been proclaimed a celebration of two hundred years of impartial government and the rule of law, two hundred years of liberty and freedom. The Constitution, declared Chief Justice Warren E. Burger, gave Americans "a new kind of freedom" and people everywhere hope for a better life. "In this 200th anniversary year of our Constitution," President Ronald Reagan told Congress, "you and I stand on the shoulders of giants, men whose words and deeds put wind in the sails of freedom." No document in history, affirmed Strom Thurmond, a member of the federal bicentennial commission, did more "to give people freedom and opportunity." If those are the grounds for commemorating the anniversary of the Constitution, they reveal a perverse and limited reading of the American past. It is to read American history without the presence of black men and women, to define them out of American identity, to exclude a people who enjoyed neither liberty, impartial government, nor the equal protection of the law. It is to read out of American history a long legacy of slavery and segregation. The same "wind in the sails of freedom" perceived by President Reagan condemned some seven hundred thousand black men and women to nearly three-quarters of a century of unfreedom. The same nation that boasted of its dedication to the proposition that "all men are created equal" was based on the most enormous of human inequalities.

The history of black America is not the history of a chosen people conquering the wilderness, extending democratic institutions, and progressing toward a more perfect union. The history of black America is a history of betrayed expectations, a history which has more often than not contradicted the democratic creed and the success ethic. It is the history of individual and collective efforts by black men and women to build a community and a culture that could sustain them in a society that refused to acknowledge their humanity. It is the paradoxical history of a people denied the rights and opportunities of American citizens yet required to demonstrate the same quality of patriotism as their more privileged white brethren. It has afforded black Americans for more than two hundred years a very different perspective on this country and its most revered traditions and celebrations. "The rich inheritance of justice, liberty, prosperity and independence, bequeathed by your fathers," Frederick Douglass told a white audience on July 5, 1852, "is shared by you, not by me. The sunlight that brought light and healing to you, has brought stripes and death to me. This Fourth of July is *yours,* not *mine. You* may rejoice, *I* must mourn."

The significance of race in the American past can scarcely be exaggerated. Those who seek to diminish its critical role invariably dismiss too much of history—the depth, the persistence, the pervasiveness, the centrality of race in American society, the countless ways in which racism has embedded itself in the culture, how it adapts to changes in laws and public attitudes, assuming different guises as the occasion demands. No wonder the history of attempts to substitute class consciousness for race consciousness in this nation is largely a history of futility, failure, and betrayal. For black Americans, there has been no exclusively economic way out. Hence that old folk wisdom, "Even after a revolution the country will be full of crackers."

The history of black America is inseparable from the experience of the United States. For two centuries Afro-Americans, by their sheer presence, have furnished the severest test of the quality and depth of America's loyalty to its professed ideals and values; they have been, as Ralph Ellison suggests, keepers of "the nation's sense of democratic achievement, and the human scale by which would be measured its painfully slow advance toward true equality." No matter how loudly Americans proclaimed themselves a "city on the hill," no matter how fervently they embraced the idea that "all men . . . are endowed by their Creator with certain unalienable rights," no matter how frequently they paraded their virtues before the world, no matter how often a Woodrow Wilson proclaimed the flag of the United States to be the flag of humanity, none of them could escape a history that revealed profound contradictions between profession and practice, ideals and realities. Some one hundred years after the Constitutional Convention, Alexander Crummell reminded the American people that the democratic experiment was still being tested. It is not the Negro who is on trial, he insisted. "It is the nation which is on trial. The Negro is only the touch-stone. By this black man she [the nation] stands or falls. If the black man cannot be free in this land . . . neither can the white man."

Since the American Revolution, black spokesmen had proclaimed their identity as Americans. The affirmation grew more insistent as many of the intellectual and political heirs of the Founding Fathers embraced deportation and colonization as a solution to the race problem. In response, black spokesmen stressed their American loyalties and claimed the Declaration of Independence and the Constitution as the heritage of all Americans, black and white. Like the revolutionary generation, blacks asserted their readiness to resist tyranny, to contend for the same rights to life, liberty, and property. In a Richmond, Virginia, courtroom, an accused black insurrectionist testified, "I have nothing more to offer than what General Washington would have had to offer, had he been taken by the British and put to trial by them. I have adventured my life in endeavouring to obtain the liberty of my countrymen, and am a willing sacrifice in their cause." For his daring and violent strike for independence and freedom for his people, Nat Turner initially selected the fifty-fifth anniversary of American independence and freedom, the Fourth of July 1831. When Martin R. Delany threatened in the 1850s to kill anyone who entered his house in search of a fugitive slave, he made clear his inspiration, "All the ideas I have of liberty and independence I obtained from reading the History of the Revolutionary Fathers." And when James Lynch in 1865 addressed a Fourth of July rally in Augusta, Georgia—the first such celebration in a free Georgia—he identified his newly freed people with the glorious achievements of the American Revolution and the manifest destiny of the United States "to elevate humanity."

That is why Reconstruction—which attempted to define the meaning of freedom in American society—held such promise for black Americans, and why it posed such a challenge to this nation, a critical test of America's commitment to the democratic ideal. The early years of freedom injected into black lives the excitement of anticipation. The sight of black occupation troops, the opening of schools and churches, the reunion of families, the bargaining sessions with former masters over compensation and conditions of labor, the participation in democratic politics as voters and officeholders—this had to be a heady experience. There was bold talk of new ways of living and working, of opportunities to better themselves in this world. The first generation born outside the discipline of slavery found reasons to be optimistic about their chances, to think they could aspire to the same goals, the same possessions and careers, the same prospects as white youths.

The optimism proved short lived; expectations were quickly disappointed, if not betrayed. Whatever aspirations black youths held, most learned to curb them as they were initiated into the racial mores of the society. Generations of black youths shared a common training and education based on their early racial experiences and perceptions. For most of them, race consciousness came early, as it did for those who experienced the tension, intimidation, and violence that marked white responses to Radical Reconstruction. In the community in North Carolina in which Pauline Fitzgerald grew up in the 1870s, the talk was of Klan terrorists, floggings, barn burnings, and hangings. T. Thomas Fortune remembered the threats to his parents and to their home in Marianna, Florida, where his father's prominence as a Republican legislator earned him the reputation of a "dangerous nigger." Oliver Bell learned as a child in Alabama the varied meanings of a "dangerous nigger": Klansmen harassed his father and murdered his two uncles, not because they were Republican activists, but because "dey wuz makin' money" and the Klan leader "didn't 'low de niggers ter have nuthin'."

The terror visited on black homes and families impressed on all blacks their powerlessness and vulnerability. Some seventy years later, Millie Bates still could not put out of her mind the day a white mob murdered her neighbor. "It still makes de shivvers run down my spine and here I is ole and you all a settin' around wid me and two mo' wars done gone since dat awful time." They hanged him to a persimmon tree, she recalled, they refused to permit his family to cut him down, and the body remained there until it fell to pieces. "Dem days wuz wors'n de war. Yes Lawd, dey wuz worse'n any war I is ebber heard of." Equally vivid memories of a walk into the nearby woods long remained with Susan Smith, ten years old when freedom came.

> I see a man hangin'...when I was pickin' blackberries. His tongue was hangin' out. De buzzards fly down on his shoulder. When de breeze blow, it set him to swingin' and de buzzards fly off. I go and tell de people. Dey come and tek him down and bury him. He a fine young cullud man. I don' know why dey done it. De folks miss him but dey didn't know what become of him.

The language and demeanor of blacks defined their "place" in society, and white people were sensitive, especially after emancipation, to any deviation from expectations, to any semblance of individuality. Early in their lives, then, blacks came to appreciate the narrow boundaries of their world, the limited options, the need to learn the appropriate social usages, to weigh carefully every word, gesture, and movement. Richard Wright, who spent his childhood in Mississippi, Tennessee, and Arkansas in the early twentieth century, remembered most vividly the fear of making the wrong move, the "sustained expectation of violence" that forced him to curb his impulses, speech, manner, and expression. "Tension would set in at the mere mention of whites and a vast complex of emotions, involving the whole of my personality, would be aroused.... In my dealing with whites I was conscious of the entirety of my relations with them, and they were conscious only of what was happening at a given moment." Personal security lay in repressing any impulses toward individuality or assertiveness in the presence of whites. A black woman born into an impoverished family in Durham, North Carolina, remembered a childhood in which she was admonished to contain her feelings. "My problem started when I began to comment on what I saw. I insisted on being accurate. But the world I was born into didn't want that. Indeed, its very survival depended on not knowing, not seeing—and, certainly, not saying anything at all about what it was really like."

Even as black families imparted lessons in survival, they handed down from generation to generation a culture and a history. No child's education was complete without hearing family stories and anecdotes of life under slavery, not only tales of brutality but also stories of resistance, deception, and trickery, of outwitting and outtalking their owners, standing up to the whites, finding ways to protect their family and friends. "My story goes a long way back," wrote Sidney Bechet, who was born in New Orleans at the turn of the century. "It goes further back than I had anything to do with.... the stories my father gave down to me.... are all I know about some of the things bringing me to where I am."

For many young blacks, hearing the stories proved to be traumatic, unforgettable experiences, for the narrator as for the listener, evoking feelings of both anger and compassion. The tales of brutality Mary Church Terrell heard from her grandmother affected both of them deeply. "She was rarely able to finish what she began. I tried to keep the tears back and the sobs suppressed, so that Grandmother would carry the story to the bitter end, but I seldom succeeded." Kathryn L. Morgan's great-grandmother, Caddy, showed her children and grandchildren the marks that the whip had left on her back. "They were thumb deep, but she didn't want them to forget what slavery was like." It was as a young girl in Baltimore in the early 1920s, entrusted with the care of her great-grandmother, a former Virginia slave, that Billie Holiday came to learn of her slave past. "We used to talk about life.

And she used to tell me how it felt to be a slave, to be owned body and soul by a white man who was the father of her children."

The folk memories, the family histories helped to shape blacks' perceptions of the white world, and of themselves. Mamie Garvin Fields, born in Charleston in 1888, contrasted the lessons she learned in the public school with those taught by cousin Lala in the informal neighborhood school in the rear of the house. In the public school, she was drilled by a white teacher in "the Rebel tradition," and learned to sing "Dixie" in Negro dialect, along with Stephen Foster favorites. "This was what they wanted to instill in us." But from cousin Lala, she learned "things that you didn't get at public school.... I learned about slavery as our relatives had experienced it and what it meant.... She taught us how strong our ancestors back in slavery were and what fine people they were. I guess today people would say she was teaching us 'black history.'" Benjamin E. Mays, born in rural South Carolina in 1894, the son of slaves, learned enough of the history of his people at home to remember that his earliest heroes were black. "Booker T. Washington meant more to me than George Washington; Frederick Douglass was more of a hero than William Lloyd Garrison; Dunbar inspired me more than Longfellow."

Statistics of black education in the late nineteenth century describe a dreary ending to the commitment to equal public education made during Reconstruction. W. E. B. Du Bois did not exaggerate when he called it "enforced ignorance." Nor did Booker T. Washington, in comparing appropriations for white and black schools, when he thought it too great a compliment to the Negro to suppose he could learn seven times as easily as the white child. By the turn of the century no one pretended to take seriously the Supreme Court order commanding separate but equal schools, and by the time Pauli Murray reached public school in North Carolina around World War I separate and unequal education was already taking a heavy toll. "It was never the hardship which hurt so much," she recalled, "as the contrast between what we had and what the white children had.... Our seedy run-down school told us that if we had any place at all in the scheme of things it was a separate place, marked off, proscribed and unwanted by the white people." The separate and inferior place assigned black pupils prepared them for the adult world they would soon enter.

What the black child learned in school was geared to a moral and productive life. Grammars, spellers, and primers inculcated in their readers the Protestant work ethic and the need to work hard and to be model employees. America was defined as a democracy of equal opportunity, in which success came ultimately to the hard-working, the sober, the honest, and the educated, to those who served their employers faithfully, practiced economy, respected property and the sanctity of contract, cultivated habits of thrift, cleanliness, and temperance, and led moral, virtuous, Christian lives. Self-improvement manuals circulating in the black community taught the same moral lessons.

The experience of black Americans, however, belied the civics and moral lessons taught by teachers, politicians, preachers, and editors. Faithful adherence to the work ethic brought most of them nothing. No matter how hard they labored, no matter how much trust they put in the free labor ideology and in abstract notions of democracy and equality, no matter how fervently they prayed, the chances for making it were less than encouraging, the basic rules did not change.

> Our father, who is in heaven,
> White man owe me eleven and pay me seven,
> Thy kingdom come, thy will be done,
> And if I hadn't took that, I wouldn't had none.

A native Mississippian described the people with whom he grew up as "hard-working, God-fearing, church-going folk who prayed trustingly to an Almighty God. Six days a week most of them toiled like beasts of burden—but to little avail. Their lives did not change materially; they simply got older, grew weary, took sick and died."

Even if blacks managed to accumulate some savings and used the savings to purchase land, they needed to exert as much resourcefulness to retain the land as they had expended to acquire it. "Soon as I got to where I could have somethin for sure and was makin somethin of myself," remembered Ned Cobb, an Alabama sharecropper born in 1885, "then they commenced a runnin at me." The fears of black success and independence that provoked much of the violence of Reconstruction proved equally devastating when blacks posed no political threat. "The more a Negro owned," Mays recalled, "the more humble he had to act in order to keep in the good graces of the white people."

The historical record is replete with examples of violence aimed at successful blacks, those suspected of having saved their earnings, those who had just made a crop, those determined to improve themselves. Fannie Lou Hamer, born in 1917 to a Mississippi sharecropper family, recalled how her father kept cropping until he saved enough to purchase some wagons, plow tools, and mules. But whites came to his lot and poisoned the mules. "It killed everything we had.... The poison knocked us right back down flat. We never did get back up again. That white man did it just because we were getting somewhere. White people never like to see Negroes get a little success." The arguments of black spokesmen who still believed in the success ethic took on a desperate quality by the late nineteenth century. The racial violence, the lynchings, Douglas observed in 1893, may actually be "a favorable symptom. It is proof that the Negro is not standing still...that he is making progress."

Although discouraged from aspiring to the same rights as white Americans, blacks were asked to fight in wars to defend those rights. For many whites, however, the sight of a uniformed black man was as intolerable as the sight of a successful or educated black man—anything that suggested a black in a position of authority or trying to "act like a white man." No wonder mobs singled out for assault blacks returning from the Spanish-American War, World War I, and World War II. To strip them of their uniforms and decorations was to strip them of any illusions about the land to which they returned and the rights to which they were entitled. After observing several such incidents, Ned Cobb could only shake his head at the depth of white hypocrisy.

> I've had white people tell me, "This is a white man's country, white man's country." They don't sing that to the colored man when it comes to war. Then it's all *our* country, go fight for the country. Go over there and risk his life for the country and come back, he ain't a bit more thought of than he was before he left.

Two wars waged by the United States to make the world safe for democracy ended with struggles waged by black people to make the United States safe for themselves.

If generations of blacks came to perceive, as did Cobb, that white folks "hated to see niggers livin like people," they also came to learn that neither accommodation nor property assured them their civil rights, or even their lives. The quality of the racial violence that gripped the South between the 1880s and World War I made it distinctive. The victims more often than not were the sons and daughters of the former slaves, those, said a white leader, who had been "born into the false teachings of Reconstruction." If the violence impressed on blacks their vulnerability, it also exposed the moral character of the "superior race." "The lynch mob came," a Mississippi woman remembered. "I ain't ever heard of no one white man going to get a Negro. They're the most cowardly people I ever heard of."

To count the lynchings and burnings, to detail the savagery, the methodical torture prolonged for the benefit of the spectators, to dwell on the voyeuristic sadism that characterized these ritual murders and blood rites in the name of enforcing deference and submission is to underscore the degree to which many whites by the late nineteenth century had come to think of black men and women as less than human. That made it easier to violate black rights and bodies and to ignore the cries of the victims. To dismiss the atrocities as the work of crazed fiends or the lower orders of white society is to miss how terrifyingly normal these people were, the class and racial solidarity they displayed, the deep popular feelings they reflected, and how convinced they were that they had participated in a necessary act, in a rite of racial self-preservation.

No matter how many whites deplored lynching and terrorism, the dominant racial views that fed the violence remained unchanged. If mobs lynched blacks with calculated sadistic cruelty, the academic sciences were no less resourceful in providing the intellectual under-pinnings of racist thought and behavior, footnoting the subhumanity of black people and helping to justify on "scientific" grounds a complex of racial laws, practices, and beliefs. No group of scholars was more deeply implicated in the miseducation of American youth and did more to shape the thinking of generations of Americans about race and blacks than historians. The scholarly monographs and textbooks they au-thored perpetuated and reinforced an array of racial stereotypes and myths and easily justified the need to repress and quarantine black people.

Historians taught the superiority of Anglo-Saxon institutions and ways of thinking and acting; they caricatured blacks as the least civilized of the races—irresponsible, thoughtless, foolish, childlike people, content with their lowly place in American life, incapable of self-control and self-direction. The history of black people was a history of submission gladly endured and of services faithfully rendered. Transported from the darkness of heathen Africa to the civilized and Christian New World, slaves found contentment and happiness, enjoying what one text called "comprehensive social security." Illustrations depicted well-fed, carefree blacks frolicking in the fields; amiable, deferential Uncle Toms greeting their masters, hat-in-hand, evincing a demeanor of contentment, docility, and faithfulness. The occasional malcontent, like a Nat Turner, was said only to have launched a "horrible massacre" that killed many white people. The treatment of Reconstruction, as in David Muzzey's popular text, depicted black ignorance and inexperience enthroned, with the Ku Klux Klan as the freedom fighters of the 1870s, redeeming Anglo-Saxon civilization from alien rule. When in 1930, Samuel Eliot Morison coauthored an influential college textbook, *The Growth of the American Republic,* he had only to draw on the distortions, half-truths, and evasions of his professional colleagues to pen his classic portrait of enslavement: "As for Sambo, whose wrongs moved the abolitionists to wrath and tears, there is some reason to believe that he suffered less than any other class in the South from its 'peculiar institution.' The majority of slaves were adequately fed, well cared for, and apparently happy."

Careful to hone their texts to the demands of the market, publishers succumbed to what was fashionable and profitable, and in doing so helped to reinforce and perpetuate the distortion and bias. Of course publishers and textbook writers were followers, not leaders; they reflected the current state of scholarship. In the early twentieth century, both historian U. B. Phillips and political scientist Woodrow Wilson came to perceive the period of enslavement as a necessary civilizing process; indeed, for Wilson, whose *History of the American People* was used to footnote D. W. Griffith's *Birth of a Nation,* Reconstruction was little more than "a host of dusky children untimely put out of school." Frederick Jackson Turner never permitted slavery—a mere "incident" in history—to intrude on his romantic celebration of frontier democracy. Those who imagined that slaves were unhappy, thought Turner, were imposing their own feelings and reactions on blacks; the slaves had been adequately fed and clothed and were given every "opportunity for expressing the natural joyousness of the African temper-

ament." And whatever new frontiers in historical interpretation Charles
A. Beard may have charted, he trod a traditional, uninformed path
when it came to black Americans: the passivity and loyalty shown by
slaves to their masters during the Civil War demonstrated to Beard
"their contentment, their affection for their owners, their inertia, or
their helplessness—or all four combined." When W. E. B. Du Bois
came to write *Black Reconstruction* in the 1930s, he examined the
historical literature on slavery and its aftermath. He was prepared for
bias, for distortion, for omission. Even so, he came away appalled by
what he had read. "I stand at the end of this writing, literally aghast
at what American historians have done to this field.... [It is] one of
the most stupendous efforts the world ever saw to discredit human
beings, an effort involving universities, history, science, social life and
religion."

Seldom did textbook writers, historians or publishing houses stop
to consider the consequences of their work. Seldom did they stop to
consider the impact of such history on black readers as well as white.
"I am ashamed," a twelve-year-old black pupil wrote in 1903, "of the
names that we are called in the standard history, 'slaves and niggers,'
and when we read that part of it the white children look at us real
funny." The history of the world Du Bois learned in graduate school
at Harvard, and again in Germany, only complemented his earlier
training. It was the history of the superior race: "Manifestly that [race]
which had a history, the white race... Africa was left without culture
and without history." Booker T. Washington remembered his first geography book and how it chose to depict the white and black races:
a picture of George Washington was placed beside one of a naked
African wearing a ring in his nose and holding a dagger in his hand.
"Naturally all this made a deep and painful impression upon me."

In the history and civics courses taught in the schools, the Constitution and liberty took on mystical dimensions, with the United States
boasting a code of laws and a judicial system superior to that of any
other nation on earth. The most glaring example of the contradiction
between the Constitution, the law, and the lives of most blacks, however, lay in the perversion of justice and in the deep complicity of the
criminal justice system, the enforcement agencies, and the legal profession in that perversion. The law made few pretenses of impartiality if
any; it was all white, and it functioned largely to advance and reinforce

the economic and social repression of blacks. The distinction between law and lawlessness became so blurred, in fact, as to be almost indistinct. The history of black people is not simply a history of extralegal violence; it is a history of legal violence, of violence sanctioned by the law. The "better class" of whites furnished the lawyers and judges and many of the jurors. And in the aftermath of mob violence, their silence, if not their acquiescence, implicated them in the very crimes they sometimes denounced.

The odds were formidable. Every black person sensed that. The law was to be feared, not respected. Guilt and innocence lost their meaning. "Dere ain' no use," a Richland County, South Carolina, black testified:

> De courts er dis land is not for niggers.... It seems to me when it come to trouble, de law an' a nigger is de white man's sport, an' justice is a stranger in them precincts, an' mercy is unknown. An' de Bible say we must pray for we enemy. Drap on you' knee, brothers, an' pray to God for all de crackers an' de judges an' de courts an' solicitors, sheriffs an' police in de land.

Both whites and black leaders expressed dismay over the degree to which the black lawbreaker came to be viewed in the black community not as a criminal, but as a martyr and a victim; the community not only sheltered the accused but in some instances honored him—especially if whites alone had suffered from his alleged crimes. When Robert Charles, a black laborer in New Orleans, clashed with police in July 1900, shooting twenty-seven whites (killing seven of them, including four police officers), he almost immediately assumed legendary proportions. No wonder the police chose to bury him hurriedly and secretly, before dawn, under military guard, in an unmarked grave in potter's field. His exploits inspired a song that, in the words of Jelly Roll Morton, "never did get very far. I once knew the Robert Charles song, but I found out it was best for me to forget it...."

To read the documents of the Department of Justice, housed in the National Archives, is to be exposed to a vast record of white injustice, terrorism, and intimidation: blacks driven off the lands they were working, victimized by a violence that went unpunished, abused on chain gangs, denied the right to "pay out" their debts, held in peonage to work for the profit of others. "In the underground of our unwritten history," Ralph Ellison has observed, "much of that which is ignored

defies our inattention by continuing to grow and have consequences."
To read this dreary record, along with the desperate appeals from the
victims themselves, is to be reminded that the crimes committed by the
powerful and the wealthy, by some of the same people sworn to uphold
the law, invariably exceed the crimes committed by the relatively
powerless.

> They got the judges
> They got the lawyers
> They got the jury-rolls
> They got the law
>   They don't come by ones
> They got the sheriffs
> They got the deputies
>   They don't come by twos
> They got the shotguns
> They got the rope
>   We git the justice
> In the end
>   And they come by tens.

Generations of blacks came to be deeply impressed with the mechanisms of white repression and with the extraordinary ways those
mechanisms shaped their day-to-day behavior. Remaining inoffensive
in the eyes of white men and women became a way of life and of
survival. But even as black people learned to accommodate, to mask
their feelings and emotions, they found ways to impart meaning to
their lives. Against formidable odds, they persevered and learned to
help themselves. Excluded from the white world, they created the institutions and shaped the culture that would provide the inner resources
necessary for survival. Some maintained a faith in education, and some
used their skills and training to move into the lower middle class, or
even higher, capitalizing in some instances on the special business opportunities created by segregation. Some found comfort in the church,
the most venerable of black institutions, and in the sense of participation and community the church imparted.

But for growing numbers of blacks in the 1890s, none of the traditional institutions and outlets offered any solace: neither the family,
the school, nor the church. Exiles in their own land, empty of belief
or hope, volatile, numbers of young blacks opted to live by their wits

on the fringes of society, where they carried on what one observer described as "unceasing psychological scrimmage with the whites." As a child in Mississippi, Richard Wright had watched with awe black men who cursed and violated the laws, sneered at the taboos and customs, mimicked the antics of white folks, and prided themselves on outwitting them. But eventually, Wright observed, they paid a terrible price for their freedom. "They were shot, hanged, maimed, lynched, and generally hounded until they were either dead or their spirits broken."

What helped to sustain Afro-Americans through bondage and a tortured freedom was a rich oral expressive tradition. Nowhere at the turn of the century did black southerners articulate their values more vividly, nowhere did they pour out their frustrations and bitterness with as much feeling as in the music they created. It was in those years, in the 1890s and the 1900s, in the Mississippi Delta, for example, that the blues began to be heard—in the train stations, in the cafés, jook joints, and brothels, in the crossroads stores, in the lumber and turpentine camps. It was the music of the poorest, the most marginal, often illiterate blacks. It was the music of the first generation of southern blacks born in freedom. They aspired to be masterless men, and to a remarkable degree they succeeded, though not without paying a heavy price.

> I got stones in my passway and my road seems dark as night
> I got stones in my passway and my road seems dark as night
> I have pains in my heart, they have taken my appetite.

The blues had its roots in gospel music and in the field hollers, shouts, chants, and work songs of black field hands and roustabouts. But it was also strikingly different—more personalized, more individualistic, more intense, more painful: "The blues is a low down aching old heart disease / And like consumption, killing me by degrees." It was more violent, subversive, and threatening, as in the chilling fantasy described by Furry Lewis, born in 1900 and raised in the Delta at Greenwood:

> I believe I'll buy me a graveyard of my own.
> I believe I'll buy me a graveyard of my own.
> I'm goin' kill everybody that have done me wrong.

Some thought it to be "the devil's music," and it had a language of its own, touching on aspects of black life seldom addressed. It reflected a growing separation from the norms and values of conventional society—a disengagement from church, from school, from family, from the workplace, from white culture. More directly than any other form of expression, it captured the consciousness, the day-to-day experiences, anxieties, and despair of a new black generation. It could be heard in the bluesy dirge sounded by Charley Patton, born near Edwards, Mississippi, in the early 1880s:

> Ev'ry day, seem like murder here
> Ev'ry day, seem like murder here
> I'm gonna leave tomorrow, I know you don't want me here;

or in the defiance articulated by an anonymous Memphis bluesman:

> I feel my hell a-risin', a-risin' every day;
> I feel my hell a-risin', a-risin' every day;
> Someday it'll burst this levee and wash the whole wide world
> away;

or in the plaintive, tormented cry of Robert Johnson, born in 1911, who spent his youth in the upper Mississippi Delta and left this epitaph:

> You may bury my body, down by the highway side
> Baby, I don't care where you bury my body when I'm dead
> and gone
> You may bury my body, ooooo, down by the highway side
> So my old evil spirit can get a Greyhound bus, and ride.

Eloquent black spokesmen in their own right, yet none of them—Charley Patton, Son House, Robert Johnson, Willie Brown, Tommy Johnson, Skip James—are to be found in the dictionaries of American or Negro biography, the histories of southern literature, or the encyclopedias of southern history. But to listen to them is to feel—more vividly, more intensely than any mere poet, novelist, or historian could convey them—the terrors, tensions, and personal betrayals that pervaded the lives of blacks coming to adulthood in the early twentieth century.

> I got to keep moving, I got to keep moving
> Blues falling down like hail, blues falling down like hail
> And the days keeps on 'minding me
> There's a hellhound on my trail
> Hellhound on my trail, hellhound on my trail.

The euphoric optimism with which many blacks had greeted and acted upon emancipation never survived into the twentieth century. Reconstruction had promised to bring black people fully within the meaning and protection of the Constitution. It had promised to end the violence, robbery, humiliation, insult, and sexual exploitation associated with enslavement. But for the nearly eight million black men and women who lived and worked in the South in 1900 (90 percent of the nation's black population), that promise had been forcibly betrayed; the amended Constitution had become mostly inoperative. For the nearly nine hundred thousand blacks in the North, although their lives differed in quality from those of their southern brethren, the dominant racial assumptions dictated a proscribed place in American society. When President Theodore Roosevelt wrote in 1906 "that as a race and in the mass they [Negroes] are altogether inferior to the whites," he articulated the belief of most Americans, a belief that was being acted out not only in Alabama, Georgia, and Mississippi, but also in Latin America and Asia.

Like many children of former slaves, Ned Cobb learned to obey whites and to avoid trouble. That was the legacy he inherited.

> They'd have dealins with you . . . but you had to come under their rulins. They'd give you a good name if you was obedient to em, acted nice when you met em and didn't question em bout what they said they had against you. You begin to cry about your rights and the mistreatin of you and they'd murder you.

Charles Wingfield grew up in Lee County, Georgia, a few miles from Albany. Like Ned Cobb, he came to learn that his people lived and acted by different rules than whites, that self-preservation dictated a measured response to the world around him. He thought about the meaning of his life, about his prospects, even as he prepared to enter adulthood.

I wondered what it was like to live.... Countless nights I cried myself to sleep.... I must have asked God why a thousand times but I never got an answer. Was nine of us kids in the family and we all had to work. I stayed out of school a lot of days because I couldn't let my mother go to the cotton field and try to support all of us. I picked cotton and pecans for two cents a pound. I went to the fields six in the morning and worked until seven in the afternoon. When it came time to weigh up, my heart, body and bones would be aching, burning and trembling. I stood there and looked the white men right in their eyes while they cheated me, other members of my family, and the rest of the Negroes that were working. There were times when I wanted to speak, but my fearful mother would always tell me to keep silent. The sun was awful hot and the days were long.... The cost of survival was high. Why I paid it I'll never know.

Generations of black youths had already paid the same price. When Wingfield pronounced that judgment on his life, he was 16 years old, Ned Cobb was nearing 80, the Emancipation Proclamation was 100 years old, the Constitution 176 years old. Ned Cobb knew when "to fall back," but he refused to demean himself, he refused to become one of the "white men's niggers." For that refusal, and for his activities in the Alabama Sharecroppers Union, he spent twelve years in an Alabama prison. Wingfield organized a protest at the Lee County Training School, where he was an honors student. He was immediately expelled. He enlisted in SNCC—the Student Nonviolent Coordinating Committee.

In the mid-twentieth century, the civil rights movement, which W. E. B. Du Bois observed from exile in Ghana, which Ned Cobb watched with fascination from his Alabama farm, and which Charles Wingfield joined, struck down the legal barriers of segregation and disfranchisement in the South and challenged the economic and educational barriers that had crippled black aspirations in the North. It left its mark on the nation. Hundreds, thousands took to the streets, mostly young people, defying the laws, defying the apathy of their elders, disciplined by nonviolence, insisting on bringing the Constitution and the nation's professed values into closer harmony, embracing the promise of a new reconstruction, more sweeping, more enduring than the last.

What they achieved was impressive, far reaching in the ways it changed the face of the South—if not the nation. But it was revealing, too, for the paradoxes and contradictions it exposed. For all the political gains, the dismantling of Jim Crow, the mass marches, the optimistic rhetoric, many of the same tensions and anxieties persisted and festered, the same quiet despair, the same desperate struggle for survival, the familiar sense of expectations betrayed, of promises not kept. Even as the civil rights movement struck down legal barriers, it failed to dismantle economic barriers. Even as it ended the violence of segregation, it failed to diminish the violence of poverty. Even as it transformed the face of southern politics, it did nothing to reallocate resources, to redistribute wealth and income. Even as it entered schools and colleges, voting booths and lunch counters, it failed to penetrate the corporate boardrooms and federal bureaucracies where the most critical decisions affecting American lives were made.

The brutalizing effects of more than two centuries of slavery and another century of enforced segregation and miseducation continue to shape race relations in the late twentieth century, continue to hold up a mirror to Americans, to test the democratic experiment, the principles and values Americans embrace. Although usually expressed with more subtlety, racism remains pervasive; its terrors and tensions are still with us, and it knows no regional or class boundaries. Twenty years have passed since the Kerner commission warned that the United States was "moving toward two societies, one black, one white—separate and unequal." That process continues. No matter how it is measured—by where blacks live, their income, the schools they attend, or their future prospects—this nation remains in critical ways two societies, separate and unequal. And the implications for the twenty-first century are devastating.

The deepening economic disparities between whites and blacks, the growing gap between haves and have-nots, the deteriorating quality of public education (the struggle is no longer to keep blacks out of the public schools but to keep whites in), the emasculation of the principle and enforcement structure of civil rights, the controversy over special efforts to redress two hundred years of special exploitation, the revived racist epithets and slurs, the acts of racial terrorism and harassment, and the insensitivity in high places (the White House and the Department of Justice), the contempt for human rights and racial justice—all suggest the forcefulness of the warning sounded by W. E. B. Du Bois in the 1930s: that black Americans face, not simply the rational, conscious determination of whites to oppress them, but "age-long complexes sunk now largely to unconscious habit and irrational urge." The problem, Du Bois concluded, was no longer to educate whites to the special problems blacks faced. White America knew the facts and remained indifferent and unmoved. Du Bois came to realize in the 1930s what Martin Luther King, Jr., would articulate some thirty years later: to reform the laws and the existing institutions was not enough, "you've got to have a reconstruction of the entire society, a revolution of values."

Some thirty-five years ago, when I was an undergraduate at Berkeley, a friend (a graduate student in history) called and asked me to come over to his house; he said someone wanted to meet me. I was ushered into the living room, and his guest soon entered from another room. I recognized him immediately—it was W. E. B. Du Bois. Of course I was deeply impressed; I had read his books. But why had he singled me out? He wanted, he said, to meet an undergraduate in history. He wanted to know what I was learning about slavery and Reconstruction. My response was in two parts: the textbook (by John D. Hicks) reflected familiar distortions and biases; the lectures did not, and their content impressed and astonished Du Bois; they revealed new ways of thinking about both slavery and Reconstruction. The person teaching the course was a young assistant professor, Kenneth M. Stampp.

No doubt Du Bois would be encouraged by the advances made in historical study since that day, the new perspectives, the varieties of historical documentation, the array of voices brought to the writing and teaching of Afro-American and American history. No field of historical scholarship has undergone such a profound transformation in the past thirty years, and the pioneering efforts of long-ignored black scholars have finally achieved their deserved recognition. No doubt Du Bois would also express admiration for the ways in which the civil rights movement and the courts finally forced a recognition of constitutional rights guaranteed blacks more than a century earlier.

But even as he applauded such achievements, Du Bois might still share with the black leaders of a century ago considerable skepticism about the proposed celebration of the anniversary of the Constitution. Major commemorations of historical events, like the recent celebration of the Statue of Liberty, have a tendency to deteriorate into mindless evocations of the American Dream—patriotic, self-congratulatory, ritualistic orgies with little substantive content. The centennial of the Civil War, for example, celebrated largely lost causes and military skirmishes, not the abolition of human slavery, black armies of occupation, and black initiatives to secure freedom. The celebration of the Constitution, under the grandiose title "Miracle at Philadelphia," also threatens to become shrouded in mythology.

This is less a time to celebrate miracles than to reflect on what was left undone at Philadelphia two hundred years ago. This is a time to recall the struggle that had to be waged to bring all Americans, black and white, men and women, within the meaning of the Constitution. The abolitionists, the slave rebels, the Reconstruction Congress, the civil rights and women's movements, the men and women who, by asserting their rights and questioning the assumptions and wisdom of those who held power, helped to strengthen the Constitution—all these people deserve a prominent place in the bicentennial celebration. "Those who profess to favor freedom and yet deprecate agitation," Frederick Douglass declared in 1857, "are men who want crops without plowing up the ground, they want rain without thunder and lightning. They want the ocean without the awful roar of its many waters." In that spirit, on this two-hundredth birthday of the Constitution, we need to examine American values and the American character. But with even greater urgency, in looking to the twenty-first century, we need to assess this nation's use and abuse of its power, wealth, and resources. That is our responsibility as historians, as teachers, and as Americans.

The bicentennial, then, affords us an opportunity to think in different ways about our heritage. It is easy enough to study, teach, and honor the Founding Fathers. They have left us ample testimony, weighty theoretical treatises, and an impressive document—The Constitution. The place of the Founding Fathers in our history is secure. But where do we place, how do we choose to remember the men and women, losers in their own time, outlaws, rebels who—individually or collectively—as much as any one of the Founding Fathers, tried to flesh out, tried to give meaning to abstract notions of liberty, independence, and freedom? How do we remember them? How do we honor them? That is a more formidable task.

Sterling Brown remembers a pilgrimage to the place where Nat
Turner fell:

> She wanted to know [this old white woman] why folks would
> come miles
> Just to ask about an old nigger fool
>   "Ain't no slavery no more, things is going all right,
>   Pervided that's a good goober market this year.
>   We had a sign post here with printing on it [to mark the
> spot Nat fell]
>   But it rotted in the hole, and thar it lays,
>   And the nigger tenants split the marker for kindling.
>   Things is all right, now, ain't no trouble with the niggers
>   Why they make this big to-do over Nat?"
> As we drove from Cross Keys back to Courtland,
> Along the way that Nat came down upon Jerusalem,
> A watery moon was high in the cloud-filled heavens,
> The same moon he dreaded a hundred years ago.
> The tree they hanged Nat on is long gone to ashes,
> The trees he dodged behind have rotted in the swamps.
>
> The bus for Miami and the trucks boomed by,
> And touring cars, their heavy tires snarling on the pavement.
> Frogs piped in the marshes, and a hound bayed long,
> And yellow lights glowed from the cabin windows.
>
> As we came back the way that Nat led his army,
> Down from Cross Keys, down to Jerusalem,
> We wondered if his troubled spirit still roamed the Nottaway,
> Or if it fled with the cock-crow at daylight,
> Or lay at peace with the bones in Jerusalem,
> Its restlessness stifled by Southamptom clay.
>
> We remembered the poster rotted through and falling,
> The marker split for kindling a kitchen fire.

2

Schooling the Hopi: Federal Indian Policy Writ Small, 1887–1917

DAVID WALLACE ADAMS

• *Evidence of Indian existence in what is now North America dates back more than 25,000 years. When Christopher Columbus first sailed to the New World in 1492, there were perhaps three million people already resident on the continent. Europeans called them Indians because of the belief that the Americas were the outer reaches of the East Indies.*

Over the course of the next five centuries, the original Americans were pushed slowly westward, where many died in battle or from strange diseases introduced by the new settlers. Ultimately, the white man decided to confine the Indians to reservations, where they could be kept out of the way until they were properly Americanized. Education was of course a favorite method of changing Indian behavioral patterns and of teaching the superiority of Western ways and European culture.

The Hopi were a particularly sedentary farming people who had special skills in pottery, basketry, and textiles. Concentrated in what is now Arizona, they lived peacefully in mesa villages even after Coronado's men visited the area in 1540. After 1820, their primary enemies were the more numerous Navaho, who in 1843 were even given control of most of the Hopi reservation. The following essay by David Wallace Adams focuses on a less violent but equally serious threat—the educational policies adopted by federal officials whose assumptions about "progress" and "savagery" placed little value on tribal traditions.

Although historians have acknowledged the important role of education in late nineteenth-century federal Indian policy, they have failed

to examine this subject in much depth. To date, a study of the federal
Indian boarding school system does not exist. Yet for many years the
"friends of the Indian" looked to the boarding school as an essential
ingredient of the government's plan to civilize the "savage." This void
in the literature is striking since the boarding school—its organization,
formal instruction, and day to day routine—was a major setting for
the clash of Native American and white cultures. A deeper understanding of this phase of Indian policy can be gained by examining its
application to a single Indian tribe—the Hopi. Several scholars have
highlighted various aspects of Hopi-white relations, but none has discussed in great depth the critical role of education in this interaction.
This study examines that subject, and in doing so, it integrates tribal
and institutional history within the larger context of Indian-white
relations.

Late nineteenth-century federal Indian policy was essentially philanthropic in its approach to the Indian question. It was rooted in a series
of premises and propositions about what the Indian was and what he
ought to become. The pivotal notion was that all cultures could be
classified on a scale according to their degree of civilization or savagism.
Philanthropists believed that throughout history, which was viewed as
a progressive and evolutionary process, only a few societies in the world
had reached the upper levels of this scale; the greater proportion of
the world's population remained steeped in savagism. American civilization, of course, exemplified the former and Indian culture illustrated
the latter.

Those responsible for the formulation of Indian policy were sure of
one thing: the Indian could not continue to exist as an Indian. As the
Commissioner of Indian Affairs William A. Jones stated in 1903: "As
a separate entity he cannot exist encysted, as it were, in the body politic
of this great nation." The Indian had to choose, then, between civilization or extinction. Philanthropists were genuinely sincere when they
expressed hope that the Indian would choose to learn the ways of the
white man rather than become a victim of American progress. By the
1880's the Indian Office had settled upon the means of achieving ab-
sorption into white society. The Indian's willingness to accept the gift
of the common school was presumed to be his only chance for survival.
As Commissioner Jones remarked in 1903: "To educate the Indian in

the ways of civilized life . . . is to preserve him from extinction, not as an Indian, but as a human being." Education, then, was the means of moving the Indian along the scale of civilization and ultimately into the mainstream of American culture. Moreover, education was seen as the only way of saving the Indian from extinction, but at a considerable price—by eliminating his Indianness.

In the late 1870's, the Indian Office had found cause for renewed hope in the assimilationist potential of education. The source of this hope lay in the apparent success of Captain Richard Henry Pratt in educating Indians at Carlisle Indian Boarding School. Pratt opened Carlisle in 1879 with the philosophy: "Kill the Indian and save the man." Shortly thereafter, all who visited the institution came away with two key impressions: first, that Indians could be civilized, and second, that education was the way to accomplish it. On the surface, at least, it appeared that, if a young Indian was removed from the savage influence of the reservation and kept for several years in the civilized environment of the boarding school, he might be successfully transformed into a copper-colored white man. Following the Carlisle experiment an elaborate three-tiered system of education was developed in the far West; it was composed of the reservation day school, the reservation boarding school, and, finally the Carlisle-type nonreservation boarding school. In the 1880's the Indian Office began to turn its attention to a remote tribe living on three mesas high above the Arizona desert—the Hopi.

In 1882, Indian agent J. H. Fleming decided to visit the Hopi. With a wagon and mules he followed a very "difficult and circuitous" route and finally reached Oraibi, the largest village of the Hopi. Fleming later recorded that "such an event I am told, had never been known in the history of the town; a span of mules and wagon on the streets of Oribi [*sic*] was indeed a novelty!" Fleming was now part of a continuous stream of Indian agents in the last quarter of the century who formed impressions of this remote people. Those agents who could move beyond their own ethnocentricity—and they were few—noted that the Hopi did not seem to fit the traditional model of savagism. They were not nomadic hunters. The Hopi had achieved instead a high level of agriculture in the almost barren desert. Nor did they live in temporary shelters made of animal skins or brush, but dwelled in well-constructed, stone and plaster houses. Furthermore, they were not warriors, but as the word Hopi implied, a people of peace. Indian agent John H. Sullivan observed in 1881:

> They are a peculiar people, and to me a very interesting branch of the human family, presenting some of the best characteristics known to civilized man, occasionally giving strong proof of the fact of their fathers having once enjoyed the advantages of a high degree of intelligence, the vestiges of which have come to them through a long line of succession from son to son. Their faults as seen by us from our standpoint are the results of their system of education, which being so different from our own, we find cause to complain, and doubtless criticize with unjustifiable severity.

Most agents were not so sensitive to the richness and uniqueness of Hopi culture. In 1890, for instance, agent C. E. Vandever, while admitting that the Hopi had an "unexpected capacity for intelligent reflection," still noted that upon reaching maturity, Hopi children "invariably sink into a state of mental apathy." Leo Crane, one of the most hated of the agents and superintendents during this period, declared in his annual report for 1912 that "the average Hopi has no morals in the white man's sense of morality. They begin as children to live on a moral plane little above their livestock." Crane, who was fond of including snapshots with his reports to Washington to demonstrate "the never-improving moral problem of these people," pointed out on one occasion: "Hopi children of both sexes often go nude in the summer, and in some of the villages boys and girls of twelve and over may be discovered practically nude."

But if nudity bothered Crane's Victorian sensibilities, the cultural characteristic that most offended him was Hopi ceremonialism. "The greatest obstacle to Hopi advancement is the dance," he stated. Crane held a special distaste for one of the most traditional and sacred of Hopi ceremonies, the famous Snake Dance. He noted in 1915 that it showed no signs of "deterioration as a barbaric Indian specticle" [sic]. All agents to the Hopi agreed that while this unique people possessed some enobling characteristics, their religious practices alone condemned them to a lower rung on the ladder of civilization. As one agent noted thirty years prior to Crane's arrival: "The dark superstitions and unhallowed rites of a heathenism still infects them with its insidious poison, which, unless replaced by Christian civilization, must sap their very life blood." In a letter to the Secretary of Interior in 1890, the Commissioner of Indian Affairs Thomas J. Morgan concluded that the solution lay in education: "If their children can be kept in school . . . , they will make very satisfactory progress in the ways of civilization."

The opening of Keams Canyon Boarding School in 1887 signaled the beginning of an uninterrupted effort to educate Hopi youth in the ways of civilization. Initially government officials had every reason for optimism about Hopi responsiveness to education. A boarding school established for the Hopi in 1875 had met with some success before closing a year later. Furthermore, the Hopi agent had written to the Commissioner in 1884 that the Hopi manifested "an earnest desire" for a white education, and he claimed to have received assurances from village leaders that out of a total Hopi population of about two thousand, the government might expect 250 students. It was no surprise, then, that after the Keams Canyon School got under way, Agent James Gallaher reported the venture "a complete success."

Within two years, however, the school was experiencing major difficulties in maintaining enrollments. As a reservation boarding school, students were permitted to return to their village for extended vacation periods. The problem was that many never came back. The Hopi were having second thoughts about turning their children over to the government for education. Thus, just two years after the opening of Keams Canyon, the Commissioner of Indian Affairs received word from agency headquarters that there existed a "disinclination of parents to send children."

At this point five Hopi headmen were invited to Washington for a conference with the Commissioner of Indian Affairs. The government sought to emphasize to the Hopi its determination to enforce school attendance. The trip was also designed to impress this remote people with the wealth and power of white civilization. The journey seems to have had the desired effect. When Chief Lololomai from Oraibi spoke with Commissioner Morgan on June 27, 1890, he began:

> My people are blind. Their ears are closed. I am the only one. I
> am alone. They don't want to go in the white man's ways, al-

though I am chief...I am thankful to see you and I want your advice as to what to do with my people who are hard headed.

Rather than reply directly to Lololomai's question, Morgan chose to discuss the power of white civilization and the importance of education:

As you see the white people are very much greater in numbers than you are. They are increasing very fast, and are very prosperous. They live in good houses and have good clothes and plenty to eat. Two things make them prosperous, one is that they educate all their children and keep them in school year after year, and they learn about books and how to do all kinds of things. The white people educate the women too, as you see here, and then when they are educated they all work. These are the two things, we educate all our children and we all work.

After a visit to Carlisle, Pennsylvania, where the chiefs witnessed the civilizing power of education in its most developed form, they returned home to proclaim the necessity of cooperating with Washington.

Their appeal went unheeded. Most Hopi remained adamant in their refusal to send their children to the Keams Canyon school. "While the headmen were willing for the children to come," reported the agent, "they had few children of their own, and referred me to the parents, while the fathers said the mothers controlled the children, and the mothers said the children would cry, and hence they would not send them." Finally, at wits end, the Office of Indian Affairs resorted to force. In December 1890 and again in July 1891 federal troops were sent to the village of Oraibi. After this show of force, the Hopi peaceably handed over their children. By the end of 1891, the agent was able to boast of a respectable enrollment of a hundred pupils at Keams Canyon.

Hopi resistance to education did not end, however. In fact, by the turn of the century the Hopi had divided into two factions, the "friendlies" and the "hostiles." As the names imply, the former were more willing than the latter to cooperate with the government's civilization policy. In the main village of Oraibi relations between the two groups degenerated. The village split in 1906, and the hostiles were forced to leave the village. The center of Hopi opposition to government policy thereafter centered in the new hostile village of Hotevilla. Its determined leader was Yukeoma, a traditional Hopi who held an ardent dislike for white ways in general and schools in particular. The persistent refusals of the Hotevilla residents to send their children to school finally brought action in 1911. A troop of cavalry was sent out with orders to force the villagers to give up their children for a white education.

Despite the continued opposition of many Hopi to the government's education policy, a steady stream of Hopi children left the mesas to learn the white man's ways after 1890. While some were eased into the white world by attendance first at one of the village day schools established in the 1890s, many directly entered the reservation boarding school at Keams Canyon. After the turn of the century an increasing number of Hopi attended the nonreservation schools at Phoenix, Arizona, and the Sherman Institute at Riverside, California. It was in the boarding school environment, both reservation and nonreservation, that Hopi pupils received their heaviest dose of civilization.

The Hopi child who came to the boarding school directly from the village received a most abrupt introduction to white society. In the first few days, they were subjected to a process, which for lack of a better term, must be called de-Indianization. The belief was that before Indians could begin to acquire the knowledge, skills, and attitudes of the white world, they must be stripped of all outward signs of their savage heritage. This process involved a threefold attack on their personal appearance and tribal identity. They were forced to abandon traditional dress for a school uniform. For some students, of course, this was a welcome exchange, especially if the Indian clothing was inferior to school apparel in its capacity to keep them warm in winter months. Others objected strongly to the change in dress. Emory Sekaquaptewa, for instance, arrived at Keams Canyon wrapped in a fine new blanket woven for him by his grandfather. At school it was exchanged for the standard issue of blue shirt, mustard-colored pants, and heavy shoes. As for the blanket, he recalled, "I saw it later, in the possession of the wife of the superintendent." After a change of dress, the new recruit was subjected to a haircut. This process, too, many Hopi regarded as an unwelcome assault on their person. Finally, there was the need to change an Indian's name. Where possible the Indian Service preferred that an Indian name be only slightly altered or merely translated into English. Often, however, pupils received a new one altogether; some even acquired names of historical distinction. At Keams Canyon in 1889, for instance, a Ki-Ki-tu was recorded as Albert Gallatin and a Ma-ku-si as Michael Angelo.

De-Indianization was only the beginning stage of an institutional process devoted to totally transforming the subjects. The Hopi received the rudiments of an education; its goal was to teach them to speak and write the English language, provide some knowledge of United States history and constitutional government, and convey an elementary understanding of basic subjects such as science, mathematics, and geography. But if instruction in academic subjects was an important aspect of the Indian's education, it was clearly secondary to instruction in manual and vocational trades. Most male graduates of the boarding school, it was assumed, would return to their western homes and support themselves as farmers or tradesmen. Thus, the average Indian's academic education emphasized reading the local newspaper, writing a short letter, and handling numbers sufficiently well to discover whether the reservation trader was cheating.

The preference for the practical over the theoretical was also rooted in the notion that the Indian's success at agricultural pursuits was the principle measuring rod for indicating his progress toward civilization. This belief found expression in the Phoenix Indian School's weekly newspaper, the *Native American*, which had etched over its masthead the declared purpose of the school: to transform "the man with a gun" into a "man with a hoe." This slogan missed the mark in the case of the Hopi, who were well known for their peaceful nature as well as their capacity to make the desert bloom, but it did serve to emphasize the practical orientation of a boarding school education. Consequently Indian boys at Keams Canyon, Sherman, and Phoenix spent half of their academic day on the school farm or in the shop learning basic carpentry skills. Hopi girls spent an equivalent period learning the skills thought appropriate for their sex in a Victorian age—ironing, sewing, and arranging a table setting consistent with the standards of civilized dining.

The emphasis placed on manual and vocational training had a much deeper purpose than merely teaching skills. It was also a means of instilling in the Indian values and attitudes thought essential to being an "American." Specifically, the Indian had to learn the virtue of work, the principle of private property, and the spirit of acquisitiveness even to the point of selfishness. According to United States Senator Henry L. Dawes, the best solution to the general problem was to take the

Indian "by the hand and set him upon his feet, and teach him to stand alone first, then to walk, then to dig, then to plant, then to hoe, then to gather, and then to *keep*." Merrill E. Gates, president of the Lake Mohonk Conference, spoke in similar terms when he told fellow philanthropists that the primary challenge before Indian educators was to awaken "wants" in the Indian child. Only then could the Indian be gotten out "of the blanket and into trousers,—and trousers with a *pocket that aches to be filled with dollars!*" This was to remain an enduring objective of Indian education for years to come, and therefore, it is not surprising that in 1907 Commissioner Francis E. Leupp stressed the same point when speaking to a group of Indian educators in Los Angeles. After noting that a group of Hopi boys from Oraibi had just arrived at Sherman Institute, he pointed to the Sherman flag monogrammed with the letters S.I. and commented that the design came "pretty near being a dollar mark." And then he added: "Sordid as it may sound, it is the dollar that makes the world go around, and we have to teach the Indians at the outset of their careers what a dollar means." This concept was for Leupp "the most important part of their education."

Leupp and other philanthropists were convinced that the Indian's survival hinged on the acceptance of this economic principle. After the Indian had been taught the ways of civilization, including the "value of things," Leupp explained, he must be left alone to "dig out his own future." He admitted that "a considerable number will go to the wall," but "those who survive will be well worth saving." It followed that the message of materialism and rugged individualism must be learned well; so well in fact that it could not be entrusted to any single area of the academic program. It must pervade all aspects of the Indian's education. The *Native American* gave poetic expression to the American ideal of success in a piece entitled "The Man Who Wins."

> The man who wins is the man who works—
> The man who toils while the next man shirks....
> And the man who wins is the man who hears
> The curse of the envious in his ears
> But who goes his way with head held high
> And passes the wrecks of the failures by—
> For he is the man who wins.

Another area of Indian education that preoccupied boarding school officials was the student's religious conversion. Because philanthropists had historically perceived an essential relationship between Christianization and civilization, missionaries had always been allowed to assume a prominent role in Indian education. By the turn of the century, Catholic, Mennonite, and other missionaries had had opportunities to convert the Hopi, but with limited success. Undaunted by these failures, the Commissioner of Indian Affairs urged the various religious denominations to exert themselves to the utmost so as not to leave "an inch of pagan territory uncovered." Boarding schools were part of this "pagan territory" in that they housed young Indians, many of whom had never come in contact with Christianity. At Keams Canyon the American Baptist Home Missionary Society was invited to offer Sunday morning services as well as two hours of religious instruction during the week. At the larger nonreservation boarding schools, such as those in Phoenix and Sherman, more than one denomination was permitted to compete for the student's loyalty.

As a result, the Indian student was subjected to religious pressures that struck at the very heart of his tribal heritage. To give in to these pressures was to deny the ways of his ancestors; to reject them was to be condemned to savagery and, if the missionaries were right, to everlasting fire and brimstone. Under these pressures many Hopi, for a time at least, professed conversion to Christianity, if only to please the superintendent. Don Talayesva, a Hopi from Oraibi, rejected the Christian message during his stay at Keams Canyon, but once at Sherman he was moved publicly at one point to declare his intention to return eventually to his village and preach the Scriptures "to my people in darkness." When reflecting on this experience at Sherman, Talayesva later recalled: "At that time I was half-Christian and half-heathen and often wished that there were some magic that could change my skin into that of a white man."

Since the Indian Bureau sought a total transformation of the Indian, every aspect of school life was devoted to this end. The structure and organization of the school environment took on special significance. A careful look at the operation of these schools reveals that they were militaristic in both atmosphere and organization. Literally every aspect of the student's life was regimented and routinized, with each day beginning and closing with the sound of a bugle. Every daily activity—

learning, working, sleeping, eating, and playing—was scheduled with the neat precision of a military encampment. The boarding school was not just a place where the Hopi learned the white man's religion, language, and skills; it was also a place where he virtually marched and drilled his way toward civilization. One Hopi who attended Sherman in 1914 later recalled: "When I entered school it was just like entering the school for Army or soldiering. Every morning we were rolled out of bed and the biggest part of the time we would have to line up and put guns in our hands.... When a man gave a command we had to stand at attention, another command grab our guns, and then march off at another command."

As this recollection suggests, the emphasis on regimentation was not mandated by the organizational difficulties involved in feeding, housing, and educating several hundred young Indians. The reasons went far deeper and had to do with what anthropologist Bernard L. Fontana has recently called the Indian's sense of "natural time" compared to the European-American's concept of "clock time." Because the notion of clock time was closely associated with such positive virtues as work, money, and progress, school officials assumed that the Indian was hopelessly bound to savagery until he internalized the mechanical and disciplined movements of clockwork and gained an appreciation for the belief that "time" was a valuable resource to be spent on civilized pursuits rather than on savage idleness. The *Sherman Bulletin* reminded its pupils that it was not enough "to do the right thing and in the right way, but it must be done at the right time as well if we would reap the rewards of our labor." Lest students miss the relationship between time and money, they were informed that "many of our most successful businessmen date their success from the time they commenced to practice the virtue of being on time." Indeed, the habit of punctuality was not an end in itself, but rather a habit that, if carried into life, became "one of the main instruments in making real success."

Still another reason for the militaristic organization of the schools was the Indian Office's conviction that the student must be taught the value of obedience. In addition to having close links with punctuality, the emphasis on obedience seems to have been rooted in the philanthropic belief that civilization—especially as it was emerging in the modern context—required the acceptance of rules, regulations, and restraints. Since most believed that the young Indian was the product of a way of life that operated on the principle of wild impulse, the lesson of obedience was seen as an essential element in his elevation. The *Sherman Bulletin,* for example, informed students that the first law of life was the word "obey."

> Obedience is the great foundation law of all life. It is the common fundamental law of all organization, in nature, in military, naval, commercial, political, and domestic circles. Obedience is the great essential to securing the purpose of life. Disobedience means disaster. The first disastrous act of disobedience brought ruin to humanity and that ruin is still going on. "The first duty of a soldier is obedience" is a truth forced upon all soldiers the moment they enter upon the military life. The same applies to school life. The moment a student is instructed to do a certain thing, no matter how small or how great, immediate action on his part is a duty and should be a pleasure.... What your teachers tell you to do you should do without question. Obedience means marching right on whether you feel like it or not.

The emphasis on order and regimentation also had a political motivation. A major purpose of the boarding school was to sever forever the ties that bound the Indian to his tribal government and to transfer his loyalty to the nation state. Classroom instruction in American history and government could not be counted upon alone to accomplish this objective. Given the tragic history of Indian-white relations, there were special problems connected with winning the young Indian's allegiance to the federal government. Only by actual participation in patriotic and military rituals, officials thought, could Indians be expected to internalize and then identify with national symbols, institutions, and leaders. The world of flags, uniforms, and parades was devoted to this end. The use of military spectacle, especially when combined with a holiday celebration or the visit of a public figure, was seen as a particularly effective method of forging new political loyalties. One Hopi, for instance, remembered that on Decoration Day at the Keams Canyon school the students were handed small flags and bunches of flowers and then "marched out to the graves of two soldiers who had come out here to fight the Hopi and had died." When President William McKinley visited Phoenix Indian School in May 1901, he watched the entire school population march in rank and assemble before him in perfect military fashion. According to the *Native American* account, "The movement was executed like clockwork, unmarred by a single mistake or bungle. There they stood for an instant, 700 pairs of eyes gazing sharply and intently at the 'greatfather.' " And then upon the command of a bugle call, the Indians shouted in unison: "I give my head and my heart to my country; one country, one language, and one flag."

This was what education for civilization was all about: one country, one language, and one flag. This goal combined with de-Indianization, Christianization, and finally, setting the Indian on his feet so that he might "dig out his own future" outfitted in trousers with a "pocket that aches to be filled with dollars" together constituted the multiple purposes of Indian education. These objectives were formulated and universally agreed upon by philanthropic groups and governmental agencies devoted to the noble goal of preserving the red man from extinction in the face of white civilization. The price that the Indian had to pay for his continued existence is revealed in the remarks made by Indian Commissioner Morgan at another boarding school ten years before McKinley visited Phoenix. After listening to some religious songs sung by an Indian choir, Morgan remarked to the students: "As I sat here and listened with closed eyes to your singing, you were not Indians to me. You sing our songs, you speak our language. In the days that are coming there will be nothing save his color to distinguish the Indian from the white man."

To the disappointment of the Indian Office, many students, after returning to their villages, rejected much of their boarding school education and returned to the old Hopi ways. Don Talayesva is a case in point. Talayesva first attended the day school at Oraibi and then spent several years at Keams Canyon. A bright student, he recalled that after one year in boarding school he had learned many English words, could recite part of the Ten Commandments, knew how to pray to Jesus, and could eat with a knife and fork. He also learned that the earth was round, that it was improper to go naked in the presence of girls, and perhaps most important of all "that a person thinks with his head instead of his heart." Talayesva then moved on to Sherman Institute. When he left Sherman in 1909, he considered himself a prosperous young man, possessing among other things a five-dollar watch and a respectable looking suitcase. After a ride on the Santa Fe Railroad and another by horsedrawn wagon, he was back in Hopi country again. Like every other returned student, he tried to fit together the pieces of his life. The first night home he lay on the roof of a Hopi pueblo, and while gazing at the clear Arizona sky, he considered the meaning of his education:

> As I lay on my blanket I thought about my school days and all that I had learned. I could talk like a gentleman, read, write, and cipher. I could name all the states in the Union with their capitals, repeat the names of all the books in the Bible, quote a hundred verses of Scripture, sing more than two dozen Christian hymns and patriotic songs, debate, shout football yells, swing my partners in square dances, bake bread, sew well enough to make a pair of trousers, and tell "dirty" Dutchman stories by the hour.

With the exception of the dirty Dutchman stories, the Indian Office would have been pleased with Talayesva's remembrance. About this returned student's future intentions, however, philanthropic enthusiasm would have been substantially dampened. For after recounting all that he had learned of the white man's world, Talayesva now "wanted to become a real Hopi again, to sing the good old Katcina songs, and to feel free to make love without fear of sin or rawhide."

Don Talayesva became part of what the Indian Office commonly referred to as the "problem of the returned student." The original faith placed in the boarding school was based on the assumption that the returned student would not only withstand the pressures to "backslide" into savagery, but that he would serve as a progressive example to those Indians amenable to advancement up the scale of civilization. This was the theory. In fact, however, the nonreservation boarding school system had scarcely been created when it came under heavy criticism for failing to live up to its promise. The problem was not the inability of the boarding school to bring about a dramatic transformation in the Indian child. Indeed, while under the watchful eye of school officials and within the regimented atmosphere of institutional routine, the young Indian appeared to adopt the ways of civilization rather quickly. The change occurred after the student's return to the reservation. Agents frequently noted the problem of the "retrograde" student or the "return to the blanket."

In a long letter to the Indian Office in 1917, Superintendent Leo

Crane described how the process of relapse affected the Hopi. From the time of birth to the age of seven the Hopi child, Crane reminded officials, "learns Indian legends, attends Indian dances and ceremonies much more colorful and appealing than any later white man's entertainment." At the age of seven he attended a day school located near his village and for the next six years continued his education in the shadow of the pueblo. "Everything learned during the day has been ironed out of him by night, through ridicule and adverse criticism of that fool white teacher, who is obeyed only because behind him is a greater and stronger fool, the Agent." During this period the child was subjected to the competing world views of the white man and the Hopi. One day he "hears of Jesus," and on the next he "attends a dance to propitiate the snake gods." After several years the child was understandably "a little confused."

Later he was sent to the reservation boarding school at Keams Canyon. At this point in his education, the Hopi child was only partly won over to the cause of civilization. While he now understood "that white people have a kindly sympathy for him," and while he genuinely appreciated the clean clothes, regular food, and clean bed that came with boarding school life, once beyond the eyes of the teacher he "still plays Indian games" and "will unconsciously sing Indian chants." He was, in effect, "AN INDIAN under instruction." At the end of his term at Keams Canyon, he might even become an "INDIAN CITIZEN," a phrase Crane never defined, but in the context of his remarks seems to imply a half-civilized status; the student essentially retained his Indian identity and manner of life, while simultaneously he felt a strong sense of political loyalty to the national government and possessed a general understanding of white ways. In any event, this outcome was the best that could be hoped for. After the reservation boarding school, Crane thought the Hopi's education should end.

Crane believed the root of the returned student problem was found in the notion that the student should continue his education at the nonreservation boarding school. Crane felt the nonreservation school was an ill-conceived "white washing process," a doomed endeavor to turn the Indian into an "imitation white man." The education the Hopi received away from the reservation was tragically irrelevant to the conditions under which the returned student lived after graduation. Indeed, surrounded by the modern conveniences at Phoenix or Sherman, the Hopi student might reflect on the contrast with his life at home. "He remembers the thirteenth century mesa, insufficient food at home, shortage of fuel in winter, struggle for crops in summer, lack of water, hard work for everything. Perhaps he thinks he is wasting his time, knowing to what he will return." Perhaps, too, he had learned a trade he would probably never be able to practice. Had anyone ever considered, Crane mused, that he would have to apply his modern skills in a thirteenth-century pueblo "located in the heart of the desert one hundred miles from a town or a railroad?" And finally, the student was sent home with a "little pin-money and WITHOUT TOOLS."

Then came the shock of adjustment. "The hand that has been firmly thrusting between his shoulder blades for fifteen years, has suddenly been removed." At first he traveled to the agency seeking employment and an opportunity to apply his newly acquired skills, but in all like-lihood this was an impossibility. He was in the ludicrous position of being a blacksmith where there were no forges, a carpenter where lumber was scarce, a tailor where flour-sacks were used for clothes, a shoemaker where moccasins were worn, and a painter where there was nothing to paint. The inevitable process of relapse soon began: "First, the money goes; then the good clothes and the 'Regal' shoes wear out; third, nature is busy on his hair. He binds up his hair with a gaudy handkerchief, as do the others; he begins to make a pair of moccasins." In the meantime, tribal elders, "in strict patriarchal fashion," remind him of the small corn field, a few horses, and some sheep that they have set aside for him. "Gradually he accepts that which he has. He ceases his visits to the Agency asking for a job. The old life is before him. He has, apparently, become an Indian of the Indians."

Despite this depressing scenario, Crane was unwilling to state that the returned student had gone back to the blanket. The educated Hopi was in fact decidedly different from those Hopi who had never been schooled in the white man's ways. While the returned student might soon appear at the agency a trifle unkempt, "he does speak English when not fearful that some stranger will laugh at his grammar, and he has not come as a beggar." Moreover, if he was shown the advantage of a modern convenience or utility, he was more likely to desire it than the Hopi who had never been to school. And perhaps most importantly: "It will be easier to obtain his children for their education, and the hold of the medicine man has been somewhat loosened." Crane felt these were not unimportant consequences of the Hopi's education. He believed the returned student was a failure only to the extent that he was *"not what the tax-payer expected him to be."* Again, Crane remained critical of the nonreservation school. If the Hopi was destined to live a simple life in the vast Arizona desert, then he asked: "Why insert this artificial period in his education?"

Criticism of the nonreservation school caused school officials to search for ways to prepare their graduating students for reservation life. A psychological tactic often used by schools was the "returned student conference." Such conferences not only enabled recent graduates to renew their institutional association with the source of their cultural elevation and to hear again the inspiring message of civilization, it also offered an opportunity to impress upon graduating students just how immense the pressures for conformity were back on the reservation. In 1910, for instance, one school official at Phoenix told members of a conference:

> I most sincerely trust that you who are leaving the school for your homes this year do not underestimate the influence your homes will have to draw you away from what you have learned at this school.... I know you feel so well grounded... in your hope of doing good... on your reservations that you do not realize what you will have to overcome. Remember you are but one against many and among that many... are relatives and friends even dearer than any friendships formed in this school. Remember too, they believe themselves just as much in the right in their beliefs as you do in yours.... Your lessons of industry, civilization and Christianity have been taught to you but very few years compared with the many years during which customs have been growing in your people.

There was a fatal flaw in how school officials attacked the problem of relapse, and it goes to the very heart of this chapter in Indian-white relations. They assumed that the difficulty was due to the conservative nature of tribal elders and a certain character flaw of the returning students, their inability to withstand ridicule and hardship for the sake of civilized principles. They ignored altogether the charge of superintendent Crane that the nonreservation boarding school was itself to blame because it prepared the Indian student for a life that did not exist on the reservation. They ignored too the possibility that many returning students readopted the old culture out of conscious preference for the Hopi way. Neither the Indian office in Washington nor school officials in the field ever considered the possibility that the real source of the returned student problem lay in the questionable premises that had historically shaped the nation's Indian policy—premises relating to such ethnocentric conceptions as "savagism," "civilization," and "progress." It is not surprising that this last explanation was never considered. To have done so would have required a painful reexamination of the entire rationale by which white Americans had justified the dispossession of the Indian's land and culture. Given all that was at stake, it was simply too much to ask.

3

The Outlaws: The Legend of Jesse Jar
and His Gang

ALBERT CASTEL

● *Long before Frederick Jackson Turner gave his famous 1893 address on "The Significance of the Frontier in American History," the idea of the West was important to Americans. In a vast, almost unexplored and unknown land, the men and women who first faced the wilderness and the savages were obvious candidates for hero-worship. Oral legends circulated about a Tennessee backwoodsman named Davy Crockett even before he was dead; when he fell at the Alamo in 1836, his place in folklore was assured. Kit Carson, Wild Bill Hickok, and Buffalo Bill were among other superhuman heroes who shaped a national ideology of self-reliance, energy, and optimism.*

Of course the image of the West did not conform to reality; the average frontiersman did not kill wild animals with his bare hands, and the streets of Dodge City did not regularly run with the blood of high noon shootouts. Contrary to the popular Hollywood stereotype, the Plains Indians were not incompetent strategists who rode around in circles until white marksmen could shoot them off their mounts. And at no time in the nineteenth century did the West account for as much as 10 percent of the national population.

Yet the images and the legends live on. The Western outlaw is a popular candidate for mythology, not only because he operated outside the existing legal system, but because he seemed to personify a restless national spirit. The image of the gunfighter is often that of a good and decent man driven to a life of violence and early death by evil and unfortunate circumstances. So it was with Jesse and Frank James and the

Reproduced through the courtesy of Cowles Magazine, publisher of *American History Illustrated*.

founger brothers. They were America's most famous des-
perados, and there was a high price on their heads. The
complexity of their experience is expertly captured by the
following essay of Albert Castel.

On August 7, 1863 the Liberty, Missouri *Tribune,* a pro-Union newspaper, carried the following item:

> THREE SOUTHERN GENTLEMEN IN SEARCH OF THEIR RIGHTS—
> On the morning of the 6th of August, Franklin James, with two
> others of the same stripe, stopped David Mitchell, on his road
> to Leavenworth, about 6 miles west of Liberty, and took from
> him $1.25, his pocket knife, and a pass he had from the Provost
> Marshall to cross the plains. This is one of the rights these men
> are fighting for. James sent his compliments to Major Green, and
> said he would like to see him.

Such was the first recorded robbery committed by Frank James.
During the next two decades he, his brother Jesse, and their sidekicks,
the Younger brothers, became America's most famous outlaws. Today,
a century after Jesse's murder and Frank's surrender in 1882, they still
possess that distinction. Here is the story of their rise to fame, along
with the sometimes brutal facts behind it; facts which have been concealed by legend like a bandit's face by a mask.

Alexander Franklin James and Jesse Woodson James were born,
respectively, on January 10, 1843, and September 5, 1847, on a farm
near Kearney, Missouri, a town twelve miles northeast of the Clay
County seat at Liberty and twenty-seven miles from downtown Kansas City to the southwest. Their father, Robert James, was an or-
dained minister; their mother, Zerelda Cole, attended school at a
Catholic convent. In 1842, shortly after being married, Robert and Zerelda left their native Kentucky to settle in Clay County, where Robert became pastor of a Baptist church, acquired a farm and slaves,
and helped found William Jewell College at Liberty. Thus the family
background of Frank and Jesse seems to have been quite solid and
respectable.

But it did not remain so for long. In 1850 Robert joined the rush to
California in quest of gold; instead he found illness and death. Zerelda
remarried twice: first, Benjamin Simms, who soon left her and then

died; next, in 1859, Doctor Reuben Samuel, a quiet, acquiescent man who devoted himself to working the James' farm. Zerelda bore him four children, two boys and two girls. How young Frank and Jesse reacted to their father's departure and death, their mother's remarriages, and the influx of half brothers and sisters is unknown, as is any authentic information about their boyhoods.

In the summer of 1861 the Civil War came to Missouri. Most of the population remained loyal to the Union. However, in the hemp-growing and slaveholding counties of western Missouri many people supported the Confederacy. Among them was the James-Samuel family. Frank, now a lanky, callow-looking youth of eighteen, joined the pro-Confederate Missouri forces of Major General Sterling Price and took part in the battle of Wilson's Creek (August 10, 1861) and the siege of Lexington, Missouri (September 12–20, 1861). But when Price retreated into Arkansas early in 1862 Frank, as did many other discouraged Missouri Rebels, deserted and returned home. There he took an oath of allegiance to the United States and posted $1,000 bond for future good behavior.

Meanwhile guerrilla war had broken out in Missouri. Bands of Kansas jayhawkers ravaged the western border, and Unionist militia persecuted and plundered Confederate sympathizers. In defense and retaliation the latter formed gangs of "bushwhackers" who raided into Kansas and terrorized Unionists in Missouri. The most successful and notorious of these gangs was that of William Clarke Quantrill, an Ohio-born renegade. One of Quantrill's followers was tall, muscular Thomas Coleman Younger. Cole joined Quantrill in January 1862, at the age of eighteen, after jayhawkers burned his father's livery stable at Harrisonville and threatened to kill him. Subsequently they did murder his father, imprisoned his sister, and drove his mother out of the family home, which they burned. Contrary to the assumption of some writers, he in no way was related to the Jameses.

By July 1862 bushwhacking was so rampant that the governor of Missouri ordered every man of military age to enroll in the state militia. Since this had the effect of forcing pro-Confederates to side with enemies against friends, many of them promptly "took to the brush." Among them was Frank James. In time he became a member of a Clay County guerrilla band headed by William "Bloody Bill" Anderson, a

ferocious killer who decorated the bridle of his horse with the scalps
of Federal soldiers.

On August 21, 1863, Anderson and his gang, Frank included, joined
Quantrill in a raid on Lawrence, Kansas, where they helped massacre
upwards of 160 helpless men and boys. Six weeks later, on October
6, 1863, they participated in the slaughter of nearly one hundred Union
soldiers at Baxter Springs, Kansas. During the winter of 1863–64 the
bushwhackers camped near Sherman, Texas, where they robbed and
occasionally murdered civilians. Many of them by then were crossing
the line, always narrow, between guerrilla war and sheer banditry.

In the spring of 1864 Anderson's band returned to its "stomping
grounds" in Missouri. Soon afterward Jesse, now seventeen, joined the
group. More than likely he would have done so in any case, but during
the past summer Union militia had tortured Dr. Samuel, abused the
pregnant Mrs. Samuel, and administered a whipping to Jesse, thereby
removing any hesitation he might have felt. Under Anderson, and riding
behind Frank, he took part in numerous raids, robberies, ambushes,
fights, and massacres. The most gruesome of the latter occurred on
September 27, 1864, at Centralia. First Anderson's men stopped a train,
robbed all of its passengers, and then murdered nearly thirty of them,
mostly unarmed Federal soldiers home on leave. Next they attacked
and overwhelmed 147 militiamen, slaughtering 124 of them and mu-
tilating their corpses. If the testimony of Frank is to be credited (a risky
thing to do), Jesse distinguished himself in this "battle" by shooting
the militia commander, Major A. V. E. Johnston.

A month later Anderson was killed in a fight outside of Richmond,
Missouri, by militiamen who subsequently cut off his head and
mounted it on a telegraph pole. At the same time the Federals routed
Price's army, which had invaded Missouri in a last desperate attempt
to secure it for the Confederacy. Most of the bushwhackers, including
Jesse, followed Price into Texas, where they spent the winter. However,
Frank joined a number of guerrillas who went with Quantrill to Kentucky. There, on July 26, 1865, after the capture and death of Quantrill,
Frank and the other survivors of this ill-starred expedition surrendered
to the Federal authorities, who released them as soon as they took the
oath of allegiance.

Meanwhile, in Missouri most of the remaining Quantrill-Anderson men
did likewise upon returning from Texas in the spring and finding that

with the collapse of the Confederacy it was pointless to continue their war-within-a-war. Jesse, however, was not one of them. According to his family and friends, he was on the way to Lexington, Missouri, to sign parole papers when a squad of Union soldiers shot and badly wounded him. Possibly this is true; certainly Jesse spent the summer and fall of 1865 at his mother's home recuperating from a wound. In any event he never surrendered.

As was to be expected, Missouri Unionists viewed the ex-guerrillas with resentment and subjected them to varying degrees of harassment, in a few instances driving the more notorious ones from their homes. Even so, the majority of the bushwhackers who wanted to settle down and lead a peaceful, law-abiding life were able to do so. The trouble was that some of them did not want to, or at least did not try very hard. This was especially true of those whose criminal tendencies had been developed and confirmed by bushwhacking. Finding a humdrum, poverty-tinged existence on a farm tedious after the exciting life and easy money of wartime, they could not resist the temptation to make use of the skills acquired under Quantrill and Anderson.

On the afternoon of February 13, 1866, a dozen former bushwhackers looted the Clay County Savings Bank in Liberty of nearly $60,000, in the process murdering a student from William Jewell, the college Frank's and Jesse's father helped establish. It was the first daylight bank robbery in American history, not counting the plundering of two banks in St. Albans, Vermont, in 1864 by Confederate raiders operating out of Canada. It also marked the beginning of a series of bank holdups by gangs of ex-guerrillas: Lexington, Missouri, October 30, 1866; Savannah, Missouri, March 2, 1867; Richmond, Missouri, May 22, 1867; and Russellville, Kentucky, March 20, 1868.

Probably Frank and Jesse participated in at least some of these robberies, although at the time they occurred neither the authorities nor the newspapers accused them of involvement. But then, on December 7, 1869, in Gallatin, Missouri, two men entered the Daviess County Savings Bank, where one of them cold-bloodedly shot the cashier, a former Union militia officer, through the head and heart. As they left the bank carrying several hundred dollars, townsmen opened fire. The bandit who murdered the cashier was unable to mount his excited horse, whereupon he jumped up behind his companion and together they galloped out of town. Several citizens identified the abandoned horse as a mare belonging to Jesse. A posse pursued the bandits to the James-Samuel farm, only to see Frank and Jesse dash out of a barn on fresh horses and escape.

The James brothers denied responsibility for the Gallatin murder and robbery and even obtained affdavits (of dubious worth) from people in Clay County swearing to their innocence. However, they refused to submit to arrest and stand trial, claiming—with good cause—that they would be lynched like several other former bushwhackers suspected of crimes. Hence they became, if they were not already, professional outlaws.

Little that is reliable is known about the beginning of Cole Younger's bandit career. If we are to believe his own story, which is filled with distortions and exaggerations, following the end of the war he settled down on a farm near Lee's Summit, Missouri (now a Kansas City suburb) and tried to lead a lawful, peaceful life. But vindictive Unionists forced him to go into hiding in order to avoid arrest for an alleged wartime murder; then they falsely blamed him and his brother Jim, also an ex-Quantrillian, for every crime committed in the area. Finally, out of sheer desperation, they decided to live up to their reputations and so teamed up with the Jameses.

Between 1870 and 1876 the James-Younger gang ranged from Kansas to Kentucky and from Iowa to Texas robbing banks, holding up stages, and sticking up trains. The latter especially excited the public imagination, being both novel and dramatic. Although the Reno brothers of Indiana were the first bandits to engage in train robberies, those committed by the Jameses and Youngers received far greater publicity. Furthermore, they did not necessarily get the idea from the Renos; as already noted, Frank and Jesse were with Bloody Bill Anderson when his band waylaid a train at Centralia in 1864.

Soon the "James boys" and "Younger brothers" were household names over America. Newspapers headlined their exploits, often attributing to them deeds they could not possibly have performed unless they had a supernatural knack for being in two widely separated places simultaneously. The *Police Gazette* and similar magazines published vivid accounts, accompanied by garish drawings, of their supposed doings. And hack writers made them the protagonists of highly imaginative stories published in crudely illustrated dime novels which were sold at depots and aboard trains, among them the very trains they robbed!

Sheriffs and police officers throughout the West tried to track down the famed outlaws, as did the Pinkerton Detective Agency. Their efforts were invariably and sometimes absurdly futile. Besides their own bumbling ineptitude, they were handicapped by the fact that thousands of pro-Southern Missourians believed that the Jameses and Youngers were innocent victims of Unionist-Republican persecution and hence were more than willing to help them. Foremost among this element was newspaper editor John N. Edwards, a former Confederate major and the close friend of Frank and Jesse. Not only did he defend them, he glorified them with purple prose in his various writings. Thus, following their robbery of the gate receipts at the Kansas City Fair on September 26, 1872, during which they accidentally shot a little girl in the leg, he published an editorial in the Kansas City *Times* entitled "The Chivalry of Crime" in which he compared them to the Knights of the Round Table.

Missouri sympathy for the bandits peaked early in 1875. On the night of January 26 a group of Pinkerton detectives, three of whose colleagues had been gunned down by the Jameses and Youngers in recent encounters, sneaked up to the James-Samuel home and tossed what they later claimed was a flare lamp through a window. The Samuels shoved the flaming device into the fireplace where it exploded, killing nine-year-old Archie Samuel and mangling Mrs. Samuel's right arm so badly that it had to be amputated below the elbow. Neither Frank nor Jesse was captured, although evidently at least one of them was present.

This tragic event aroused indignation throughout Missouri and led to the introduction of a bill in the legislature which provided for the pardoning of all ex-bushwhackers for their wartime deeds and promised them a fair trial for all alleged postwar crimes. But before the legislature could act Frank and Jesse murdered—or so it was thought—a neighbor whom they suspected of aiding the Pinkertons. As a result the trend of public sentiment turned against them and the bill failed.

So far all of the robberies perpetrated by the Jameses and Youngers had taken place in regions they were familiar with and where friends or relatives could aid escape. Then, late in the summer of 1876, following a July 7 train stickup at Rocky Cut near Otterville, Missouri, a member of the gang known as Bill Chadwell (real name William Stils) persuaded the others that his home state of Minnesota offered rich and easy pickings. As a consequence, on the morning of September 7 eight men, all dressed in long, linen dusters, rode into Northfield, Minnesota. They were Frank and Jesse James, Cole, Bob and Jim Younger, Chadwell, and two ruffians called Clell Miller and Charlie Pitts.

Three of the men dismounted and entered the First National Bank. They ordered cashier Joseph Heywood to open the vault. He refused. One of the bandits, probably either Jesse or Frank, shot him. The teller, A. E. Bunker, ran out the back door, undeterred by a bullet in the shoulder. Meanwhile several townsmen, having perceived that a robbery was in progress, opened fire with rifles and shotguns on the mounted men outside the bank. Two of them—Chadwell and Miller— tumbled dead from their horses. Bullets from the robbers' revolvers in turn killed the sheriff and a Swedish immigrant who understood neither English nor what was happening. The outlaws inside the bank rushed out, remounted, and along with the others galloped away under a hail of bullets. Bob Younger's horse went down; Bob, whose right elbow had been shattered by a rifle bullet, was picked up by a companion, most likely Cole, then continued his flight.

As hundreds of grim-faced possemen scoured western Minnesota, the unsuccessful raiders sought to make their way back to Missouri. But they were slowed down by their ignorance of the countryside, heavy rains, and above all by the badly wounded Bob Younger. According to some accounts, Frank and Jesse proposed abandoning, even killing him. Cole, however, refused to allow it. Eventually the Jameses went off alone and reached home safely.

The Youngers and Pitts were less lucky. On September 21 near Madelia, Minnesota, a posse cornered them in a swamp. A short, onesided gun battle ensued. Pitts was killed and the Youngers, literally riddled with bullets, surrendered. After recovering sufficiently they stood trial for murder and attempted robbery. They pleaded guilty and were sentenced to life imprisonment in the Minnesota State Penitentiary at Stillwater.

For three years following the Northfield fiasco Frank and Jesse lay low. Contrary to the billboards of certain present-day tourist traps, neither then nor at any other time did they hide out in caves. Instead they lived under assumed names with their wives and children in places like Nashville, St. Louis, and even Kansas City. As Frank once remarked, "Most people look alike in the city." Given the primitive identification devices and the haphazard police communications of the era, it was not necessary for them to adopt disguises or take elaborate precautions. In fact, law enforcement agencies lacked both photographs and detailed descriptions. All they knew was that they were tall, lanky, and bearded, which was not much to go on.

Then, in spectacular style, the James boys—or at least Jesse—came out of retirement. First, on October 8, 1879, a gang led by Jesse ransacked a safe aboard a train at Glendale, Missouri. Next, on July 15, 1881, they held up a Rock Island train near Winston, Missouri, murdering the conductor and a passenger. And on the night of September 7, 1881 (fifth anniversary of the Northfield raid), the gang robbed both the safe and the passengers on a Chicago & Alton train at Blue Cut, east of Independence. The engineer of the latter stated that the leader of the bandits, before riding off, shook hands with him and said, "You are a brave man . . . here is $2 for you to drink the health of Jesse James with tomorrow morning." In addition, a Jackson County farmer who had been arrested for participating in the Glendale affair testified in court that Jesse had recruited him and provided him with a revolver and shotgun. As a result, only fanatics like Edwards continued to call Frank and Jesse guiltless victims of persecution.

Thomas T. Crittenden, the newly installed Democratic governor of Missouri, decided to put an end to the Jameses once and for all. They had caused Missouri to become known as the "outlaw state," they were bad for business, and they were furnishing political ammunition to the Republicans, who accused the Democrats of not really trying to apprehend them. Accordingly he announced a reward of $10,000 (to be paid by the railroad companies) for information leading to the capture, dead or alive, of either Frank or Jesse.

Crittenden's offer produced results. Among the new members of the James gang were two more brothers—Charles and Robert Ford. On December 4, 1881, Bob Ford and a veteran bandit named Dick Liddil killed Wood Hite, also an outlaw and Frank and Jesse's cousin, in a quarrel over a woman. Fearful that Jesse would slay him in revenge, Liddil arranged to surrender to Sheriff James A. Timberlake of Clay County after first obtaining assurances of leniency from Crittenden if he helped apprehend Jesse. On learning of this, Bob Ford realized that Jesse surely would suspect him as a friend of Liddel. Hence he too contacted Timberlake and Crittenden, with the result that he and his brother agreed to tip off Timberlake as to the time and place of the gang's next operation. For his part Crittenden promised the Fords immunity from punishment and a share of the reward money.

Late in March 1882, the Fords went to the house in St. Joseph, Missouri, where Jesse, under the alias of Thomas Howard, had been living with his wife and two children since November. Together with Jesse they planned to rob the bank in nearby Platte City on April 4. However, on the morning of April 3, while eating breakfast with the Fords, Jesse read in the Kansas City *Times* that Liddil had surrendered to the authorities. Immediately Bob Ford sensed that Jesse now knew the Fords intended to betray him. So when Jesse removed his pistol belt—something he had never done before—and stood on a chair to dust a picture on the wall, Bob Ford thought two things: first, that Jesse was seeking to throw him off guard by pretending to have complete confidence in him; second, that "Now or never is your chance. If you don't get him now he'll get you tonight." So Bob pulled out the revolver that Jesse had given him the day before and fired. The bullet tore through the back of Jesse's skull behind the right ear and, in Bob Ford's own words, "he fell like a log, dead."

Brought to trial in St. Joseph on a charge of murder, Charles and Bob Ford pleaded guilty, were sentenced to death, and were promptly pardoned by Crittenden. Ten years later, in Creede, Colorado, Bob Ford himself fell victim to a murderer's pistol, having achieved the gloomy notoriety of being "that dirty little coward that shot Mr. Howard." Charles Ford committed suicide in 1896.

By 1882 Frank James was thirty-nine and at least semi-retired from banditry. The murder of Jesse convinced him that if he was going to reach forty, he had better make peace with the law. Therefore, with Edwards serving as his intermediary, he surrendered to Crittenden at Jefferson City on October 5, 1882. Twice, once at Gallatin, Missouri, and again at Muscle Shoals, Alabama, he stood trial for his alleged crimes, and each time a sympathetic jury acquitted him for lack of convincing evidence. It never was proved in a strictly legal sense that the James boys ever committed so much as a single robbery!

During the years that followed his second acquittal, Frank eked out a shabby existence as a shoe store clerk, theater guard in St. Louis, and horse-race starter at county fairs. Meanwhile a group of Missourians sought pardons for the Younger brothers, who in hopes of parole were model prisoners. In 1901 the governor of Minnesota granted conditional paroles to Cole and Jim—Bob had died of tuberculosis in 1889—but required them to remain in the state. Soon after his release Jim, despondent because the parole board refused him permission to marry, committed suicide in a St. Paul hotel room. In 1903 the Minnesota authorities gave Cole a complete pardon, and he returned to his old home at Lee's Summit. He now was a fat, bald, old man. Only his hard, cold eyes bespoke the tough young bushwhacker and bandit of yore.

For a while Frank and Cole traded on their notoriety by touring with the "Cole Younger—Frank James Wild West Show." Then they separated, with Frank spending most of his time at the old James-Samuel farm, where he charged visitors fifty cents apiece for a tour. On February 18, 1915, he died. As for Cole, he gave lectures on "What Life Has Taught Me," published an autobiography in which he claimed that the only robbery he ever took part in was at Northfield, and was the center of attention at the annual reunions of the survivors of Quantrill's band. One year after Frank's death, he too went to his reward.

Thus Frank and Cole ended their long careers as living legends—legends somewhat tarnished, however, by the very fact that they were living and had to make a living. Jesse on the other hand achieved the perfect legend. Even before he died he was more famous than Frank, in part because of the alliterative quality of his name, in part because he had a stronger personality and was more active, at least in the later years. His death and the manner of it wiped away, in the popular mind, the harsh reality of his deeds and transformed him into the classic bandit-hero whose daring and cunning render him invincible until he is brought down by base treachery. In this sense Bob Ford did Jesse a favor: It would not have been the same if he had died in bed, like Cole and brother Frank, from old age.

4

Florida's Black Codes

JERRELL H. SHOFNER

• *The surrender terms offered by General Ulysses S. Grant to Robert E. Lee's proud but dwindling Army of Northern Virginia were among the most generous in history, especially in view of the suffering, anguish, and emotion which accompanied the Civil War. At Appomatox Court House, the commander of the Union Army was both magnanimous and sensitive. All that was required was that Confederate soldiers put down their arms and go home in peace.*

But the battlefield result did not immediately make clear what the political future would be for those Southern whites who had led their states out of the Union. According to tradition, and to a considerable segment of Northern sentiment, such men were traitors to the United States. Southern voters understandably took a different view and promptly returned many leaders of the secessionist movement to Washington as members of Congress. Simultaneously, other firebrands of the old Confederacy gained dominance over the various state legislatures and promptly began to limit the social, political, and economic rights of the former slaves.

The result was a series of racist and repressive laws known to history as the "black codes." They were intended both to guarantee the subservience of the entire black population and to assure the continued division of Southern society along strict racial lines. Although they varied from state to state in severity, the black codes generally prevented African-Americans from bearing arms or from working at occupations other than farming and domestic service.

As Jerrell H. Shofner makes clear in the following article, these initial inhibitions proved to be only the first set of a long series of measures designed to preserve the "Southern way of

Reprinted with permission of the editor from *Florida Historical Quarterly*, January 1977.

life." The black codes were followed by the "Jim Crow" laws between 1890 and 1910. These new restrictions, which legalized segregation in public facilities and which introduced such concepts as the literacy test, the "grandfather clause," the white primary, and the poll tax, made it almost impossible for blacks to rise above the lowest rung of the economic ladder, or indeed even to protest effectively. Thus a rigidly enforced segregation system came to dominate all aspects of Southern life. Even after two decades of militant civil rights activity, this legacy has just begun to be erased.

In October 1956, Dr. Deborah Coggins, health officer for Madison, Jefferson, and Taylor counties, sat down to lunch in Madison, Florida, with a public health nurse to discuss a matter of mutual official concern. Because of their busy schedules the lunch hour was the only mutually available time for the meeting. But since the doctor was white and the nurse black, the business luncheon led to the dismissal of the doctor by indignant commissioners of the three counties. Her "breach of social tradition" had been so serious, according to the commissioners, that it rendered her unfit to continue in the office to which she had been appointed about six months earlier. While Governor LeRoy Collins disagreed, and incensed citizens of South Florida condemned the commissioners, most white North Floridians nodded approval. As they saw it, Dr. Coggins had violated one of the strictest taboos of her community when "she ate with the darkies." As a native of Tampa married to a descendant of an old Madison County family, she should have known better.

Social intercourse between whites and blacks was forbidden by both law and custom in Florida in the 1950s. And it had been that way as long as most people then living could remember. The one brief period following the Civil War when things had been different had merely proved that segregation was the best way for all concerned. This belief was reinforced by all the myths and folk tales, social institutions, and statute laws with which Floridians of the 1950s were acquainted.

Those few years following the Civil War had been crucial ones for white Floridians, most of whom had sympathized with and supported the Confederate war effort. Defeated, disorganized, and bankrupt in 1865, they had taken heart when President Andrew Johnson announced his plans for reconstructing the nation. Guaranteeing former Confederates retention of all their property except slaves, he appointed William Marvin as provisional governor to oversee the formation of a new government. To gain readmission to the Union, Florida had only to repudiate slavery, secession, and debts incurred in support of the Confederacy, and recognize all laws enacted by Congress while the state was out of the Union. Marvin repeatedly told white audiences that if they would change the laws to provide civil rights to the newly freed blacks that he believed they would not be required to implement Negro suffrage. Retrospectively this implied promise seems to have been an unfortunate one. Radical congressmen had been contending with Abraham Lincoln and later Andrew Johnson for control of Reconstruction policy. What white Floridians regarded as major concessions to former slaves was far less than Radical congressmen believed necessary. The latter watched with growing concern as the southern state governments created by President Johnson enacted their "black codes" which distinguished between black and white citizens. And the final decision on Johnson's Reconstruction program rested with Congress.

The delegates to the 1865 constitutional convention and the members of the 1865–1866 legislature who enacted the Florida black code had spent their lives as members of the dominant white class in a society whose labor system was based on racial chattel slavery. They brought to their law-making sessions all their past experiences gained from a lifetime acquaintance with a comprehensive ideological and legal framework for racial slavery. They believed that blacks were so mentally inferior and incompetent to order their own affairs that subjection to the superior white race was their natural condition. Whites benefited from the labor of blacks, and they were in turn obligated to provide guidance and welfare for their workers. Now that slavery was abolished these men met to comply with Andrew Johnson's requirements, while, at the same time, trying to salvage as much as possible of that system under which whites with their paternalistic responsibilities to blacks, and Negroes with their natural limitations, had lived peacefully.

Florida had a comprehensive slave code regulating almost every activity touching the lives of blacks. Because "free Negroes" had constituted an anomaly in a society where racial slavery was so central, there was also an extensive set of laws regulating their affairs. It was understandable that the lawmakers of 1865–1866 should draw on their past experiences and on the codes regulating slaves and free blacks. But in doing so they invited criticism from suspicious Radicals in Congress who believed that the president had erred in his lenient requirements.

A three-member committee was named by the constitutional convention of 1865 to recommend to the first legislature, scheduled to meet the following year, changes in the old laws necessary to make them conform to the postwar situation. The committee's report did nothing to assuage congressional suspicions. It urged the legislature to preserve, insofar as possible, the beneficial features of that "benign, but much abused and greatly misunderstood institution of slavery." It strenuously asserted the legislature's power to discriminate. Such power had always been executed by all the states of the Union, including those of New England. Slavery had been abolished, but nothing had been done to the status of the "free negro." Certainly, therefore, "Freedmen" could not possibly occupy a higher position in the scale of rights than had the "free negro" before the war.

Provisional Governor William Marvin, who had been appointed by President Johnson in 1865, warned that Congress was likely to intervene unless the state legislature accepted the concept of Negro freedom and extended to freedmen equal protection of the law. Despite this warning, the legislature followed the committee's recommendations. It enacted laws dealing with crime and punishment, vagrancy, apprenticeship, marriages, taxation, labor contracts, and the judicial system which were collectively referred to as the black code. The code clearly established a separate class of citizenship for blacks, making them inferior to whites.

A long list of crimes was enumerated and penalties assigned. The death penalty was imposed for inciting insurrection, raping a white female, or administering poison. Burglary was punishable by death, a fine not exceeding $1,000, or a public whipping and the pillory. Malicious trespass, buying or selling cotton without evidence of ownership, defacement of public or private property, and other crimes of similar nature were punishable by fines, imprisonment, or whipping and the pillory. Whipping or the pillory was also the prescribed punishment for injuring someone else's livestock, hunting with a gun on another's property, or unauthorized use of a horse whether in the employ of the owner or not. According to an antebellum statute continued in force by the 1865–1866 legislature, Negroes were specifically denied the right to carry firearms, bowie knives, dirks, or swords without a license from the probate judge. The punishment was forfeiture of the weapon and a whipping, the pillory, or both. This provision reflected some concern among white Floridians at the time about a rumored Negro insurrection, which had no substantive basis.

"AN ACT to punish Vagrants and Vagabonds" made all persons subject to arrest who could not demonstrate that they were gainfully employed. Aimed at preventing congregation of freedmen in the towns, this law was especially alarming to Radical congressmen. A convicted vagrant could post bond as a guarantee of good behavior for the following year, but if no bond was posted, he could be punished by the pillory, whipping, prison, or by being sold for his labor up to one year to pay his fine and costs. "AN ACT in relation to Apprentices" allowed the courts to apprentice the children of vagrants or paupers to persons who could supervise their activities, provide for them, and teach them a trade. It applied to both races, but in the aftermath of emancipation most of the children affected were black. This was only a slight extension of an antebellum law requiring that all free blacks over twelve years of age have a duly registered white guardian.

For the first time, a statute defined a Negro as any person with one-eighth Negro blood. Although that standard still left much to interpretation, some such ruling was necessary to the enforcement of several acts intended to separate the races. Both blacks and whites were enjoined from attending the meetings of the other race. They were also required to ride only in railroad cars designated for their respective races. Marriages between Negro men and white women were prohibited. White violators of the enactment could be fined $1,000, jailed for three months, or both. In addition to the fine, Negroes could be made to stand in the pillory for one hour, receive thirty-nine lashes, or both.

One of the most controversial enactments was "AN ACT to establish and enforce the Marriage Relation between Persons of Color." Negro couples were given nine months to decide whether they wished to continue living together. After that time they had either to separate or be legally married. This method of correcting a problem arising from slavery and its abolition caused so much criticism in the northern press that the legislature in November 1866 simply passed a law declaring all freedmen living as man and wife to be legally married.

Even the revenue laws seemed discriminatory. There was a provision for a five-mill property tax on real property and a capitation tax of three dollars on every male between twenty-one and fifty-five. The Negroes often did not learn of the tax in time or did not have the money to pay it. If they were delinquent they could be arrested and sold for their labor for a period long enough to liquidate the obligations incurred. Several cases of tax-delinquent blacks being sold for a year's labor soon caught the attention of the northern press. Such an exorbitant punishment for failure to pay a three-dollar tax seemed to some congressmen to be a substitute for the bonded servitude which had just been abolished.

Although the legislators followed closely a system already established by the military commanders, their "ACT in relation to Contracts of Persons of Color" also distinguished between the races. Contracts were to be in writing and witnessed by two white persons. If Negroes broke their agreements, they could be punished as common vagrants by being whipped, put in the pillory, imprisoned, or sold for up to one year's labor. They could also be found in violation of their contract for "willful disobedience," "wanton impudence," "disrespect" to the employer, failure to perform assigned work, or "abandonment of the premises." If the employer broke the contract, the laborer could seek redress in the courts. Although the state attorney general ruled the law unconstitutional, the next legislature rewrote it so as to apply to both races in occupations limited almost entirely to Negroes.

An early crop lien law was intended to keep tenants on the land. A landlord was empowered to seek a writ placing a lien against growing crops on rented land if the rent was not paid within ten days of the due date. If a tenant did not pay out at the end of the year, the lien could be extended to the next year and he could be legally held on the land. Attracting little attention as part of the black code at the time, this statute, with subsequent additions, contributed largely to an agricultural system which kept many tenants in economic bondage for years after the Civil War.

Central features of the black codes were "AN ACT to extend to all the inhabitants of the State the benefits of the Courts of Justice and the processes thereof" and another "prescribing additional penalties for the commission of offenses against the State, and for other purposes." The convention-appointed committee in its recommendations

to the legislature had bemoaned the loss of that highly efficient institution which had existed on the plantations for punishing those "minor
offenses to which Negroes are addicted." Since those offenses were
now under the jurisdiction of the judiciary, the committee declared that
circuit courts would be unable to handle the increased volume of liti-
gation. It accordingly proposed that criminal courts be established in
each county and the legislative assembly complied. These courts were
soon handling cases, but the heritage of slavery days was too much for
them. The legislators had permitted Negroes the right to testify only
in cases involving blacks, and juries were made up of white men only.
These whites had lived in a society where Negro slaves had had no
standing in the courts, and they were now unwilling to accept the word
of blacks. The courts were abject failures as legal remedies for freedmen
accused of crimes or seeking redress of wrongs committed by whites.

The law "prescribing additional penalties" was a response to the
special committee's recommendation that "whenever a crime be punishable by fine and imprisonment we add an alternative of the pillory
for an hour or whipping up to thirty-nine lashes or both at the discretion
of the jury." This discrimination was "founded upon the soundest
principles of State policy, growing out of the difference that exists in
social and political status of the two races. To degrade a white man
by physical punishment is to make a bad member of society and a
dangerous political agent. To fine and imprison a colored man . . . is to
punish the State instead of the individual."

The Floridians who enacted the "black code" were surprised and
angered by the national reaction they caused. Thomas W. Osborn,
assistant commissioner of the Freedmen's Bureau in Florida, intervened
to prevent the administration of corporal punishment. Radicals in Congress pointed to the discriminatory legislation to show that Negroes
could not expect equal treatment as long as the antebellum Florida
leaders remained in power. With similar legislation in other former
Confederate states, the Florida black code helped the Radicals convince
their moderate colleagues that President Johnson's Reconstruction plan
had failed to furnish necessary protection to newly-freed persons. In a
mammoth executive-legislative struggle which lasted through most of
1866, Congress overturned the Johnson governments in the South and
implemented Congressional Reconstruction in 1867–1868.

Based on Negro suffrage—which Provisional Governor Marvin had said would not happen—and military supervision, the congressional plan seemed to Floridians to be a broken bargain. In late 1866 Governor Walker complained that the state had complied with President Johnson's Reconstruction requirements, but that Floridians were still being denied their rights. The subsequent implementation of Negro suffrage, enactment of the 1868 constitution, and the election victory of the newly-founded Florida Republican party were considered by local whites as unwelcome and unwise invasions of the rights of the state.

These developments also embittered them toward their former slaves. When Negro suffrage was first announced, the planters assumed that they could control the freedman's vote. At assemblages throughout the black belt counties former owners competed with "carpetbaggers" for the allegiance of the new voters. When the blacks quite understandably ignored their former masters in favor of the new Republican leaders, the native whites lost most of their paternalistic sentiment toward the freedmen. They determined to resist Negro suffrage and Republican hegemony by every means they could muster.

Landowners and storekeepers applied economic pressures on black voters. Politicians resorted to ingenious political tactics. Conservatives in the legislature blocked action whenever possible by dilatory parliamentary maneuvers. But by far the most visible, and in the long run the costliest, method was violence. With black legislators sitting in the Capitol, black marshals advertising their tax-delinquent property for sale in the county seats, and white Republicans wielding power dependent on black voting majorities, white Floridians believed that destruction of Republican power was a goal which justified any successful means. According to one sympathetic historian who lived in post-Reconstruction Pensacola, "in this contest for a very necessary supremacy many a foul crime was committed by white against black." According to their reasoning, Republican politicians in Washington had overpowered reasonable, well-meaning President Johnson and had implemented, over his vigorous vetoes and in violation of agreements already made with southern leaders, and contrary to sound constitutional theory, a policy of Negro suffrage. Although it was not the fault of the blacks, this policy had subjected an educated, property-owning class to the mismanagement and corruption of ignorant Negroes and their carpetbagger leaders. This wrong had to be corrected regardless of the methods necessary. But in permitting the use of violence for this purpose, the white leaders unleashed a force which was almost impossible to stop.

As soon as the military commander turned over control of the state to Republican Governor Harrison Reed in July 1868 and withdrew his troops to garrison duty, violence began increasing. At first night-riding bands of hooded horsemen attempted to frighten rural Negroes into submission. But partially because many blacks showed more courage than expected and partially because it was easy to commit excesses against helpless people while shrouded in the anonymity of darkness and disguise, the scare tactics soon degenerated into merciless beatings and murder. Threats were delivered and when they went unheeded, recipients were ambushed. Dozens of white Republicans and Negroes were assassinated throughout the Florida black belt from Jackson County on the Apalachicola River to Columbia County on the Suwannee and southward to Gainesville. In Jackson County alone between 1868 and 1871, more than 150 persons were killed.

Congress responded with corrective legislation. A national elections law empowered the United States government to place supervisors at every polling place in Florida and the other southern states. Military guards were also to be deployed during elections to potentially dangerous locations. Two enforcement acts authorized President Grant to declare martial law and employ soldiers where disorder was beyond the ability of state governments to control. Before the 1872 election the worst of the violence had subsided in Florida, as much from the belief among native whites that it had achieved its purpose as from the presence of United States military forces. This episode nurtured the growth of two important aspects of the evolving myth of the Lost Cause: the idea that helpless white Southerners were being mercilessly suppressed by the military power of a hostile central government, and that they were driven to the use of violence to correct an even greater wrong—dominance of the state by an ignorant Negro electorate.

After years of delay due to opposition from Conservative-Democrats and some of the white Republicans, the legislature of 1873 enacted a civil rights law calling for equal accommodations in public places, although it *permitted,* without requiring, integrated schools. Within months of its enactment it was essentially nullified by a Leon County jurist. When several Negroes complained that they had been denied access to a skating rink in Tallahassee, the judge ruled that private owners or commercial establishments had the right to refuse service to anyone they chose. Although it remained on the books for a time, the 1873 civil rights law was a dead letter. Because its principles were opposed by a majority of white Floridians, it did nothing to change social conduct.

During the four years following President Grant's reelection in 1872 the Reconstruction process continued with diminishing velocity. Most southern states were recaptured by native white Conservative-Democratic parties despite the efforts of the Grant administration. A national depression, repeated scandals in the administration, and other matters caused northern interest in the South to wane. As the 1876 presidential election approached, many Northerners were anxious for a settlement of "the southern question." The stage was set for the final episode in the growth of the myth of the Lost Cause. When the campaign of Samuel J. Tilden and Rutherford B. Hayes for president ended in an uncertain election, the nation was subjected to nearly four months of anxiety. Hayes was ultimately inaugurated after tacitly agreeing to withdraw United States soldiers from the South. This resolution of the disputed election became known as the "compromise of 1877." When he withdrew the troops, all remaining Republican administrations in the South collapsed, and Conservative-Democratic regimes took over in their places. The men who headed those new governments came to be called "Redeemers" who had ousted the carpetbaggers and restored "home rule" in the southern states.

Left to their own devices, white and black Republicans were unable to maintain themselves. During the next few years the southern Republican parties became permanent minorities and eventually almost disappeared. The United States Supreme Court's 1883 decision in the *Civil Rights Cases* was regarded as national acceptance of the failure of Reconstruction and restoration of white supremacy in the South. In that decision the court limited the civil rights guarantees of the fourteenth amendment so that they applied only against official discrimination. Thus, while it was unconstitutional for a state to pass a law discriminating on grounds of race, it was legal for private owners of hotels, restaurants, and theaters to refuse service to blacks.

Cautiously at first, but with increasing confidence, white Floridians began rewriting their laws with a view to establishing a society similar to that envisioned in the black codes of 1865–1866. The 1868 constitution was regarded as a carpetbagger document, imposed on the state by outsiders supported by a black electorate and military force. The demand for its replacement swelled in the early 1880s. Attended by a minority of Republicans, only seven of whom were Negroes, an 1885 convention wrote a constitution which prepared the way for disfranchisement of blacks and dissolution of the Republican Party. It authorized a poll tax as a condition for voting and required that all officeholders post bonds before assuming office. The latter was intended to make it difficult for blacks to qualify for office if they were able to win in the northern counties where there were overwhelming majorities of blacks. But the poll tax provision was most important. The 1889 poll tax law required that potential voters pay their tax for two years immediately prior to elections. If the county records did not show the tax paid, then the would-be voter was required to produce receipts to prove that he was eligible to vote. An accompanying statute required separate ballot boxes for each office. These made it necessary that the voter be able to read the names on the boxes in order to place his ballots in the correct places and have them counted. The result was dramatic. Statewide Republican candidates received more than 26,000 votes in 1888; in 1892 they received fewer than 5,000.

The legal changes were accompanied by incessant racist rhetoric from public officials and the state press. School histories taught young children that the "Redeemers" had saved the state from the excesses of "Radical Reconstruction." When white Floridians divided on policy matters, Conservative-Democratic politicians reminded the voters that whites must stand together or risk a return to "Negro rule."

This tactic prevented the sundering of the paramount white man's party, but it also increased the gap between the races. Violence had declined after 1872, but it had never ceased. As the possibility of federal intervention diminished in the 1880s and the doctrine of white supremacy became more firmly entrenched, violence as a means of repressing blacks increased. The brutal Savage-James lynching at Madison in 1882 went without serious investigation. Another in Jefferson County in 1888 resulted in the arrest of five white men, but all of them were acquitted by all-white juries. Two especially repugnant lynchings in the mid–1890s led Governor William D. Bloxham to deplore the practice in his 1897 inaugural address, but he offered no remedy. The praise of white supremacy and persistent reminders of its alternatives from prominent men perpetuated a climate of tolerance for violence by whites against blacks.

Floridians were reinforced in their views by similar developments in other southern states. Worse yet, racial developments in the South coincided with a growing racial theory throughout the United States. Relying on Joseph Gobineau and other European racist writers, social theorists in the United States were preaching the idea of Anglo-Saxon superiority and the corresponding inferiority of blacks to a receptive audience. At the same time the United States acquired the Philippine Islands, and a little later Theodore Roosevelt added his "corollary" to the Monroe Doctrine. Our decision to uplift our "little brown brothers" in the Philippines and "protect" our Latin American neighbors from European interference by intervening in their internal affairs added powerful impetus to the growing racial theories in our country.

By the turn of the century the Lost Cause myth was virtually beyond question in the South and was gaining adherents elsewhere. It placed little emphasis on the demise of slavery and the failure of secession. Rather it focused on the unsuccessful efforts at postwar Reconstruction. President Johnson had been willing to permit Southerners to reform their society along lines that allowed for the innate inferiority of blacks. But a misguided Radical-controlled Congress had taken direction of Reconstruction away from him. These crusading Northerners had attempted to change natural conditions by legislative fiat, causing immense difficulties for all involved in an experiment which was doomed by nature to failure. Finally seeing the errors of their ways, they had withdrawn from the struggle, leaving Southerners to solve their own racial problems. This was a powerful and satisfying rationale for a caste system which ultimately degraded Negroes to the point where they had absolutely no defense against the worst excesses of the most lawless elements of white society.

Beginning in 1889 a series of Jim Crow laws were passed which gave legal sanction to the segregation which already existed by custom. These laws went far beyond the earlier black codes in separating the races, but they did little more than legalize existing conditions. Racial segregation in Florida was more extensive in 1900 than it had been in 1865.

An 1895 statute prohibited anyone from conducting a school in which whites and Negroes attended either the same classes, separate classes in the same building, or classes taught by the same teachers. Fines and jail sentences were provided for violators. Others soon followed. In 1903 intermarriage was forbidden between white persons and Negroes, including anyone with at least one-eighth Negro blood. Either or both parties to such a marriage could be punished by up to ten years imprisonment or $1,000 fine. A 1905 enactment required separation of the races on street cars and required companies operating them to provide separate facilities. Failure of the company to do so was punishable by a $50 fine with each day constituting a separate offense. Passengers violating the statute were subject to fines of $25 or up to thirty days in jail. Negro nurses travelling with white children or sick persons were exempt. Since slavery days there had been almost unlimited contact between the races where the blacks were in a servant capacity, and this continued. Segregation was a class rather than a physical matter.

In 1905 constables, sheriffs, and others handling prisoners were forbidden to fasten white male or female prisoners to colored prisoners, subject to fines up to $100 or sentences up to six months. The same legislature required terminal and railroad companies to provide separate waiting rooms and ticket windows for whites and Negroes. The penalty for failure was a fine up to $5,000. A 1909 statute required "equal" and "separate" railroad cars or divisions of cars.

These legal reinforcements of existing practices had great significance. Law and custom had been in harmony during antebellum slavery days. The 1865–1866 black code reflected the social experiences of those who enacted them. Then it was overturned by national legislation which ran counter to the beliefs of the dominant groups of Florida society. Because they disagreed with the Reconstruction legislation and the circumstances of its enactment, native white Floridians not only overturned the laws but also developed a rationale—the Lost Cause myth and its corollary of the necessity for white supremacy—which justified and reinforced their actions following the celebrated 1876 election dispute. The Jim Crow laws were the final necessary step. By the early twentieth century white Floridians were living in a society whose customs, ideology, and law code were once more in harmony.

The first third of the twentieth century was the nadir of race relations in Florida and the nation. Although segregation seemed to be permanently entrenched, whites did not let the matter rest. Politicians always referred to it in their campaigns. Newspapers carried editorials dealing with racism and news stories casting obloquy and odium on Negroes. Creative writers dealt with the subject in the same way. There was a widespread movement to solve the race problem by sending the blacks to Africa. A strong advocate of the idea was Frank Clark, an influential Florida congressman who once declared that "Mr. Lincoln said that this nation could not exist 'half slave and half free.' I think it is equally true that this nation can not exist *half white* and *half black*." Likewise, progressive Florida Governor Napoleon B. Broward went so far as to propose mass removal of Negroes from the United States in his 1907 message to the legislature.

Without political rights, economic strength, or legal status, blacks had no defense. Their best hope was to keep away from whites unless they were fortunate enough to identify with someone who would assist them in legal and economic matters. Usually tied to the land by perpetual indebtedness and dependent on the good will of a white man for whatever security they had, blacks in the early twentieth century occupied a social position not significantly different from that of the antebellum "free Negro" who had been obliged by law to have a white guardian. But this unofficial paternalism was not available to all, and it was inadequate to prevent physical abuse on those occasions when blacks came into contact with unruly whites. Insults and petty violence could sometimes be borne in silence. But at other times it was impossible to avoid trouble. With no legal or social restraints, white ruffians and sometimes ordinary citizens angered by some incident assaulted blacks without fear of reprisal.

In 1911 Mark Norris and Jerry Guster of Wadesboro, Leon County, were arrested on a charge of stealing and resisting arrest. B. B. Smith, a sawmill owner who had been deputized especially to arrest them, had struck Norris with a pistol while doing so. In the justice of the peace court in Miccosukee, the two Negroes were acquitted. When they went to Smith's home to talk about the matter, a gun fight ensued, and Smith was killed. A group of blacks gathered to defend the two men against an anticipated mob, but they quietly surrendered when two deputies arrived to arrest them. Ultimately, ten Negroes were arrested, six of whom were charged with murder. A crowd gathered in Tallahassee, and talk of lynching increased. Six of the men were smuggled out of Tallahassee and taken to Lake City for safekeeping. A few evenings later several men drove to Lake City and got the blacks out of jail on a forged release order, took them to the edge of town, and riddled all six with bullets for more than a half hour. No one in Lake City went to investigate the shooting until the assassins were driving away; thus there were no witnesses to the crime. Governor Albert Gilchrist offered a $250 reward for information about the lynching, but a cursory investigation was shortly abandoned without success.

There was almost no provocation for an incident at Monticello in 1913. Sheriff's deputies went into Log Town, a black section, at about eleven o'clock one Saturday evening just "scouting around." Seeing a group of blacks walking down the road, the deputies called on them to stop to be searched. The Negroes ran. The deputies fired and three blacks were wounded; one of them permanently paralyzed by a shot in the back. No weapons were found on any of them. Walking down the road on a Saturday night seemed to be sufficient cause for a presumption of guilt only in the case of blacks.

When J. A. McClellan shot and killed Charlie Perry, a black, in 1918, the coroner's jury found the shooting to have been in self-defense. It was true that an argument between them had been started by Perry. But the reason for the altercation was that McClellan and others had broken into Perry's house and had searched it without either a warrant or the owner's permission. During the 1920 general election, July Perry of Ocoee, Orange County, caused a disturbance when he tried to vote without having paid his poll tax. He even threatened election officials, but it is inconceivable that the aftermath would have been the same had he been white. Whites followed Perry home and ordered him out of his house. He fired on them. When the altercation was over three days later, the entire Negro section of Ocoee had been burned and four innocent people consumed in the fire. The grisly episode ended only after a mutilated July Perry was finally put to death by the mob which had tired of torturing him. Three years later at Rosewood, near Cedar Key, a white mob charged into the black community searching for an alleged rapist, burned six houses and a church, and killed five blacks. This time the blacks fought back and two whites also died.

The lynching of Claude Neal in Jackson County in 1934 was so shocking that it stimulated a renewed effort in Congress to enact antilynching legislation. Neal was accused of murdering a white girl with whom it was charged he had had an illicit relationship. Transferred from jail to jail in West Florida and in southern Alabama he was finally overtaken by a mob in the latter state and brought back to Marianna. He was tortured and mutilated, dragged behind a car, and finally displayed on the streets before crowds, including school children, who attacked the then lifeless body. The corpse was hanged on the courthouse square. On the following day mobs threatened blacks on the streets of Marianna, and order was not restored until the militia was called in. The NAACP published a report of the incident which aroused considerable ire across the nation, but nothing was done. The attorney general ruled that the recently enacted federal law against kidnapping across state lines did not apply because a monetary ransom had not been the purpose of the mob. And as always there was no remedy under state law.

Violence was only the extreme and most visible surface of a racially segregated society. Many whites who deplored violence still obeyed the infinite daily reinforcements of their segregated system: separate dining facilities, theaters, restrooms, waiting rooms, railroad cars, and drinking fountains, as well as the customary racial divisions of labor. While blacks and whites often worked at comparable jobs at the lower end of the economic spectrum, nearly all the professional and white collar jobs were limited to whites and the most menial tasks were overwhelmingly filled by blacks. Even where employment of blacks and whites was comparable, compensation was disproportionate. For example, black school teachers in the 1930s in one north Florida county earned from $37.50 to $40 per month, slightly less than half the salaries of their white counterparts. At that time Confederate veterans were drawing pensions of $37.50 per month. Even the New Deal programs of the national government, designed to relieve the poverty of the 1930s, were affected by racism. Relief administration in Jacksonville established a formula which gave forty-five percent of the available funds to Negroes and fifty-five percent to whites, while black relief families outnumbered white by three to one. Florida Negroes were often denied access to the work-relief programs of the Civilian Conservation Corps and the National Youth Administration on the grounds that they were unqualified to meet admission standards.

By the time Claude Neal was lynched in 1934 forces outside the state were already undercutting the racial status quo. Negro migration into northern cities had created potential black political power. Breaking traditional ties with the Republican party, large numbers of urban blacks voted for Franklin D. Roosevelt in 1936, beginning an alliance with the national Democratic party which still exists. The NAACP had gained considerable attention by its publicity of lynching statistics and its lobbying for an antilynch law. It won its first school desegregation case at the graduate level in 1937. In World War II blacks made significant gains in the armed services and in defense jobs at home. Further migrations out of the South occurred. The Truman administration called for fair employment practices and the 1948 Democratic platform endorsed the idea. The military services were integrated in 1949.

Despite all these changes, the 1954 United States Supreme Court decision in *Brown* v. *Board of Education of Topeka* and its 1955 directive to integrate the public schools with "all deliberate speed" fell like a bombshell on Florida and the other southern states. The Florida attorney general sent to the court the results of a study by social scientists showing that attempts to integrate the state's schools would cause violence. On the basis of the report he asked for a stay of execution of the decision. Some public officials said the court decision was too soon; others said it was an invasion of state rights and a usurpation of legislative power by the courts. State Senator John Rawls of Marianna introduced a resolution in the legislature which emphasized that the constitution of Florida added "legal force to the time honored custom and native inclination of the people of Florida, both negro and white, to maintain...a segregated public school system...integration...in the public schools...would tend to encourage the...unnatural, ...abhorrent, execrable, and revolting practice of miscegenation."

White Floridians girded themselves to resist. With a full range of laws requiring segregation and the widespread belief in state rights, theirs was a formidable defensive arsenal. Because the segregation laws conformed so closely to the social values of white Floridians, they emphasized the primacy of state legislation and branded the United States Supreme Court an usurper. Opponents of integration eventually destroyed much of the creditability of the national court system by emphasizing the clash of state law with the court. It was at this point that the Jim Crow laws were crucial. Instead of having to face the basic question of how a state could distinguish between its citizens by law, segregationists were able to attack the integrity of the agency which raised the question. It was much more satisfying to defend the right of the state against invasions of the national court than to defend the Jim Crow system on its dubious merits.

Governor LeRoy Collins's unwillingness to defy the court was a setback, but he promised to use all lawful efforts to maintain segregation while at the same time calling on Floridians to obey the law of the land. The legislature went beyond the governor's position, passed a resolution calling on him to interpose the authority of the state to protect Florida citizens from any effort of the national government to enforce the Brown decision, and enacted legislation providing for the closing of the schools if the national government used force to integrate them. Representative Mallory Horne of Leon County led an effort to restrict the authority of the court, and many Floridians prepared to *defend the law by resisting* the Brown decision.

The moderation of Governor Collins made an immense difference in Florida. Despite the attorney general's warnings of incipient violence, and amidst reports of disruptions in other states, Florida passed through this "Second Reconstruction" with markedly little actual violence. Although there was almost no progress toward school integration for years after the Brown decision, the civil rights movement broadened to other areas and accelerated. White Floridians retreated slowly, resisting each attack on their social system by referring to the state laws. Gradually the national court system negated those laws. With constant pressure from the courts, and belatedly from Congress and the president, the legal framework of segregation crumbled.

But the initiative came almost entirely from outside the state. Some Floridians, exasperated at the national government's interference, argued that they had been gradually working out solutions for the racial problem before the Brown decision. Some social scientists argue that as a rural, agricultural society becomes urban and industrialized, racial segregation breaks down because it cannot function in such a society. However that may be, there was little change in the racial caste system in Florida until the nation once more became interested in it. The hideous lynchings of the early twentieth century ceased when Congress started seriously considering antilynching legislation. Education funds went to Negro schools in larger quantity as the NAACP began winning its desegregation cases. New congressional legislation on civil rights, public accommodations, and voting spearheaded changes in these areas.

With assistance from the national courts and marshals, blacks moved from the back of the buses, sat down at public lunch counters, came down out of the theater balconies, attended previously all-white schools at least in small numbers, and moved into the mainstream of Florida society in countless ways which had been denied them by both law and custom in the past. It was still a piecemeal movement, and social approval of segregation was still strong among whites, but the Jim Crow legal system had been nullified by the late 1960s.

Florida society still retains some of its traditional segregation. Negroes still live mostly in the less desirable sections of towns. Many white families have taken their children from the public schools and sent them to "Christian" schools which cropped up rapidly after 1968. But there is a significant difference. Supported by custom *and the law* only a few years ago, segregation and its correlative of white supremacy and black inferiority were taken for granted by most political and other opinion leaders. Some applauded it as beneficial and even necessary for the South. Gubernatorial candidate Bill Hendricks campaigned throughout Florida in the 1950s as the Ku Klux Klan candidate. White supremacists rested confidently and comfortably with their views, knowing that they were supported by the laws of the state.

That has changed. Few Floridians now speak publicly against basic civil rights for blacks. Racial jokes have moved from most drawing rooms into the restrooms. Denial of the legal sanction for segregation has reversed the burden of public approval. It is no longer popular to advocate segregation, at least directly. Those who believe in it are on the defensive. In the 1974 election, Jeff Latham, a candidate for statewide office, ruined his creditability and his chances for election when he admitted appealing for support from a racist organization.

It is difficult to change the values of society by law—or in the jargon of the capitol hallways "You can't legislate morality"—but it is possible to take away the legal basis for repugnant practices. Jim Crow legislation had provided an immense reinforcement of a segregated society and the rationale for it. Its repeal was difficult because it complemented the values of the most powerful groups of Florida society. But once that legislation was nullified, segregationists found themselves on the opposite side of the law. Interposition was a last-ditch effort to justify the system in terms of state sovereignty along lines enunciated by John C. Calhoun more than a century earlier and negated by the Civil War. The state rights defense was gradually discredited in the 1960s by repeated revelations of southern law enforcement officials using the color of law to commit criminal acts in defense of segregation.

Finally forced to the basic question of how to justify segregation on its merits in terms of mid-twentieth century America and without the support of Jim Crow laws—much as their ancestors had had to deal with the problem of converting slaves to freedmen in 1865–1866—white Floridians have exerted remarkable effort to overcome their segregationist views. They have come far from the time when violence was justified on the ground of the necessity for white supremacy. Many people who still prefer a segregated society restrain themselves from open advocacy of it. And most important of all, most Floridians are willing to accept recent changes, albeit sometimes reluctantly, because they are reinforced by the law.

Racial divisions of American society persist and have become a national problem, but they are no longer being dealt with at the level to which they had descended in the early twentieth century. Americans have probably gone as far toward an integrated society as legal changes will take them. Difficulties encountered with the Supreme Court's "busing" decisions reveal the limits on law as a positive force. Legal provisions cannot diverge too far from custom and belief without disruption. But the disparity is not as great in 1977 as in 1867–1868 when the black code was replaced by laws calling for equality. With time—history—and tolerance, custom and the law will once more coincide as they did for white Floridians before 1860.

5

Civil Disorder and the American West: The Role of the Army in Controlling Labor and Ethnic Violence

CLAYTON D. LURIE

• *One of the most enduring images in American history is that of the cavalry riding to the rescue of beleaguered pioneers in the decades after the Civil War. As John Wayne depicted in* She Wore a Yellow Ribbon, *and as hundreds of novels and movies have repeatedly emphasized, tough horse soldiers cleared the Great Plains of hostile Indians and opened a vast territory for white settlement.*

The reality of course was more complex. For one thing, the native population more often fell victim to the white man's diseases and whiskey than to his bullets. For another, the army occasionally intervened to protect unpopular immigrant groups from racist attacks. As Clayton D. Lurie reminds us in the following essay about Wyoming in 1885, when striking miners against the Union Pacific Railroad took out their frustrations on politically weak Asian newcomers, twenty-eight Chinese workers died in a single afternoon of fury. Coming to the rescue of the Chinese workers, the army stopped the violence and remained in Rock Springs for fourteen years. The real winner, however, was the Union Pacific Railroad, which essentially used the army to keep wages low and to restore peace.

Amidst campaigns against Indians and aiding frontier civil authorities in maintaining law and order, the U.S. Army was called on several occasions in the late nineteenth century to respond to domestic disorder resulting from labor disputes. The president is authorized by the Constitution and by Congress to call on the military to protect state gov-

Reprinted from Clayton D. Lurie, "Civil Disorder and the Military in Rock Springs, Wyoming: The Army's Role in the 1885 Chinese Massacre," *Montana: The Magazine of Western History*, 40 (Summer, 1990), 44–59.

ernments against insurrections, domestic disorders, and threats to existing authority and systems of government, to enforce federal laws and court orders, and to enforce laws guaranteeing civil rights.

On one occasion in 1885 the army was called to suppress a labor-related race riot in southwestern Wyoming involving Chinese immigrants. Although domestic military interventions had occurred previously in American history, interventions to protect immigrant groups from nativist or racist attacks were unique. Initially, both the federal government and the army were unsure how to respond. Outside of military intervention in the South during Reconstruction, the anti-Chinese riots of 1885–1886 in Wyoming represented the army's first experience with a labor-related racial disorder.

Within months of their deployment in Wyoming, federal forces were also called to quell racial disturbances between whites and Chinese in Washington Territory and were summoned, but not sent, to deal with similar racial disturbances in Silver City and Raton, New Mexico. The lessons civil and military officials learned from these interventions reinforced the concept of using regular army forces as a first resort for suppressing race riots in other forms of domestic violence during the next sixty years.

Such civil disturbance duty forced the army to define an internal defense mission where none had existed before and formulate a doctrine to support that mission. The process took decades to complete with the result that most of the army's responses to civil disturbances remained ad hoc until well into the twentieth century. Successful intervention in the anti-Chinese riots in Rock Springs in 1885, nonetheless, prompted more frequent requests for the army to act as a national constabulary to quell both racial and labor disputes in the decades that followed—a role army commanders and enlisted personnel neither sought nor desired.

The first Chinese immigrants to the western United States arrived on the Pacific Coast after gold was discovered in California in 1848 and were welcomed initially as a source of labor. In the 1860s, railroad and mining companies imported Oriental laborers for similar reasons. During construction of these first transcontinental railroads, the Chinese gained a reputation for being extraordinarily diligent workers, willing to labor long hours under miserable and dangerous conditions for less pay than whites. Despite protests from labor unions and white residents of the Pacific Coast, the United States signed the Burlingame Treaty with China in 1868. The treaty made Chinese immigration easier and provided them with "most favored nation" rights, privileges, and protections. Under the treaty, for example, Chinese immigrants did not need to declare their intention of becoming U.S. citizens to reside or work in the country.

Although Asians formed a small percentage of the nearly 23.5 million foreign-born immigrants to enter the United States between 1880 and 1919, their presence aroused significant social prejudice. Indeed, as late as 1870 only 63,000 Chinese resided in the United States, a figure that did not surpass 100,000 until the 1880s. Increasingly, however, racial differences, economic competition, and what was perceived by whites as a threatening Chinese presence fueled prejudice against them among American nativists, who disliked all immigrant groups but especially the Chinese. Such attitudes were frequently reflected in contemporary journal and newspaper articles, which heightened racial distrust. In turn, racial tensions were exacerbated by job competition between Americans, European immigrants, and Chinese, all of whom by the 1870s were caught up in the larger context of labor strife in the trans-Mississippi West.

To western mine owners and other corporate leaders, nativist and working-class fears of Chinese competition were secondary to the potential of using Oriental workers to minimize labor costs, maximize profits, and stymie the growth of budding labor unions. Western corporations hired large numbers of Chinese laborers for mining, railroad construction, and lumber industries. According to the accepted business philosophy of the time, these policies made good economic sense. Not surprisingly then, the staunchest defenders of Chinese immigrant workers were those business, industrial, and government leaders with vested interests in continued unrestricted Chinese immigration and favorable Sino-American relations.

Consequently, corporations used their wealth and influence at territorial, state, and federal levels to support legislation that would assure continued Chinese immigration as well as protect Chinese immigrants already in the United States from the resentment of Americans in general and labor unions in particular. The exaggerated testimonials of business and industrial leaders to Chinese industry, thrift, morality, honesty, and cleanliness were nearly the opposite of exaggerated nativist claims derogating Chinese immigrants and were soon overcome by the shrill attacks of nativists, unionists, and members of the working class.

Labor unions throughout the nation were struggling for mere recognition, as well as higher wages and improved living and working conditions. Chinese immigrants who either were excluded or refused to join unions and support strikes threatened to undermine union gains and presented Caucasian workers in the West with the prospect of permanent unemployment. Labor unions therefore joined nativist ranks in demanding restrictions on Chinese immigration and in calling for exclusion of Chinese laborers from logging, railroad, and mining industries. The Knights of Labor and later the American Federation of Labor, among others, bolstered nativist claims that the Chinese drained American wealth, took jobs from U.S. citizens, and became union-busting pawns for large corporations. Unions also alleged that Oriental peoples were morally depraved, unclean, and culturally and racially inferior.

Nativist and labor groups, meanwhile, were making themselves heard in Washington, D.C. Consequently, on October 31, 1880, the United States modified the 1868 Burlingame Treaty and required China to recognize and accept the American right to limit or suspend Chinese immigration, although not prohibit it absolutely. Business interests supported the treaty changes in lieu of outright exclusion, but nativist and labor organizations continued to seek stronger restrictions and exclusion.

Subsequent passage of the Exclusion Act of 1882, however, met labor's demands in part. With its passage, the immigration of Chinese laborers was suspended until 1892, all Chinese were declared ineligible for citizenship, and Chinese labor was prohibited in certain industries. The 1882 law was to be reviewed each decade and renewed or amended if necessary. To the chagrin of nativist and labor groups, however, the United States agreed to continue to protect the 105,000 Chinese already working in America.

Unions remained frustrated over the lack of comprehensive restrictive legislation and over widespread corporate evasion of prohibitory statutes. Immigrant brokers continued to smuggle Chinese workers unlawfully into treaty-forbidden western industries such as mining, timber, and railroad construction, where they were promptly hired. Commenting on this illicit traffic, General John Pope, commanding general of the Division of the Pacific, noted that the practice made Chinese people conspicuous in the small, previously all-white towns of the interior West. Pope doubted that juries could be found to punish those guilty of attacks upon the Chinese. Union frustration combined with racial bigotry to prompt violent attacks upon Chinese laborers.

Such violence had erupted as early as the 1860s, and massive anti-Chinese riots had followed in Los Angeles and San Francisco in 1871. Twenty-one Chinese died in the San Francisco riot, and six years later mobs in the city burned twenty-five Chinese business establishments during the Great Railway Strike of 1877. Anti-Chinese disturbances also occurred in Denver in 1880.

Despite statements to the contrary, corporate and territorial authorities seemed unwilling or unable to protect the Chinese from labor and nativist mobs. In seeking federal military intervention against anti-Chinese rioters, businessmen and politicians often sought to portray labor unions as the cause of the racial unrest. Unions, they claimed, served as a breeding ground for racism and European-style radicalism dedicated to destroying free immigration, human liberty, and free enterprise. If the public accepted such views, business leaders reasoned, corporations could be assured of a continued supply of cheap Chinese labor, high profits, and less opposition from weakened labor organizations.

In response to the continued illegal hiring of Chinese workers, the Knights of Labor initiated a campaign for more effective enforcement of the 1882 Exclusion Act. Union members and others argued that Chinese workers who were hired in violation of the law were not entitled to legal protection. Their confidence in normal legal channels shaken by blatant hiring violations, those who opposed Chinese labor determined to take the law into their own hands. Racial violence seemed only a matter of time, and indeed, the first of several violent riots occurred in Rock Springs, Wyoming, in September 1885.

Located in southwestern Wyoming halfway between Rawlins and Evanston, Rock Springs was a small mining community of one thousand inhabitants, most of whom worked in the coal mines of the Union Pacific Railroad. Racial tensions had been present in the town for at least a decade. Prior to 1875, the Union Pacific's mines had been worked exclusively by whites. But a strike for higher wages that year prompted the company to fire striking white workers and replace them with 150 Chinese immigrants brought in under contract with the firm of Beckwith, Quinn, and Company. A Union Pacific spokesman said during the strike, "if the white men will not dig the Company's coal for pay, who will blame the company for hiring yellow, black, or red men, who are ready and willing to do what white men will not do." At least 150 striking white miners lost their jobs to the Chinese newcomers, while fifty other whites returned to work with no increase in wages.

Ten years later, the Union Pacific employed 842 workers in Rock Springs, including 552 Chinese and 290 predominately European whites. The Chinese did not live among the white miners, but in remote areas "where law and authority are feeble," wrote Wyoming Territorial Governor Francis E. Warren, "and where race prejudice may be precipitated on the slightest pretext.

As racial tensions festered nationwide, white contempt for Chinese miners in Rock Springs grew stronger during the summer of 1885. More Chinese were hired illegally and paid wages lower than those paid to whites. Moreover, the new Chinese miners, who were excluded from membership in the Knights of Labor and other unions, showed little interest in labor organizations and even less support for anticipated labor protests. Rumors were rife among white miners that the Chinese received special treatment from "pit bosses," who often accepted bribes to hire them. The Rock Springs *Independent* reported that "white men had been turned off . . . and hundreds could not get work while the Chinese were shipped in by the carload and given work." Company officials insisted publicly that Chinese laborers received similar pay, worked under the same regulations, and were not meant to supplant white miners. But the company's privately contracted labor agent, A. C. Beckwith, confirmed that the Chinese miners were paid three dollars a day, compared to four dollars a day for whites.

Union Pacific officials remained undaunted by rising racial tensions and later claimed they were unaware of any problems. On the company's right to hire Chinese, however, railroad officials were adamant. Union Pacific official S. R. Callaway defended the railroad's policy in the summer of 1885:

When the company can be assured against strikes and other outbreaks at the hands of persons who deny its owners the right to
manage their property, it may consider the expediency of abandoning Chinese labor; but under all circumstances and at any
cost or hazard it will assert its right to employ whom it pleases
and refuse to ostracize any one class of its employees at the
dictation of another.

Anti-Chinese resentment climaxed on September 2, 1885, with fighting between white and Chinese miners in the coal pits. At 6 A.M. a
group of white youths startled Chinese workers exiting Mine No. 6 by
stoning them, and at noon, seventy miners, joined by an equal number
of unemployed men, left local saloons and stormed the Chinese area
of town. The mob first sent three men to warn the Chinese miners to
leave town in one hour but grew impatient lest their quarry completely
elude them. Reaching the Chinese area a half hour early, the mob
burned and plundered dwellings and killed twenty-eight Chinese, some
of whom perished in their burning homes. Fourteen other Chinese were
severely injured. Property damage was estimated at $140,000. The
remaining Chinese in Rock Springs were panic-stricken and fled to the
surrounding hills. When the mob disbanded, company officials collected terrified survivors and put them on a train bound for Evanston
one hundred miles to the west.

Shortly thereafter, D. O. Clark, assistant superintendent of the Union
Pacific's coal mining department, and Sweetwater County Sheriff Joseph Young wired Governor Warren for military aid. Warren forwarded the request to Brigadier General Oliver Otis Howard,
commander of the Department of the Platte, suggesting that one or
more companies of federal troops be sent to Rock Springs from Fort
D. A. Russell. Howard, in turn, sent the request to General John M.
Schofield at division headquarters in Chicago.

Anticipating a slow response through military channels, the Union
Pacific's general traffic manager in Omaha, Thomas I. Kimball, convinced Warren to request help directly from Secretary of War William
C. Endicott. In his telegram to Endicott, Warren reported that an
"armed mob of white men" had attacked Chinese miners, that county
authorities were powerless to prevent further violence, and that the
territory lacked a militia to end the crisis. Warren then asked whether

the federal government could "afford military protection to life and property at Rock Springs."

During the following days, Charles Francis Adams, president of the Union Pacific Railroad, son and grandson of two former U.S. presidents, and former ambassador to England, wrote the War Department repeatedly asking for military intervention. Adams insisted that the Union Pacific had no intention of negotiating with the miners until order had been restored.

Endicott was absent from Washington, D.C., and the messages from Warren and Adams went to Adjutant General Richard C. Drum. Drum located the vacationing Endicott on September 3 at Salem, Massachusetts, and advised the secretary of the crisis. Endicott advised Drum to consult Attorney General A. H. Garland on a course of action. Garland was also out of town, however, so Drum referred the messages to Secretary of State Thomas F. Bayard.

While Drum sought a responsible federal official in the nations's capital, Warren, in the company of several Union Pacific officials, visited Sweetwater County to investigate the riot. In conference with Sheriff Young in Rock Springs, Warren learned that widespread hatred of the Chinese made assembling a reliable posse to track down the massacre's perpetrators impossible. Later, while in the Sweetwater County seat of Green River, Warren received a telegram from Sheriff J. J. Le Cain of Uinta County advising that the Chinese who had fled to Evanston had now regrouped and armed themselves. As a result, Evanston contained hundreds of armed and angry men of two races and threatened to explode into even greater bloodshed than had been experienced at Rock Springs. Still lacking a response to his request for federal military aid, Warren urged Le Cain to raise as many deputies as possible. Le Cain could recruit only twenty men.

The imminent spread of open racial warfare in southwestern Wyoming forced Warren to make a direct but procedurally complicated appeal to President Grover Cleveland. In his September 3 telegram, Warren repeated what he had told Endicott, adding that "immediate assistance is imperative to preserve life and property." Uncertain how the Constitution or federal statutes on domestic disturbances might apply to a federal territory and to crimes against foreign nations, Warren avoided reference to either. Schofield and Howard urged him to correct this omission on September 4, however, with an amended request.

On his second request Warren appropriately cited Revised Statute 5298, which authorized the president to dispatch federal forces to counter insurrection in the territories, aid and protect civil authorities and populations, enforce federal laws, and prevent destruction of federal property. Warren informed Cleveland that "unlawful ... combinations and conspiracies exist among the coal miners and others in Uinta and Sweetwater Counties which prevent individuals and corporations from enjoyment and protection of their property and obstruct execution of territorial law." He described the Rock Springs situation as an "open insurrection" with sheriff's officials powerless to prevent further violence without "organized bodies of armed men."

Because Wyoming lacked a territorial militia, Warren requested federal regulars "to support civil authorities until order is restored, criminals arrested, and the suffers relieved." At Drum's urging, Warren submitted a third request on September 5, adding that the "legislature of Wyoming is not in session and cannot be convened in time to provide for the emergency." It was an irrelevant addition. Warren was not asking for aid under Revised Statute 5297, the law covering state requests, but rather that Cleveland enforce federal laws.

While Warren formulated his requests, Bayard conferred with Drum and agreed that regulars should be deployed in Sweetwater County "to prevent any interruption to the United States mail or the routes over which they are received," but not to protect Chinese or Union Pacific property. Troops therefore were committed in Wyoming under the authority of laws passed on July 2, 1864, and July 27, 1866, more commonly known as the Pacific Railway acts. The acts had initiated construction of the transcontinental railroads and provided for their federal protection as "military roads" and "postal routes."

Bayard's decision appears odd because regulars could have been committed under the provisions of either the 1880 or 1882 treaties with China, which guaranteed federal protection to Chinese in the United States, or under provisions of Revised Statute 5298.

Concrete evidence is lacking, but Bayard's decision may have been motivated by one or more factors. The secretary probably hoped calm could be restored rapidly without excessive publicity and without involving the Chinese government. Bayard also probably wanted to avoid the appearance of sending federal troops to protect an unpopular minority against working-class whites, whose grievances (though not necessarily their actions) were condoned by much of the general public.

Bayard's primary motivation, however, probably was to avoid setting the precedent of committing federal troops to quell what eventually became widespread anti-Chinese rioting in the West. The army lacked the manpower, time, and resources to suppress scores of race riots. Indeed, in the weeks following the violence at Rock Springs, anti-Chinese rioting erupted in at least thirty towns and cities along the West Coast, primarily in California. Whatever their motivations, Bayard and Drum hoped the mere presence of federal troops would intimidate those bent on further violence against the Chinese or on destruction of railroad property, and Secretary Endicott endorsed their plan.

On September 4, Schofield authorized Howard to send troops to Rock Springs and any other place in Wyoming where their presence might deter anti-Chinese violence. Howard had only 3,259 troops in the entire Department of the Platte. Nonetheless, he ordered two companies of the Seventh Infantry at Fort Steele, under Lieutenant Colonel Henry L. Chipman, and two companies of the Ninth Infantry at Fort D. A. Russell under Lieutenant Colonel Thomas M. Anderson, to travel by Union Pacific Railroad to Rock Springs and Evanston. The troops arrived the following day.

When Chipman's troops got to Rock Springs, the violence had subsided and Sheriff Young had begun to arrest men suspected of participating in the anti-Chinese attacks. His pretext was that their actions interfered with the proper operations of the Union Pacific as a military road and federal mail route. Anderson's forces in Evanston also prevented violence, but the colonel predicted more trouble when Chinese workers returned to the mines. To meet that exigency, Anderson asked for a ten-man Gatling gun detachment from Fort D. A. Russell, which arrived on the afternoon train on September 6.

Facing an unstable situation, Warren telegraphed Cleveland on September 7, warning that unlawful organized mobs in possession of coal mines ... will not permit Chinamen to approach their own homes, property, or employment.... From the nature of outbreak sheriff of county cannot rally sufficient posse and Territorial government cannot sufficiently aid him. Insurrectionists know through the newspapers and dispatches that troops will not interfere under present orders and moral effect of presence of troops is destroyed. If troops were known to have orders to assist sheriff's posse in case driven back, I am quite sure civil authorities could restore order without actual use of soldiers; but unless U.S. Government can find a way to relieve us immediately, I believe worse scenes than those at Rock Springs will follow and all Chinamen will be driven from the territory.

Adams repeated Warren's requests on September 7 and 8, and emphasized the importance of protecting county authorities who were guarding the mines and non-striking workers.

The urgency of Anderson's request for a Gatling gun and the continued pleas of Warren and Adams convinced Schofield to expand the army's role in Wyoming. Lacking a presidential proclamation under the Constitution, U.S. treaties with China, or Revised Statute 5298, Schofield decided to act under the authority granted by Congress in the Pacific Railway acts, as Bayard had done. Schofield argued that the obstruction of any portion of the Union Pacific's transportation system jeopardized the nation's communication and strategic links to the West Coast, and he urged Drum to extend protection to all trains, rails, and coal mines held by the Union Pacific.

Diplomatic considerations added weight to the efforts of Warren, Adams, and Schofield. Cleveland deemed it imperative to honor Article II of the November 17, 1880 treaty with China, protecting all resident Chinese, although he hoped to do so without using federal troops. When troops were committed initially, however, their use was not to protect the Chinese. Without abandoning the goal of safeguarding the mail, Cleveland ordered the army to protect Chinese laborers and railroad property wherever there was threatened or actual violence.

The president further authorized Schofield to aid civil authorities and, "if necessity actually exists," to arrest "those committing offenses against the laws." To insure that troops did not come under direct control of Wyoming's territorial governor or other civil officials, Cleveland insisted that field commanders confer directly with Schofield when they received requests from civil authorities.

On September 7, five days after the riot, Schofield informed his field commanders at Rock Springs and Evanston that the president had ordered the army to protect Chinese laborers. In detailed guidance the next day, he cautioned that, in protecting the Chinese and aiding civil authorities, commanders were to limit their actions "to the necessary measures of defense. . . . Further action such as arrest and confinement of offenders, or other aid to civil authorities was to be taken in each case only upon [Schofield's] express orders."

Schofield explained that he would authorize arrest and confinement only after local commanders had received a request for help, investigated the case, and related the facts to him. Chipman and Anderson were to prepare daily situation reports and send them through department headquarters to division headquarters. He instructed his commanders to caution their troops "that it is no part of their duty to punish offenders, but rather to prevent, so far as possible, any commission of the specific offense apprehended and to protect those in danger of attack in the absence of civil protection." Schofield enclosed a copy of his instructions to Warren and urged him to inform local commanders fully of any facts that might justify an appeal for troops to arrest or confine federal offenders.

Howard decided that four companies of troops were inadequate to carry out this expanded mission and ordered Colonel Alexander McDowell McCook of Camp Murray, Utah, to dispatch six companies to Evanston on September 8. Leading a detachment of three companies of the Ninth Infantry, Captain Alfred Morton reached Evanston on September 9 and assigned two companies to Anderson. With the remaining units, Morton escorted several hundred Chinese by rail to Rock Springs. All entered town without incident at 4 P.M., and Morton placed his detachment under Chipman's command. Warren conveyed his appreciation to Drum for such prompt assistance and predicted that the show of force would preclude further hostilities.

The sudden reappearance of hundreds of Chinese, accompanied by four additional companies of federal regulars, convinced white miners that the Union Pacific Railroad was determined to use federal military

aid to reinstate Chinese miners and oust them from the area. The Rock
Springs *Independent* claimed that the

> action of the company in bringing back the Chinese means that
> they are to be set to work in the mines and that American soldiers
> are to prevent them from again being driven out. It means that
> all [white] miners at Rock Springs, except those absolutely re-
> quired, are to be replaced by Chinese labor. It means that the
> company intends to make a "Chinatown" out of Rock Springs.
> ... Let the demand go up from one end of the Union Pacific to
> the other, "The Chinese must go."

Anti-Chinese newspapers in Wyoming continued to bristle at federal
intervention. In its September 9 edition the Rock Springs *Independent*
asked:

> Is it not a ... damnable disgrace to see a rich and powerful cor-
> poration ... claiming and receiving the assistance of American
> soldiers to enforce the employment of leprous aliens? ... Why
> even the soldiers themselves curse the duty that compels them to
> sustain the alien against the American.

Workers were inflamed by the rhetoric of a union lawyer who denounced "the blighting influence of monopoly and its attendant slavery." They passed a resolution declaring that "the presence of Federal
bayonets at Rock Springs and Evanston [were unnecessary to protect]
either life or property, but a power wielded solely in the interest of a
grasping corporation ... to force a revolting system of slave labor upon
the country." Intimidated by the presence of Chipman's command,
however, the miners made no attempt to harm the Chinese during the
day. But a different situation reigned at night. To escape white ven-
geance, frightened Chinese laborers huddled for safety in railroad box-
cars guarded by federal troops.

Despite union protests, railroad officials were determined to have
Chinese workers return to the mines as quickly as possible. The Chinese
balked at returning to work, however, until federal troops stood guard
at every mine shaft. As a result, company officials complained to Howard on September 12 of Chipman's reluctance to deploy troops at the
mines before violence had actually occurred.

After consulting with Schofield, Howard ordered Chipman to post his men at the mines. For reinforcements, Howard summoned another company of the Twenty-first Infantry from an instructional camp at Goose Creek, Wyoming, on September 17. Drum overruled both officers the next day, declaring preemptive deployment of troops at the mines exceeded Schofield's instructions of nine days earlier.

While Howard reinforced his contingent at Rock Springs, the Chinese government prepared to investigate the events of September 2. With approval from the War Department, Cheng Tsao-Ju, the Chinese minister to the United States, sent two consular officials from San Francisco to Wyoming. Under army protection, they interrogated witnesses and company officials for eight days. Their report, which Imperial Chinese officials read with great interest, concluded, among other things, that the attackers, like the victims, were aliens and not citizens of the United States. Still, the Chinese government insisted that the United States was legally and morally responsible for protecting Chinese residents under treaty obligations. Failing that, the U.S. government should indemnify the Chinese government for the abuse of its subjects and property damage. Such obligations were stated clearly and simply by treaty.

Ignoring the Chinese view, the Cleveland administration denied that the United States owed anything either to the Chinese government or to Chinese laborers at Rock Springs. The Chinese ambassador wrote Bayard on November 30, 1885, however, reminding him of American treaty obligations and that the "administration of justice and the protection of life and property are functions of the federal government in a territory," according to the Constitution.

Bayard responded on February 18, 1886, correcting the ambassador's interpretation of the Constitution and noting "that the territory of Wyoming enjoyed local self-government with full authority to maintain order and administer justice.... The local authority and responsibility is in practice as self-contained in a territory as in a state." The massacre occurred in an area, he argued,

where there were few representatives of formal, recognized authority. The Chinese went there voluntarily. There was no representative of the United States Government or Territory of Wyoming among the assailants; hence, no official insult or wrong.

Assailants, as well as assailed, were aliens; so there was nothing national in what occurred.

Under the circumstances, he added, the United States was not obligated to indemnify, and had no official liability but, "in view of the shocking outrages and the complete failure of police authorities, generosity and pity might induce the President to recommend that Congress indemnify the Chinese."

The government's position was soundly condemned by many Americans, especially those residing in the East, who were appalled and outraged at the massacre and subsequent lack of government sensitivity. E. L. Godkin of the *Nation* wrote in March 1886:

> It is the duty of every sovereign state either to provide the necessary legal machinery for the fulfillment of its international obligations or else to make good the damage which any foreigner may have sustained through its failure to do so.... The Chinese, in claiming damages for this great national disgrace, stand as firmly on the law as they stand on abstract justice.

As the secretary of state had indicated, President Cleveland, without any admission of national guilt or responsibility, recommended that Congress pay something. On February 24, 1887, Congress approved a payment of $147,748.74 to the Chinese government.

While Chinese officials conducted their investigation at Rock Springs, Schofield informed Drum of his intention to go to Rock Springs for a first-hand look at the situation. His plans apparently leaked out because the Knights of Labor, which by then viewed the Army as a partisan supporter of the Chinese and Union Pacific Railroad, ordered a walkout along the rail line west of Nebraska to disrupt his visit. Speaking off the record during a stopover in Omaha, Schofield warned the Knights of Labor that any tampering with the operation of a "military road," in violation of the Pacific Railway Acts, would be treated as an "act of war" against the government. The walkout never materialized.

Before Schofield reached Rock Springs, McCook wrote Howard that any attempt by civil authorities to punish those involved in the riots would be a waste of time because of public prejudice against the Chinese. A Sweetwater County grand jury had already convened and interviewed witnesses but failed to return any indictments. It found instead that "whatever crimes may have been committed, the perpetrators thereof have not been disclosed by evidence before us." Reflecting local sympathies, the grand jury also concluded that "there appears to be no doubt of abuses existing that should have been promptly adjusted by the railroad company and its officers." In view of the local situation, McCook recommended establishing a military commission to try the accused and cited as precedent the commission that tried the Modoc Indians, including "Captain Jack," accused of killing Edward S. Canby in 1873. Schofield considered McCook's suggestion as he traveled west to Rock Springs.

Following Schofield's arrival on September 21, the Union Pacific reopened its mines. When a hundred Chinese entered the shafts, union workers ceased operation of weighing and loading machines in protest. The company, seeking to rid its operations of troublesome white union workers, replaced them immediately, as it had with Mormon strikebreakers from Utah in the 1870s. Confident that idle white miners would not make trouble with federal troops on hand, Schofield dismissed McCook's recommendation for a military commission. He did order an additional company of the Twenty-first Infantry to Rock Springs from Fort Sidney, Nebraska, bringing the total number of companies in the town to eight. Schofield left Rock Springs on September 22 and headed for Cheyenne to reassure Warren that the army was in firm control and would maintain the peace.

The military buildup in southwestern Wyoming peaked on September 25 with 203 regulars occupying Rock Springs and another 120 troops in Evanston. By early October Schofield was convinced that a withdrawal of troops could begin. Eleven days later Howard reduced Chipman's command to two companies of the Seventh Infantry and the Gatling gun crew of the Twenty-first Infantry. At Evanston, Howard reduced the force to one company of the Ninth Infantry. Worried by such substantial reductions, Warren asked Howard to retain the last three companies for several more months. Howard consented and ordered construction of semipermanent encampments named "Pilot Butte" at Rock Springs and "Medicine Butte" at Evanston on October 20. Benefiting directly from the army's peacekeeping mission, the Union Pacific agreed to construct and pay for the necessary buildings at both locations by the end of November 1885.

Assured of an on-going military presence in Wyoming to keep the peace, protect its property, and safeguard its Chinese laborers, the Union Pacific proceeded to break the miners' union and rid its operations of union influence. In late 1885, company officials fired forty-five white miners whom it considered participants in the riot, while offering to let other white miners return to work under the same conditions that existed before the violence in September. Some workers, primarily union members and sympathizers, chose not to return to the mines with Chinese workers and were offered free rail transportation out of Wyoming.

When a majority of white miners rejected such stipulations in hopes of winning concessions, company officials hired 120 more Chinese laborers to replace them, raising the total number of Chinese miners to 457. By December 1885, only eighty-five white miners remained, and the mines returned to full production—with Chinese labor and without a union. The Union Pacific had succeeded through the vehicle of anti-Chinese violence and federal military aid, to break the Knights of Labor in Rock Springs and gain a cheaper, more controllable non-union work force. As if to justify their actions, company officials claimed increased coal production. In contrast to the 1,450 tons of coal mined in August 1885, the company reported producing 1,610 tons in December 1885, and implied that employment of non-union Chinese miners, rather than recently installed drilling equipment, explained improved production.

Federal troops remained in southwestern Wyoming for fourteen years. All troops stationed at Evanston were gone by April 1887, but the last company of the Twenty-fourth Infantry at Rock Springs did not depart for Fort Assinniboine, Montana, until March 1899. During these years of garrison duty, the regulars had little to occupy their time beyond countless marches and rifle practice. Concerted anti-Chinese violence erupted in Wyoming on only one other occasion, when a group of whites, allegedly including a few federal troops, assaulted five Chinese miners in 1896.

The anti-Chinese riots at Rock Springs caught the Cleveland administration by surprise and revealed government confusion over the objectives and procedures of military intervention. At the outset, Adjutant General Drum had agreed with Secretary of State Bayard and Secretary of War Endicott that federal troops might be used in advance of a presidential proclamation to protect the mails and the railroad routes over which they were carried. Later, General Schofield suggested broadening protection to include all rails of any transcontinental line designated by Congress as a "military road." President Cleveland later added protection of the Chinese to those objectives, in fulfillment of federal obligations under the nation's 1880 treaty with China.

General Howard's troops occasionally overstepped the bounds set by the Posse Comitatus Act of June 1878, which prohibited the military from usurping the powers and duties of civil authorities and law enforcement officials without specific authorization from the president and Congress. But his troops succeeded in suppressing violence and prevented damage to railroad and mining company property. To a lesser extent the U.S. Army also prevented further violence against Chinese immigrants and ensured their safety.

The army accomplished all these civil disturbance missions without violence. The prolonged military presence in Wyoming aided in destroying labor organizations in the region, however, and kept union organizers at bay. Railroad and mining companies, such as those operated by the Union Pacific, also prevented union activity by importing Chinese laborers who spurned all organizing efforts.

While anti-Chinese violence requiring federal military intervention diminished in Wyoming after 1885–1886, the struggle between management and organized labor over the importation and use of Chinese labor continued for the next four decades. Commenting on the anti-Chinese violence in Wyoming, Terrance V. Powderly, leader of the Knights of Labor, clearly placed the blame for racial violence on Congress. Powderly declared:

> The recent assault upon the Chinese at Rock Springs is but the outcome of the feeling caused by the indifference of our lawmakers to the just demands of the people ... no blame can be attached to organized labor for the outbreak perpetrated at Rock Springs ... if Congress had listened to union organizations about Chinese, if Congress had penalized those breaking immigrant laws, if Congress had not "winked" at violations, and refused to listen to those wronged, men at Rock Springs would not have had to take the law into their own hands.

In response to popular resentment of Chinese labor, pressure from labor groups, and a desire to avoid further violence, Congress produced a flurry of legislation in the years following 1886. The restrictions of the Exclusion Act of 1882 were renewed in 1892 and again in 1902, and new restrictions were added in the Scott Act of 1887. Immigration quotas for Chinese and all other foreign groups were established by the Immigration Act of 1924.

With each additional piece of restrictive legislation, the number of Chinese immigrants entering the country declined. Concomitant with this decline there were fewer racial incidents. Through legislative means the United States solved what was termed the "Chinese problem," which precluded further use of federal troops to quell anti-Chinese violence.

6

"An Italian Is a Dago": Italian Immigrants in the United States

HUMBERT S. NELLI

● *The United States is a nation of migrants and immigrants, a place where every group is a minority. As early as the 1640s, when New York City was still known as New Amsterdam and when the little seaport counted fewer than 3,000 inhabitants, more than sixteen languages could be heard on its narrow streets. And this was more than two centuries before the great wave of immigrants would begin to pour through Castle Garden and Ellis Island en route to a new life in a new land.*

Between 1820 and 1930, about forty million Europeans crossed the Atlantic Ocean for the United States. Throughout the middle years of the nineteenth century, the bulk of the newcomers were from the British Isles or Germany. After 1880, however, emigration from those countries tapered off, and a pronounced shift toward eastern and southern Europe became apparent. The two largest groups were Jews, most of whom were fleeing oppression in the area known as the Pale of Settlement, and Italians, most of whom hailed from the impoverished southern portion of their native land. The experience of this second group, in some ways typical and in others unusual, is the subject of this thoughtful essay by Professor Humbert S. Nelli of the University of Kentucky.

To Americans the Italian immigrants who poured into the country in the late nineteenth and early twentieth centuries did not resemble heirs of the noble Roman Empire or the glorious Italian Renaissance. Instead, they appeared to be the dregs of a broken and defeated race. Woodrow Wilson, while still a professor at Princeton University, reflected a widely held view when he wrote in his *History of the American People* that

Italian immigrants had "neither skill nor energy nor any initiative of quick intelligence." Even "the Chinese were more to be desired, as workmen if not as citizens, than most of the coarse crew that came crowding in every year at the eastern ports."

Indeed, during the decades of large-scale immigration before World War I, Italian immigrants generally were the objects of prejudice and contempt. Thus a railroad construction boss appearing before a Congressional committee in 1890 was asked: "You don't call... an Italian a white man?" "No, sir," the surprised construction boss responded to what seemed to be a ridiculous question. "An Italian is a Dago."

In *The Italian in America,* published in 1905, Eliot Lord summarized prevailing prejudices toward Italian immigrants:

> It is urged that the Italian race stock is inferior and degraded; that it will not assimilate naturally or readily with the prevailing "Anglo-Saxon" race stock of this country; that intermixture, if practicable, will be detrimental; that servility, filthy habits of life, and a hopelessly degraded standard of needs and ambitions have been ingrained in the Italians by centuries of oppression and abject poverty; that they are incapable of any adequate appreciation of our free institutions and the privileges and duties of citizenship; that the greater part are illiterate and likely to remain so... and that there is no material evidence of progress and prospect of relief without the enforcement of a wide ranging exclusion.

In the decades since, Italians and their descendants have worked successfully to overcome the stigma of being "a Dago," "a Greaseball," an unskilled, unlettered, and poverty-stricken slum dweller. By the 1990s the majority of Italian Americans had attained middle-class status. Nevertheless, many of the stereotypes and myths from the immigrant era remain, holdovers from the years of mass immigration.

A total of more than five million Italians entered the United States after 1820, when American immigration statistics were first kept. The peak period, when nearly four million arrived, was between 1880 and the beginning of World War I in 1914. Following the end of the war immigration picked up again until virtually ended by restrictive legislation in 1924. Nevertheless, more than half a million Italians immigrated during the twenties. Eighty percent of the post–1880 immigrants came from the *Mezzogiorno,* the provinces south of Rome and the island of Sicily.

For the vast majority of southern Italian peasants, emigration offered the best hope, perhaps the only hope, for improving their lives. The grandeur and glory of the ancient Roman Empire had long since disappeared, and Italy by the nineteenth century was a poverty-stricken land with but one major natural resource: people.

"Purely economic causes," reported the United States Immigration Commission in 1911, were responsible for "practically all emigration from Italy." The emigrants were driven by a desire to escape abject and wretched poverty and a vicious system of taxation, the burden of which fell almost exclusively on peasants and especially those in Italy's South. At the same time, they were attracted by the hope of bettering their miserable conditions through seasonal or temporary labor elsewhere in Europe or overseas. In 1882 the Italian government asked provincial officials throughout the country to investigate their jurisdictions and provide accurate information as to the basic factors responsible for emigration from the homeland. The answers were nearly unanimous in ascribing emigration to three factors: "destitution, lack of work, and a natural desire to improve their condition."

A major characteristic of Italian immigration to the United States was its seasonal nature. As one observer in 1906 noted, "they form a stream of workers that ebbs and flows from Italy to America in instant response to demand." Southern Italians were, in this view, "the most mobile supply of labor that this country has ever had." Indeed, a very large proportion of the immigration was composed of migratory laborers who came here to work on construction or other seasonal jobs for eight or nine months of the year and then returned to spend the winters in Italy. Others left the United States during the winter months to work as agricultural laborers in Latin America. The seasons in South America are the reverse of those in the United States and Europe, and many Italians stayed in the Southern Hemisphere from November to March. The greatest Latin American economic opportunities were in Argentina and Brazil and that is where most of the immigrants went.

Because of their migratory ways, the immigrant laborers in the United States came to be known as "birds of passage." In Latin America, similar designations were used. Argentinians, for example, referred to Italian laborers as *golondrinas,* or swallows. Eventually most of the immigrants settled in the New World, but in many cases the trips back and forth to Italy, Latin America, or elsewhere were repeated several times.

Some contemporaries noted that in the years after 1900 the return migration to Italy was especially heavy during bad economic periods in the United States. Thus in the depression year of 1904 more than 134,000 Italian immigrants returned to Europe. This reverse migration served as a type of safety valve for depressed industrial towns and cities in the United States.

Despite the departure of less successful workers during depression periods, Italian immigration after the turn of the century became more stable as women and children joined the men who had earlier come to America seeking their fortunes. More than 95 percent of the Italians coming to the United States landed in New York City. From there they fanned out through the country although the majority remained close to the port of arrival or settled in urban-industrial centers of the Middle West. Of a total 2,284,601 Italians who came to the United States between 1899 and 1910, approximately three-quarters went to the heavily urbanized states of New York (993,113), Pennsylvania (429,200), Massachusetts (154,882), and New Jersey (118,680). Another 111,249 were attracted to Illinois and 58,699 to Ohio, largely because of the economic opportunities available in the cities of Chicago and Cleveland. Northern Italians were still drawn across the continent to California and particularly to the city of San Francisco, which in 1910 contained 16,918 Italian immigrants. A very limited number of Italians were attracted to farming, mostly to agricultural colonies formed in Texas, Arkansas, Mississippi, Louisiana, and Alabama. Some immigrants settled in New Orleans, prior to the 1890s a magnet for southern Italians and especially Sicilians.

As early as 1901 the United States Industrial Commission recognized that after a few years of travel back and forth to Europe or Latin America, either the family was brought over or, if the man was single, he "marries and settles down here, becoming a permanent member of the community." The arrival of Southern Italian family units in the period after 1900 was the last link in a migratory chain that began in the 1880s and 1890s with the efforts of padrones to supply labor for American employers. Padrones, or labor agents, generally recruited unskilled southern Italians for railroad or other construction or maintenance work. Although the padrone system played a key role in the early stages of the immigration, once the movement was firmly under-way the services provided by labor agents were no longer necessary and the system declined.

As the early immigrants became acquainted with American conditions and practices, they were better able to look after themselves and help later arrivals. During this intermediate stage in the migration process, individual male workers assisted male relatives and friends of working age to emigrate. Demographer J. S. McDonald noted in 1964 that "new arrivals generally traveled directly to the relatives or friends who had financed their passage, and relied on them to find their first lodgings and employment." Not an organized process, this sequence involved a series of individual decisions and actions and accounted for a large proportion of the male immigration from Italy.

The final stage came when adult male immigrants concluded that it was no longer advantageous, economically or otherwise, to continue the periodic travel overseas, and sent for their families. Not only did the migrants save money by not traveling back and forth to Italy, but because wives and children were brought to the United States and put to work, family incomes rose. Some of the immigrants who settled in America did not, however, send for the families left behind in Italy. They simply broke off all contact and, without bothering to obtain divorces from Old World spouses, married again and raised new families in America. This manner of "closing" the "chain of migration" was, as one immigration scholar has put it, "a rather ordinary experience for many Italians."

Whether in New York, Chicago, or some other city of the East and Middle West, where the majority of Italian immigrants settled, the typical pattern of settlement began with the founding of the immigrant community by northern Italians, who tended to predominate until the 1880s. The original enclave started in or near the center of the city—that is, the business district—and was characterized by the outward movement of economically successful newcomers from the slum area ethnic settlement into the wider American community. Newcomers from southern Italy swarmed into the colony in the years after 1880, filling vacancies and creating or contributing to problems in over-crowded and rapidly deteriorating neighborhoods.

The earlier-arriving northern Italians regarded their brethren from the southern provinces as "an army of barbarians encamped among us." In fact, as one scholar of American ethnic history recently observed, "the northern Italians openly repudiated the southern Italians—perhaps more forcefully than any other American ethnic group has repudiated others of the same nationality."

Living conditions in urban immigrant neighborhoods were indeed abominable. The Italian colony in New York City's Lower East Side was in 1893 described as "probably one of the most filthy localities in the city. Here, surrounded by tall brick tenements and frame rookeries, amid the sickening odors of decaying vegetable matter and filth, the streets crowded with swarthy men, women and children, dirty but picturesque withal—here can be found the home of the Italian." In the tenements, "families upon families" were "huddled together, living, eating and sleeping in one room; indeed, in many cases a room barely 8 × 10 feet will hold as many as ten persons." American observers concluded that the immigrants were attracted to such unpleasant living conditions. The Italian "seems to thrive on dirt and as a consequence, is not in the least troubled by it." Writing in 1887, a *Chicago World* reporter maintained that "It is not abject poverty which causes such nasty and cheap living; it is simply an imported habit from Southern Italy."

Early in the immigration process, southern Italians recognized the benefits that accrued from involvement in politics. Political machines in New York, Chicago, and other cities granted patronage jobs to Italians (and to members of other immigrant groups as well) in exchange for support on election day. Work included street cleaning, garbage collecting, custodial jobs in public buildings, road maintenance, and assignments in public transportation networks and sewage systems, besides construction work on tenements, bathhouses, and parks. In addition to jobs, the successful political boss obtained exemptions from city ordinances for core-area businessmen; arranged bail and obtained pardons; sponsored picnics, parades, dances, social and athletic affairs, bazaars, and community church functions; distributed turkeys and presents during the holiday season; gave fuel and food to needy residents; sent flowers to the sick; and attended funerals.

In Italian wards, political bosses generally came from Irish backgrounds and found that they needed an intermediary between themselves and the Italian masses. The machine found it expedient to employ as go-betweens men who spoke the language of the community and who knew its customs, prejudices, and the best means of molding public opinion and winning votes.

Despite diligent efforts, Italians enjoyed only limited success in winning elective office. Up to the 1930s, the level of achievement was on the ward and, occasionally, the city level and even more rarely, in state office. "In national affairs," Robert F. Foerster noted in 1919, "the Italians have so far been all but negligible."

Italians did, however, benefit from patronage. They began to move into public employment by at least the early 1890s. Such employment generally offered to unskilled laborers relatively steady income and job security, while to the ethnic group it gave convincing proof of the benefits to be gained from participation in local politics. With the turn of the century, Italians moved into this employment sector in ever-increasing numbers, even though in the last years of the nineteenth century much work came increasingly under the control of civil service commissions. This shift was important because it introduced the element of education at a time when tenement dwellers generally did not have much schooling. To Italians and other immigrants, civil service meant the loss of a job to a middle-class resident in a neighborhood on the periphery of the city.

Although Italians benefitted from opportunities in both public and private employment, and from which some realized great financial success, most Italian immigrant males remained laborers throughout their lives. For these men, success was achieved if they were able to rise to semi-skilled or skilled status. They and their compatriots who remained unskilled laborers contributed substantively but anonymously to the economic growth of the nation, performing construction, mining, factory, or maintenance work. As S. Merlino, himself an immigrant, wrote in 1893, the Italian laborer in America "tills the soil, builds railroads, drains swamps, opens here and there to the industry of American workmen new fields which would not perhaps be opened but for his cheap labor."

The typical immigrant worked a long and hard day for low pay. The United States Commissioner of Labor surveyed living and working conditions in Italian neighborhoods of Baltimore, Chicago, New York, and Philadelphia in the years 1893 and 1894, and found that common laborers put in a sixty-hour week for an average weekly wage of between six and nine dollars. In order to pay for food, housing, clothes and other necessities (which were often exorbitantly high), many found it necessary to put as many family members as possible to work.

Two problems facing the immigrant generation were child labor and the employment of women. By the age of fourteen and often earlier, children were removed from school and sent into the job market to supplement the family income. Few parents of the pre–1914 period recognized the value of education. As Nathan Glazer and Daniel P. Moynihan, authors of *Beyond the Melting Pot,* observed, "It was the 'bad' son who wanted to go to school instead of to work, the 'bad' daughter who wanted to remain in school instead of helping her mother." The conflict between immediate financial gain and long-range educational advantage was common to immigrant groups. Foreign-born children, including Italians, often left school at the first opportunity because of unpleasant classroom experiences.

To a newly arrived immigrant child whose family spoke English poorly or not at all, school could be a frightening experience. Lack of family support for formal education provided another serious obstacle to success in school. Educational apathy, an Italian-language newspaper editor stated in 1902, resulted as a carryover "on the part of Italian parents, especially those of the south of Italy, of an old-country attitude." Mario Puzo, author of *The Godfather* and an American-born son of Neapolitan immigrants recalled. "My mother wanted me to be a railroad clerk. And that was her highest ambition; she would have settled for less.... She was illiterate and her peasant life in Italy made her believe that only the son of the nobility could possibly be a writer."

In a break from European habits, women went out to work or brought piecework home. In New York, Chicago, and other manufacturing centers, Italian women were heavily represented in the garment industry and in the manufacture of lace, artificial flowers, candy, paper, and tobacco products. As early as 1902 Mable Hurd Willett, who studied the employment of women in the clothing trades in New York City, found that Italians had gained "a complete monopoly of part of the work, the felling and finishing of ready-made clothing." By 1910 Italian women constituted the largest proportion (36.2 percent) of the female work force in the New York garment industry. They dominated the artificial flower industry, totaling 72 percent of the entire work force in that line of activity. Italian women (along with women of other immigrant groups) went into this kind of work because the peculiar nature of such industry often permitted them to work at home. Production processes were decentralized and the factory work, if the job could not be done at home, required little or no machinery. Such conditions suited women with small children, and also made it possible to put girls under sixteen years of age to work.

Whether at home or in a factory, Italian women worked long hours for low pay under sweatshop conditions. In 1895 reformer Jacob Riis described the experience of a New York City school teacher who decided to visit the home of one of her students because the "little Italian girl, hardly yet into her teens, stayed away from her class in the Mott Steet Industrial School so long" that the teacher was worried. The teacher went to the girl's apartment and "found the child in a high fever, in bed, sewing on coats with swollen eyes, though barely able to sit up." Sickness, Riis concluded, "unless it be mortal, is no excuse from the drudgery of the tenement."

In 1919 social reformer Louise Odencrantz observed that in the prewar era of large-scale immigration, "the assertion was frequently heard that the Italian girl underbids her fellow-workers in every occupation she enters, that the most poorly paid home work is largely in her hands, and that Italian standards of living are a menace to American industry." Yet Italian women did not always accept these conditions without complaint. By the eve of World War I they had begun to join labor unions. Although less active than Eastern European Jews, they seemed to be more amenable to organization than Slavic women, or even Americans. Thus Italian women did indeed adapt to their new urban industrial environment.

The immigrants had left a largely pre-industrial rural country. In Italy the social structure of the village was founded on the family, whose interests and needs determined an individual's attitudes toward church, state, and school. Sociologist Floyd Mansfield Martinson stated that "there was intimate interplay of the [southern Italian] peasant family with religious practices, the planting and gathering of food, the celebration of feasts and holidays, the education of the children, the treatment of sick, the protection of the person, and all other aspects of small-village folk life."

Each family member was expected first of all to uphold family honor and to fulfill his or her particular duties and responsibilities. The father, the interpreter of all needs and interests, maintained his authority with strict discipline. Even if he did not deserve it, the wife obeyed her mate's wishes. A saying summed up Southern Italian attitudes toward wives: "Like a good weapon, she should be cared for properly; like a hat, she should be kept straight; like a mule she should be given plenty of work and occasional beatings. Above all, she should be kept in her place as a subordinate, for there is no peace in the house where a women leads her husband." This encapsulated the male version of the ideal marriage mate. In reality, the mother, although subordinate, had a voice in family decisions and mediated between the father and the often numerous offspring.

Parents expected respect and obedience from children, who assumed responsibilities at an early age. Families were large and the children, especially the boys, represented economic assets. Not only did sons seek employment while still quite young, but most—if not all—of the wages earned were turned over to the parents. All sons in a family had greater social value than did female children.

The process of settlement in the United States profoundly affected the family as well as other institutions. Within the typical immigrant family two cultures came into conflict, a recurring theme explored by numerous Italian American novelists. Immigrant parents wanted to conduct family life according to Old World patterns, and attempted to establish relationships as they remembered them. The children, on the other hand, wanted to behave in what they considered to be "the American way." As the children learned English, whether in school or on the streets, family roles and relationships began slowly to alter. The children rather than the parents understood the world in which they lived—or at least, they thought they did. As a result, the young gained a voice in family affairs. Dependence on children was especially difficult for the father to accept because it deposed him from his position of authority. Unlike the homeland, where peasant-class youngsters existed for the benefit of their parents, at least until they married, immigrant children in America learned to live their own lives and to pursue their own interests and welfare. Gradually the children began to break away from parental control and to exert their individualism. The boys typically escaped into the streets to seek companionship and a sense of security in neighborhood youth gangs.

Particularly troublesome to immigrant parents was the altered role for daughters. Sons had traditionally been allowed some freedom of action, befitting their future roles as heads of families. Expected, in the old country, to prepare for wifehood and motherhood, daughters in America grew into new roles largely because of economic necessity. Because the family had to send as many members out to work as possible in order to increase income, wives and daughters as well as sons took jobs.

Careful study of documentary material for 1896 and 1911 led historian Elizabeth Pleck to conclude that "Italian wives were as likely to work as German or Irish wives and more often employed than Polish or Russian Jewish married women.... Nor did Italian traditionalism prevent daughters from working in American sweatshops and factories, generally with parental approval."

A survey of working women in New York City published in 1919 found that 91 percent of Italian daughters fourteen years of age and older worked for wages. When a girl became a wage earner, she gained a sense of independence completely alien to her counterparts in Southern Italy. One New York Italian colony girl described the problem of unmarried young immigrant women in the United States: "Our parents think you can sit home and wait for a man to come asking for your hand—like a small town in Italy. They don't realize that here a girl has got to get out and do something about it." Courtship patterns emerged that were a mixture of rural-Italian and urban-American dating customs.

The majority of the southern Italian immigrants in the United States were between eighteen and forty-five years of age. Most married and raised families in the new homeland. Marriage generally took place in the late teens or early twenties, a later age than was generally the case in Italy. In another change from Old World behavior, offspring demanded the right to have a voice in choosing their mate and to base their decision on the principle of romantic love, although parental consent was sought. Even the girls began to demand this right. As social worker Ida L. Hull observed in a speech delivered at the National Conference of Social Work in 1924, the Italian girl brought up in America "is apt to be a rebel. She insists on having some part in choosing a husband for herself, perhaps by the elimination of several admirers before she picks out the most favored one."

Immigrant youngsters generally married within the Italian group, although increasingly they chose mates from outside the village or province of family origin. Among the second generation, marriage to non-Italians and even to non-Catholics became more common, especially in prosperous families. Studies conducted at least as early as 1916 noted a tendency on the part of upwardly mobile young men "to marry girls of other nationalities who they meet in the peer contacts of American life." Doctors, lawyers, and other professionals, merchants, politicians, policemen and others in public employment, married women of Irish, German, Polish, Jewish, Scandinavian, or English background. Because of their more sheltered upbringing, girls generally did not meet as many outsiders as did male family members, but as they found employment among non-Italians, their range of choices also expanded. The majority of marriages, however, remained within the ethnic group.

World War I profoundly affected immigration and immigrant colonies in America. Manpower needs in the belligerent countries of Europe and the extreme difficulties of ocean passage during wartime cut sharply into the number of newcomers arriving from overseas. Italian immigration declined steeply, from 283,738 in 1914 to 49,689 in 1915 and to 5,250 in 1918, the last year of the war. The virtual cessation of immigration ended the constant replenishment of labor reserves in the United States. Combined with military manpower needs in the period after the United States entered the war in April 1917 (in the United States Army alone were an estimated 300,000 Italian Americans, including 89,662 immigrants), labor shortages offered wider job opportunities than ever before and at higher wages to immigrants already in the country and their children.

With the passage of federal legislation in 1917, 1921, and 1924, the United States reversed its traditional policy of free immigration. Social workers and other liberal elements among the American population joined Italians and other urban ethnics (under the guidance of Jewish organizations) in the fight against immigration restriction; but the outcome was never in doubt when business groups aligned themselves with organized labor in support of restriction. Organized labor traditionally supported the passage of federal legislation to restrict immigration in the belief that the constant stream of unskilled labor undermined unionizing efforts. During the war years, with traditional overseas sources of unskilled labor cut off, American industry discovered the availability of alternate sources of manpower. Mexicans and blacks from the American South removed industry's need for European immigrants. This development, along with emotional factors like antiradicalism, religious bias, and racism, brought about the closing of America's "Golden Door" and the adoption of clearly discriminatory quota laws. According to historian William E. Leuchtenburg, the Immigration Act of 1924 (the Johnson-Reed Act) "reflecting racist warnings about a threat to the 'Anglo-Saxon' stock, aimed at freezing the country ethnically by sharply restricting the 'new' immigration from southern and eastern Europe."

Large-scale immigration resumed after the war but was again blocked, this time by the restrictive legislation of the twenties. In 1920, before the legislation went into effect, 95,145 Italians immigrated and another 222,260 arrived in the following year. Under the provisions of the Johnson-Reed Act a maximum quota of 150,000 immigrants a year was admitted to the United States, based on country of origin. Italians were assigned a yearly quota of 3,845.

The major era of Italian and other European immigration to the United States had ended.

7

Hull House in the 1890s:

A Community of Women Reformers

KATHRYN KISH SKLAR

● *The settlement house idea began in 1884, when two students from Oxford University moved into a run-down neighborhood in East London. Their purpose was simple: to bridge the gap between the rich and the poor, between the middle-class periphery and the inner-city slums. They converted a building into a combination library, educational center, and a residence hall and made plans to become permanent residents so that they might learn as well as teach.*

The movement spread quickly across the Atlantic. In 1891, there were six settlement houses in the United States; by 1897 the number had jumped to seventy-four; and by 1910 there were more than four hundred. The great majority were located in the large cities of the Northeast and Midwest, and they included such venerable and long-lived institutions as Lillian Wald's Henry Street Settlement on the Lower East Side of Manhattan, Graham Taylor's Chicago Commons in the Windy City, and Robert Wood's South End House in Boston. Usually each settlement contained at least a half-dozen permanent residents. Stressing the principle of "neighborhood sovereignty"—that is, mutual self-help and co-operation among immigrants in the urban villages—the settlement workers tried to teach the English language, offer training in labor skills for the unemployed, and instill respect for law and order and an understanding of the political workings of American democratic government. Because they actually lived in a working class neighborhood they saw problems from a fresh perspective and became active in myriad reform activities.

From *Signs* Vol. 10, no. 4 (1985): 658–77. Reprinted by permission of the author and The University of Chicago Press.

Easily the most famous of the social settlements was Hull House in Chicago, and the most influential of the early residents was its founder, Jane Addams. Indeed, she was considered to be the most respected woman of her generation. Born in Rockford, Illinois, she founded Hull House in 1889 and devoted her life to the lower classes and to the cause of active local government. As the following essay by Professor Kathryn Kish Sklar of the State University of New York at Binghamton suggests, however, there was another dimension to the Hull House experience. It enabled women reformers to develop their capacity for political leadership.

What were the sources of women's political power in the United States in the decades before they could vote? How did women use the political power they were able to muster? This essay attempts to answer these questions by examining one of the most politically effective groups of women reformers in U.S. history—those who assembled in Chicago in the early 1890s at Hull House, one of the nation's first social settlements, founded in 1889 by Jane Addams and Ellen Gates Starr. Within that group, this study focuses on the reformer Florence Kelley (1859–1932). Kelley joined Hull House in 1891 and remained until 1899, when she moved to Lillian Wald's Henry Street Settlement on the Lower East Side of New York, where she lived for the next twenty-seven years. According to Felix Frankfurter, Kelley "had probably the largest single share in shaping the social history of the United States during the first thirty years of this century," for she played "a powerful if not decisive role in securing legislation for the removal of the most glaring abuses of our hectic industrialization following the Civil War." It was in the 1890s that Kelley and her colleagues at Hull House developed the patterns of living and thinking that guided them throughout their lives of reform, leaving an indelible imprint on U.S. politics. This essay attempts to determine the extent to which their political power and activities flowed from their collective life as coresidents and friends and the degree to which this power was attributable to their close affiliation with male reformers and male institutions.

The effects of both factors can be seen in one of the first political campaigns conducted by Hull House residents—the 1893 passage and the subsequent enforcement of pathbreaking antisweatshop legislation mandating an eight-hour day for women and children employed in Illinois manufacturing. This important episode reveals a great deal about the sources of this group's political power, including their own collective initiative, the support of other women's groups, and the support of men and men's groups. Finally, it shows how women reformers and the gender-specific issues they championed helped advance class-specific issues during a time of fundamental social, economic, and political transition.

One of the most important questions asked by historians of American women today is, To what degree has women's social power been based on separate female institutions, culture, and consciousness, and to what degree has it grown out of their access to male spheres of influence, such as higher education, labor organization, and politics? This essay advances the commonsense notion that women's social power in the late nineteenth century depended on both sources of support. Women's institutions allowed them to enter realms of reality dominated by men, where, for better or for worse, they competed with men for control over the distribution of social resources. Thus although their own communities were essential to their social strength, women were able to realize the full potential of their collective power only by reaching outside those boundaries.

.   .   .   .

The community of women at Hull House made it possible for Florence Kelley to step from the apprenticeship to the journeyman stage in her reform career. A study of the 1893 antisweatshop campaign shows that the community provided four fundamental sources of support for her growth as a reformer. First, it supplied an emotional and economic substitute for traditional family life, linking her with other talented women of her own class and educational and political background and thereby greatly increasing her political and social power. Second, the community at Hull House provided Kelley with effective ties to other women's organizations. Third, it enabled cooperation with men reformers and their organizations, allowing her to draw on their support without submitting to their control. Finally, it provided a creative setting for her to pursue and develop a reform strategy she had already initiated in New York—the advancement of the rights and interests of working people in general by strengthening the rights and interests of working women and children.

As a community of women, Hull House provided its members with a lifelong substitute for family life. In that sense it resembled a religious order, supplying women with a radical degree of independence from the claims of family life and inviting them to commit their energies elsewhere. When she first crossed the snowy threshold of Hull House "sometime between Christmas and New Year's," 1891, Florence Kelley Wischnewetzky was fleeing from her husband and seeking refuge for herself and her three children, ages six, five, and four. "We were welcomed as though we had been invited," she wrote thirty-five years later in her memoirs. The way in which Kelley's family dilemma was solved reveals a great deal about the sources of support for the political activity of women reformers in the progressive era: help came first and foremost from women's institutions but also from the recruited support of powerful men reformers. Jane Addams supplied Kelley with room, board, and employment and soon after she arrived introduced her to Henry Demarest Lloyd, a leading critic of American labor policies who lived with his wife Jessie and their young children in nearby Winnetka. The Lloyds readily agreed to add Kelley's children to their large nursery, an arrangement that began a lifelong relationship between the two families. A sign of the extent to which responsibility for Kelley's children was later assumed by members of the Hull House community, even after her departure, was the fact that Jane Addams's closest personal friend, Mary Rozet Smith, regularly and quietly !helped Kelley pay for their school and college tuition.

A bit stunned by her good fortune, the young mother wrote her own mother a summary of her circumstances a few weeks after reaching Hull House: "We are all well, and the chicks are happy. I have fifty dollars a month and my board and shall have more soon as I can collect my wits enough to write. I have charge of the Bureau of Labor of Hull House here and am working in the lines which I have always loved. I do not know what more to tell you except this, that in the few weeks of my stay here I have won for the children and myself many and dear friends whose generous hospitality astonishes me." This combination of loving friendship and economic support served as a substitute for the family life from which she had just departed. "It is understood that I am to resume the maiden name," she continued to her mother, "and that the children are to have it." It did not take Kelley long to decide to join this supportive community of women. As she wrote Friedrich Engels in April 1892, "I have cast in my lot with Misses Addams and Starr for as long as they will have me." To her mother she emphasized the personal gains Hull House brought her, writing, "I am better off than I have been since I landed in New York since I am now responsible *myself* for what I do." Gained at great personal cost, Kelley's independence was her most basic measure of well-being. Somewhat paradoxically, perhaps, her autonomy was the product of her affiliation with a community.

One significant feature of Hull House life was the respect that residents expressed for one another's autonomy. Although each had a "room of her own," in Kelley's case this room was sometimes shared with other residents, and the collective space was far more important than their small private chambers. Nevertheless, this intimate proximity was accompanied by a strong expression of personal individuation, reflected in the formality of address used at Hull House. By the world at large Kelley was called Mrs. Kelley, but to her close colleagues she was "Sister Kelley," or "Dearest F. K.," never Florence. Miss Addams and Miss Lathrop were never called Jane or Julia, even by their close friends, although Kelley occasionally took the liberty of calling Addams "gentle Jane." It was not that Hull House was bleak and business-like, as one resident once described male settlements in New York, but rather that the colleagues recognized and appreciated one another's individuality. These were superb conditions for social innovation since the residents could draw on mutual support at the same time that they were encouraged to pursue their own distinct goals.

This respect for individuality did not prevent early Hull House residents from expressing their love for one another. Kelley's letters to Jane Addams often began "Beloved Lady," and she frequently addressed Mary Rozet Smith as "Dearly Beloved," referring perhaps to Smith's special status in Addams's life. Kelley's regard for Addams and Addams's for her were revealed in their correspondence after Kelley left in 1899. Addams wrote her, "I have had blows before in connection with Hull House but nothing like this"; and Mary Rozet Smith added,

"I have had many pangs for the dear presiding lady." Later that year Addams wrote, "Hull House sometimes seems a howling wilderness without you." Kelley seems to have found the separation difficult since she protested when her name was removed from the list of residents in the *Hull House Bulletin*. Addams replied, "You overestimate the importance of the humble Bulletin," but she promised to restore Kelley's name, explaining that it was only removed to "stop people asking for her." Fourteen years later in 1913 Addams wrote "Sister Kelley," "It is curious that I have never gotten used to you being away from [Hull House], even after all these years!"

One source of the basic trust established among the three major reformers at Hull House in the 1890s—Jane Addams, Julia Lathrop, and Florence Kelley—was similarly of family background. Not only were they all of the upper middle class, but their fathers were politically active men who helped Abraham Lincoln found and develop the Republican Party in the 1860s. John Addams served eight terms as a state senator in Illinois, William Lathrop served in Congress as well as in the Illinois legislature, and William Kelley served fifteen consecutive terms in Congress. All were vigorous abolitionists, and all encouraged their daughters' interests in public affairs. As Judge Alexander Bruce remarked at the joint memorial services held for Julia Lathrop and Florence Kelley after their deaths in 1932, "Both of them had the inspiration of great and cultured mothers and both had great souled fathers who, to use the beautiful language of Jane Addams in speaking of her own lineage, "Wrapped their little daughters in the large men's doublets, careless did they fit or no.' "

These three remarkable women were participating in a political tradition that their fathers had helped create. While they were growing up in the 1860s and 1870s, they gained awareness through their fathers' experience of the mainstream of American political processes, thereby learning a great deal about its currents—particularly that its power could be harnessed to fulfill the purposes of well-organized interest groups.

Although Hull House residents have generally been interpreted as reformers with a religious motivation, it now seems clear that they were instead motivated by political goals. In that regard they resembled a large proportion of other women social settlement leaders, including those associated with Hull House after 1900, such as Grace and Edith

Abbot, whose father was Nebraska's first lieutenant governor, or So-
phonisba Breckinridge, daughter of a Kentucky congressman. Women
leaders in the social settlement movement seem to have differed in this
respect from their male counterparts, who were seeking alternatives to
more orthodox religious, rather than political, careers. In, but not of,
the Social Gospel movement, the women at Hull House were a political
boat on a religious stream, advancing political solutions to social problems that were fundamentally ethical or moral, such as the right of
workers to a fair return for their labor or the right of children to
schooling.

Another source of the immediate solidarity among Addams, Lathrop,
and Kelley was their shared experience of higher education. Among
the first generation of American college women, they graduated from
Rockford College, Vassar College, and Cornell University, respectively,
in the early 1880s and then spent the rest of the decade searching for
work and for a social identity commensurate with their talents. Addams
tried medical school; Lathrop worked in her father's law office; Kelley,
after being denied admission to graduate study at the University of
Pennsylvania, studied law and government at the University of Zurich,
where she received a much more radical education than she would have
had she remained in Philadelphia. In the late 1880s and early 1890s,
the social settlement movement was the right movement at the right
time for this first generation of college-educated women, who were able
to gain only limited entry to the male-dominated professions of law,
politics, or academics.

While talented college women of religious backgrounds and inclinations were energetically recruited into the missionary empires of
American churches, those seeking secular outlets for their talents chose
a path that could be as daunting as that of a missionary outpost. Except
for the field of medicine, where women's institutions served the needs
of women physicians and students, talented women were blocked from
entering legal, political, and academic professions by male-dominated
institutions and networks. In the 1890s the social settlement movement
supplied a perfect structure for women seeking secular means of influencing society because it collectivized their talents, it placed and
protected them among the working-class immigrants whose lives
demanded amelioration, and it provided them with access to the male

political arena while preserving their independence from male-dominated institutions.

Since Hull House drew on local sources of funding, often family funds supplied by wealthy women, Jane Addams found it possible to finance the settlement's activities without the assistance or control of established religious or educational institutions. In 1895 she wrote that Hull House was modeled after Toynbee Hall in London, where "a group of University men . . . reside in the poorer quarter of London for the sake of influencing the people there toward better local government and wider social and intellectual life." Substituting "college-trained women" for "University men," Hull House also placed a greater emphasis on economic factors. As Addams continued, "The original residents came to Hull House with a conviction that social intercourse could best express the growing sense of the economic unity of society." She also emphasized their political autonomy, writing that the first residents "wished the social spirit to be the undercurrent of the life of Hull-House, whatever direction the stream might take." Under Kelley's influence in 1892, the social spirit at Hull House turned decisively toward social reform, bringing the community's formidable energy and talents to bear on a historic campaign on behalf of labor legislation for women and children.

Meredith Tax's *Rising of the Women* contains the most complete account of this campaign, which culminated in the passage of landmark state legislation in 1893. There Tax justly reproves Jane Addams for assigning Hull House more than its share of the credit for the campaign. The settlement did play a critical leadership role in this venture, but it was never alone. Indeed it was part of a complex network of women's associations in Chicago in the 1890s. About thirty women's organizations combined forces and entered into local politics in 1888 through the Illinois Women's Alliance, organized that year by Elizabeth Morgan and other members of the Ladies Federal Union no. 2073 in response to a crusading woman journalist's stories in the *Chicago Times* about "City Slave Girls" in the garment industry. The alliance's political goals were clearly stated in their constitution: "The objects of the Alliance are to agitate for the enforcement of all existing laws and ordinances that have been enacted for the protection of women and children—as the factory ordinances and the compulsory education law. To secure the enactment of such laws as shall be found necessary. To investigate all business establishments and factories where women and children are employed and public institutions where women and children are maintained. To procure the appointment of women, as inspectors and as members of boards of education, and to serve on boards of management of public institutions." Adopting the motto "Justice to Children, Loyalty to Women," the alliance acted as a vanguard for the entrance of women's interests into municipal and state politics, focusing chiefly on the passage and enforcement of compulsory education laws. One of its main accomplishments was the agreement of the city council in 1889 "to appoint five lady inspectors" to enforce city health codes.

The diversity of politically active women's associations in Chicago in the late 1880s was reflected in a list of organizations associated with the alliance. Eight bore names indicating a religious or ethical affiliation, such as the Woodlawn branch of the Women's Christian Temperance Union and the Ladies Union of the Ethical Society. Five were affiliated with working women or were trade unions, such as the Working Women's Protective Association, the Ladies Federal Union no. 2703, and (the only predominantly male organization on the list) the Chicago Trades and Labor Assembly. Another five had an intellectual or cultural focus, such as the Hopkins Metaphysical Association or the Vincent Chatauqua Association. Three were women's professional groups, including the Women's Press Association and the Women's Homeopathic Medical Society. Another three were female auxiliaries of male social organizations, such as the Lady Washington Masonic Chapter and the Ladies of the Grand Army of the Republic. Two were suffrage associations, including the Cook County Suffrage Association; another two were clubs interested in general economic reform, the Single Tax Club and the Land Labor Club no. 1; and one was educational, the Drexel Kindergarten Association.

Florence Kelley's 1892 entrance into this lively political scene was eased by her previous knowledge of and appreciation for the work of the alliance. Soon after its founding she had written the leaders a letter that was quoted extensively in a newspaper account of an alliance meeting, declaring, "The child labor question can be solved by legislation, backed by solid organization, and by women cooperating with the labor organizations, which have done all that has thus far been done for the protection of working children." In Chicago Kelley was perceived as a friend of the alliance because in 1889 and 1890 she had helped organize the New York Working Women's Society's campaign "to add women as officials in the office for factory inspection." According to Kelley, the Society, "a small group of women from both the wealthy and influential class and the working class, ... circulated petitions, composed resolutions, and was supported finally in the years 1889 and 1890 in bringing their proposal concerning the naming of women to factory inspectorships to the legislature, philanthropic groups and unions." As a result in 1890 the New York legislature passed laws creating eight new positions for women as state factory inspectors. This was quite an innovation since no woman factory inspector had yet been appointed in Great Britain or Germany, where factory inspection began, and the only four previously appointed in the United States had been named within the last two years in Pennsylvania. Writing in 1897 about this event, Kelley emphasized the political autonomy of the New York Working Women's Society: "Their proposal to add women as officials in the office for factory inspection was made for humanitarian reasons; in no way did it belong to the goals of the general workers' movement, although it found support among the unions." Thus when Kelley arrived at Hull House, she had already been affiliated with women's associations that were independent of trade unions even though cooperating with them.

For Kelley on that chilly December morning the question was not whether she would pursue a career in social reform but how, not whether she would champion what she saw as the rights and interests of working women and children but how she would do that. The question of means was critical in 1891 since her husband was unable to establish a stable medical practice, even though she had spent the small legacy inherited on her father's death the year before on new equipment for his practice. Indeed so acute were Kelley's financial worries that, when she decided to flee with her children to Chicago, she borrowed train fare from an English governess, Mary Forster, whom she had probably befriended at a neighborhood park. Chicago was a natural choice for Kelley since Illinois divorce laws were more equitable, and within its large population of reform-minded and politically active women she doubtlessly hoped to find employment that would allow her to support herself and her children. Although the historical record is incomplete, it seems likely that she headed first to

a different community of women—that at the national headquarters
of the Women's Christian Temperance Union (WCTU). She had been
well paid for articles written for their national newspaper, the *Union
Signal*—the largest women's newspaper in the world, with a circulation
in 1890 of almost 100,000—and the WCTU was at the height of its
institutional development in Chicago at that time, sponsoring "two day
nurseries, two Sunday schools, an industrial school, a mission that
sheltered four thousand homeless or destitute women in a twelve-month
period, a free medical dispensary that treated over sixteen hundred
patients a year, a lodging house for men that had... provided temporary housing for over fifty thousand men, and a low-cost restaurant."
Just after Kelley arrived, the WCTU opened its Women's Temple, a
twelve-story office building and hotel. Very likely it was someone there
who told Kelley about Hull House.

The close relationship between Hull House and other groups of
women in Chicago was exemplified in Kelley's interaction with the
Chicago Women's Club. The minutes of the club's first meeting after
Kelley's arrived in Chicago show that on January 25, 1892, she spoke
under the sponsorship of Jane Addams on the sweating system and
urged that a committee be created on the problem. Although a Reform
Department was not created until 1894, minutes of March 23, 1892,
show that the club's Home Department "decided upon cooperating
with Mrs. Kelly [*sic*] of Hull House in establishing a Bureau of Women's
Labor." Thus the club took over part of the funding and the responsibility for the counseling service Kelley had been providing at Hull
House since February. (Initially Kelley's salary for this service was
funded by the settlement, possibly with emergency monies given by
Mary Rozet Smith.) In this way middle-and upper-middle-class clubwomen were drawn into the settlement's activities. In 1893 Jane Addams successfully solicited the support of wealthy clubwomen to lobby
for the antisweatshop legislation: "We insisted that well-known Chicago women should accompany this first little group of Settlement folk
who with trade-unionists moved upon the state capitol in behalf of
factory legislation." Addams also described the lobbying Hull House
residents conducted with other voluntary associations: "Before the passage of the law could be secured, it was necessary to appeal to all
elements of the community, and a little group of us addressed the open
meetings of trades-unions and of benefit societies, church organizations,

and social clubs literally every evening for three months." Thus Hull House was part of a larger social universe of voluntary organizations, and one important feature of its political effectiveness was its ability to gain the support of middle-class and working-class women.

In 1893 the cross-class coalition of the Illinois Women's Alliance began to dissolve under the pressure of the economic depression of that year, and in 1894 its leaders disbanded the group. Hull House reformers inherited the fruits of the alliance's five years of agitation, and they continued its example of combining working-class and middle-class forces. In 1891 Mary Kenney, a self-supporting typesetter who later became the first woman organizer to be employed by the American Federation of Labor, established the Jane Club adjacent to the settlement, a cooperative boardinghouse for young working women. In the early 1890s Kenney was a key figure in the settlement's efforts to promote union organizing among working women, especially bookbinders. Thus the combination of middle-class and working-class women at Hull House in 1892–93 was an elite version of the type of cross-class association represented by the Illinois Women's Alliance of the late 1880s—elite because it was smaller and because its middle-class members had greater social resources, familiarity with American political processes, and exposure to higher than average levels of education, while its working-class members (Mary Kenney and Alzina Stevens) were members of occupational and organizational elites.

By collectivizing talents and energies, this community made possible the exercise of greater and more effective political power by it members. A comparison of Florence Kelley's antisweatshop legislation, submitted to the Illinois investigative committee in February 1893, with that presented by Elizabeth Morgan dramatically illustrates this political advantage. The obvious differences in approach indicate that the chief energy for campaigning on behalf of working women and children had passed from working-class to middle-class social reformers. Both legislative drafts prohibited work in tenement dwellings, Morgan's prohibiting all manufacturing, Kelley's all garment making. Both prohibited the labor of children under fourteen and regulated the labor of children aged fourteen to sixteen. Kelley's went beyond Morgan's in two essential respects, however. Hers mandated an eight-hour day for women in manufacturing, and it provided for enforcement by calling for a state factory inspector with a staff of twelve, five whom were to be women. The reasons for Kelley's greater success as an innovator are far from clear, but one important advantage in addition to her greater education and familiarity with the American political system was the larger community on which she could rely for the law's passage and enforcement.

Although Elizabeth Morgan could draw on her experience as her husband's assistant in his work as an attorney and on the support of women unionists, both resources were problematic. Thomas Morgan was erratic and self-centered, and Elizabeth Morgan's relationship with organized women workers was marred by sectarian disputes originating within the male power structure of the Chicago Trades and Labor Assembly. For example, in January 1892, when she accused members of the Shirtwaist Union of being controlled by her husband's opposition within the assembly, "a half dozen women surrounded [her] seat in the meeting and demanded an explanation. She refused to give any and notice was served that charges would be preferred against her at the next meeting of the Ladies' Federation of Labor." Perhaps Morgan's inability to count on a supportive community explains her failure to provide for adequate enforcement and to include measures for workers over the age of sixteen in her legislative draft. Compared to Kelley's, Morgan's bill was politically impotent. It could not enforce what it endorsed, and it did not affect adults.

Kelley's draft was passed by the Illinois legislature in June 1893, providing for a new office of enforcement and for an eight-hour day for women workers of all ages. After Henry Demarest Lloyd declined an invitation to serve as the state's first factory inspector, reform governor John Peter Altgeld followed Lloyd's recommendations and appointed Kelley. Thus eighteen months after her arrival in Chicago, she found herself in charge of a dedicated and well-paid staff of twelve mandated to see that prohibitions against tenement workshops and child labor were observed and to enforce a pathbreaking article restricting the working hours of women and children.

Hull House provided Kelley and other women reformers with a social vehicle for independent political action and a means of bypassing the control of male associations and insitutions, such as labor unions and political parties; at the same time they had a strong institutional framework in which they could meet with other reformers, both men and women. The drafting of the antisweatshop legislation revealed how this process worked. In his autobiography, Abraham Bisno, pioneer organizer in the garment industry in Chicago and New York, described how he became a regular participant in public discussions of contemporary social issues at Hull House. He joined "a group ... composed of Henry D. Lloyd, a prominent physician named Bayard Holmes, Florence Kelley, and Ellen G. [Starr] to engage in a campaign for legislation to abolish sweatshops, and to have a law passed prohibiting the employment of women more than eight hours a day." Answering a question about the author of the bill he endorsed at the 1893 hearings, Bisno said, "Mrs. Florence Kelly [*sic*] wrote that up with the advice of myself, Henry Lloyd, and a number of prominent attorneys in Chicago." Thus as the chief author of the legislation, Florence Kelley drew on the expertise of Bisno, one of the most dedicated and talented union organizers; of Lloyd, one of the most able elite reformers in the United States; and, surely among the "prominent attorney," of Clarence Darrow, one of the country's most able reform lawyers. It is difficult to imagine this cooperative effort between Bisno, Kelley, and Lloyd without the existence of the larger Hull House group of which they were a part. Their effective collaboration exemplified the process by which members of this remarkable community of women reformers moved into the vanguard of contemporary reform activity, for they did so in alliance with other groups and individuals.

What part did the Hull House community, essential to the drafting and passage of the act, have in the statute's enforcement? Who benefited and who lost from the law's enforcement? Answers to these questions help us view the community more completely in the context of its time.

During the four years that Kelley served as chief factory inspector of Illinois, her office and Hull House were institutionally so close as to be almost indistinguishable. Kelley rented rooms for her office across the street from the settlement, with which she and her three most able deputies were closely affiliated. Alzina Stevens moved into Hull House soon after Altgeld appointed her as Kelley's chief assistant. Mary Kenney lived at the Jane Club, and Abraham Bisno was a familiar figure at Hull House evening gatherings. Jane Addams described the protection that the settlement gave to the first factory inspection office in Illinois, the only such office headed by a woman in her lifetime: "The inception of the law had already become associated with Hull House, and when its ministration was also centered there, we inevitably received all the odium which these first efforts entailed.... Both Mrs. Kelley and her assistant, Mrs. Stevens, lived at Hull-House; ... and one of the most vigorous deputies was the President of the Jane Club. In addition, one of the early men residents, since dean of a state law school, acted as prosecutor in the cases brought against the violators of the law." Thus the law's enforcement was just as collective an undertaking as was its drafting and passage. Florence Kelley and Alzina Stevens were usually the first customers at the Hull House Coffee Shop, arriving at 7:30 for a breakfast conference to plan their strategy for the day ahead. Doubtlessly these discussions continued at the end of the day in the settlement's dining hall.

One important aspect of the collective strength of Kelley's staff was the socialist beliefs shared by its most dedicated members. As Kelley wrote to Engels in November 1893, "I find my work as inspector most interesting; and as Governor Altgeld places no restrictions whatever upon our freedom of speech, and the English etiquette of silence while in the civil service is unknown here, we are not hampered by our position and three of my deputies and my assistant are outspoken Socialists and active in agitation." In his autobiography Bisno described the "fanatical" commitment that he, Florence Kelley, and most of the "radical group" brought to their work as factory inspectors. For him it was the perfect job since his salary allowed him for the first time to support his wife and children and his work involved direct action against unfair competition within his trade. "In those years labor legislation was looked on as a joke; few took it seriously," he later wrote. "Inspectors normally ... were appointed from the viewpoint of political interest.... There were very few, almost no, court cases heard of, and it was left to our department to set the example of rigid enforcement of labor laws." Although they were replaced with "political interests" after the election of 1896, this group of inspectors showed what could be accomplished by the enactment of reform legislation and its vigorous enforcement. They demonstrated that women could use the power of the state to achieve social and economic goals.

Kelley and her staff began to take violators of the law to court in October 1893. She wrote Lloyd, "I have engaged counsel and am gathering testimony and hope to begin a series of justice court cases this week." She soon completed a law degree at Northwestern University and began to prosecute her own cases. Kelley found her work enormously creative. She saw potential innovations in social reform all around her. For example, she thought that the medical chapter of her annual report would "start a new line of activity for medical men and factory inspectors both." True to her prediction, the field of industrial medicine later was launched at Hull House by Alice Hamilton, who arrived at the settlement in 1897. Thus the effects of this small band of inspectors continued long after their dispersal. The community of women at Hull House gave them their start, but their impact extended far beyond that fellowship, thanks in part to the settlement's effective alliance with other groups of women and men.

. . . .

Historians of women have tended to assume that protective labor legislation was imposed on women workers by hostile forces beyond their control—especially by men seeking to eliminate job competition. To some degree this was true of the 1893 legislation since, by closing tenement dwellings to garment manufacture and by depriving sweatshop contractors of the labor of children under fourteen, the law reduced the number of sweatshops, where women and children predominated, and increased the number of garment workers in factories, where men prevailed. Abraham Bisno was well aware of the widespread opposition to the law and took time to talk with offenders, "to educate the parents who sent their children to work, and the employers of these children, the women who were employed longer than eight hours a day, and their employers." Jane Addams also tried to help those who were deprived of work by the new law: "The sense that the passage of the child labor law would in many cases work hardship, was never absent from my mind during the earliest years of its operation. I addressed as many mothers' meetings and clubs among working women as I could, in order to make clear the objective of the law and the ultimate benefit to themselves as well as to their children."

Did the children benefit? While further research is needed on this question, recent scholarship pointing to the importance of working-class support for the schooling of working-class children has revised earlier estimates that children and their families did not benefit. At best the law was a halfway measure that encouraged but could not force parents to place their children in school. Nevertheless, Florence Kelley was pleased with the compliance of parents and school officials. As she wrote Henry Demarest Lloyd, "Out of sixty-five names of children sent to the Board of Education in our first month of notifying it when we turned children under 14 yrs. of age out of factories, twenty-one were immediately returned to school and several others are known to be employed as nursegirls and cashgirls i.e. in non-prohibited occupations. This is good co-operation." While schools were inadequate and their teachers frequently prejudiced against immigrants, education was also an important route out of the grinding poverty that characterized immigrant neighborhoods. Thus it is not surprising that a large minority of parents complied with the law by enrolling their children in school.

The chief beneficiaries of the law, apart from those children who gained from schooling, were garment workers employed in factories. Most of these were men, but about one in four were women. The 1893 law was designed to prevent the erosion of this factory labor force and its replacement by sweatshop labor. Bisno described that erosion in his testimony before the state investigating committee early in 1893, stating, "Joseph Beifeld & Company have had three hundred and fifty employees some eleven or twelve years ago inside, and they have only eighty now to my knowledge, and they have increased their business about six times as much as it was eleven years ago." This decline of the factory population inevitably caused a decline of union membership since it was much more difficult to organize sweatshop workers. Thus as a union official Bisno was defending his own interests, but these were not inimical to all women workers.

Demonstrating the support of women unionists for the law's enforcement, members of the Women's Shoemakers Union chastized the Chicago Trades and Labor Assembly in February 1894 for their lukewarm support of the by-then-beleaguered eight-hour restriction. They "introduced resolutions, strongly condemning the manufacturers of this City for combining to nullify the state laws. . . . The resolutions further set forth that the members of the Women's Shoemakers Union effected as they were by the operation of the Eight hour Law unanimously approved the Law and for the benefit of themselves, for their sister wage workers and the little children, they pleaded for its maintenance and Enforcement." Although some women workers—particularly those who headed households with small children—must have opposed the law's enforcement, others, especially single women and mothers able to arrange child care, stood to gain from the benefits of factory employment. In a study completed for the Illinois Bureau of Labor Statistics in 1892, Florence Kelley found that 48 percent of Chicago working women lacked the "natural protectors" of fathers or husbands. Viewing them as a permanent feature of the paid labor force, she pointed to the importance of their wages to their families, thereby refuting the notion that all working women were supported by male wage earners. Although the historical evidence does not reveal how many, some young women who had formerly worked in sweatshops and whose families relied heavily on their wages doubtlessly benefited from the legislation by moving into larger factories with better working conditions.

The 1893 statute made it possible for women as well as men to move from exploitative, low-paying sweatshops into larger shops and factories with power machinery, unions, and higher wages. While the law's prohibition of tenement manufacturing obviously enabled such mobility, its eight-hour clause was no less instrumental since it attacked the basic principles of the sweating system—long hours and low wages. The average working day in the garment industry was about ten hours, but in some sweatshops it could be as long as twelve, thirteen, or fourteen hours. Reducing the working day from ten to eight hours did not significantly decrease production in factories with electric or steam-powered machinery since productivity could be raised by increasing a machine's speed or a worker's skill level. However, the eight-hour law drove many subcontractors or "sweaters" out of business since it eliminated the margin of profit created by workers' long hours at foot-powered sewing machines. From the sweatshop workers' perspective, it reduced wages even further since they were paid by the piece and could finish a much smaller amount of goods in eight hours. The wages of factory workers, by contrast, were likely to remain the same since negotiations between employers and employees customarily included a consideration of what it cost to sustain life, a factor absent from the sweaters' calculations.

Another group who benefited indirectly from this "antisweating" legislation were the men who worked in industries employing large numbers of women workers. Historians of protective labor legislation in England and the United States have noticed the tendency of male co-workers to benefit from legislation passed to protect women. This was true as early as the 1870s in Massachusetts and as late as the 1930s, when many states had laws limiting the hours of women but not the hours of men. The strategy of extending the legislation de facto to men seems to have been a deliberate intent of Kelley and her staff in the mid-1890s. At a high point in her experience as a factory inspector, Kelley wrote Engels on New Year's Eve, 1894: "We have at last won a victory for our 8 hours law. The Supreme Court has handed down no decision sustaining it, but the Stockyards magnates having been arrested until they are tired of it, have instituted the 8 hours day for 10,000 employees, men, women and children. We have 18 suits pending to enforce the 8 hours law and we think we shall establish it permanently before Easter. It has been a painful struggle of eighteen months and the Supreme Court may annul the law. But I have great hopes that the popular interest may prove too strong." When the eight-hour clause of the law was declared unconstitutional in 1895, therefore, it was beginning to affect industrywide changes in Chicago's largest employer, extending far beyond the garment industry.

The biggest losers from the enforcement of the 1893 legislation, as measured by the volume of their protest, were Chicago's manufacturers. Formed for the explicit purpose of obtaining a court ruling against the constitutionality of the eight-hour law, the Illinois Manufacturers' Association (IMA) became a model for other state associations and for the National Association of Manufacturers, formed in 1895. After 1899, when Kelley embarked on a thirty year campaign for state laws protecting working women and children, the National Association of Manufacturers was her constant nemesis and the chief rallying point of her opposition. Given the radical ideas and values behind the passage and enforcement of the 1893 legislation, it is no surprise that, at this stage of her career, Kelley's success inspired an opposition that remained her lifelong foe.

After the court decision the *Chicago Tribune* reported, "In far reaching results the decision is most important. It is the first decision in the United States against the eight-hour law and presents a new obstacle in the path of the movement for shorter hours." An editorial the next day declared: "Labor is property and an interference with the sale of it by contract or otherwise is an infringement of a constitutional right to dispose of property.... The property rights of women, says the court, are the same as those of men." For the first but not the last time in her reform career Florence Kelley encountered opponents who claimed the banner of "women's rights." In 1921 with the introduction of the Equal Rights Amendment by Alice Paul and the National Woman's Party, the potential conflict between women's rights and the protection of women workers became actual. Nearly a generation earlier in 1895 the opposition was clearly a facade for the economic interests of the manufacturers.

What conclusions can be drawn about the Hull House community from this review of their activities on behalf of antisweatshop legislation? First, and foremost, it attests to the capacity of women to sustain their own institutions. Second, it shows that this community's internal dynamics promoted a creative mixture of mutual support and individual expression. Third, these talented women reformers used their institution as a means of allying with male reformers and entering the mainstream of the American political process. In the tradition of earlier women's associations in the United States, they focused on the concerns of women and children, but these concerns were never divorced from those of men and of the society as a whole. Under the leadership of Florence Kelley, they pursued gender-specific reforms that served class-specific goals.

In these respects the Hull House community serves as a paradigm for women's participation in Progressive reform. Strengthened by the support of women's separate institutions, women reformers were able to develop their capacity for political leadership free from many if not all of the constraints that otherwise might have been imposed on their power by the male-dominated parties or groups with which they cooperated. Building on one of the strengths of the nineteenth-century notion of "women's sphere"—its social activism on behalf of the rights and interests of women and children—they represented those rights and interests innovatively and effectively. Ultimately, however, their power encountered limits imposed by the male-dominated political system, limits created more in response to their class-specific than to their gender-specific reform efforts.

8

Theodore Roosevelt: Image and Ideology

EDWARD N. SAVETH

● *Theodore Roosevelt, twenty-sixth President of the United States, manipulated the press as well as anyone in American history. A snob and a publicity hound, he managed to overcome his delicate early health to become an avid outdoorsman and a successful politician. He first gained prominence between 1895 and 1897, when he became head of the New York City Police Board. In a flash, Roosevelt became the most famous law enforcement official in the land. Although he did not initiate any major reforms and was an ineffective administrator, he won acclaim and public affection by appearing to be an independent crime fighter. Thereafter, he organized a volunteer regiment that won fame as the Rough Riders during the Spanish-American War. Riding the crest of his hero status, Roosevelt was elected governor of New York in 1898 and vice president of the United States in 1900.*

When President McKinley was assassinated six months after taking office, Theodore Roosevelt immediately became the nation's chief executive. At age 42, he had inexhaustible vitality and enthusiasm and the ability to coin vivid phrases. His administration won fame for "trust-busting," and he glorified military strength. By the end of his second term, Roosevelt was the most popular man in America, and he virtually dictated the nomination of his presidential successor William Howard Taft.

Who was Theodore Roosevelt? What made him complex? The following essay by Professor Edward N. Saveth examines the "inner man" behind the popular image.

Facing the American political scene in the late nineteenth century, the American patrician had these options: He could take refuge in the

Reprinted with the permission of the editor of *New York History* and Edward N. Saveth, Distinguished Professor of History Emeritus, SUNY.

uncompromising political morality of high Mugwumpery, hoping that preachment and education would have an uplifting effect upon mass political behavior. He could avoid the rough and tumble of electoral politics and aspire to appointive office. He could play the role of behind-the-scenes adviser to the powerful, as Henry Adams was to John Hay when the latter was secretary of state. He could serve unequivocally and cynically the political machine as did Boise Penrose, or make some compromise with it, which was Theodore Roosevelt's style. Philanthropy and participation in the work of voluntary organizations provided retreats from politics or, alternatively, avenues of entry into political life. There were opportunities in business, the professions and the life of the mind, the latter permitting failing remnants of those who first came here, to deliver jeremiads about the American scene, from which the patrician was alienated—judgments tinged with pessimism, racism and complaints about "failure of nerve," especially his own. Finally, the patrician could become an idler or even retreat into the vices of those whom Roosevelt called "the idle rich."

Theodore Roosevelt wanted to be a member of the governing class. To that end his choice was politics, requiring a blend of his patrician background with whatever was required to be elected. Americans were and still are intrigued by the mystique surrounding "the man of family, property and education," as John Adams defined the American patrician. On the other hand, conditioned by egalitarianism, the electorate was sensitive to elitism.

Roosevelt was as close to being an aristocrat as anyone in a nation which was traditionally anti-aristocratic; he was a relatively rich man at a time when men of wealth were under increasing public scrutiny. He was a man of family in an environment which changed so rapidly that the rigidities of family culture could be a liability, as was true of Henry Adams. He was an educated man, a cultivated man when education and cultivation were frequently identified with snobbery and femininity—with "dudes that part their name in the middle; man-milliners ... who rode side-saddle," who were unmindful that political parties were built by determined masculine effort and not "by deportment, or by ladies' magazines, or by gush."

Roosevelt disassociated himself from what the public disliked and distrusted about the man of family and the cultivated man. Part of Roosevelt's self-definition was in terms of negative reference groups.

Roosevelt made plain his aversion to aristocrats, idlers, clubmen, snobs, and "special apostles to culture" of the Mugwump variety. "Bitter, sour, ineffective men," Roosevelt called the Mugwumps, "who possess much refinement, culture, knowledge of a highly unproductive type." Evolving identity from disassociation, Roosevelt made it plain that he was not one of these.

Roosevelt built into his image positive elements of activism and masculinity. "I wish," he wrote, "to preach not the doctrine of ignoble ease, but the doctrine of the strenuous life, the life of toil and effort, of labor and strife." The strenuous life began with Roosevelt's childhood struggle against illness, spurred by his father's injunction "to make his body." This was followed by Roosevelt's involvement with athletics, especially contact sports like boxing and wrestling, in which he participated directly, and football which his sons played at Groton and which he followed closely. Baseball was a bit tame for him even, as he feared the consequences of football injuries upon young bodies.

The model was father. "I owe everything I have or am to Father," Roosevelt wrote in his *Autobiography*. "He did everything for me and I nothing for him ...I realize more and more each day that I am as much inferior to Father morally and mentally as physically." From father, Roosevelt inherited wealth and high social status in the New York community; the determination to conquer illness by sheer force of will—to "make" his body. Father repeatedly advised son Theodore to be mindful of his morals and to live like a Christian gentleman. Being a Christian gentleman implied responsibility to those less-fortunately endowed, a paternalistic attitude toward the poor with overtones of patriarchalism and the vocation of stewardship. Theodore Sr. was active in numerous civic and philanthropic organizations—an inveterate member of the board. His son was determined to "lead such a life as Father would have wished me to" and to "do something to keep up his name."

Roosevelt meant every word of this. Yet, repeated testaments to father overlooked or neglected important differences. Father was not the politician that his son was. Nor did the son share father's frenzied philanthropic impulse. The son never really confronted the fact that father was a noncombatant in the Civil War. Brother Elliott, apparently, was not affected by the moral example of father in the way that

Theodore was. Elliott was a poor student, played too much, drank too much, was a bad husband to his wife Anna, and a bad father to his daughter Eleanor, who married Franklin Delano Roosevelt. Theodore was blunt in asserting his dislike for the life Elliott led and the company he kept, the "unhealthy" excitements and excesses which led to "nothing." Why Elliott failed to adopt father as a model in the way that Theodore did is one of the imponderables of family history that is lost in a jungle of unknown and probably unknowable variables.

Father and ancestry provided Roosevelt with a somatic relationship to the American past; the equivalent of a proprietary interest in the affairs of the Republic. In turn, Roosevelt believed, as he once said, that the people had "a proprietary interest in him."

Roosevelt's antecedents included Isaac Roosevelt who, along with Jay, Livingston, Schuyler, Stephen Van Rensselaer, and James Duane, Roosevelt considered among the "best and ablest leaders of the New York community during and after the American Revolution." Isaac was a relative rarity among Roosevelt's ancestors insofar as he was involved politically. Most of the early Roosevelts were businessmen rather than politicians, and even Isaac was not a major political figure. Roosevelt merged Isaac with more distinguished cohorts and characterized the resulting group as a "caste," whose most prominent member, John Jay, became for Roosevelt a reference individual, almost a reference ancestor. To Roosevelt, Jay was "both an aristocrat and a patriot," whose support for the American cause during the Revolutionary War represented a triumph of patriotism over "aristocracy." Political decisions, Roosevelt added, were more difficult for men like Jay and Gouverneur Morris than for Sam Adams and Patrick Henry because Morris and Jay "had to choose between caste and country."

Jay's struggle against the dictates of "caste" assumed personal meaning for Roosevelt in terms of his own political decision making. In 1884, Roosevelt was a reformer within the ranks of the Republican party, faced with the necessity of deciding whether to support James G. Blaine, who had a reputation for corruption, or to bolt the party along with the Mugwumps. Roosevelt believed that to follow the dictates of "caste" would have committed him to an impractical reformism and, not incidentally, political impotence. The decision for Blaine, Roosevelt believed, was in the tradition of Jay's forsaking caste.

Actually, the Mugwump revolt against Blaine was in the premodern political style of Jay. Refusing to join this defection in Republican ranks, Roosevelt embraced political modernism including professionalism in politics, political machines, and aggressive appeals for the votes of the electorate. This was not Jay's way, to whom politicians were men "raised from low degrees ... rendered giddy by elevation," who were more susceptible to the whims of "prevailing fashions" in politics rather than "the utility of their goods to those who are to wear them." They brought out what was bestial in the "lower class of mankind," who Jay regarded as deficient in "virtue."

Nor was it the way of Gouverneur Morris. Roosevelt defended Morris as a practitioner of republican virtue insofar as he had abandoned a comfortable private life and, out of a sense of duty, entered the public realm. At the same time, Roosevelt found Morris cynical about politics, unable and unwilling to get along with people whose status was beneath his own.

"His own conduct," Roosevelt wrote of Morris, "affords a conclusive condemnation of his theories as to the great inferiority of a government conducted by the multitude, to a government conducted by the few who should have riches and education. Undoubtedly he was one of these few; he was an exceptionally able man, and a wealthy one; but he went farther wrong ... than the majority of our people—the 'mob' as he would have contemptuously called them—have ever gone at any time...."

Roosevelt did not develop the theme that Jay and Morris, along with others of the founders, were the inheritors of the ideal of republican virtue which was inherited from the classicists via the Renaissance and the English gentry. Republican virtue vested leadership in an elite which would put aside personal interests and the joys of private life in order to serve the community. This elite found republican virtue limited for the most part to themselves and not widely distributed among the mass of mankind. Republican virtue was sustained by deference to natural aristocrats and the hope that there was sufficient virtue among the mass of people to cause them to choose their superiors as governors.

Roosevelt rejected this brand of politics because it was elitist and patently doomed in an era of mass suffrage. Indeed, the most likely heirs of republican virtue were the Mugwumps who accepted the responsibilities of public service, sometimes grudgingly, even as they made known their dislike of political modernism. Roosevelt did not address republican virtue as such. (Only recently have historians been sensitized to the concept of republican virtue.) Instead, Roosevelt's emphasis was upon "character" which subsumed much of what was involved in republican virtue but was less elitist and more available to everyman. Republican virtue evoked ancestry and past achievement; character signified the individual bucking the odds. Republican virtue represented the man of family; character the self-made man. Roosevelt's self image was that of the man of family who was self made.

Roosevelt's concept of character included the "homely virtues" such as common sense, honesty and especially "the great virile virtues, the virtues of courage, energy and daring; the virtues [that] beseem a masterful race...." Some attributes of republican virtue were included but, on the whole, character was more robust, more democratic, less elitist, and more accessible to a democratic constituency. It was also less intellectual than republican virtue and more inclusive of a "naturalist-vitalist" trend in late nineteenth-century American life and culture. Character was manliness, virility, and courage; a gutsy concept. Roosevelt said repeatedly that his preference was for character over intellect.

Roosevelt did not say that the Mugwumps lacked character; rather that their character lacked virility. Mugwump politics were essentially premodern and in the tradition of republican virtue. Mugwumps were uncomfortable with professional politicians, political machines, and the substitution of aggressive campaign tactics for deference. To Roosevelt, the Mugwumps were "political hermaphrodites." On the other hand, to the extent that the professional politician was self made, Roosevelt endowed him with character and political masculinity. Told by patrician friends that he was unlikely to meet gentlemen at the Republican headquarters of New York's Twenty-first Assembly District and that he would encounter only saloon keepers and the like, Roosevelt's reply was: "If that is so, the groom and the saloon keeper are the governing class and you confess weakness. You have all the chances, the education, the position, and you let them rule you. They must be better men. So, I went."

Roosevelt's first experience with electoral politics resulted in his election to the New York State Assembly in 1881. Seven years later, when James Bryce was collecting material for the *American Commonwealth*, Roosevelt assured him that the machine was no worse than the men who manned it. "In good city districts the 'machine' is also generally good. Thus in our three New York districts, the 'brownstone front' ones, we have good machines ... the assemblymen and aldermen are all gentlemen—club men, of 'Knickerbocker' ancestry, including a Hamilton, a Van Rensselaer, etc., etc. In none of these districts is there the least difficulty now, in a decent man's getting into the machine...."

Relying on the machine, Roosevelt was above it with a reputation as a reformer and good government man. He was definitely not New York's counterpart of Pennsylvania's Boise Penrose whose ancestry was probably more distinguished than Roosevelt's and whose intellect may have been superior. Penrose, like Roosevelt, began as a reformer. Later on, Penrose took demonic pleasure in immersing himself in the intricacies of the Pennsylvania political machine, his huge bulk literally wallowing in political corruption while concomitantly enjoying whoring and gluttony.

Roosevelt was no Penrose. Still, one wonders what Roosevelt's father would have thought of his son's involvement with the machine and with those who made politics a profession. Father's political ambitions, not as strong as his son's, had been defeated by Roscoe Conkling, who controlled New York's politics in the way that Penrose, at a later date, controlled Pennsylvania's. Roosevelt's cousin Emlen believed that father "would not have liked it," which might have been a projection of Emlen's own opinion.

Father died in 1878, three years before Roosevelt's initiation into public life. There followed in rapid succession Roosevelt's marriage, the death of his wife in childbirth, his final acrimonious break with the Mugwumps over the Blaine nomination. There were personal as well as political reasons for changing his environment.

Roosevelt's investment of part of his inherited wealth in a ranch in the Dakotas was not altogether unusual for someone of his background. Other scions of wealthy and prestigious eastern families, bored with life in the East and seeking excitement and the opportunity to be on one's own among adventuresome surroundings, were doing the same thing. Like Roosevelt, they looked to the West to escape from the restraints of the eastern environment, to experience the "beat of hardy life," to acquire toughening and masculine experience. From Dakota,

Roosevelt wrote to Henry Cabot Lodge: "The Statesman (?) of the past has been merged, I fear for good, into the cowboy of the present."

The ranch, like the political clubhouse, provided Roosevelt with a proving ground for masculinity. Cowboy and politician were redolent of the common man. The politician, however, did not lend himself to the kind of romanticizing that the cowboy did. Owen Wister and other writers portrayed the cowboy as a "natural aristocrat," a "cavalier" of the plains. At a later date the politician does emerge as a positive if not a romantic figure. Historians and journalists have aided in the refurbishment of the Tweeds and the Flynns. So has that quintessential patrician, Dean Acheson, who hailed Alfred E. Smith at the 1928 Democratic convention as another Bonnie Prince Charlie leading the political troops. We may be hearing more of this, as the sound byte may make the politician as obsolete as the cowboy, becoming like the cowboy a subject of nostalgic fantasy.

Roosevelt, of course, was never the proletarian of the plains, which is what the cowboy, unglamorous and unromanticized, was. He was the patrician proving himself, in encounters with bullies, bears, and frontier flotsam—all sorts of derring-do including rifles at ten paces. Almost all of this was publicized by Roosevelt, a natural and fluent writer, in print media.

Thus imaged, Roosevelt could direct verbal salvos, replete with righteousness, at the idle rich, who sought only enjoyment; the "criminal rich," who thought only of enhancing wealth; the "bourgeois type," who, while honest, industrious, and virtuous, was also "not unapt to be a miracle of timid and short-sighted selfishness." Also coming under the Rooseveltian fire was the "timid good" who formed a "most useful as well as a most despicable part of the community." Roosevelt included the timid good with the semi-cultivated classes; "flabby types," whose low character "eats away the great fighting qualities of our race." The same indictment was made of a "few doctrinaires and educated men." Roosevelt expected little from the small farmers, agricultural laborers, mechanics, and workmen. Still, Roosevelt said time and again that men should be judged as individuals rather than as types.

The warrior was for Roosevelt the epitome of the virile virtues. The Spanish-American War provided Roosevelt with the opportunity to act out his fantasy of the warrior image. Frederick Remington's painting of Roosevelt leading the charge up San Juan Hill, which was commissioned by Roosevelt, depicted the warrior-hero who was expendable in the service of his country.

The patricians and cowboys who, among others, constituted the Rough Rider regiment, First Volunteer U.S. Cavalry, that Roosevelt led into battle in Cuba, received the bulk of the regiment's publicity. Press reports of combat denied what patricians feared about themselves as well as some public expectation—that the patrician, facing the ultimate test of manhood, might flinch in battle. This expectation was shattered in bad verse. Wrote a correspondent of the *Denver Evening Post:*

> We was somewhat disappointed, I'll acknowledge, fur to see
> Sich a husky lot o'fellers as the dandies proved to be,
> An' the free an' easy manner in their bearin' that they had
> Sort o' started the impression that they mightn't be so bad.

In the words of another versifier in the Chicago *Tribune:*

> They scoffed when we lined up with Teddy.
>   They said we were dudes and all that;
> They imagined that "Cholly" and "Fweddie"
>   Would faint at the drop of a hat.
> But let them look there in the ditches,
>   Blood-stained by the swells in the van,
> And know that a chap may have riches,
>   And still be a man!

A dispatch by correspondent Richard Harding Davis likened the war to an Ivy League football match. "For the same spirit that once sent these men down a white-washed field against their opponents' rush-line was the spirit that sent Church, Channing, Devereux, Ronalds, Wrenn, Cash, Bull, Larned, Goodrich, Greenway, Dudley, Deans, and a dozen others through the high hot grass at Guasimas, not shouting, as their friends the cowboys did, but each with his mouth tightly shut, with his eyes on the ball, and moving in obedience to the captain's signals."

"Not shouting" and "mouth tightly shut" subtly distinguished patrician from cowboy. So did Roosevelt's uniform which was tailored by Brooks Brothers.

Remington's portrait of Roosevelt, sabre brandished, was representative as well of Roosevelt as a political campaigner. Roosevelt vested in political issues the kind of moral coloration that found expression in the war against Spanish decadence. Demonstrating the political style of the crusader who was at the same time sensitive to political chances, he struck out vigorously against the evils that he saw as plaguing the nation. The image that he projected was that of an honest, strong, competent, sincere, fearless, and above all, masculine advocate—reinforced by emphatic gestures and body language. Teeth dominated his facial expressions as they did cartoon representations of him. "Teethadora," a newspaper reporter dubbed him. The reformer, Jacob Riis, noted how Roosevelt "snapped his teeth together and defied the party leaders." A popular couplet during the Spanish-American War described how

> Teddy came runnin' with his glasses on his nose
> And when the Spaniards saw his teeth,
> you may well believe they froze.

Teeth are symbolic of oral aggression. As an extension of the toothy half-grin, Roosevelt would lean forward and point his index finger at the audience as if to impress each of his hearers. Not to be underestimated is the impact of the man of high status enunciating high ideals! In an era that knew not radio, television, or even voice amplification, an era that was a heyday of vaudeville—Roosevelt was one of the better acts around.

Roosevelt's image exuded masculinity but not sexuality. Imagery was attuned to home and fireside, to purposeful ejaculations in the marriage bed for the production of children, spurred by thoughts of the imminence of race suicide. "The woman who flinches from childbirth," Roosevelt wrote Hamlin Garland, "stands on a par with the soldier who drops his rifle and runs in battle."

Family, Roosevelt believed, was the measure of the good society and "the prime duty, the inescapable duty of the *good* citizen . . . is to leave his or her blood behind him in the world." Large families reared by eugenically superior people were essential to the progress of civilization. "A race must be strong and vigorous; it must be a race of good fighters and good breeders . . . no capacity for building up material prosperity can possibly atone for the lack of the great virile virtues." Old families, like his own, to which he linked eugenic soundness, should have at least six children. No role for a woman ranked higher, in Roosevelt's scale, than motherhood.

As the family went, so went the nation. Eugenically sound families were mentors to Americans of lesser cultural and biological inheritance. This was a facet of the dignity-deference relationship and of the stewardship role of old families. Not only domestically but also in underdeveloped areas of the world, the extended family of English-speaking peoples were destined to play such a role. English speaking but not Anglo-Saxon. Roosevelt believed that there were no Anglo-Saxons and that the Englishman who "was commonly mistaken for an Anglo-Saxon was actually a medley of low Dutch, Celtic, Scandinavian and Norman elements with the Germanic strain predominant." The typical American, Roosevelt said, was much the same in make-up because the basic English strain, itself a compound, was reinforced by immigration mainly from Dutch and German sources, followed by a lesser infusion from Ireland and the Scandinavian peninsula and Huguenots. These ethnic elements were represented in his own ancestry, and in terms of his conception of the ethnic composition of the average American, Roosevelt saw himself as typical.

Finley Peter Dunne, the humorist, in his newspaper column had challenged Roosevelt for an alleged belief in Anglo-Saxon superiority. Roosevelt's reply to Dunne was a denial of anglophilism and presentation of himself as the image of the composite nation. Not altogether accurately because, as Roosevelt well knew, none of the stocks from southern, central, and eastern Europe, who came to the United States in large numbers after 1880, were represented in his ancestry. Therefore, when he spoke of his polygenesis and of America as a melting pot, he had in mind mainly the nationalities from which he was derived. While paying homage to the melting-pot image, Roosevelt did not define with too much precision what he meant by it. The public Roosevelt was not the strong advocate of immigration restriction that his friend Henry Cabot Lodge was. On this issue, Roosevelt was a great maker of "weasel paragraphs" and "lynx-eyed" statements and his private feelings were stronger than his public statements. He said more than once that "the representatives of many old-world races are being fused together into a new type," that was the composite American.

Yet, at a time of national crisis prior to World War I, Roosevelt insisted that the crucible in which all the new types are melted into one was shaped from 1776 to 1789, and our nationality was definitely fixed in all its essentials by the men of Washington's day.

"There is nothing against which I protest more strongly," Roosevelt wrote Dunne, "socially and politically, than any of us looking down upon decent Americans because they are of Irish or German ancestry; but I protest as strongly against any similar discrimination against or sneering at men because they happen to be descended from people who came here some three centuries ago...." Roosevelt presented himself to Dunne as an old-stock underdog smeared by unfair allegations of snobbery. Roosevelt neither wanted nor expected priority because of his derivation. (Had he insisted on priority, he would not have received it.) Instead, Roosevelt, in the underdog role, asked for himself and others like him, no more and no less in the way of fair political treatment than was received by men named Reilly and Schwarzmeister—that he not be penalized by the widespread but erroneous belief that the older stocks were aloof, snobbish, and "aristocratic."

The melting-pot image was expedient for Roosevelt insofar as it was sufficiently ambiguous to please almost everyone. It was an image of unity without indication of who was included or excluded. It also served Israel Zangwill who dedicated his play, *The Melting Pot*, to Roosevelt. Neither man defined melting pot in depth and, conceivably, they could have been talking at cross purposes. The ethnics, except for a minority of unmeltable ones, were more or less accepting of the melting-pot image since it, like the political clubhouse, gave them an all-important sense of belonging to a larger entity. Roosevelt was not a pluralist in the sense that Horace Kallen and Randolph Bourne were. Neither were the majority of ethnics, who were eager to embrace, if not Roosevelt's ancestors, then what they represented.

Roosevelt possessed an abiding sense of race which he defined in various ways, his racial thought changing with his extensive reading on the subject. Race, however defined, drove him insofar as it became integrated with qualities that he held dear: virility, manhood, and a sense of national purpose. His preferences, generally, were for people of his own origin and for carriers of the culture of the English-speaking peoples. He accepted peoples of southern and eastern European origin as members of the white race, but only insofar as they abandoned old-world cultures and allegiances and adopted the mold of American nationality as shaped by earlier arrivals whose ethnicity and ideals were similar to Roosevelt's own. He spoke of "making a new race, a new type in this country," but this was to take many generations and it is questionable how much Roosevelt wanted the new type to differ from the old. He was very dubious whether peoples of color would ever be successfully integrated into the American society.

Had Roosevelt not been in politics, it is possible that his views on race would have been more pronounced. Political exigency undoubtedly softened his racial attitudes as did traditional Middle States population heterogeneity. Politically, Roosevelt could not afford the anti-Semitism of Henry Adams nor the biases against southern and eastern European immigrants expressed by Lodge, main author of the National Origins immigration legislation of 1924, which discriminated against peoples of southern and eastern European origin.

As with everything else he did, Roosevelt played the politics of the melting pot with a certain zest. He had good memories. Invited during his post-presidential tour of Europe to dine with the Italian royal family, Roosevelt was expected to walk in with the "queen on my arm, and my hat in my other hand—a piece of etiquette which reminded me of nothing with which I was previously acquainted, except a Jewish wedding on the East Side of New York, where the participants and guests of honor wear their hats during the ceremony, and where, on the occasions when I was Police Commissioner, and occasionally attended such weddings, I would march solemnly in to the wedding feast with the bride, or the bride's mother, on one arm, and my hat in my other hand. Both at the Italian Court and at the East Side weddings, however, some attendant took the hat as soon as I sat down at the table."

Which is an appealing story of what happened long ago when, for all the semi-mythic character of the melting pot, Americans seemed to want it to work as part of a consensus. Whatever Roosevelt's private reservations, more important is his willingness to behave politically, and to image himself accordingly, as if the ideal was reality, which, to some extent, it was and is.

The melting pot was symbolic of national unity, which was a Roosevelt goal. More than ethnic and racial contention, however, Roosevelt feared class conflict. He did not, in so many words, identify an eth-class. He told Congress in his Second Annual Message on December

2, 1902, that "we need to remember that any kind of class animosity in the political world is, if possible, even more wicked, even more destructive to national welfare, than sectional, race or religious animosity." Mindful of the destructive effects of class warfare on earlier republics, Roosevelt stated that "no true patriot will fail to do everything in his power to prevent substitution of class hatred for loyalty to the whole American people." He would resolve the problem of class tensions by treating each man "not as a member of a class, but on his own worth as a man." He urged political organizations not to draw what was described as "an exclusive social line."

The Progressive party seemed to do just that, in part as a reaction to the control of the Republican party by businessmen and political professionals. Among the reasons why Roosevelt in 1912 became the Progressive nominee for the presidency was his almost paranoid fear of social disorder, or destabilization. Leadership of the Progressives would provide Roosevelt with the opportunity to resolve perplexing and threatening social problems, to express in his own image the ideal of a united nation. The latter was to be achieved by means of the socio-political controls advocated in Herbert Croly's *The New Nationalism,* some of which were written into the platform of the Progressive party.

The Progressive goal of an ordered and controlled society represented social controls. It was also reminiscent of father's stewardship role, his "maniacal benevolence" involving philanthropies, board memberships in voluntary organizations, personal services to the poor and, finally, his work during the Civil War with the United States Sanitary Commission. The son tried to emulate father, believing as he did in "the gospel of works as put down in the Epistle of James." However, what worked for father did not work for the son. Roosevelt tried "faithfully to do what Father had done" but found himself doing it "poorly ... in the end, I found out that we have each to work in his own way." Roosevelt thought philanthropy was discredited by the extremely noxious individuals who went into it with ostentation to make a reputation.

Nevertheless, he clung to the image of stewardship. In a speech at Osawatomie, Kansas on August 31, 1910, Roosevelt characterized the national government as belonging "to the whole American people" and "the executive power as the steward of the public welfare." In this context the Progressive party platform could be considered a modernization of stewardship with an arbitrated social policy directed by the

executive and administered by "service-intellectuals." The latter were
not of the Mugwump stripe, not "educated and cultivated" in the
traditional, classical sense, but a technical intelligentsia who were more
likely graduates of the University of Wisconsin than of Harvard, whose
training, not unlike the class background of patricians, made them
impartial in matters of class conflict. "The most important thing for
this class of men to realize," wrote Roosevelt, "is that they do not form
a class at all."

Roosevelt aspired to a government capable of steering between the
"Scylla of mob rule and the Charybdis of the reign of mere plutocracy"
which he characterized as the worst of all aristocracies. How to realize
the Burkean ideal of wealth made "obedient and laborious in the service
of virtue and public honor"? Roosevelt believed, or seemed to believe
that the Progressives might achieve this goal with the cooperation of
a body of public service intellectuals.

Following the Progressive defeat in 1912, Roosevelt wrote to Sir
Edward Grey, then England's prime minister, that he had not expected
to win. He added: "There is something to be said for government by
a great aristocracy which has furnished leaders to the nations in peace
and war for generations." However, there was no such class in the
United States. Between 1912 and 1916, Roosevelt became increasingly
critical of the Progressives. They had, said Roosevelt, few "practical
men" and "under such circumstances the reformers tended to go into
sheer lunacy." Moreover, the Progressives were not his kind of people.
Virtually at the start of Roosevelt's involvement with the Progressives,
Henry L. Stimson warned him that the movement for change was in
the wrong hands and directed by the wrong people. Stimson urged
Roosevelt in 1910 not to weaken Republican solidarity. Stimson
explained:

> The Republican party, which contains, generally speaking, the
> richer and more intelligent citizens of the country, should take
> the lead in reform and not drift into a reactionary position. If
> instead the leadership should fall into the hands of either an
> independent party or a party composed, like the Democrats,
> largely of foreign elements, and if the solid business Republicans
> should drift into new obstruction, I fear the necessary changes
> could hardly be accomplished without much excitement and pos-
> sible violence.

Following the Progressive interlude, Roosevelt actually did go home to the kind of people who, Stimson believed, should guide reform. Home included a patrician friendship circle that embraced national and international personalities who were welcome in the best houses in Washington, including the White House and especially the adjoining houses of Henry Adams and John and Clara Hay. This was less a salon than occasional gatherings of those who "belonged." (Roosevelt considered salons effeminate.) Tensions within this group were not unlike those which occurred within a family.

Henry Adams, whose home was opposite the White House and across Lafayette Park, in 1906 wrote of Roosevelt's "middle-class reforms" as "amusing" but "conservative." Adams believed that they should have happened long ago. In 1912, Adams assailed the Progressive Roosevelt for appealing to the mob—"a sort of Moses and Messiah for a vast progressive tide of humanity symptomatic of the degradation of energies." Adams considered reviving his "old theory that Theodore is insane, not only in his opinions but in his personal behavior. Déséquilibré . . . the asylum is the end. . . . " Nevertheless, Adams added, "socially and personally Roosevelt touches us all very closely." Roosevelt's "sheer energy the like of which never existed outside a lunatic asylum" never bored "us." A lunatic, perhaps, but Roosevelt remained one of "us."

In other ways, Roosevelt returned to "us." Understandably, Dr Michael Pearlman has subtitled his volume, on the movement to prepare America to fight in World War I, *Patricians and Preparedness*. Patricians were in the vanguard of the preparedness movement and Roosevelt, atavism kindled, was the most outspoken among them. Aspiring to forge maximum national unity, Roosevelt now embraced segments of the business community of which he had once been critical as well as the Republican party hierarchy which had deprived him of the nomination in 1912. Roosevelt was home indeed. He would gladly have become a symbol of national unity in wartime by fulfilling a long-time wish to die on the battlefield. This was the penultimate image. Alas, the Wilson administration refused Roosevelt permission to lead a company of volunteers as he once did in Cuba. The closest to martyrdom that Roosevelt came was the death of one of his sons in combat and the wounding of two, which afforded Roosevelt a seemingly unnatural satisfaction.

Roosevelt's concern with national unity and his efforts to image himself as symbolic of that unity, may have been due in part to fractures in his own personality. Ike Hoover, the White House usher, who greatly admired Roosevelt, believed the president to be "forcing himself all the time; acting, as it were, and successfully." Gamaliel Bradford wrote of Roosevelt as "playing a game ... forcing optimism, forcing enjoyment with the desperate instinctive appreciation that if he let the pretense drop for a moment, the whole scheme would vanish away." Owen Wister detected wistfulness blurring Roosevelt's eyes: "the misty perplexity and pain, which Sargent caught so well ... the sign of frequent conflict between what he knew and his wish not to know it, his determination to grasp his optimism tight, lest it escape him in the many darknesses that rose around him all along his way." According to a perceptive biographer, "black care, for all the phenomenal pace he maintained through his life clung to him more than he let on."

What saved Roosevelt from these languors was a strong sense of inner direction, supplemented by psychic strength derived from ancestry or tradition direction. Not that he would have or could have revived the Federalist world of John Jay, Gouveneur Morris and his supreme hero, Alexander Hamilton. On a personality scale marking at one extreme tradition direction, inner direction and at the opposite extreme, other direction, Roosevelt is a classic inner-directed type, leaning more toward tradition direction than other direction. Roosevelt, who accepted that aspect of political modernization which was centered in political machines and professional politicians, was not involved in political modernization's latest phase: fabricated personality and canned imagery. Dead at the age of sixty, Roosevelt could have been worn out by strenuous living, but not by the psychic strain of living up to his imagery. Roosevelt *was* his imagery.

Imagery compensated for status uncertainty. Roosevelt once described Gouverneur Morris as having "a smothered doubt as to one's real position." So did Roosevelt. In 1909, during his post-presidential tour of Europe, Roosevelt was received by a group of Austrian aristocrats to whom he attempted to define his status in the context of the American and Austrian social structure. In a letter to the English historian, George Otto Trevelyan, Roosevelt relates how he told the Austrians that there was no American counterpart to them as an aristocracy. Roosevelt had no objection to aristocracy and kingship in

Europe, adding that they had no place in America. "Their people and our people," could meet "on a footing of entire equality and good will, but with full recognition of the fact that any attempt at too intimate relations would result in showing utter discordance.... If we came too close we should find that our systems of life were fundamentally irreconcilable." Roosevelt also made clear his opposition to intermarriage between European aristocrats and the American upper class.

On a more personal note, Roosevelt related that "even the extremely aristocratic Austrians seemed eager to see me, just because I did represent something new to them. They regarded me as a characteristically American type, which however had nothing in common with the conventional American millionaire; to them it was interesting to meet a man who was certainly a democrat—a real, not a sham democrat— both politically and socially, who was yet a gentleman...."

He was all the more acceptable, Roosevelt continued, because of his reputation as a soldier and big-game hunter and because he had attacked while president "the big financial interests, and because I frankly looked down on mere monied men, the people of enormous wealth who had nothing but their wealth behind them.... Men who had done these things, they could understand; and they also understand men who did things that their own bourgeois class did; but what puzzled them was to find the two characters combined."

Roosevelt neither imaged nor projected himself as bourgeois. But there was a coincidence between business careers, self made, and the strenuous life. Roosevelt was respectful of the risk and daring of entrepreneurship as an aspect of strenuous living even as he disdained greed. His sons, Roosevelt told the Austrians, would have to work for a living. His oldest son, Ted, "as soon as he had left Harvard ... had gone into a mill, had worked with a blouse and tin dinner pail, exactly like any other workman for a year, and when he had graduated from the mill had gone out for the same firm to San Francisco, where he was selling carpets...."

Self-made represented character, inner direction, and strenuosity. It involved, as well, tradition direction. Early in the eighteenth century, William Byrd II, the Virginia patrician, distinguished "2 sorts of nobility: those ... that made noble themselves and those that had their Titles by Inheritance." Later, John Adams and Thomas Jefferson compared the "artificial" aristocracy of birth and the "natural" aristocracy of talent and achievement. Neither Byrd nor Adams and Jefferson gave sufficient weight to the advantages of birth which enabled them to become achievers. Similarly, Roosevelt habitually understated the amount of money he had inherited and which made possible his political career.

Self made, however, did not provide a core of patrician identity sufficiently unique to yield what Antonio Gramsci described as a "historically organic" ideology likely to elicit mass "spontaneous consent." Nor was the American patriciate a class which, in the words of George Sorel, was possessed "of serious moral habits imbued with feelings of its own dignity and having the authority to govern." Had such a sense of identity and ideology developed, they could have displaced imagery or produced a different kind of imagery—possibly with deference written on its face. They also might have changed the nature of American politics in-sofar as Roosevelt and patrician politicians, before him and after, would have been armed with "grand theory" as an instrument for imposing order upon a society characterized by Professor Morrison as having the potential for "anarchy, disorder, and wanton bloodshed." Instead, Morison continues, Roosevelt strived to achieve "acceptable working agreements between the dissident elements that make up society." Imagery was part of Roosevelt's pragmatism. Would ideology have been more effective in preserving social peace and national unity? Not likely.

9

Commerce in Souls: Vice, Virtue, and Women's Wage Work in Baltimore, 1900–1915

PAMELA SUSAN HAAG

• *Whether or not it is the world's oldest profession, prosti-tution dates back at least to ancient Greece and Rome and has been common in most human societies ever since. In the Middle Ages commercial sex flourished, and licensed brothels were a source of revenue to municipalities. In the United States the "social evil" appeared early in the colonial period, and by the late nineteenth century virtually all major cities had "red-light districts" that operated in conjunction with other forms of crime and vice.*

Periodically, American reformers took aim at open sexual-ity and attempted to end the practice whereby a female offered herself to an adult male for monetary gain. Usually the cam-paigns were accompanied by great fanfare and well-publicized police raids. Prostitution of course survived, and it is probably true that anti-vice crusades revealed more about the societies which launched them than about the practices they intended to stamp out. Prostitution, for example, often involved many persons other than those who were physically intimate. En-trepreneurial landlords and saloonkeepers recognized that commercial sex meant high rents, stable profits, and upward mobility. The police and the politicians enjoyed a regular source of graft, while the prostitutes involved often received lucrative remuneration, albeit at the cost of extreme personal exploitation.

The following essay on Baltimore is about female sexuality in its larger context. Reformers were apt to call anything prostitution, even the acceptance of a gift from a boyfriend

" 'Commerce in Souls' ": Vice, Virtue, and Women's Wage Work in Baltimore, 1900–1915." *Maryland Historical Magazine*, volume 86, number 3, 1991. Article is reprinted courtesy of the Maryland Historical Society.

if he expected to take liberties as a result of his generosity.
These reformers attempted to regulate behavior at the work-
place and at the dance hall, they wanted to enforce a sharp
line between dating and sex, and they wanted to direct wom-
en's energies toward acceptable pursuits. Thus marriage and
motherhood were appropriate areas for female labors. In es-
sence, this essay reveals how long older Americans have been
uncomfortable with the freedoms enjoyed by their children
and grandchildren.

Baltimoreans animated the summer of 1915 with lurid talk of urban
vice and the "ways of immorality." An elite, fourteen-member Maryland Vice Commission had spent three years plumbing the sexual "underworld" of Baltimore's young working women and then cautiously
meted out its hefty report to the public. The Maryland commission
and forty-three similar committees zealously convened across the nation
between 1900 and 1917 ostensibly sought to investigate only "commercialized vice." Yet Maryland's investigators, at least, found that
"the new methods of dress and make-up on some women's and girl's
faces, together with their actions," prevented the commissioners from
differentiating "the streetwalker from the respectable girl."

Consequently members of the commission cast a probing eye across
the entire landscape of women's work and leisure. They diligently cat-
alogued not only the unabashedly "fallen" brothel "inmate" who
"loved the society of real sports" and was "just out for the coin," but
also the seventeen-year-old salesgirl "E.S.," who merely "flirted with
every man in sight" and had "plenty of new clothes." They recounted
trips to "questionable" shore parks that boasted vaudeville stages, well-
supplied drinking pavilions, and Turkish theaters—hang outs for girls
who worked in day time and went out at night—where "all sorts of
smutty and suggestive dances are permitted" and girls eventually "wander out into the woods for sexual relations." They expressed outrage
at the novel practice of throwing "parties," where women and men
would drink a great deal and engage in "unrestricted and promiscuous
behavior." In short, the commission "exposed" a robust sexual tableau
that seemed to involve virtually all young women and gave Baltimoreans much to whisper, worry, and write about. Baltimore's eight-
hundred-page vice report contributed modestly to the almost one billion

pages written on "vice" nationwide between 1900 and 1920. Never before had prostitution ignited such an explosion of widely circulated, sensational tales. As an observer noted in 1921, "it was not until the early years of the twentieth century that the whole country awoke to the disgrace of a system of commercialized vice." A pattern of polite neglect had prevailed through most of the previous century. What suddenly prompted reformers' interest in the plight of a marginalized, socially alienated element of Baltimore's population; why did the Maryland Vice Commission construe "prostitution" and sexual commerce in such inclusive—and imprecise—terms?

Progressive reformers "discovered" prostitution when a growing and flamboyant population of middle-class, "respectable" young women—often newly emigrated from Maryland's rural regions—began to engage in wage labor for consolidated industries and postpone reproductive labor expected in marriage. For a generation of elite reformers who defined "respectable" femininity rather rigidly as motherhood and wife-hood and suspected laboring women of being promiscuous or danger-ously sexual, the difference between earning a wage in a factory and earning a fee for prostitution was by no means obvious. Indeed, Pro-gressives in the early 1900s attempted to clarify and redefine, by such means as Baltimore's vice crusade, virtue in a "modern manner."

Victorian conceptions of the "scarlet woman," foundered in the drast-ically transformed urban culture that reform-minded Baltimoreans con-fronted in the early twentieth century. With a population of 450,000—a 100 percent increase from 1870—Baltimore in 1913 displayed a panoply of cultures and "public women," female wage earners who walked the streets, socialized in dance halls and alleyways, adorned themselves with make-up and, with these traits, complicated the urban middle class's attempts to understand their morality with the anach-ronistic nineteenth-century terms of virtue and vice. As one Baltimorean observed in 1914, "the street is the social meeting place.... It is the playground ... its glitter and glare, its lights and shadow ... attract boys and girls.... The call of the street is irresistible."

Progressive reformers—all college-educated, predominantly of the professional or entrepreneurial classes, dramatically represented in Bal-timore's *Social Register*—found Baltimore's newly incorporated econ-omy and the "lights and shadows" it generated profoundly disturbing and compelling. To the professional or independent businessman, the industrial sector embodied simultaneously the city's hopes for healthy development and the threat that the consolidation of capital through incorporation and the profits of mass production would deny the middle class financial and, by extension, political or social sovereignty. Hence Progressives envisioned a militaristic opposition between themselves and retailers such as Louis Stewart, who had amassed fortunes rapidly, even mercilessly, in the waning days of Gilded Age prosperity and speculation. The father of Stewart's department stores, Eliot Samuel Posner, first established a neighborhood notion and dry goods store in 1875. By 1891 he was able to open a new store downtown, for which he gratefully thanked the public in a newspaper advertisement. "We are, have always been, the devoted servers of your interest," Posner declared. "We deem it a duty to confer with you, since your best good is interwoven with our own far more than the vine is wound about the oak." When in 1901 Louis Stewart purchased and incorporated Posner's downtown store, however, the vine loosened from the public oak until in 1902 the store had become a subsidiary of the Associated Merchants Company and, fourteen years later, the National Dry Goods Association. As Baltimore's elite realized, the number of "independent businessmen" in the city had dwindled. This distressing trend colored almost every reform effort of the Baltimore Progressive alliance, including the anti-vice campaign.

During the tumultuous economic expansion of the late nineteenth and early twentieth centuries, Baltimore's industrial and corporate growth lagged behind that of New York, Boston, and Philadelphia, yet daunting socioeconomic changes did occur in the city. By 1900 Baltimoreans had invested an estimated $100 million in Southern railroads (Baltimore had been dubbed the commercial "Gateway to the South"), streetcars, cotton mills, coal, iron, and municipalities. Twenty-three oyster-packing companies formed the first Baltimore corporation in 1878, intent on abolishing price-cutting and competition. Between 1881 and 1890, the number of corporations soared from thirty-nine to ninety-seven. By 1905, 17.3 percent (374) of all industrial establishments had incorporated. Together they produced 52 percent of the city's goods and employed 50 percent of the working population.

Particularly vibrant industries included tobacco, foundry work, tobacco processing, canning, and clothing production. As these businesses relentlessly competed with New York for the West Coast market, they mushroomed into many-storied factories with hundreds of workers. H. Sonneborn and Company, clothing manufacturers, employed roughly 2,500 workers in an eight-story downtown factory; Bethlehem Steel engaged 2,000 male workers; tin manufacturers Matthai, Ingram and Co. operated a 617-acre factory in South Baltimore, and A. Booth and Co., another clothing manufacturer, employed 1,100 workers. Sprawling industrial plants "developing in a haphazard way," according to one 1915 survey, supplanted the waterfront homes of "old seafaring families" who had evacuated to the upland districts. As with the Stewart's retailing chain, local companies also came under national jurisdiction, an even more ominous trend than local consolidation. Standard Oil, for example, effected an 1877 merger of almost every city refinery into the Baltimore United Oil Company, further mocking the community's capacity to regulate its economic and political future. The reordering and consolidation of Baltimore's social and economic landscape led reformers to ask, "would a fairly simple soul who tended to a machine all day long ... be the same ... lover of his God that he had been when he patiently carved or fashioned a pair of shoes?" An 1897 Baltimore *Sun* editorial answered negatively that monopolies were hostile to the "best interest of American life."

The *Sun's* idealized "American life" included a world in which middle-class women, at least, escaped wage labor and the sentence of "becoming only machine[s] capable of so much net product." In addition to immigration, mechanized production sparked an exodus— especially in Maryland—of women from rural regions into the city and factories where they became menial laborers. By 1900, 48 percent of Baltimore's industries had been mechanized, and most of these businesses employed women as machinists. Known as "working girls," "women adrift," or "homeless women," white female laborers assumed a visible role in Baltimore's "public" sphere during the early 1900s. Thirty percent of Baltimore's female workers were women who had left their families to find room and board in the city. Supporting themselves and often sending money to their families, these women were to be found in any industry where the work was light and consisted of a series of regular, simple operations. In canning factories women far exceeded the number of men due to the simplicity of mechanized can production and labeling. Similarly, the use of a cigar mold to streamline production opened the way for Baltimore tobacco factories to employ women as a cheap source of labor. The female to male ratio in Baltimore's tobacco factories leapt from 1:10 in 1880 to 1:2 in 1900, and by 1912, women occupied 40 percent of the cigar and cigarette making jobs. The largest Baltimore industry, men's apparel, usurped a high percentage of the female labor force as the city embraced the "Boston system" of production by which whole garments were manufactured in one factory. Shirt manufacturers divided production into fourteen discrete operations performed by a population of 14,000 working women and girls. Alluring department stores and office buildings employed over 1,500 women as well.

Seasonal employment for women included oyster shucking. "The oyster shucking women are a very hard working, good tempered, not very clean community," commented one observer. "Their morals are not very strict, if their conversation is a criterion." For most unskilled jobs the average daily wage hovered around $1.25, although women uniformly earned less than men.

The immigrant woman might have preferred working for exploitative wages as low as $1.00 per day to conditions in Europe. One Baltimore woman recalled, "The Polish women practically worked for nothing. But they were doing a hell of a sight better than in Poland ... they all said so!" In winter and spring the women shucked oysters on Fell Street, and in summer they skimmed tomatoes brought in from Pennsylvania. To the native woman, work outside of the home, however monotonous or taxing, might have inspired ambitions of economic achievement. For older women with children to support, prospects for economic security appeared bleaker; as they struggled to integrate the care of their children with wage work. In one vegetable industry where men, women, and children—"laughing and singing"—worked together, women often nursed their offspring "while hulling peas for their own living."

Although many of Baltimore's native-born working girls continued to board with their parents, often at a cost of one to three dollars a week, an increasingly noticeable percentage took up residence with friends or alone, perhaps in one of the city's "furnished rooms" that the commission feared encouraged immorality. "E.B.," for example, a twenty-two-year-old sales clerk, had emigrated from rural Maryland because her parents opposed her engagement. She never married her fiancé, however, and earned six dollars a week at a department store, out of which she paid three dollars and fifty cents for a furnished room.

Her workday ran from 8:00 A.M. to 8:25 P.M., broken by a half-hour lunch break in which employees used to dance until they became "so free and vulgar in their movements" that management put a stop to the ritual. One-third of E.B.'s colleagues were recent immigrants, and there were a few older, divorced or married women. According to one exasperated investigator, "clothes formed the principle object of conversation (punctuated with vulgarity) among them, with men for an occasional change." In the evenings and on Sundays E.B. and her counterparts frequented public and private shore parks as well as the much-talked-of-dance halls, where the commission surmised that E.B. supplanted her income by going out with men: "She says she would rather starve than not dress well."

It is important to place the 1913 Maryland vice investigation in historical context because the social reformers' goal in the anti-prostitution campaign mirrored and stemmed from their larger goal of battling the reign of capital and the "parasitic" urban structures that made its acquisition so easy. As the Baltimore Women's Civic League proclaimed in its opening meeting on 5 April 1911, the Progressives had initiated the "Crusade Against Ugliness: The organization of the Civic Association marks an epoch in American development, the coming of the time when the reign of the almighty dollar is to be disputed by the love of beauty." To the Progressive sensibility, nothing provided a more effective or lurid object lesson on the general tyranny of the "almighty dollar" in the age of consolidated capital than the corruption of female virtue endemic to the red-light district. The prostitute's world had changed in step with the industrialist's, and by 1900 a system of commercialized vice had permanently displaced the unorganized, comparatively solitary solicitation of centuries before. Progressives feared that a "corporate merger" between saloon owners, merchants, dance hall workers, cab drivers, and so on had created a protective wall about the "commerce in souls" and blurred the boundaries between respectable and illicit female labor. Baltimore's reformers sustained an interest in vice precisely because they conceived of prostitution on the one hand and female, waged labor in massive, impersonal work environments on the other as structurally identical examples of femininity commodified and feminine virtue corrupted.

The Maryland Vice Commission included four doctors—chairman George Walker, J. M. T. Finney, William Howell, and Women's League

member Lillian Welsh—lawyer Louis Levin and several Baltimore businessmen, including Frederick Gottlieb and Simon Stein. Other participants included Anna Herkner, Jesse Brown, Walter Denny, George
Dimling, J. W. Magruder, and Howard Schwarz. Rockefeller Foun-
dation member George Kneeland, chairman of the "Committee of Fourteen" that investigated prostitution in New York City, wrote the
precedent vice commission report (*Commercialized Vice in New York
City*) and in 1913 piloted the Maryland Vice Commission as well.
Kneeland construed vice in New York as a corporate malaise, a social
evil organizationally and structurally linked to the greediness of "big
business." His report sensationally concluded not only that prostitution
had become a business, its "army of women" exploited in "a thoroughly
business-like way," but that "no legitimate enterprise is more shrewdly
managed" or adjusts more promptly to conditions. The hierarchy of
managers, owners, and prostitutes in a certain vice district of Manhattan, in Kneeland's description, produced extraordinarily high re-
turns for the man who proved capable of maintaining business
conditions. "The King," as Kneeland described him, presided over a
group consisting of thirty-eight men who owned and operated twenty-
eight one-dollar houses. The profits collected from the prostitution
cooperative, Kneeland calculated, "are sufficiently staggering," hov-
ering somewhere around $325 per week per house in the region. If the
houses investigated comprised even half of the total number, roughly
$2 million each year would be paid to the inmates, half of which was
turned over to the house.

Conditions in Baltimore were not so extreme, yet they grew in proportion to Baltimore's corporate-industrial development. Perhaps due
to Kneeland's presence on the Maryland Vice Commission, the theme
of repudiating the corporate structure that defined the New York report
anchored the Baltimore study as well. The commission noted that in
Baltimore, too, vice had become a consolidated enterprise. In the eastern and western red-light districts, situated on Fleet and Josephine
streets, respectively, one man owned thirteen brothels at an average
cost of twenty-two dollars a month, two other men jointly owned five
houses, two women owned four houses, and one woman owned two
houses. Between 1900 and 1903, in contrast, Baltimore had sported
350 separate houses with a total of 1,400 "inmates."

Maryland's vice commission exhibited an obsessive interest in the apparent lawlessness generated by the simultaneous consolidation of the vice enterprise and Baltimore's "legitimate" industries and viewed the regions as geographically interlocked. Investigators surmised that places of female employment in Baltimore—chiefly clothing, canning, or cigar factories and department stores—dotted the path to the vice district. Baltimore Progressive journalist E. Cookman Baker described what he perceived as the perilous merger of the female laborer's and the prostitute's world: "The streets upon which these houses of shame are located are near the playgrounds of the poor ... and through these streets the factory girls pass to and from their work.... Many fall, to rise no more to the things that are pure and good." Baker and his contemporaries objected not primarily to the existence of vice but to its reconfiguration as an inescapable fixture of Baltimore's geography, one that their idealized "virtuous young woman" confronted each day and to which she would invariably succumb.

The commission feared, however, that structural similarities between vice and women's work extended beyond the geographic. Investigators finally condemned both the corporate boss and the brothel madam for "capitalizing" on commodified womanhood. The Maryland commission reported that "there are many safe and 'respectable' persons and institutions who, as this investigation shows ... contribute to the existence of the system." Madams, in short, were only as successful as the "legitimate" entrepreneurs they cajoled into supporting their trade. Like the business profiteer, madams who colluded with merchants to effect mergers in the red-light districts most "willfully and maniacally converted the wretchedest of all bargains between men and women into an organized industry."

The vice commission portrayed the madam—usually thirty to fifty years old and "herself a former inmate"—as a figure entirely beyond redemption. "We are disposed to believe that there does not exist a more shrewd, callous and rapacious type," the commission stated, although it gestured at the few madams they judged "kindly and motherly." The madam attended to the daily operation of the house, an endless routine that allowed for few activities "outside of [her] miserable trade," and remained in the trade until forced to retire due to sheer decrepitude. "One," the commission noted, "a poor fat, old rheumatic, [was] still hobbling about with painful stiffened joints and grabbing at the few quarters which the girls hand her." If not begging their subsistence, they might "marry worthless men and spend the rest of their lives quarreling." Paradoxically, the commission also surmised that madams frequently became solvent through their profession. Out of her career, the investigators estimated, a madam might save as much as $100,000 if she operated one of the better houses that cleared up to $200 to $250 a week. One madam who owned three houses with ten girls claimed that each prostitute averaged four men a night and earned $20 per day, of which the madam exacted one-half of the total earnings. Fifty-cent or one-dollar houses cleared $75 a week after they paid $6 in rent, $14 for a servant, and $5 for gas and electricity.

In their greedy indifference to the "cost in humanity" of financial profit, admonished the commission, madams embodied in a more dramatic form the values of a corporate economy and society at large, kept running by (male) profiteers. National commentators tended to poise an unprincipled male alliance of pimps, merchants, and liquor dealers against the victimized "girl" who produced barely a subsistence from the "cold-blooded traffic." In contrast, Baltimore's investigators ascribed the commercial structure of vice to the madam's cunning, yet they simultaneously preserved their belief in a naturally gentle—and easily beguiled—feminine disposition by treating the shrewd madam as a mutant strain of womanhood: she appeared most often as the ominous androgyne who snared girls into lives of debauchery. Whereas the prostitute was the "girl," the madam was the "old rheumatic," one of the "more intelligent few," one of a "few individuals," a "former inmate," or the "most rapacious type." In effect, she was the (male) "overseer," evocative of exploitative entrepreneurs more broadly construed.

The starkest links between the "legitimate" economy and the sex economy surfaced when the madam sought to procure fresh "inmates" for the brothel. It was "her business to acquire and to exhibit the youngest and most innocent girls," the commission said, because the greater the girl's "charm or delicacy, the greater profit she can yield." Once under her "sinister subjection" the madam ensured that "captured" girls were on hand for clients. The commission did not specify the means of procurement, although one madam, who "had no reason to tell anything which was not true," recalled that during her career in the brothel six to eight men came to her house every week and offered to furnish girls at a price ranging from ten to fifty dollars. In keeping with the rapid in-state migration to Baltimore in the 1910s, the Maryland commission speculated that madams might procure inmates from rural areas by "picturing to the country girl the ease of the life to which they invite her."

The commission surmised, however, that most recruitment took place at the confused intersection of legitimate wage work and the "underground" economy with its allure of rapid profit, and in so theorizing conflated the persona of the madam with that of the corporate boss. In some cases, madams apparently cultivated literal bonds with managers or owners of factories and stores employing young women. Two men in an unnamed Baltimore "firm," the commission reported, colluded with a madam who had "free reign over department store girls. Recently she came twice on one day and openly admired one of the young girls and complimented her on her beauty." Alternatively, a madam might wander through stores and lure saleswomen into "the life" with promises of fingers "loaded with diamonds" and "rich men who would give her money and presents," according to the commission's report.

Even if owners or managers did not explicitly create partnerships with madams, the commission implicated them in the vice enterprise, insofar as any suspected sexual transgression or interchange between female employee and boss constituted either a form of prostitution or a prelude to the girl's eventual demise. By this device, the commission identified all bosses as madams, all employees as potential if not actual prostitutes, and all madams as paradigmatic of exploitative bosses. One firm, for example, consisted of five men, two of whom "very much frightened" the female employees: "As soon as one of these men entered the store," the commission reported, "word is passed around among the girls and they are all on the lookout." In several department stores employers purportedly tried to induce "nice girls" to go out with them, sometimes under the promise of presents or increased wages. Floorwalkers and buyers, especially, raised suspicions. "Floor-walker X" had been married three times and called department store girls "dearie or sweetie," although the girls "do not seem to think anything is meant by this freshness, and say he treats them kindly."

Before even confronting the perils of the licentious department store, girls might have fallen victim to unscrupulous employment agencies or middlemen that for a fee of one dollar, would help convert "an innocent girl into a prostitute." The commission concluded, perhaps hastily, that above-ground agencies in the city only placed male workers—employment agencies presumed that women who inquired for "work" implicitly meant or would accept the job of prostitution. The commission accused hotel and office workers, particularly "negro janitors," as independently facilitating procurement as well. One hotel janitor maintained a list of girls on whom he could call when he had a guest or customer at the hotel who requested a prostitute. Bellboys offered similar lists, one commenting, "last year there were a number of ... women who came to the hotel and gave their names and addresses, so that [I] might arrange a meeting with a man for them."

A motley cast of secondary exploiters shared the ill-gotten profits of commodified womanhood—male procurers, female procurers, cab drivers who lured visiting women into the district, merchants who colluded with madams to overcharge prostitutes, and druggists who offered fraudulent remedies for pregnancy or venereal disease. As with the division of labor in the factory, each of these characters (the "bosses" in the vice system) reaped some profit from the ignorance of female underlings and the abuse of women's productive energies.

Significantly, the commission cited their interviews with local merchants as "one of the most surprising and painful discoveries of the whole investigation" because "most of the merchants in the city [proved] willing to enter into an agreement ... whereby a defenseless group is outrageously cheated." Investigators posing as madams proposed to all the leading merchants of the city that they overcharge prostitutes for clothes on a kick-back basis. Of the interviews conducted, only seven out of sixty merchants "flatly refused" the offer, thus substantiating the reformer's pervasive fear that Baltimore's collective quest for the "almighty dollar" had superseded "the love of beauty." One investigator reported that merchant "M.B.Y." "said if she didn't accept my offer, somebody else would, probably some rich Jew who did not need the money as badly as she did. She herself was a perfectly moral woman, but in a strictly business matter she thought her dealing with my class of women was justified." M.A.M. responded that "he would add 20 percent to all gowns made. He asked me whether the girls looked and acted like ladies, because he would not want his fashionable trade to know he did business with the 'sporting class.' He said of course one person's money is as good as another and he would be glad to have my trade." From these exchanges the commission surmised that leading merchants colluded with madams to such an extent that their "legitimate" business interests had seamlessly fused with the corrupt.

The vice commission's investigation of "business conditions" in Baltimore suggested that institutions buttressing vice embraced the entire spectrum of the consolidated urban economy, and that employers who utilized female productive energies for profit often explicitly colluded with madams in "shamelessly exploiting women" for illegitimate financial gain. More interestingly, however, the commission situated female wage work along a continuum of vice-related activities, such that the salesgirl who endured a floorwalker's "suggestive comments" was judged to be involved in an exploitative sexual transgression vaguely linked or preparatory to prostitution. Finally, it shifted the definitional boundaries of "vice" from a sexual barter or exchange for explicit financial reward to any morally or sexually ambiguous interaction that occurred as women participated in the wage or market economy. In sum, the reformer's treatment of employment conditions in Baltimore both literally and figuratively conflated structures of "legitimate" business enterprise with the illegitimate red-light industry.

Reginald Kauffman's *The House of Bondage,* a muckraking novel that went through four editions in the early 1900s, explicitly and sensationally made the connection between feminine virtue, prostitution, "wage slavery," and an unprotective, corporate culture which the Maryland commission described in more cautious terms. "Anything like financial independence was ... impossible" in the brothel, Kauffman wrote, for "the slaves of [the madams] were as much slaves as any mutilated black man of the Congo or any toiling white man of the factory.... The social system was too mighty. [The prostitute] could not prevail against it." Although Progressive reformers averred from any explicit critique of capitalism, they consistently characterized prostitutes as ensnared in the same expansive net of social ills that entrapped the working girl, and more generally assumed that any female productive labor commodified women's sexual nature and thus paid a "wage of sin." Reformers cared about the prostitute in large part not because they viewed her as metaphorically similar to female workers but rather because they did not perceive many meaningful, literal distinctions between the structures of urban sexual commerce and other degrading forms of women's wage work.

Young women's uses of their bodies as marketable objects, whether in the brothel or the factory, profoundly disrupted Victorian, middle-class gender identities, which were predicated on a separation between the "public," where men labored, and the privatized feminine domain of the family—a haven from the heartless world of the labor market. Because reformers had few means by which to understand the moral implications of "respectable," middle-class women "working out," they tended to evaluate and define women's experiences in all work environments through the prism of prostitution, assuming that any wage-paying work for young women entailed their sexual commodification and subsequent "dehumanization." Social reformer Anne Brown, for instance, characterized the "evil" of both prostitution and women's work as one of "impersonality—the regarding of persons as things."

In the act of utilizing their labor power for discrete, mechanical tasks, women relinquished what to the Victorian sensibility had always made them human—their identities as mothers and wives rather than laborers. As Margaret Drier charged in 1914, the working girl, modeling herself after the prostitute, "found it easy to do as the unmoral kind had always done—she entered into the barter and sale of [herself] for an income."

Because they viewed prostitution as the metaphor for women's work in the public sphere, members of Maryland's vice commission devoted two volumes of their report solely to the "industrial conditions" in Baltimore that purportedly encouraged vice and nebulous "moral lapses" among women workers. Without question, below-subsistence wages in department stores and tobacco factories prompted many young women living away from home to at least occasionally accept money or gifts from "fellows" in order to make ends meet or simply to enjoy an evening of "city pleasures" that would break monotonous work routines. Baltimore's investigators explicitly rejected primarily attributing young women's moral failings to dangerously unfair wages, however. Instead the commission "exposed" subtler causes of vice they viewed as intrinsic to the types of work and work environments created by factory production and consolidated industry.

The commission conducted an exhaustive investigation of places employing women to illustrate what they saw as the conflation of overt prostitution and "respectable" work. Office work especially outraged Baltimore's reformers as an insidiously disguised prostitution. "We found nothing more reprehensible than some of the immoral practices of a number of Baltimore's esteemed and prominent business men," the commission reported. "The practices of the red-light district are pale and mild compared to the acts of these Christian gentlemen." An "attorney of some prominence," for example, had told an investigator that he would not hire a girl unless he could "have relations" with her, and female office workers interviewed often reported having affairs with executives. "S.O.N.," a private secretary earning seven dollars a week, "had additional income from a businessman in her building," who gave her money and sent her roses. "They have been together to dinner at the Madison," an investigator recounted, and the "girl knows all about the private places in Baltimore." An employer's "seductive" behavior toward a secretary today might constitute sexual harassment because the meanings of women's jobs are more carefully drawn and distinguished from the explicitly sexual labor of prostitution. Baltimore's reformers in the early twentieth century, however, made few meaningful distinctions between women's work and sexual barter. Investigators characterized the office affair as indigenous to the work environment itself—a "commercial bargain [in which] one buys what the other has to sell ... until the commodity diminishes in value." By the same logic, waitressing appeared a dangerously imprecise profession to investigators, who speculated that the ambiguous meanings of "tips" and "gifts" from customers presented "an open door to immorality." Waitress "R.B.N." had been taken out twice for "immoral purposes" by men who frequented her restaurant, and she knew about contraception.

Waitressing and office work, however, absorbed a comparatively select subgroup of Baltimore's female working population. By 1915 Baltimore boasted several mammoth department stores that satisfied an extravagant array of needs and whims. The commission examined three stores, each employing from six hundred to seven hundred young women, who would parade out of work at 10 P.M. on Saturday nights "all dolled up to meet men at the front door to accompany them to dance halls." Department stores "seduced and endangered" Baltimore's young women, the commission theorized, because they chaotically confused social boundaries. The salesgirl each day fondled beguiling, luxurious merchandise she could ill afford, women worked closely with male store managers, "the colored help ate in the same room with white people," women's dressing rooms were congested, and "on bargain days there is a rush of all kinds of people" who exposed young women to relentless sexual temptation. "The men are seen, more or less openly, to handle the girls in the most disgusting and vulgar fashion and are never called down," the commission decried. Telephone exchanges in public places, similarly, threw "the operator into contact with a number of men," such that the women "are known to be more or less immoral."

Even sex-segregated, enclosed work environments ignited investigators' suspicions. Baltimore's tobacco factories, employing over three thousand women, permitted "hardened" older women to mingle with—and finally corrupt—the young. "A woman employed in the factory says that she has worked with common prostitutes but has never heard them talk as do these young girls," the commission reported. Nearly all the girls adorned themselves with jewelry that they wore very conspicuously and tirelessly recounted "which pieces were given them by individual men in much the same fashion as an Indian displays the scalps in his belt." By conflating the tobacco operative's "leisure" activities—her mercenary "scalping" of men—with her factory labors, the commission underscored that even work as regimented and ostensibly unambiguous as tobacco processing existed along a spectrum of urban sexual commerce, and that the blending of classes and moral "types" in the workplace encouraged eventual overt prostitution.

It bears emphasis that Baltimore's reformers did not enthusiastically endorse the popular and statistically evident conclusion that low wages encouraged women's "bartering" with men for dinners, gifts, and, sometimes, explicit monetary reward. Instead, investigators condemned the very phenomenon of women's wage work—however generously remunerated—produced by consolidated capital and large-scale industry. Office workers, waitresses, salesgirls, and telephone operators often fulfilled such diffuse and ill-specified tasks for employers that the commission probably correctly identified a nebulous grey area between wage work and sexual work characteristic of Baltimore's emerging "service" industries in the early 1900s. Significantly, however, investigators defined "pay" in such all-inclusive terms (e.g., from explicit wages to "gifts" such as dinners and roses) that they effectively erased differences between "legitimate" wages and the "wages of sin." Along these lines, they also described all premarital sexual relationships as entailing some form of economic exchange in which the woman accrued a wage, however intangible, for her "services." Office worker "Miss N," for example, who worked for a prominent businessman downtown, reported that her boss had given her a diamond ring and taken her out several times to dinner. Because Baltimore's elite reformers had difficulty envisioning a sexual practice—today recognized as "dating"—between the extremities of prostitution and the wifehood–motherhood tandem, they could only view "Miss N's" affair as a commercialized sexual exchange. The practice of dating may have begun with the urban working class in the early 1900s, but it would not emerge as a sanctioned cultural institution until the late 1920s.

Although reformers generally did not recognize distinctions between prostitution and dating, or leisure activities and the "workaday world," Baltimore's young working women upheld their own criterion of vice and virtue, one that distinguished between prostitution and having a "fellow" on precisely the grounds that if a woman labored, her wage derived only from her job, and her activities in amusement parks, dance halls, and saloons constituted a realm of pleasures distinct from "work" altogether.

One investigator, stationed at an amusement park on the Back River, recorded the nuances of an exchange with a "charity girl," the commission's label for women who consented to sexual relations for little or no reward aside from perhaps an "ice cream or a glass of beer." The woman invited the investigator to go out with her one afternoon, and when he "asked her price," she seemed quite upset, and said, "I'm no common whore. I'm not looking for money," and hinted that she might accept a dress. For this young woman, "gifts" and presents constituted morally legitimate tokens of affection from men, stridently demarcated from monetary payments gained through the woman's "real" work in a department store. In distinguishing between salaries and gifts or "treats," women construed their sexual relations in terms subtler than the Progressive's dichotomy. For them, Baltimore's dance halls and parks created a third, sexually exciting realm separate from both the (private) family and the (public) workplace. Mazie, a twenty-one-year-old cigar maker, assured an investigator that although her "fellow" might buy her a drink or treat her, "she had never taken a cent in [her] life" and merely had a "regular Saturday night friend to dance with." "O.R.Y," employed as a hatter, went with boys two or three times a week, and saw that she'd never get a dance partner if she "went around prim." She underscored, however, that she "could not pick up the nerve to ask for money," because then—and presumably only then—"the fellows put you down as a 'whore.'"

In their analysis of the sexual economy, Baltimore's reformers assigned moral meanings to various forms of female labor and leisure in an economically transformed city. Their tales of moral peril and demise implicitly reaffirmed marriage and motherhood as appropriate, "safe" arenas for women's labors. Meanwhile, their conflation of various forms of female wage labor, from prostitution to retail sales, redefined "prostitution" as a phenomenon endemic to any contractual relations between men and women outside of the marital contract. Significantly, the Progressives depicted the difference between legitimate and illicit female employment as one of degree rather than kind. Although the prostitute was more dramatically marginalized from proper society, the working woman also suffered the demoralizing effects of "industrial" prostitution. The anti-vice investigation of Baltimore's most margin-alized women, then, ironically led reformers back to the heart of the city's socioeconomic transformation—it expressed larger anxieties con-cerning the implications of women's wage work in the transitional period from a Victorian middle-class morality based on the "cult of domesticity" to a sexual morality more characteristic of life in the "modern manner." As the Maryland vice crusade illustrates, a city's response to economic change and class reconfigurations always involves an attempt to reconcile pre-existing notions of social order—princi-pally, ideas of appropriate gender roles and gendered notions of "work"—with material exigencies that often render these ideals un-realistic and contestable.

10

World War I: European Origins and American Intervention

JOHN MILTON COOPER, JR.

● *World War I is the central event of the twentieth century. The first truly global conflict, it caused the deaths of at least ten million people, including practically an entire generation of the young manhood of Russia, Germany, France, and Great Britain, and it led directly to the Russian Revolution of 1917. Had Germany won the conflict, which seemed entirely possible as late as May 1918, or at least achieved a stalemate, the dislocations which led to the rise of Adolf Hitler and ultimately to World War II would not have been likely.*

Although Americans played a relatively minor role in World War I, arriving in force only eight months before the Armistice, their participation was crucial to Allied success. The great German offensive of 1918, which carried virtually to the suburbs of Paris, was halted because of the presence and tenacity of American reserves who were thrown into the gap. Exhausted after four years of horrible trench warfare, the Kaiser's soldiers were demoralized by the appearance of fresh troops from across the ocean.

Because World War I was so momentous and because American intervention tipped the balance against Germany and thus changed the course of history, President Woodrow Wilson's attitudes and actions have understandably attracted considerable attention. Having won reelection in 1916 on his record of keeping the United States neutral, he decided on April 2, 1917, to shift his course. In the following essay, John Milton Cooper, Jr., recounts the pivotal events which determined that boys from Iowa and Brooklyn would fight and

Reprinted with permission from *Virginia Quarterly Review* 56 (Winter 1980), 1–18. © *The Virginia Quarterly Review.*

*sometimes die in the tiny villages and devastated fields of
northern France.*

One day in July 1955 the ground around the town of Messines, Belgium,
trembled from an underground shock. It was not an earthquake. It was
the explosion of a cache of munitions buried nearly 40 years before.
For eleven months, during 1916 and 1917, British troops had dug 21
mineshafts deep under the German lines in that part of Flanders and
had filled them with five hundred tons of explosives. Early in the morning of June 7, 1917, the British had detonated the charges, causing a
blast that had awakened people as far away as London, 130 miles
distant. Only 19 of the loaded mineshafts had blown up, however. The
rumbling in 1955 signaled the explosion of one of the two remaining
charges. The other lies somewhere in the Flemish earth, still unexploded
but practically certain to go off someday.

That incident of the explosives planted deep and their continuing
after-effects is emblematic of the impact of World War I both on its
own time and on the subsequent history of the 20th century. The war
appeared to many contemporaries as a gigantic explosion or earthquake; those were two of the most popular terms used to describe the
conflict. In longer perspective, too, the war looks like an explosion or
earthquake in a metaphorical sense. It undermined an international
dispensation under which European nations dominated among the
world's major powers and ruled over much of the globe through their
colonial empires. Likewise, the war shattered the domestic stability of
those nations, sapping the authority of traditionally dominant groups
and giving rise to violent extremism at both ends of the political spectrum. The shocks generated by the crumbling of that international and
domestic order have precipitated the greatest events of the last 60 years,
since the end of the war, and their final tremors are yet to be felt.

From its outbreak, nearly everyone recognized the momentousness
of World War I. The suddenness and magnitude of the conflict that
erupted in August 1914 tended to throw imaginations out of kilter.
Observers instinctively grasped for non-human terms to describe it.
Natural catastrophes, like an explosion or earthquake, came readily to
mind. Henry James called the war "the plunge of civilization into this
abyss of blood and darkness." Theodore Roosevelt believed that it was

"on a giant scale like the disaster to the Titanic." Others resorted to supernatural terms. In the United States, which was so strongly influenced by Bible-reading Protestantism, the most widely used name for the war came to be "Armageddon," the nation-shattering miracle preceding the Last Judgment in the book of Revelation. "Now Armageddon has a real meaning," announced one American magazine. "If this be not Armageddon, we shall never suffer the final death grip of nations." Those who have witnessed later occurrences in this century may balk at that assertion, but no one can doubt that people at the time of World War I knew that they were living through one of history's greatest events.

Such knowledge was not an unalloyed advantage to the participants. The ready comparison of the war to events that did not have human origins betokened an attitude that the war was also beyond human control. That attitude, not the destruction and carnage, was what made World War I so profoundly disheartening. World War II claimed more lives, laid waste more land and cities, and introduced more terrible weapons. Yet that later war has legitimately exciting, hopeful, and noble aspects. The difference between the world wars involved more than the fixity of the first versus the movement of the second. Rather it is a question of why they differed in that way, and the answer lies less in the technology or art of war and more in the imagination and grasp of the civilian and military leaders of the belligerent powers.

"The Second World War in some ways gave birth to less novelty and genius than the First," writes Sir Isaiah Berlin, who compares the literary production of the two wars. "Yet," Berlin adds, "perhaps there is one respect in which the Second World War did outshine its predecessor: the leaders of the nations involved in it were, with the significant exception of France, men of greater stature, psychologically more interesting than their prototypes." One does not have to agree with all of Berlin's judgments of individual leaders to concede the truth of his observation. H. H. Asquith, Sir Douglas Haig, Erich Ludendorff, and Kaiser Wilhelm, for example, contrast so hollowly with Winston Churchill, George S. Patton, Erwin Rommel, and even Adolf Hitler, because those earlier figures made themselves captives rather than masters of events. World War I produced only two authentic world leaders, Woodrow Wilson and Vladimir Lenin, because they alone of all the national leaders grappled with the task of controlling the war itself. In their conflicting ways, Wilson and Lenin offered the only lights in the drab field of leadership in World War I.

What really made the war so staggering to people's sensibilities was its human origin: for the first time in history the deeds of men seemed to match the accidents of nature and the acts of God. World War I sprang from two related breakdowns in mankind's proudest creations at the beginning of the 20th century—the highly civilized nation-states of Europe. One breakdown, which was immediate and obvious, lay in relations among those nation-states. Although Europe had not experienced a general conflict for a hundred years before 1914, its state system had shown unmistakable signs of instability for at least a generation. All the main European powers except Great Britain held grudges against each other, and their grudges involved such intractable matters as control of territories and populations and assertions of political and economic influence that were considered vital. The relative detachment of the British afforded no safety, either, since the general instability also threatened them. Imperial expansion during the generation before the war had sometimes deflected rivalries from European concerns, but in the end controversies over colonies and spheres of influence in Africa and Asia had exacerbated tensions among the home countries. Moreover, the colonial and naval dimensions of the European rivalries had alarmed the British and drawn them into the struggle in ways that strictly continental controversies probably would not have done.

It seems clear now that of all the instigators of the war which broke out in 1914 Germany bore the heaviest responsibility. During the preceding ten years Europe had witnessed a series of crises initially occasioned by conflicts in the Far East, North Africa, or the Balkans. The Germans had either fomented those crises or rushed into them, each time in hopes of sowing discord among their rivals and reaping gains for themselves and their client states. Those German actions had reflected more than a normal but reckless desire to get ahead at the expense of adversaries. As Fritz Fischer and other German historians have shown, an expansionist consensus had grown up since the 1890's behind the proposition that Germany must become a "world state" with a "world mission." Further, a number of German leaders had become convinced that their nation's destiny could be fulfilled only through what the Foreign Minister in 1913 called "the coming world war." By 1914, diplomatic setbacks in the Balkans and the Near East and foreign economic uncertainties had created what Fischer terms a "crisis of German imperialism." The government in Berlin therefore greeted the dispute following the Austrian Archduke's assassination at Sarajevo in a mood of desperate hope. The Germans not only gave the Austrians a "blank check" in their dealings with Serbia, but they encouraged their ally to go to war. As Fischer concludes, "It is impossible to speak seriously either of Germany's being 'towed in Austria's wake' or of her being 'coerced.'"

Laying such responsibility at the Germans' door does not mean that they should once more be arraigned for "war guilt," as the victorious Allies did in 1919 in the Treaty of Versailles. No one has yet examined British, French, or Russian moves with the same access and assiduity that Fischer has studied the German role in the coming of the war. It seems likely that closer examination of French or, if it were possible, Russian sources might uncover at least a few comparable actions in goading Germany toward confrontation. Some elements in France did seek and welcome war in 1914. There, too, a nationalist revival had been flourishing, with increasingly shrill assertions of French destiny and revanchism toward Alsace and Lorraine. Even Britain, which was the last and most reluctant major power to enter the war in 1914, does not appear entirely blameless. For a number of years the British Foreign Secretary, Sir Edward Grey, had been giving assurances to the French of backing in the event of war. Grey had kept those assurances secret not only from Parliament but also from the full Cabinet, and though he had never explicitly promised British intervention, he had made commitments to the French that could not realistically be honored without fighting at their side. As events transpired, the German violation of Belgian neutrality averted a political crisis over Britain's entry into World War I. Defending "brave little Belgium" forestalled debate and rallied people to the colors in Britain in 1914 much as Pearl Harbor did in America in 1941.

Responsibility for the war was also generalized among the European nations in another way besides their diplomatic conduct. The second breakdown that contributed to the outbreak of World War I lay in the internal affairs of the countries involved. Foreign policy never exists in a vacuum, and in 1914 the actions of all the nations that became

belligerents reflected domestic conditions. The Kaiser's regime ruled
Germany in a mood of constant, though often exaggerated, insecurity.
A plethora of proscriptions and legal disadvantages had not availed to
prevent the Social Democrats from emerging as the strongest single
party, and in 1913 and 1914 some conservative spokesmen had advocated war as a means of curbing rising Socialist strength. In France
socialism and nationalism had competed for the allegiance of the working classes, and only the fortuitous assassination of the eloquent Jean
Jaurpes in July 1914 had removed a potential rallying point for Socialist
opposition to the war. British internal discord stemmed not only from
the growing strength and militancy of the Labour Party but also from
woman suffrage agitation and, most gravely, from incipient civil war
over autonomy for Ireland. Ironically, all of the major European powers, only backward, despotic, chronically troubled Russia seemed to
be gaining in internal stability, thanks to massive industrialization and
sweeping land reform.

By 1914, the breakdown that became so evident in Europe after
World War I was already well advanced. The war undoubtedly accelerated the process, and in the case of Russia it may well have paved
the way for a revolution that might not otherwise have occurred. But
the war did not cause that internal breakdown. Instead, the breakdown
contributed to the war. The dominant mood of the leaders of the
nations that took up arms in 1914 was relief. British, French, and
German leaders all seemed glad to lay aside their troubles at home and
fight a foreign foe. David Lloyd George, the strongest figure in the
British government, told one friend in August 1914, "In a week or two
it might be good fun to be the advance guard of an expeditionary force
to the coast of France, and run the risk of capture by a German ship!"
The masses of men who went to war briefly shared such summer holiday
sentiments, but their euphoria soon gave way to gloom and despair.
Among thoughtful European observers, World War I almost at once
instilled doubts about human nature and the progress of civilization.
For men in the trenches and reflective onlookers, it was understandable
that the war might seem beyond human control. For their leaders,
however, the abdication of responsibility seems to have stemmed from
their original relief at having escaped upleasant domestic conditions.
It would seem that European leaders did not try harder to control the
war because they did not want to. They evidently preferred the carnage

of the war to the upheavals which they knew would meet its end if they did not emerge somehow triumphant.

II

Viewed from America, many aspects of World War I appeared different. Observers in the United States also immediately marveled at the immensity of the conflict, and they used the same nonhuman descriptions and bemoaned the setback to human progress. But other elements entered into reactions on this side of the Atlantic. Where Europeans initially thrilled to the adventure of war, Americans expressed relief at not being in it. Later, when the United States did enter the war, the most popular description for it would be "over there"; that phrase also expressed the basic American attitude toward World War I at its outbreak. From the American standpoint, the war was a terrible catastrophe that had befallen somebody else, far away. "Again and ever I thank Heaven for the Atlantic Ocean," wrote the American ambassador in London at the end of July 1914. People in the United States felt not only geographically but also morally removed from the war. It appeared to offer spectacular confirmation of longstanding notions about New World innocence and purity in opposition to Old World sin and decadence. In August 1914, the *New York Times*, usually a sober newspaper, contrasted the opening of the Panama Canal with the outbreak of the war by gloating, "The European ideal bears its full fruit of ruin and savagery just at the moment when the American ideal lays before the world a great work of peace, goodwill, and fair play." In short, many Americans reacted to the outbreak of World War I by figuratively repeating the Pharisee's prayer, "Thank God I am not as other men are."

That pervasive sense of removal from the war presented the most formidable barrier to eventual American intervention. But any thoughts of intervention lay well in the future. When President Wilson admonished his countrymen in August 1914 to remain "neutral in fact as well as in name," he simply seemed to be voicing the prevailing popular attitude. The following December he reiterated such sentiments when he dubbed the European conflict "a war with which we have nothing to do, whose causes can not touch us." Actually, Wilson meant to do more than convey soothing reassurance, since he had early come to fear the potential impact of the conflict on the United States. The mood of detachment lasted for the better part of the first year of the war. By the spring of 1915—despite some expressions of sympathy for the Allies, despite frictions with the British over their blockade of the Central Powers, and despite jitters at the German submarine proclamation—people appeared less concerned than ever about World War I. "Americans regard the war either as a bore," reported the British ambassador in Washington in April 1915, "or as an immensely interesting spectacle provided for their entertainment, of which they are commencing to be rather tired."

The great majority of Americans' attitudes toward World War I changed suddenly and dramatically on the afternoon of May 7, 1915. That was when the news reached the United States that a German submarine had sunk the British liner *Lusitania*, the world's largest passenger ship, killing 1,198 men, women, and children, 198 of whom were Americans. Ten years later the journalist Mark Sullivan discovered that all the people he interviewed could remember exactly where they had been when they had learned of the sinking of the *Lusitania*, what they had thought and felt, and what they had done for the rest of the day. The event left an indelible memory not only because it was another great catastrophe but also because it raised the threat of involvement in the war. Although many spokesmen fumed with outrage over the *Lusitania*, few raised cries for war. Out of 1,000 newspaper editors asked to telegraph their views to New York newspapers, six called for war. President Wilson caught the dominant public reaction when he stated a month after the sinking of the *Lusitania*, "I wish with all my heart I saw a way to carry out the double wish of our people, to maintain a firm front in respect of what we demand of Germany and yet do nothing that might by any possibility involve us in the war."

That statement defined the diplomatic dilemma that persisted until the United States entered World War I in April 1917. German-American relations did not begin a long slide toward war. A grave but polite diplomatic duel persisted between the two countries for nearly a year, until an American ultimatum forced the Germans to restrain their submarines in the spring of 1916. Thereafter, the threat of war receded for several months, and most of the friction between the United States and European belligerents involved the Allies, particularly Britain. Only Germany's launching of an expanded submarine offensive at the end of January 1917 brought the final crisis that plunged America into the war. Yet behind the ebb and flow of German-American relations lay the same conditions that Wilson had described after the sinking of the *Lusitania*. From mid–1915 onward two basic requisites existed for American intervention. Those requisites were the German use of the submarine and the presence of Woodrow Wilson in the White House.

For the last 40 years nearly all American interpreters have portrayed their nation's entry into World War I as a well-nigh inevitable event. Deploring "revisionists" and applauding "realists" have alike viewed intervention in 1917 as an outcome virtually foreordained by the machinations of great political, economic, and strategic forces. By contrast, most British interpreters and Arthur S. Link in this country have emphasized the twists and turns of specific events and the roles of individual actors. Although the two perspectives can be complementary, whether to stress the weight of overarching forces or the actions of contemporaries poses an inescapable choice in assessing American entry into World War I. Of the two perspectives, the second—the stress on specific men and events—is the correct one. When due account has been given to the influences of culture, trade, political sympathies, and strategic reckoning that may have affected the course of American policy, two incontrovertible facts remain. First, the United States would almost certainly never have entered World War I if Germany had not resorted to submarine warfare. Second, the vehicle through which the United States did enter the war was Woodrow Wilson.

The German decision to use the submarine represented one of the most fateful moves of the war. It also involved two great blunders. The first blunder occurred with the initial submarine proclamation in February 1915, when Germany threatened to sink without warning all merchant shipping in a zone surrounding the British and French coasts. By issuing that proclamation, the Germans were, as Ernest May has pointed out, doing the only thing that could have caused meaningful hostility with the Americans. British control of the seas had curtailed contacts between the United States and Germany so thoroughly that no other occasion for war or even much diplomatic friction could have arisen without the submarine. Worse, the Germans were risking a wider war for doubtful military advantage. Not only were Germany's World War I submarines small, vulnerable craft which carried few torpedoes and had a short cruising range, but in 1915 there were so few of them that they could inflict at most minimal shipping losses. Why the Germans took such a bad risk and then clung stubbornly to their intentions in the face of American protests sprang in part from tense, complicated civil-military relations within the Kaiser's regime. But the submarine policy also reflected a new and disheartening development in the history of warfare. The German submarine advocates' claims in 1915 offered the earliest example of what has become a familiar 20th-century faith in military "hardware"—the notion that some new piece of technology will bring victory that is both quick and cheap in one's own expenditure of man-power and resources. Air power and nuclear weapons would offer later fields for this faith which the submarine had first occasioned.

The second even greater submarine blunder was the decision in January 1917 to resume and widen the undersea war. The German government made that decision in full knowledge and expectation of likely American intervention. They were taking the calculated risk that their submarines could knock the Allies out of the war by cutting off their overseas supplies of munitions and food long before any American contribution could swing the balance against them. This risk in 1917 seemed considerably better than the earlier one, inasmuch as German shipyards had by then built enough submarines to make serious inroads in Allied shipping. The rate of tonnage losses inflicted in the spring of 1917 nearly crippled the British war effort. Only the timely adoption of the convoy system cut those losses to an acceptable level by providing an effective defense against the submarine.

III

The German error in 1917 lay in believing that the submarine offered the sole means to victory. By the beginning of that year, the Allies had fallen into desperate financial straits. The impending collapse of their credit in the United States was about to accomplish the same result as the German submarine offensive—cutting the Allies' overseas supply lifeline—with no risk of American intervention. In fact, the Allied financial position had deteriorated so badly that nothing could save them short of the rapid, massive infusion of money that would require American co-belligerency as a precondition. By resuming and broadening submarine warfare in January 1917 the Germans were doing the one thing that could save the Allies from collapse. To use a recent phrase,

Germany was snatching defeat from the jaws of victory. Why the Germans made this blunder evidently stemmed from two considerations. One was a simple, though inexcusable failure of intelligence. "So far as I know the Germans were totally unaware of our financial difficulty," wrote the British Treasury expert John Maynard Keynes, who talked with his German opposite numbers after the war. Such ignorance seems incredible, particularly because much of the information about the Allied financial predicament was public knowledge and a few hours of simple intelligence gathering in New York and Washington would have yielded further, convincing evidence.

A second, deeper consideration also underlay the German blunder. As the German historian Gerhard Ritter has observed, indications abounded in Berlin not only that the best chance to win the war lay in waiting to let Allied troubles mount but also that a more cautious submarine policy might keep the United States neutral. Despite those signs, the Germans went ahead with the submarine campaign because nothing less than swift, decisive military victory seemed acceptable to the men in power. That decision sprang in part, as Ritter suggests, from the ascendancy of the military, which had transformed the Kaiser's government into a dictatorship by General Ludendorff behind the figurehead of Field Marshal Paul von Hindenburg. Even more, the decision reflected the abdication by both military and civilian leaders to what they regarded as the larger than human requirements of the World War. They were simply unable to conceive of any course except riding the war through to total victory. It seems likely, therefore, as the British historian Patrick, Lord Devlin has speculated, that the German leaders would have chosen to unleash their submarines even if they had known more about the Allies' financial peril. If that were so, then the German choice of the submarine campaign was, as Edmund Burke described the French Revolution, "a fond election of evil."

The second incontrovertible fact about American intervention in World War I is what Winston Churchill recognized more than 50 years ago when he wrote of Woodrow Wilson, "It seems no exaggeration to pronounce that the actions of the world depended, during the awful period Armageddon, upon the workings of this man's mind and spirit to the exclusion of almost every other factor; and that he played a part in the fate of nations incomparably more direct and personal than any other man." Wilson's role was the opposite of that of the German submarine. If the United States would not have entered World War I except for the submarine, no one besides Wilson would have done so much to keep the country out of the war. No major American statesman of the time equaled Wilson either in representing majority opinion or in grasping basic problems. His principal rivals and critics all leaned too far toward the belligerent half of the people's "double wish," as with Theodore Roosevelt, Elihu Root, and Henry Cabot Lodge, or toward the pacific half, as with William Jennings Bryan and Robert M. La Follette. William Howard Taft and Charles Evans Hughes came closer to Wilson's middle ground, and Taft also looked beyond the immediate controversies, but they lacked Wilson's boldness and perception.

From the war's outbreak, Wilson had apprehended that his fundamental task lay in attempting to end the conflict and prevent the recurrence of anything like it. His early admonitions about neutrality and remoteness from the war had also contained urgings to remain self-controlled in order to be ready to perform great international services. That vision of service owed less to any Presbyterian idealism of Wilson's than to his convictions about the indivisibility of world peace and security. In this regard, he resembled his fellow, deeply religious Southerner, Jimmy Carter, with whom he has been compared, rather than a more worldly operator like Franklin Roosevelt. In his handling of the submarine troubles with Germany in 1915 and 1916, Wilson proved highly resourceful in hewing to the middle way between war and submission when so many others were falling away, including his successive Secretaries of State, Bryan and Robert M. Lansing, and his main confidant, Colonel Edward M. House. Moreover, all the while he was preparing for an effort to end the war and lay the basis for a new international order.

Wilson's finest hour during World War I came in the two-and-a-half months following his re-election in November 1916, when he moved simultaneously on several fronts to mediate the conflict and create a structure for peace. Shortly after the election, Wilson exercised America's financial leverage over the Allies by backing and strengthening a Federal Reserve Board warning against excessive foreign loans. Then in December 1916 he dispatched a circular note to the belligerent powers, asking them to state their peace terms and pledging American participation in a future international body empowered to maintain peace. The note went first through diplomatic channels and was made public two days afterward. Finally, on January 22, 1917, after receiving various replies from the warring nations, Wilson delivered a speech to the Senate in which he called for "a peace without victory.... Only a peace among equals can last. Only a peace the very principle of which is equality and a common benefit." In that speech he also laid down the specific principles for the war's settlement which he reiterated a year later in the Fourteen Points, and he again pledged American participation in an international concert to keep the peace.

Wilson gave an extraordinary performance. He moved deftly and calmly amid suspicions, jealousies, and recriminations abroad and at home. The Germans and the Allies responded to the American initiative by executing labyrinthine, often deceitful, maneuvers which reflected internal strains as well as mutual enmity. The mediation effort drew fire in the United States from pro-Allied stalwarts like Lodge and Roosevelt, who charged Wilson with playing Germany's game. His proposal for American membership in an international peace-keeping organization earned denunciations both from pacific isolationists, who feared involvement in foreign conflicts, and from nationalists, who rejected any abridgment of sovereignty and self-interest. Those attacks in December 1916 and January 1917, which were spear-headed by Senators Henry Cabot Lodge and William E. Borah, offered a foretaste of the postwar debate over joining the League of Nations. Besides outright opposition, Wilson also had to brook disloyalty from his top lieutenants as Secretary Lansing and Colonel House each in his own way tried to sabotage the mediation venture. Whether Wilson's attempt to gain control of the international situation at the beginning of 1917 would have succeeded if Germany had not reopened submarine warfare is doubtful. Too many factors seem to have been working against it. Yet, merely by making the attempt, Wilson had staked his claim to world leadership.

The German submarine decision transformed Wilson's task from guiding other nations toward peace to wrestling with his own country's likely involvement in war. The two months from the unleashing of the submarines to American intervention formed what Arthur Link has called Wilson's "Gethsemane." Alone of the nation's leaders, he apprehended that no quick, simple choice could be made between going into and staying out of World War I. Curiously, this most solitary of modern Presidents found himself perfectly attuned to the sentiments of the great majority of his countrymen. Studies of public opinion have shown that even after the mounting submarine sinkings and the publication of the Zimmermann telegram in February and March 1917, relatively few people favored intervention. Likewise, a number of contemporary observers noted that most members in both Houses of Congress remained undecided about entering the war right down to the night of April 2, 1917, when the President finally disclosed his decision. As it was, Wilson convinced large majorities in the House and Senate to go in, but he could almost certainly have persuaded equally large majorities to stay out.

Why Wilson chose war has remained a puzzle ever since. In recent years some doubt has been cast on the reliability of his eleventh-hour outpouring to Frank Cobb of the *New York World* about making Americans "go war-mad, quit thinking and devote their energies to destruction." But even if Wilson did not say those exact words to Cobb, he gave plenty of other indications between February and April 1917 that he hated to plunge the United States into World War I. Even more than possible hysteria at home Wilson recoiled from the loss of control abroad. To Cobb he reportedly said that intervention "means an attempt to reconstruct a peace-time civilization with war standards, and at the end of the war there will be no bystanders with sufficient power to influence the terms. There won't be any peace standards left to work with." Earlier, in his second inaugural address, on March 5, 1917, Wilson had reviewed America's relations with the war, emphasizing that "all the while we're not part of it." Americans had "grown more and more aware and more and more certain that the part we wished to play was the part of those who mean to vindicate and fortify peace." No matter what trials lay ahead, he had vowed, "nothing will alter our thought or purpose." At bottom, the problem remained how to keep Americans from surrendering to the war.

IV

Wilson made it clear in his war address on April 2, 1917, that he wanted American belligerency to serve the same ends as his peace initiative. "I have exactly the same things in mind now," he asserted, "that I had in mind when I addressed the Senate on the twenty-second of January last. . . . Our object now, as then, is to vindicate the principles of peace and justice as against selfish and autocratic power and to set up amongst the really free and self-governed peoples of the world such a concert of purpose and of action as will henceforth insure the observance of those principles." Wilson was not sounding the trumpet for a holy war. The tone of the war address was somber and low-keyed. Wilson alluded to the "solemn and even tragical character of the step I am taking," and he prefaced his conclusion by conceding, "It is a fearful thing to lead this great peaceful people into war, into the most terrible and disastrous of all wars, civilization itself seeming to be in the balance." The Allies soon painfully discovered that Wilson had not enlisted America on their side in a crusade. Rather he was still seeking to control the war. Only now he believed that he could not avoid belligerency, and he was gambling that he could make belligerency serve the same ends of reaching a just settlement and maintaining a lasting peace.

Wilson knew that the gamble might fail. He feared that belligerent means might subvert his pacific goal, but he believed that he had no choice. Interestingly, Wilson's last words in the war address, which followed his declaration that America would fight to achieve a new international order, were "God helping her, she can do no other." The phrase was, as some observers recognized, a paraphrase of Martin Luther's declaration to the Diet of Worms: "God helping me, I can do no other." The phrase had probably occurred to Wilson by chance, but it did express both his own Christian philosophy and the role in which he was casting the United States. Like Luther, he was acknowledging that men and nations could not avoid sin but must, in seeking to do God's will, "sin boldly." He was asking his countrymen to "sin boldly" in seeking to control the war and in striving to make the world better, freer, and more peaceful.

American intervention revolutionized World War I. It saved the Allies from financial collapse, which, together with the other reverses they suffered in 1917, would have insured their defeat. It gave the British and French the morale boost that allowed them to hold out on the Western Front in the spring of 1918 against the last great German offensive. It supplied fresh manpower for the counteroffensive that ended the war on November 11, 1918. Moreover, American intervention made the war for the first time a global conflict. Before April 1917, it had involved mostly European nations and had had ramifications elsewhere largely through their colonial possessions. The entry of the United States drew in the Western Hemisphere and extended connections into the Pacific. Also, because of Wilson's efforts, the war came to be about more than territorial appetites and imperial designs. Now it involved world-wide aspirations to self-government, new ways of conducting relations among nations, and attempts to create a different international order. Without Wilson and without the United States, it would have been a far different war.

Woodrow Wilson never forgot that he might be making a tragic mistake by entering World War I, and he may have. Certainly his justification for intervention helped implant the habits of glib globalizing and facile homogenizing of disparate parts of the world which have been besetting sins of American foreign policy since World War I. Similarly, despite Wilson's intentions, the war did turn into a self-righteous crusade for many Americans, thereby confirming another dangerous predilection in the nation's conduct in world affairs. The international and the domestic orders of Europe lay in ruins, and instability was going to reign there no matter who won the war. Perhaps, as the isolationists always insisted, America might have done better to have left that unhappy continent alone and might have done more for the world by setting an example of restraint. But that was not what Woodrow Wilson chose to do, and that has not been America's role in the 20th-century world. Thanks to him and to the long-running aftereffects of World War I, the United States has tried again and again to shape events that have seemed to others beyond human control. That has been America's glory and tragedy.

Henry Ford and the Jews

LEONARD DINNERSTEIN

● *Henry Ford did not invent the gasoline-powered engine, and he made no important technological contribution to early automobiles. He did not even originate the idea of an economical car for the average family. But Henry Ford was alone in sticking to it with a grim persistence, and he became the most important and successful of the industry pioneers. A Michigan farm boy who migrated to Detroit in 1879 at the age of sixteen, Ford worked variously as a machinist, a watch repairman, and an engineer, all the while tinkering with internal combustion engines and auto buggies in his backyard shop and in a tiny brick building on Bagley Avenue. In 1896 he produced his first "flexmobile," and for the next six years he tried, mostly unsuccessfully, to market at a profit improved models of the vehicle. His big break came in 1902, when his racing car won several nationally publicized races and gave Fords a reputation for toughness and reliability.*

Within the next generation, Henry Ford became a legend— the very embodiment of modern industrial technique. In 1908 he introduced a boxlike vehicle which was easy to operate, simple to repair, and dependable even under trying conditions. Dubbed the Model T—and promptly known as the "Tin Lizzie"—it remained unchanged in outward appearance for the next two decades.

By 1925 Ford was turning out nine thousand cars per day, or one every ten seconds. That such unprecedented production earned the "Flivver King" $25,000 per day and made him a billionaire did not detract from his image. In Vanity Fair, he was described as "the Colossus of Business, an almost divine Master-Mind." A study in contradictions, Ford was a salesman whose product destroyed vast areas of traditional small

Reprinted courtesy of *Moment* magazine, the Jewish Magazine for the '90s.

town life, and who, at the same time, devoted a considerable
amount of his fortune and spiritual energies to rebuilding
models of old-fashioned villages and promoting old-fashioned
square dancing. At the end of the 1920s college students were
asked to rank the greatest people of all time. Henry Ford came
in third—behind Jesus Christ and Napoleon Bonaparte.

But Ford was also a notorious anti-Semite who was at times
consumed by a hatred of Wall Street and of other major fi-
nancial institutions in which he felt that Jews exercised undue
influence. The following essay by Professor Leonard Dinner-
stein of the University of Arizona considers the causes and
consequences of the Flivver King's prejudice.

In 1987 Hebrew Union College acquired an extraordinary letter signed
by Henry Ford, the originator of the Ford Motor Company. Dated
June 30, 1927 and addressed to the Jews of the United States, it states
in part:

> For some time past I have given consideration to the series of
> articles concerning Jews which since 1920 have appeared in *The
> Dearborn Independent*. Some of them have been reprinted in
> pamphlet form under the title "The International Jew." Although
> both publications are my property ...in the multitude of my
> activities it has been impossible for me to devote personal atten-
> tion to their management or to keep informed as to their contents.
> It has therefore inevitably followed that the conduct and policies
> of these publications had to be delegated to men whom I placed
> in charge of them and upon whom I relied implicitly.
>
> To my great regret I have learned that Jews generally, and
> particularly those of this country, not only resent these publi-
> cations as promoting anti-Semitism, but regard me as their enemy.
> Trusted friends with whom I have conferred recently, have as-
> sured me in all sincerity that in their opinion the character of the
> charges and insinuations made against the Jews, both individually
> and collectively, contained in many of the articles which have
> been circulated periodically in *The Dearborn Independent* and
> have been reprinted in the pamphlets mentioned, justifies the
> righteous indignation entertained by Jews everywhere toward me
> because of the mental anguish occasioned by the unprovoked
> reflections made upon them.
>
> ...I deem it to be my duty as an honorable man to make
> amends for the wrong done to the Jews as fellow-men and broth-

ers, by asking their forgiveness for the harm that I have unintentionally committed, by retracting so far as lies within my power the offensive charges laid at their door by these publications, and by giving them the unqualified assurance that henceforth they may look to me for friendship and goodwill.

Despite his denials, there can be no doubt that Henry Ford was responsible for the outrageous slanders. He was the sole owner of the newspaper and personally supervised the development and continuation of the articles on "The International Jew," which were later collected and published in four volumes. In 1920 and 1921, he made almost daily visits to *The Dearborn Independent's* offices where he paid attention only to "Mr. Ford's Page" and the materials about the Jews. According to the 1921 testimony of his private secretary, Ernest Liebold, "*The Dearborn Independent* is Henry Ford's own paper and he authorizes every statement occurring therein."

Ford also said in his letter that he had examined the materials on the Jews carefully, was "mortified" by their content, and ordered their discontinuance immediately. "Had I appreciated even the general nature, to say nothing of the details, of these utterances, I would have forbidden their circulation without a moment's hesitation...." He pledged to withdraw all copies of "The International Jew" throughout the United States and in foreign lands as well, and pledged further that "henceforth *The Dearborn Independent* will be conducted under such auspices that articles reflecting upon the Jews will never again appear in its columns." He kept his word on that and closed down the newspaper at the end of the year.

Behind this letter lay nearly a decade of virulent anti-Semitism by the most powerful American industrialist of the twentieth century. *The Dearborn Independent's* initial series on the Jews began in May 1920, continued through January 1922, and then intermittently continued until 1927. Henry Ford was not brought to this apologizing easily.

Born on a farm in Dearbornville, Michigan, on July 30, 1863, to parents of mixed Irish, Dutch, Flemish, English, and Scottish heritage, Ford's earliest recollections were "that there was too much work on that place." At 16 he started an apprenticeship in a Detroit machine shop and later worked in power plants and serviced steam-traction engines. In his spare time he tinkered with an engine for an automobile and finally produced one in 1899. The rest is history: He started the Ford Motor Company in 1903, produced his first Model T auto in 1908 and won worldwide attention in 1914 when he announced that he would pay his workers $5 a day. Since the going rate in the United States at that time was about 22 cents an hour for laborers, men flocked to the Ford plants in Michigan from all over the world.

Ford's sudden rise to fame enhanced his sense of self-importance and he was inclined to interpret his success and its universal acclaim as proof of his unerring judgment. He began to take positions on issues about which he had little knowledge, and that included the role of the Jew in the world. Biographer Allan Nevins in his book *Ford* attributed the automaker's "spasm of violent anti-Semitism" to "ignorance and misinformation." But in looking back to Ford's youth there seems to be little doubt that he shared the values of rural America. In the farm areas of Michigan near where he was raised there was a general apprehension and mistrust of Jews. Nevins described it: "In rural communities where the only Jew ever seen was a roving peddler, where Christian and Jew were antithetical terms and where such images as Shylock and Fagin were traditional, parochialism bred strange distortions of view. An anti-Semitic thread had been observable in the garment of Populism. More than one observer noted that when Ford spoke harshly of the Jew he referred less to a race or religion than to "certain traits for which that term seemed convenient." The negative associations with Jews were so inbred that he used the term "Jew" with abandon. "He called all the moneylenders of the world 'Jews,' " his sister Margaret would later recall. He even referred to J. P. Morgan's gentile banking associates as "Jews."

Though there were no other indications of racial or religious animosity in Ford's pronouncements before 1915, the connection between Jews and banking never quite left him. He attributed the cause of World War I to international Jewish bankers who prodded the Germans to begin the conflagration.

A militant pacifist, Ford had delusions of grandeur and thought that single-handedly he could use his influence to end the war. In 1915 an American Jewish woman of Hungarian descent, Rosika Schwimmer, encouraged him to send a delegation to Europe to help end the war and Ford, inspired by the idea, launched the so-called Peace Ship whose passengers included 83 Americans. Their purpose was to go to Europe, meet with pacifists from other nations, and together wield their influence to end the war. Major newspapers mocked Ford's scheme, distinguished Americans refused his invitation to participate in the effort, and the whole thing collapsed when Ford and the ship reached Norway. The auto magnate was ill, Norwegian officials thought he was foolish, and the project was disbanded. "In later years," biographer Robert Lacey wrote in *Ford: The Men and the Machine,* "Henry Ford's virulent anti-Semitic campaigns were to make up one of the darker chapters in his life and he would hark back to his ill-starred adventure with the Hungarian Jewess as the beginning of it all. The Peace Ship incident, he would maintain, was the first time he had personal experience of the mischievous links between radicalism and the Jews."

Another difficult episode in Ford's life occurred in 1918, when he ran as a Democrat for U.S. Senator from Michigan and lost. He attributed his defeat, biographer Keith Sward tells us in *The Legend of Henry Ford,* to the nefarious influence of "Wall Street" and an "influential gang of Jews." Thereafter, Ford downright ran off at the mouth about Jews. On a camping trip with friends Thomas Edison, Harvey Firestone, and John Burroughs (a prominent naturalist) Burroughs recorded in his diary of the trip that "Mr. Ford attributes all evil to the Jews or the Jewish capitalists: The Jews caused the war; the Jews caused the outbreak of thieving and robbery all over the country; the Jews caused the inefficiency of the Navy," and so forth.

Ford's diatribes coincided with other increased manifestations of hostility toward Jews in the United States. The Bolshevik Revolution had occurred in Russia in 1917 and it gave rise to American fears about subversion in the United States. John Higham, the historian, pointed out in *Strangers in the Land* that "Jews offered the most concrete symbol of foreign radicalism. . . . Stories circulated about the streets of New York to the effect that every Jewish immigrant would become a soldier in the revolutionary army assembling in America." Public meetings and congressional hearings brought additional evidence of the alleged association of the Jews with Bolsheviks and radicals, and in March 1919, a prominent American periodical, the *Literary Digest,* expanded on these views in an article entitled "American Jews in the Bolshevik Oligarchy."

Soon after the Bolshevik Revolution occurred, a forged document,

The Protocols of the Elders of Zion, written by members of the Russian secret police in the late nineteenth century, was widely circulated. The document alleged that the Jews were engaged in a secret plot to over-throw Christian governments throughout the world and planned to take control themselves. Though it made little impact when originally written, after the Bolshevik Revolution in 1917 it emerged as a major political weapon. As historian Morton Rosenstock has observed:

> The Protocols . . . supplied a tried and tested scapegoat that could be blamed for the evils of a rapidly changing world beset by war and revolution. In America, the Protocols reinforced the anti-Jewish stereotype that already stressed the international, con-spiratorial, immoral and Mammon-driven Jewish nature.

The Protocols was published in England in February 1920, in Boston a few weeks later, and its arguments soon appeared in Ford's news-paper, *The Dearborn Independent.* The newspaper had been purchased in January 1919, with the intention of serving as a vehicle for the expression of the auto magnate's opinions on a variety of subjects. The articles published made little impression and had no national impact while the newspaper languished in oblivion. A consultant, J. J. O'Neill, was called in for advice about how to spruce up the journal and he recommended a strong and forceful series on a major topic. "Let's have some sensationalism," his report urged.

Ford found the Jew a suitable villain. Jews had allegedly encouraged the Germans to start World War I, had undermined the efforts of Ford's Peace Ship, or so he believed, and had supposedly caused his defeat when he ran for the U.S. Senate in 1918.

Moreover for some inexplicable reason, historian Morton Rosen-stock tells us, Ford, who was one of the world's wealthiest men, "felt personally threatened by the power of finance capitalism and by labor unrest. His answer, in part, was to identify the two as one and to equate both with the Jews."

It is difficult for many of us today to think of one of America's greatest industrial magnates as a simpleton but in many regards he was just that. Albert Lee, in *Henry Ford and the Jews,* notes that a con-temporary in the 1920s, Norman Hapgood, characterized Ford's mind as "that of a child. And like a child he lived in a fanciful world of his own creation. He had good guys—mainly himself, his yes men and the

Germans—and the villains—Jews, Catholics, smokers and drinkers. Reasoning was just so much talk to a man who lived only by hunches and feelings." Thus, the publication of *The Protocols* triggered his own imagination as he set out to tell the nation about the Jews among us.

Ford's public attacks against the Jews began in *The Dearborn Independent* on May 22, 1920 when the paper launched a seven-year on-again off-again series on "The International Jew." The first batch of articles ran for ninety-one consecutive weeks until they were abruptly terminated, without explanation, in January 1922. The first article informed readers that

> the Jew is the world's enigma. Poor in his masses, he yet controls the world's finances. Scattered abroad without country or government, he yet presents a unity of race continuity which no other people has achieved. Living under legal disabilities in almost every land, he has become the power behind many a throne. There are ancient prophecies to the effect that the Jew will return to his own land and from that center rule the world, though not until he has undergone an assault by the united nations of mankind.
>
> The single description which will include a larger percentage of Jews than members of any other race is this: He is in business. It may be only gathering rags and selling them, but he is in business. From the sale of old clothes to the control of international trade and finance, the Jew is supremely gifted for business. More than any other race he exhibits a decided aversion to industrial employment, which he balances by an equally decided adaptability to trade. The Gentile boy works his way up, taking employment in the productive or technical departments, but the Jewish boy prefers to begin as messenger, salesman or clerk—anything—so long as it is connected with the commercial side of the business.

"In America alone," the newspaper continued:

> most of big business, the trusts and the banks, the natural resources and the chief agricultural products, especially tobacco, cotton and sugar, are in the control of Jewish financiers or their agents. Jewish journalists are a large and powerful group here. "Large numbers of department stores are held by Jewish firms," says the Jewish Encyclopedia, and many if not most of them are run under Gentile names. Jews are the largest and most numerous

landlords of residence property in the country. They are supreme
in the theatrical world. They absolutely control the circulations
of publications throughout the country. Fewer than any race
whose presence among us is noticeable, they receive daily an
amount of favorable publicity which would be impossible did
they not have the facilities for creating and distributing it themselves. Werner Sombart, in his "Jew and Modern Capitalism,"
says: "If the conditions of America continue to develop along
the same lines as in the last generation, if the immigration statistics
and the proportion of births among all nationalities remain the
same, our imagination may picture the United States of fifty or
a hundred years hence as a land inhabited only by Slavs, Negroes
and Jews...."

In subsequent articles Ford accused Jews of trying "to twist Amer-
icanism into something else," and of exerting "more power in New
York than they have ever exerted during the Christian era in any place,
with the exception of the present Russia. The Jewish Revolution in
Russian was manned from New York...." The August 6, 1921 issue
of *The Dearborn Independent* proclaimed: "JEWISH JAZZ—MORON
MUSIC—BECOMES OUR NATIONAL MUSIC."

In an interview that the *Review of Reviews* published in December
1921, Ford tried to give the rationale for the many pieces on "The
International Jew." He claimed that he was

only trying to awake the Gentile world to an understanding of
what is going on. The Jew is a mere huckster, a trader who doesn't
want to produce, but to make something out of what somebody
else produces.

Never before in American history had there been such a blatantly
anti-Semitic series published over so long a period of time. Nor had
there ever been such a renowned figure as Henry Ford promoting such
slander. Elements in the American Jewish community reacted with
shock and anger. Shortly after the appearance of the first essay on "The
International Jew," *The American Hebrew* editorialized, "No American in the whole of our history has perpetrated so shocking an attack,
so dastardly a crime, against the Jews as has Henry Ford...." The
editors suggested that he be stripped of his citizenship and then taken
out and "tarred and feathered." Louis Marshall, president of the American Jewish Committee, then the leading Jewish defense organization

in America, called Ford's attacks "the most serious episode in the history of American Jewry." And New York's Reform leader, Rabbi Stephen S. Wise, responded:

> It is the special shame of Christendom in America to-day that the tissue of lies and forgeries known as the "Protocols," or the "Jewish Peril," is being given circulation by a confessedly nearly illiterate multimillionaire, who has taken upon himself the onus of filing the gravest charges that have ever been uttered against Jews in this or any land.

To be sure, some non-Jewish opposition also developed to both the outrageousness of *The Dearborn Independent's* series and Ford's crassness. On November 3, 1920, *The Nation* ran a story pointing out that a wave of anti-Semitism was sweeping the world and observed that "the chief responsibility for the revival of this hoary shame among us in America attaches to Henry Ford." The writer dismissed "the common source of Mr. Ford's propaganda," *The Protocols of the Elders of Zion,* as "an old and absurd forgery." A nationally known socialist writer, John Spargo, also objected to Ford's outrageous attacks upon the Jews and took it upon himself to organize a group of prominent Christians to protest the blatant bigotry. He wrote a manifesto that 119 dignitaries, including President Woodrow Wilson and former president Howard Taft, signed. The document, published in January 1921, without mentioning Ford or *The Dearborn Independent* noted

> with profound regret and disapproval the appearance in this country of what is apparently an organized campaign of anti-Semitism . . . We protest against this organized campaign of prejudice and hatred not only because of its manifest injustice to those against whom it is directed, but also, especially, because we are convinced that it is wholly incompatible with loyal and intelligent American citizenship.

A month earlier, in December 1920, the Federal Council of Churches of Christ had also publicly proclaimed its disapproval of Ford's actions. Louis Marshall and members of other Jewish organizations had been prepared to urge the Federal Council to take some action, but the Federal Council, representing the major Protestant denominations, needed no outside prodding.

But not everyone was critical of Ford's series. Ford's propaganda pieces on the Jews were reprinted in several European countries and were used extensively by the Nazi party in Germany. Adolf Hitler used them in writing *Mein Kampf* and German copies of *The International Jew* were kept on a table in the anteroom of Hitler's Munich office. *The International Jew* was also translated into more than a dozen other languages, including Arabic. A Spanish language edition of 1936 and 1937, *El Judio International por Henry Ford,* has the automaker's picture on the frontispiece.

Due to his wealth and status as folk hero, Henry Ford's sponsorship guaranteed attention. Ford forced automobile dealers selling his cars to purchase specified numbers of copies of *The Dearborn Independent* while encouraging friends and customers to take out individual subscriptions. Thus the circulation of the newspaper rose from 72,000 in 1919, to almost 300,000 in 1922, and to 700,000 in 1924. That same year the *New York Daily News,* the nation's largest daily, had a circulation of only 50,000 more. Rural Americans, especially, read *The Dearborn Independent* but no sector of society was totally oblivious to the newspaper's position. How many individuals actually endorsed the ideas presented cannot be measured, but Albert Lee, author of *Henry Ford and the Jews,* has written:

> One has only to read through the letters of encouragement in the Ford Archives—letters from otherwise compassionate people condemning the Jews, letters from numerous Christian ministers praising the anti-Semitic attacks and enclosing money for copies of *The International Jew,* letters from college professor and illiterate alike—to be impressed by how easily people would believe Ford about ethnic hatred and politics, simply because he made a car that pleased them.

The beginning of the end of the Ford diatribes occurred in 1924, when Aaron Sapiro, a Jew who had been promoting farmer cooperatives, was attacked in *The Dearborn Independent.* Sapiro had been helping the farmers increase their income since 1919. On April 23, 1924, Ford took off against him. "JEWISH EXPLOITATION OF FARMERS' ORGANIZATION" blared the headline. The story began: "A band of Jews—bankers, lawyers, moneylenders, advertising agencies, fruit-packers, produce buyers, professional office managers and bookkeeping experts—is on the back of the American farmer." Sapiro was personally attacked along with Jews generally. Sapiro demanded a formal apology and when that was not forthcoming, he brought suit against both Ford and *The Dearborn Independent*.

The case came to trial in the spring of 1927. Ford's secret investigators tried to find damaging evidence about Sapiro but they came up with nothing. With the opening of the trial Ford himself became extremely elusive. Process servers were unable to find him to serve a subpoena. Not until the court threatened to declare him in contempt did his attorney agree to produce him. The night before Ford's scheduled appearance in court, he had an automobile "accident" and was hospitalized. Some people questioned the seriousness of his condition and others thought his so-called accident might have been staged, but physicians certified that he was unable to appear in court. The chief of Ford's own private detective service, Harry Bennett, later acknowledged that the auto magnate had told him, "Harry, I wasn't in that car when it went down into the river."

As the trial proceeded, Ford's investigators attempted to co-opt some of the jurors. One of them, however, told a newspaper reporter that Ford's people were trying to influence her and the judge declared a mistrial.

A new trial date was set for the fall but the trial never took place. Historian Morton Rosenstock tells us that Ford "seemed frightened at the unpleasant prospect of appearing on the witness stand if the Sapiro case was retried." He therefore decided to end his campaign against the Jews. It is impossible to know exactly why Ford decided to avoid a court appearance but a number of factors have been suggested. Perhaps the trauma of a previous courtroom appearance remained vivid in his memory and he had no desire to repeat the experience. In 1919 the *Chicago Tribune* had called him an "ignorant idealist" and he sued the newspaper for $1 million. Although technically he won the case and was awarded 6 cents in damages, Ford was made to look foolish when he took the witness stand and told attorneys that the American Revolution had occurred in 1812 and labeled traitor Benedict Arnold "a writer." Ford also had a close relationship with a married woman who gave birth to a child in 1923 that might have been his son. No one knows, of course, what kinds of questions attorneys would ask witnesses in an open courtroom, but Ford had sufficient reason not to want to subject himself to the kind of humiliation and embarrassment a situation that he did not control might present.

But Ford also had other reasons to discontinue his vilification of the Jews. His son Edsel, as well as several friends, had been counseling him for some time to stop his attacks. The fact that the Ford Motor Company suffered from stiff competition and lower sales in the mid-1920s may also have contributed to his decision. Will Rogers allegedly joked that "Ford used to have it in for the Jewish people until he saw them in Chevrolets, and then he said, 'Boys, I am all wrong.' "

After the retrial of the case was set for the fall of 1927, Ford's emissaries contacted various Jews in positions of responsibility and ultimately made a connection with Louis Marshall: Ford was willing to apologize and do whatever was necessary to get himself out of the position of having to take the stand to defend his series on "The International Jew." Marshall then drafted a letter for Ford to sign, the automobile magnate agreed to the terms, and in June 1927, Ford formally retracted his assertions and publicly apologized to the Jewish people. That was the end of Sapiro's suit.

Ford's retraction satisfied Louis Marshall and many other Jews. Marshall claimed that the automobile maker's concessions gave him "more happiness than any action in which I have ever been engaged."

Broadway producer and song writer, Billy Rose, wrote a ditty called, "Since Henry Ford Apologized to Me," and ended it with a pledge that if the car maker ran for president he would have Rose's support. *The Atlanta Constitution* editorialized:

> Although manly and courageous, the retraction is no more than Mr. Ford should have made. The pity is it was not made long ago. And the greater pity is that a nationally circulated magazine, with the name of one of the most extensively known men of the world at its masthead, should have ever permitted such baseless attacks to have begun.

The Richmond *Times-Dispatch* noted that "in denying knowledge of the anti-Semitic policy of his magazine and in disavowing any understanding of its effect on the Jewish people, [Ford] has set himself up as a target for further ridicule."

On Ford's seventy-fifth birthday, in 1938, Adolf Hitler publicly awarded Ford the highest honor the German government could bestow on a foreigner: the Grand Cross of the German Eagle. Many people were critical of Ford for accepting this token of esteem but he defended his position. "My acceptance of a medal from the German people," he stated, "does not, as some people seem to think, involve any sympathy on my part with Nazism."

In the last years of his life, while not publicly proclaiming his anti-Semitic feelings, Ford joined the isolationist, and somewhat anti-Semitic, America First movement, which wanted to keep the United States out of World War II. Shortly before his death in 1947, a reporter asked him if the Ford Motor Company might go public. The old man allegedly rose from his sick bed and passionately replied: "I'll take my factory down brick by brick before I'll let any of those Jew speculators get stock in the company."

12

Al Capone: "I Give the Public What the Public Wants"

JOHN G. MITCHELL

● *Long before the Civil War, temperance enthusiasts had sought to make the country safe from demon rum. In 1880, Neil Dow labeled the liquor traffic "the most important political question facing the nation," and thereafter two generations of religious fundamentalists, Anti-Saloon Leaguers, and Women's Christian Temperance Union members carried on the fight. Enthusiasm for prohibition swept across the United States in the early years of the twentieth century, and it became law finally in 1919 by riding the patriotic fervor of World War I. As Frederick Lewis Allen wrote: "If a sober soldier was a good soldier and a sober factory hand was a productive factory hand, then the argument for prohibition was for the moment unanswerable."*

At best, the moral amendment to the Constitution was a mixed blessing. In part it represented the attempt of the middle class to impose its values upon inner-city residents who found that drinking eased the drabness of their daily lives. The strong desire for spirits felt by many people was not quenched by legislation. Some legitimate businesses folded and alcoholism may have declined, but much of the liquor trade simply went underground. Speakeasies replaced saloons, and underworld entrepreneurs built illegal empires out of the liquor trade.

No city was more troubled by gangster violence than Chicago, and no underworld figure was more notorious than "Scarface" Al Capone. Born in a tough neighborhood near the Brooklyn Navy Yard, Capone gained a reputation as a fighter as a youth and moved to Chicago to escape a possible

From "Said Chicago's Al Capone," *American Heritage* (February/March 1979). Reprinted by permission of International Creative Management. Copyright © 1979 by American Heritage.

New York murder indictment. Gaining the confidence and
support of the famous Johnny Torrio, Capone operated ini-
tially on Chicago's South Side before gradually expanding his
influence, usually via the gun, throughout the metropolitan
area. As John G. Mitchell notes in the following essay, Capone
simply gave the public what it wanted, thus demonstrating
the difficulty of altering standards of personal morality by
constitutional dictums.

The newspapers called him Scarface, but the sobriquet did not safely
bear repeating in his presence. It was *Mister* Capone instead, or Big
Al; or, among trusted lieutenants of his palace guard, "Snorky,"
a street word connoting a certain princely elegance. The elegance
was mostly in cloth, in expensive suits from Marshall Field, silk pajamas from Sulka, the upholstery of the custom Cadillac that was
said to have cost more than twenty grand in 1920's dollars. In his
pockets, it was rumored, he carried cash enough to buy two such
limousines; he tipped lavishly, and showered his friends with gold-
plate gifts. To hide the furrows of the scars on his left cheek, he
powdered his face with talcum and explained that the wounds were
inflicted by shrapnel while he was fighting in France with the "Lost Bat-
talion." He believed in the sanctity of the American family. "A woman's home and her children are her real happiness," he once told
a reporter. "If she would stay there, the world would have less to
worry about."

For a time, a good part of the world worried about Alphonse Capone
of Chicago, Illinois. He was a prince, all right. Beneath the elegant
veneer he was prince of the bootleggers, baron of the brothels, and
vicar of assorted vices that for more than a decade scrambled the
innards of the Second City, its labor, its industry, its law enforcement,
its municipal officialdom. He ruled an empire of corruption the likes
of which had never before and have not since been witnessed by any
American city. He commanded an army of emissaries and assassins
whose numbers at peak approached one thousand. He sat at the pin-
nacle of a society so grotesque the newspapers felt obliged to give both
its principals and its understudies nicknames: Mike de Pike, Bathhouse
John, Greasy Thumb Guzik, Hinky Dink Kenna, Two-Gun Alterie, and
Bloody Angelo; Ecola the Eagle and Izzy the Rat and Lupo the Wolf

and Duffy the Goat; Hop Toad Giunta and Blubber Bob, among dozens of others.

In Capone's supreme snorkiness there was always some wrinkle. Though the tailoring was splendid, it never quite seemed to conceal the bulge in his jacket beneath the left armpit. The Cadillac was custom-made not just for the plush upholstery but for a half a ton of armor plate, the steel visor over the gas tank, the thick, bulletproof glass, the removable rear window that converted the back seat into a machine-gun emplacement. The generous tipping was not limited to newsboys and hatcheck girls; he also tipped the eccentric William Hale Thompson a quarter-million dollars to help elect him mayor of Chicago, and Thompson later rewarded his benefactor by dismissing the city's official obeisance to gangsters as "newspaper talk." For Capone, a quarter-million was merely a fractional gratuity. His syndicate's net profits in the late 1920's were estimated by the Chicago Crime Commission at sixty million dollars a year.

There was even a wrinkle in his story about the scars, for he had never been to France in military uniform, had never felt shrapnel. He had felt instead the cutting edge of a pocketknife in a Brooklyn saloon, his reward for insulting a woman. Of which, in Capone's view of the species, there were two distinct kinds—the ones who stayed home, and the ones who didn't. "When a guy don't fall for a broad," said Big Al years later, "he's through." There was a bit of self-fulfilling prophecy in the remark. In his time, Capone no doubt dodged—and dispensed in kind—more flying metal than any doughboy who served in France. Yet it was to be his fate to die not with his spats on but in his silk pajamas, *through* at the age of forty-eight, from neurosyphilitic complications.

He was of an era that today seems more romantic than grotesque, more imagined than real. He brought to the third decade of this century much of its celebrated roar; and for that, in the minds of many Americans born too late to have heard the harsh authentic decibels, he looms as something of a folk hero, a Robin Hood of the Loop, a grand desperado much closer in style to the flamboyant two-gun type of the Old West than to today's furtive *capo* who, in stressful moments, is more likely to reach for a pocket calculator than a snub-nosed Smith & Wesson. In a society vicariously fascinated with crime and violence, it is not surprising that Alphonse Capone should be accorded such retrospective honors. He was the last of the Great American Gun-slingers.

After Big Al—notwithstanding the subsequent rise of Lucky Luciano and Vito Genovese and Frank Costello and other latter-day godfath-ers—everything changed. To be sure, the violence did not end with Capone; it simply became more sophisticated—ice picks through the eardrum instead of baseball bats about the head and shoulders, corpses consolidated with scrap metal rather than abandoned in the gutter. After Capone, the rackets diversified, dope preempted illicit booze, the crime families intermarried, and the profits proliferated. But no one ever quite managed to fill Snorky's shoes. And no other name again became synonymous with Chicago.

According to all accounts, Chicago had always been special, the dis-tinctively American town. It was the Queen of the Lake, the Wonder of the Wonderful West. Sarah Bernhardt found in it "the pulse of America." Carl Sandburg praised it as hog butcher for the world. For a time, however, part of the city's distinction was its capacity to inspire the pejorative phrase. Strangers turned away appalled by its open display of raw vice and spectacular mayhem. "It is inhabited by savag-es," wrote Rudyard Kipling. "A grotesque nightmare," said Don Mar-quis. One of its own, the alderman Robert Merriam, observed that Chicago was unique because it "is the only completely corrupt city in America." The English writer Kenneth Allsop noted in his book *The Bootleggers and Their Era* that Chicago during the 1920's "was effec-tively a city without a police force, for [the police] operated partially as a private army for the gangs." And in his informal history of the city's underworld, *Gem of the Prairie,* Herbert Asbury described the decade as a time when "banks all over Chicago were robbed in broad daylight by bandits who scorned to wear masks....Burglars marked out sections of the city as their own.... Fences accompanied thieves into stores and appraised stocks of merchandise before they were stolen."

After one especially noisy series of intergang bombings, a newspaper pundit wryly remarked that "the rockets' red glare, the bombs bursting in air / Gave proof through the night that Chicago's still there." In the United States Congress, a Midwestern senator suggested that President Calvin Coolidge recall the Marine expeditionary force then in Nicaragua and dispatch it to a place more worthy of armed intervention—Chicago.

The city's pernicious reputation was well established long before the arrival of Al Capone. By the turn of the century the Queen of the Lake had become the hussy of America. Its red-light district—out-shining even those of New York, New Orleans, and San Francisco—sprawled for block after block across the seamy South Side. The district, according to one chronicler, swarmed with "harlots, footpads, pimps, and pickpockets" operating in and out of "brothels, saloons, and dives of every description." Within the area were a number of subdistricts affectionately known as the Bad Lands, Coon Hollow, Satan's Mile, Hell's Half-Acre, and Dead Man's Alley; later these quaint neighborhoods became known collectively as the "Levee."

Among the city's most notorious whoremasters was one James Colosimo. Son of an immigrant from Calabria, Italy, Big Jim Colosimo had learned all the ropes that the Levee had to offer. He had been a bootblack, pickpocket, pimp, and bagman for the aldermen who controlled the district's votes and vices. In 1902 he met and married the brothelkeeper Victoria Moresco. Soon Big Jim was managing scores of bordellos and ancillary saloons; and from every dollar earned by a prostitute, more than half went to Colosimo. Colosimo's Café, on South Wabash Avenue, had green velvet walls and crystal chandeliers. It had the best entertainers, the most beautiful chorus girls, the largest selection of imported wines in Chicago. It established Colosimo as a man of considerable means. Inevitably, too, it marked him as a target for extortion.

Extortion was then the specialty of the Black Hand, the secret Sicilian underworld society. Colosimo, being Calabrian, was fair game. If he could afford to pay off the South Side aldermen and the police, surely he could afford some modest tribute to the society. Say, for starters, about five thousand dollars? Colosimo agreed. Then the Black Handers upped the ante. On the second scheduled payoff, Colosimo contrived to ambush the extortionists and left three of them dead under a South Side bridge. But the threats and demands continued. Colosimo needed help. He sent for his nephew in New York, Johnny Torrio, a veteran of the notorious Five Points gang. Several years later Johnny Torrio in turn would send for Al Capone.

He was the fourth of nine children born to Gabriel and Teresa Capone, who in 1893 had emigrated from Naples to the slums of the Brooklyn Navy Yard district. Gabriel was a barber. The family lived in a dingy flat heated by a potbellied stove. Dodging vegetable carts and ice wagons, the children played stickball in the streets. Nearby, according to Capone's most definitive biographer, John Kobler, were the fleshpots of Sands Street where "sailors piled ashore, clamoring for liquor and women." Alphonse attended P.S. 7 on Adams Street. One of his closest friends was a boy named Salvatore Luciana, later known as Lucky Luciano. When Al was eight, the family moved a mile south to Garfield Place. There was a new social club in the neighborhood. Gilt letters in a window identified it as the John Torrio Association.

To what extent Torrio figured in the early underworld education of Al Capone is not altogether clear. Kobler quotes Capone as having said, from the perspective of middle age, that he "looked on Johnny like my adviser and father and the party who made it possible for me to get my start." No doubt it was Torrio who steered both Capone and Luciano to apprenticeship with the Five Points gang while they were still in their mid-teens. Torrio was a man of eclectic connections and alliances. He commanded the respect of Frankie Uale (alias Yale), who specialized in murder contracts and who for ten years was national boss of the *Unione Siciliane,* a sort of institutional missing link between the Black Hand of the Old World and the Mafioso of the New. Yale hired Capone as a bouncer-bartender at his Harvard Inn at Coney Island. There, according to Kobler, young Al's "huge fists, unarmed or clutching a club, struck [obstreperous carousers] with the impact of a pile driver." In 1918 Capone married Mae Coughlin of Brooklyn. The following year, facing a murder indictment should a man he had pile-driven in a barroom brawl die, he received word from Torrio that his huge fists were needed in Chicago. Though the brawl victim survived, Big Al was already a murder suspect in two other New York cases. To Chicago he went.

It was a good time to be going to Chicago. His mentor, Torrio, was beginning to eclipse Colosimo for control of the South Side rackets. William Hale Thompson, the laissez-faire mayor, was soon to be re-elected. And Congress was preparing to make the nation dry with passage of the Volstead Act. One hour after Prohibition became the law, at midnight January 17, 1920, a whisky shipment stamped "for medicinal purposes" was hijacked on Chicago's South Side. The Anti-Saloon League had promised "an era of clear thinking and clean living." But it had misjudged the prodigious thirst of the American people. By 1929 the bootleg liquor industry was reaping an annual income of three billion dollars—a sum more than three times greater than the amount paid that year by individual taxpayers to the Internal Revenue Service. By 1930 Chicago had ten thousand speak-easies. Each speak-easy, on a weekly average, purchased two cases of liquor (at ninety dollars the case) and six barrels of beer (at fifty-five dollars the barrel). Estimated bootleg revenues each week came to $5,300,000. And sooner than later every dollar passed through the hands of one or another of Chicago's multitudinous gangs. Increasingly each year, the largest share found its way to the gang that was headed by Johnny Torrio and Scarface Al Capone.

Torrio had seized control of the South Side as early as 1920. On May 11 he had arranged for a shipment of whisky to be delivered to Colosimo's Café, and Colosimo himself was to be there to receive it. The whisky never arrived. Waiting in the café vestibule, Colosimo instead received a fatal bullet in the back of his head. Police suspected, but could never prove, that the assassin was Frankie Yale, imported from New York under contract to Johnny Torrio.

With Colosimo gone, Torrio promoted Capone to the unofficial rank of chief field general, installed him as manager of Torrio headquarters at the Four Deuces on South Wabash Avenue, cut him in for 25 percent of all brothel profits, and promised him half the net from bootleg operations. As Kobler reconstructs it: "They complemented each other, the slight older man, cool, taciturn, reserved, condoning violence only when guile failed; the beefy younger one, gregarious, pleasure-loving, physically fearless, hot-tempered. By the second year they no longer stood in the relationship of boss and hireling; they were partners."

Among Torrio's many schemes for extending his operations beyond the South Side was a dream of ruling the nearby suburb of Cicero. Cicero traditionally had been the turf of the O'Donnell brothers and their West Side gang; but Torrio, a master of crafty diplomacy, had managed to secure a beachhead in the community and soon installed Capone in new headquarters there at the Hawthorne Inn.

The final siege of Cicero began in the spring of 1924. It was election time. Joseph Klenha, the corrupt incumbent president of the village board, was facing a challenge from a slate of Democratic reformers. To counter the threat of a reform victory, the Klenha machine made an offer that Torrio and Capone could hardly afford to refuse: Ensure a Klenha landslide, the gangsters were told, and Cicero is yours. It was a task tailor-made for Al Capone.

In his detailed account of crime and politics, *Barbarians in Our Midst,* Virgil W. Peterson, director of the Chicago Crime Commission, described the Cicero election as "one of the most disgraceful episodes in American municipal history." Armed with machine guns, Capone mobsters (some two hundred by Kobler's count) "manned the polls. Automobiles filled with gunmen patrolled the streets. Polling places were raided and ballots stolen at gunpoint. Voters were kidnapped and transported to Chicago where they were held captive until after the polls closed." Apprised of the reign of terror, a Cook County judge dispatched over a hundred patrolmen and detectives from Chicago to Cicero, and gun battles between gangsters and police raged through the afternoon. Among the several fatal casualties was Big Al's brother, Frank Capone. President Klenha was handily re-elected. "And Cicero," observed Virgil Peterson, "became known throughout the nation as one of the toughest places in America, a reputation it was to retain for many years."

Capone's stunning conquest of Cicero left little doubt in the minds of rival mobsters that a new and formidable leader had arrived in their midst. From Torrio he had acquired the organizational skills to put together a tightly disciplined army of thugs, hit men, and specialists in assorted vices; and with them—after the retirement of Torrio in 1925— he proceeded to wrest from his rivals a large piece of virtually any racket he fancied.

Directly under Capone on the organizational flow chart was his good friend and business manager, Jake "Greasy Thumb" Guzik. For liaison with the *Unione Siciliane,* there was Frank "The Enforcer" Nitti. His departmental chieftains included, for bootlegging operations, Capone's brother Ralph (nicknamed "Bottles") and his cousin, Charlie Fischetti;

for brothels, Mike de Pike Heitler; and for gambling, Frank Pope. Farther down on the chart were Capone's musclemen: Jim Belcastro, the bomber of breweries; Phil D'Andrea, the sharpshooting bodyguard; and Samuel Hunt, alias "Golf Bag," so-called for the luggage in which he preferred to carry his shotgun. (Golf Bag's first intended victim survived the buckshot, Kobler notes, and was thereafter known as "Hunt's hole in one.") Other torpedoes of importance included Anthony Accardo (alias Joe Batters), Sam Giancana, Paul "The Waiter" Ricca, Murray "The Camel" Humphreys, and Jack "Machine Gun" McGurn, whose real name was DeMora and to whom police over the years attributed no fewer than twenty-two murders.

For the most part, Capone's lieutenants enjoyed an *esprit de corps* unlike that of any other mob in Chicago. There was no place in the organization for men who would not adhere to a code of unfaltering loyalty and rigid discipline. Despite the predilection of some associates for booze and cigars, Capone insisted on keeping his troops in fine fighting shape. In one headquarters spread, at the Hotel Metropole, two rooms were set aside as a gymnasium and equipped with punching bags and rowing machines.

A subsequent command post was established in the Lexington Hotel. Capone occupied a corner suite, presiding at the head of a long mahogany conference table. Framed on the wall behind him were portraits of George Washington, Abraham Lincoln, and Mayor William Hale Thompson. Two floors below, in a maids' changing room, a hinged full-length mirror concealed a secret door leading to an adjacent office building. Capone used it frequently to frustrate those who tried to pry into the pattern of his daily itinerary.

He lived constantly within a shield of armed guards. When he dined in public, the bar of the chosen restaurant would be crowded—in advance—by his trusted henchmen. When he went to the theater, twelve seats were reserved for him and his entourage in the rear of the house, where vigilance was easy. In transit, the custom-built Cadillac was always preceded by a scout car, and followed by a touring car filled with his most proficient marksmen. His headquarters swivel chair had an armor-plate back. He crossed sidewalks and hotel lobbies in a huddle of bodies three deep. Yet for all these precautions, no life insurance company would write him a policy. Capone and his kind had been going to too many funerals, and too many rivals were planning a funeral for Capone.

On the North Side, for example, there was Dion O'Banion, the choir-boy-turned-safecracker, and now ostensibly a florist, who had supplied twenty thousand dollars in wreaths and arrangements for the funeral of the slain Frank Capone. "A most unusual florist," observed Virgil Peterson, for O'Banion "not only furnished flowers ... but also provided the corpses." Chicago police said he was responsible for twenty-five murders. O'Banion detested Capone. Among the choirboy's chief lieutenants was George "Bugs" Moran, whom history remembers not only as the inspiration for a memorable Valentine's greeting from Al Capone, but as the man who first produced and directed murder-by-motorcade, a system whereby, if all went well, the victim was rapidly riddled from a slow procession of passing cars.

Swinging counterclockwise from O'Banion's North Side, one presently arrived on the turf of Roger "The Terrible" Touhy, whose headquarters were in Des Plaines and who had little traffic—or trouble, for that matter—with the mob of Capone. At nine o'clock—west lay the precincts of the aforementioned O'Donnell gang, perennial foes of the South Side Italians. At eight o'clock, in the valley between Cicero and Chicago's own Little Italy, one entered the fiefdom of Terry Druggan and Frankie Lake, pious Irishmen both. Once, hijacking a beer truck parked in front of a Catholic church, Druggan was said to have ordered the bootleggers out of the cab of the truck at gunpoint. "Hats off when you're passing the House of God," said Druggan, "or I'll shoot 'em off."

On the Southwest Side, at seven o'clock, near the site of today's Midway Airport, yet another gang skulked under the leadership of Joe Saltis and Frank McErlane, the latter being regarded by the Illinois Association for Criminal Justice as "the most brutal gunman who ever pulled a trigger in Chicago." Like Bugs Moran, McErlane was an innovator, the first gangster in America to demonstrate the superior firepower of the Thompson submachine gun.

Virtually all these mobs, at one time or another in the 1920's, were aligned against the army of Capone. In fact, there was only one independent organization with which Capone had any strong ties whatsoever, and that was the Sicilian community ruled by the six Genna brothers. Through political connections, the Gennas had obtained a license to process industrial alcohol. They processed it, all right—into bootleg whisky; and soon, under their direction, alky cooking (as Kobler recounts it) "became the cottage industry of Little Italy." The mash was powerful, the denaturing process resulted in a product capable of blinding the consumer, and in a single lot of one hundred confiscated barrels of the liquor, police were said to have found dead rats in every one. For hit men, the Gennas relied on John Scalise and Albert Anselmi, who, in the mistaken belief that garlic in the bloodstream could cause gangrene, anointed all their bullets against the possibility of a slightly misplaced shot.

Thus were the territories staked out and the players positioned when the great Chicago beer wars broke out in the fall of 1924. Sometimes the action was difficult to follow. As Virgil Peterson perceived it, "The lines of battle were constantly shifting." No matter. The florists and undertakers had never had it so good.

O'Banion was the first to go. There had been a confrontation with Torrio over sharing profits from saloons. There had been much bad blood between North Siders and the Gennas. O'Banion had ordered the hijacking of one of the Gennas' alky trucks. He had told the Sicilians to go to hell, and had boasted of outwitting Johnny Torrio. At noon on November 10, 1924, three men (two later identified as Scalise and Anselmi) called at O'Banion's flower shop while the Irishman was clipping chrysanthemum stems. Six shots were fired. None were misplaced.

On January 12, outside a restaurant at State and Fifty-fifth streets, a limousine with Hymie Weiss and Bugs Moran at the curbside windows pulled abreast of a parked vehicle. A moment earlier, Al Capone had stepped from that vehicle into the restaurant. Weiss and Moran raked the car with buckshot, wounding Al's chauffeur. The unscathed Capone later surveyed the damage, then put in a call to General Motors with specifications for a bulletproof Cadillac.

It was Torrio's turn twelve days later. Standing on the sidewalk near his apartment, he was hit in the jaw, the right arm, and the groin by buckshot and bullets from a passing limousine. At Jackson Park Hospital, Capone came and sat at his bedside, weeping. But Torrio was tough. He survived, and eagerly accepted a sentence of nine months in the Lake County Jail. It was safe there. Having served his time, he announced that he would retire and leave everything to Capone. Then he departed for Italy.

Meanwhile, in May of 1925, the O'Banionites had resumed their reprisals. They struck down Angelo Genna. He was buried in unconsecrated ground at Mt. Carmel Cemetery, within shotgun range of the grave of Dion O'Banion. Capone may have sent flowers, but he shed no tears. The lines had been shifting. He wanted control of the Gennas' alky industry. Within six weeks, two more Gennas, Michael and Anthony, were ambushed and killed. Scalise and Anselmi defected to Capone's camp. Both were captured by the police and charged with murder. There were many suspects, but no convictions.

Then the lines shifted again, to Cicero and the West Side. In the first four months of 1926, police recorded twenty-nine gangland slayings. Among the last of that group to die was the assistant state's attorney, William McSwiggin. He was cut down by gunfire in front of the Red Pony Inn, not far from Capone's Cicero command post. Capone went into hiding for three months.

It was a relatively quiet summer—a few desultory killings here and there, a gun battle on Michigan Avenue. Capone reappeared in his old haunts. On September 20 he lunched at a restaurant next door to the Hawthorne Inn. Suddenly there was a burst of machine-gun fire. Capone dove for the floor. Outside, on Twenty-second Street, an eleven-car motorcade slowly passed in review. Guns protruded from every window. The inn, the restaurant, storefronts on either side were raked by tommy guns, shotguns, and revolvers. Slugs ripped through twenty-five autos parked at the curb, and the sidewalk glittered with shards of broken glass. As the eleventh car sped away, up from the floor rose Capone, unhurt, but paler than the talc on his otherwise ruddy jowls. There is no record of what he was thinking then, but very possibly he was thinking only—and darkly—of Hymie Weiss and Bugs Moran.

And within a month, Weiss was dead, shot down from ambush in the shadow of Holy Name Cathedral, near the flower shop where O'Banion had died barely two years before. "It's a real goddamn crazy place," New Yorker Lucky Luciano was reported to have said of Chicago after a visit. "Nobody's safe in the streets."

Throughout all the vicious years, Al Capone no doubt held himself in high personal esteem. After all, he was merely providing services, the supply of which, like his brothel whores, could never quite meet the demand. "I give the public what the public wants," he told a reporter during one of his many "frank" interviews. "I've given people the light pleasures . . . and all I get is abuse."

Surprisingly, a large segment of the public seemed to share Capone's view of himself as the pleasurable benefactor. Though on one day Chicagoans might read with horror of the latest atrocity linked to his mob, on the next they might cheer his waving arrival at Charlestown Racetrack. In Evanston once, during a Northwestern University football game, an entire troop of Boy Scouts startled the crowd with the rousing cry "Yea, Al!" (He had bought them their tickets.) His fan mail was heavy. By some accounts, he was Chicago's greatest philanthropist. At the pit of the Depression, he was said to have financed a South Side soup kitchen dispensing 20,000 free meals a week. People liked to remember things like that—and liked to forget just exactly what it was the big fellow did to afford such beneficence.

But not everyone was impressed by the good-guy image. On a visit with his wife to Los Angeles, his presence came to the attention of the police; they gave him twenty-four hours to clear out of town. In Miami he was *persona nongrata* until he discovered that the mayor was a realtor. So Capone bought a house, a fourteen-room villa on Palm Island in Biscayne Bay. He promptly improved it with an encircling wall of concrete blocks and a thick, oaken portcullis. Capone liked to swim and fish and bask in the sun; the sun helped him forget all the troubles of Chicago. In fact, he was doing just that on February 14, 1929. It was Valentine's Day.

The infamous massacre of seven Bugs Moran associates in a warehouse on Chicago's North Clark Street bears no detailed recounting here (having been the focus of numerous books and movies), except to note that quite by accident Moran was not among the machine-gunned victims, and that the triggermen were the garlic anointers, Scalise and Anselmi. For these two thugs, it should further be noted, there was a strange reward. On May 7, at the Hawthorne Inn, Capone assembled a roomful of mobsters ostensibly to honor Scalise and Anselmi for their recent deeds. It was a jovial occasion until, shortly after midnight, Capone announced to the guests of honor that he was privy to their part in a budding conspiracy to dethrone him. Having passed sentence on the Sicilians, Capone signaled his bodyguards to bind and gag them; and then, according to witnesses, the good guy who gave people so many simple pleasures proceeded to club his lieutenants to death with a baseball bat.

The following week Capone was in Atlantic City, attending a business convention. Guzik and Nitti flanked him at the conference table. Joe Saltis was there, and Frankie McErlane. There was "Boo Boo" Hoff from Philadelphia. From New York there were Lucky Luciano, Frank Costello, and Dutch Schultz. Torrio had returned from Italy to preside as the elder statesman. The purpose of the conference was peace. There was to be an end to the killing. The nation henceforth was to be redistricted; the *Unione Siciliane* was to be reorganized, and the Chicagoans were to stop this petty quarreling among themselves and merge under the leadership of Capone. Big Al was delighted, except for one catch: Bugs Moran had declined an invitation to the meeting. Back in Chicago, Moran would still be after him. Back in Chicago, a dozen Sicilian gunmen were awaiting their chance to avenge the clubbing of Scalise and Anselmi.

And the risks were by no means limited to Chicago. According to crime reporter Edward Dean Sullivan, who wrote the following in 1930, "The effort to 'get' Capone became virtually nationwide. Killers in every town that Capone might reach were assigned to the job.... When he got to Philadelphia from Atlantic City, having failed to arrange a peace with the Moran outfit on any terms, Capone, charged with having a concealed weapon, was soon in prison and untroubled."

Released from Eastern Penitentiary in March, 1930, Capone returned to Chicago with a bodyguard, wrote Sullivan, "the size of which indicated his state of mind." But the climate of the windy city was such that "he left for Florida within ten days and as this is written, six months later, he has just returned to Chicago. Twenty of his enemies died in his absence."

Sullivan further noted that Capone's most frequently repeated statement was: "We don't want no trouble." As it turned out, he was about to get a large measure of trouble. By 1931 the troubles had piled up on two fronts. There were frequent raids against the Capone breweries and distilleries; G-men with sledgehammers were wrecking the old alky stills and pouring the contraband booze into the gutters. Meanwhile, as if this were not enough for Capone to contend with, agents of the Internal Revenue Service began making discreet inquiries about town as to why, after so many extravagant years of big spending, he had never once filed a tax return. In a kind of dress rehearsal for their biggest act, the IRS agents won tax-evasion indictments against Ralph Capone and Frank Nitti. Then Big Al himself was charged with twenty-two counts of failing to render unto Uncle Sam what was Uncle Sam's; and in October, 1931, in federal court, he was found guilty by jury trial, fined fifty thousand dollars, and sentenced to eleven years in prison. Capone was stunned. It would never have turned out like this in the good old days.

But the good old days were long gone. Pending an appeal, Capone was held in the Cook County Jail, where the amenable warden David Moneypenny provided his celebrated prisoner with all the comforts of home, including unlimited visitations by the likes of Jake Guzik and Murray Humphreys and Lucky Luciano and Dutch Schultz. For all such audiences, Capone insisted on absolute privacy; and Moneypenny obliged by allowing Big Al to use the most secure suite in the entire jail—the death chamber.

The appeal was denied. In the spring of 1932, handcuffed to a fellow prisoner, Capone was transferred to the federal penitentiary at Atlanta, Georgia. There he was given the identifying number 40,822 and assigned to work eight hours daily cobbling shoes. For the most part he stayed out of trouble; but his old reputation belied to authorities his new good behavior. In the retributive penal spirit of the times, he was considered an "incorrigible." And by 1934 the government had a special place for people like that. They called it Alcatraz.

Capone was among the first of the incorrigibles confined on the skullcap rock in San Francisco Bay. His new number was 85. He was assigned to Cellblock B and the laundry-room detail. He was conceded no favors. Feisty young inmates, looking for ways to enhance their own reputations for toughness, insulted Capone to his face. They called him "wop with the mop." A thug from Texas shoved a pair of barber's scissors into his back. He was jumped in a hallway and almost strangled before he managed to flatten his assailant. Capone somehow endured. But his health was failing. The syphilis which had gone so long untreated was beginning to erode his central nervous system. There were periods when lucidity escaped him. He could respond to treatment, but the disease was too advanced to hope for a cure.

In January, 1939 (with time off the original sentence for good behavior and working credits), Capone left Alcatraz for the less dismal precincts of a federal correctional institution near Los Angeles; and in November, at Lewisburg, Pennsylvania, he was released into the custody of his wife Mae and brother Ralph. In Chicago, according to Kobler, "reporters asked Jake Guzik if Capone was likely to return and take command again." Whereupon Guzik "replied in language harsher than he intended, for his loyalty had never wavered." Al, said Guzik, was "nutty as a fruitcake."

Capone lingered on in Miami, his mind confused, his sleep haunted by dreams of assassins. Finally, in January, 1947, he suffered a brain hemorrhage. The hemorrhage was soon followed by pneumonia. The body was taken to Chicago for burial. The funeral was modest; the Church had forbidden a requiem mass.

There are those who say that Scarface Al Capone bequeathed to America a legacy of corruption that prevails to this day. In 1963 Senator John L. McClellan's Subcommittee on Investigations elicited from Chicago police superintendent Orlando Wilson a remarkable statistic. Since 1919, Wilson reported, there had been 976 gangland murders in his city, but only two of the killers had ever been convicted. Wilson's choice of 1919, not being round numbered, may have seemed arbitrary to most of his listeners; but to seasoned observers of organized crime it was clearly Chicago's watershed year. For in 1919 a young man from New York had come to Chicago—an unsingular happenstance at the time, yet one that seems to have made all the difference ever since.

13

Race, Ethnicity, and Real Estate Appraisal

KENNETH T. JACKSON

• *Relentlessly, almost unconsciously, the United States has become the world's first suburban nation. Since 1950, millions of acres of brush, shrub oak, pine, and prairie have given way to crabgrass and concrete, and the suburban total of 105 million now represents the largest single element of the national population. Indeed, suburbia has become the most quintessential aesthetic achievement of the United States and has come to symbolize the fullest, most unadulterated embodiment of the American present, a manifestation of some of the most fundamental characteristics of modern society, among them conspicuous consumption, a reliance upon the private automobile, upward mobility, the breakdown of the extended family into nuclear units, the widening division between work and leisure, and a tendency toward racial and economic exclusiveness.*

Despite certain common human attitudes about "home," any residential comparison of the United States with the rest of the world will reveal that America is unusual in terms of its preference for the free-standing house on its own plot, its high degree of home ownership (about 65 percent of all households in 1994), its use of wood as the predominant building material, and its pattern of wealthy suburbs and poor inner-city neighborhoods.

Reprinted from *Journal of Urban History*, August 1980, © Sage Publications, Beverly Hills, by permission of the publisher.

AUTHOR'S NOTE: I wish to express my appreciation to Herbert J. Gans, Robert Kolodny, Peter Marcuse, William E. Leuchtenburg, and John A. Garraty of Columbia University; to Joseph B. Howerton, Jerry N. Hess, and Jerome Finster of the National Archives; to Frederick J. Eggers, Mary A. Grey, and William A. Rolfe of the Department of Housing and Urban Development; to Joel A. Tarr of Carnegie-Mellon University; to John Modell of the University of Minnesota; to Mark Gelfand of Boston College; to Joan Gilbert of Yale University; and to Margaret Kurth Weinberg of the Connecticut Governor's Office.

Why have the metropolitan areas of the United States sub-
urbanized so quickly? One might think of the plentiful land
around most cities, of the relative wealth of the nation, of the
heterogeneity of the American people, of the cheap energy and
its inducement to decentralization, of the attractiveness of the
domestic ideal, and of rapid technological advances like street-
cars and automobiles which made long-distance commuting
feasible. But government has not been an impartial observer
in the contest between cities and their suburbs. Federally fi-
nanced interstate highways have undermined the locational
advantages of inner-city neighborhoods, while income-tax de-
ductions have encouraged families to buy houses rather than
rent apartments. In the following essay, Professor Kenneth T.
Jackson of Columbia University focuses on the much-praised
mortgage policies of Uncle Sam and points out the extraor-
dinarily flagrant discrimination that was built into them from
the beginning.

If a healthy race is to be reared, it can be reared only in healthy
homes; if infant mortality is to be reduced and tuberculosis to
be stamped out, the first essential is the improvement of housing
conditions; if drink and crime are to be successfully combated,
decent sanitary houses must be provided. If "unrest" is to be
converted into contentment, the provision of good houses may
prove one of the most potent agents in that conversion.

King George V, 1919

A nation of homeowners, of people who own a real share in their
own land, is unconquerable.

President Franklin D. Roosevelt, 1933

The appeal of low-density living for more than a century in the United
States and across regional, class, and ethnic lines has led some observers
to regard it as natural and inevitable, a trend "that no amount of government interference can reverse." Or, as a senior Federal Housing Administration (FHA) official told the 1939 convention of the American
Institute of Planners: "Decentralization is taking place. It is not a policy,
it is a reality—and it is as impossible for us to change this trend as it is to
change the desire of birds to migrate to a more suitable location."

Despite such protestations, there are many ways in which government
largesse can affect where people live. For example, the federal tax code

encourages businesses to abandon old structures before their useful life is at an end by permitting greater tax benefits for new construction than for the improvement of existing buildings. Thus, the government subsidizes an acceleration in the rate at which economic activity is dispersed to new locations. Similarly, Roger Lotchin has recently begun important research on the importance of defense spending to the growth of Sunbelt cities since 1920. Military expenditures have meanwhile worked to the detriment of other areas. Estimates were common in the late 1970s that Washington was annually collecting between $6 billion and $11 billion more than it was returning to the New York metropolitan area.

On the urban-suburban level, the potential for federal influence is also enormous. For example, the Federal Highway Act of 1916 and the Interstate Highway Act of 1956 moved the government toward a transportation policy emphasizing and benefiting the road, the truck, and the private motor car. In conjunction with cheap fuel and mass-produced automobiles, the urban expressways led to lower marginal transport costs and greatly stimulated deconcentration. Equally important to most families is the incentive to detached-home living provided by the deduction of mortgage interest and real estate taxes from their gross income. Even the reimbursement formulas for water line and sewer construction have had an impact on the spatial patterns of metropolitan areas.

The purpose of this article, which is part of a much larger analysis of the process of suburbanization in the United States between 1815 and 1980, is to examine the impact of two innovations of the New Deal on the older, industrial cities of the nation.

THE HOME OWNERS LOAN CORPORATION

On April 13, 1933, President Roosevelt urged the House and the Senate to pass a law that would (1) protect small homeowners from foreclosure, (2) relieve them of part of the burden of excessive interest and principal payments incurred during a period of higher values and higher earning power, and (3) declare that it was national policy to protect home ownership. The measure received bipartisan support. As Republican Congressman Rich of Pennsylvania, a banker himself, remarked during the floor debate:

I am opposed to the Government in business, but here is where I am going to do a little talking for the Government in business, because if aid is going to be extended to these owners of small homes, the Government will have to get into this business of trying to save their homes. The banker dares not loan for fear the depositor will draw out his deposit; then he must close his bank or the Comptroller of the Currency will close it for him.

The resulting Home Owners Loan Corporation (HOLC), signed into law by the President on June 13, 1933, was designed to serve urban needs; the Emergency Farm Mortgage Act, passed almost a month earlier, was intended to reduce rural foreclosure.

The HOLC replaced the unworkable direct loan provisions of the Hoover administration's Federal Home Loan Bank Act and refinanced tens of thousands of mortgages in danger of default or foreclosure. It even granted loans at low interest rates to permit owners to recover homes lost through forced sale. Between July 1933 and June 1935 alone, the HOLC supplied more than $3 billion for over a million mortgages, or loans for one-tenth of all owner-occupied, nonfarm residences in the United States. Although applications varied widely by state—in Mississippi, 99 percent of the eligible owner-occupants applied for loans while in Maine only 18 percent did so—nationally about 40 percent of eligible Americans sought HOLC assistance.

The HOLC is important to housing history because it introduced, perfected, and proved in practice the feasibility of the long-term, self-amortizing mortgage with uniform payments spread over the whole life of the debt. Prior to the 1930s, the typical length of a mortgage was between 5 and 10 years, and the loan itself was not paid off when the final settlement was due. Thus, the homeowner was periodically at the mercy of the arbitrary and unpredictable forces in the money market. When money was easy, renewal every five or seven years was no problem. But if a mortgage expired at a time when money was tight, it might be impossible for the homeowner to secure a renewal, and foreclosure would ensue. Under the HOLC program, the loans were fully amortized, and the repayment period was extended to about 20 years.

Aside from the large number of mortgages which it helped to refinance on a long-term, low-interest basis, the HOLC systematized appraisal methods across the nation. Because it was dealing with problem mortgages—in some states over 40 percent of all HOLC loans were foreclosed even after refinancing—the HOLC had to make predictions and assumptions regarding the useful or productive life of housing it financed. Unlike refrigerators or shoes, dwellings were expected to be durable—how durable was the purpose of the investigation.

With care and extraordinary attention to detail, HOLC appraisers divided cities into neighborhoods and developed elaborate questionnaires relating to the occupation, income, and ethnicity of the inhabitants and the age, type of construction, price range, sales demand, and general state of repair of the housing stock. The element of novelty did not lie in the appraisal requirement itself—that had long been standard real estate practice. Rather, it lay in the creation of a formal and uniform system of appraisal, reduced to writing, structured in defined procedures, and implemented by individuals only after intensive training. The ultimate aim was that one appraiser's judgment of value would have meaning to an investor located somewhere else. In evaluating such efforts, the distinguished economist C. Lowell Harriss has credited the HOLC training and evaluation procedures "with having helped raise the general level of American real estate appraisal methods." A less favorable judgment would be that the HOLC initiated the practice of "redlining."

This occurred because HOLC devised a rating system which undervalued neighborhoods that were dense, mixed, or aging. Four categories of quality—imaginatively entitled First, Second, Third, and Fourth, with corresponding code letters of A, B, C, and D and colors of green, blue, yellow, and red—were established. The First grade (also A and green) areas were described as new, homogeneous, and "in demand as residential locations in good times and bad." Homogeneous meant "American business and professional men"; Jewish neighborhoods or even those with an "infiltration of Jews" could not possibly be considered "Best."

The Second security grade (blue) went to "still desirable" areas that had "reached their peak," but were expected to remain stable for many years. The Third grade (yellow) or "C" neighborhoods were usually described as "definitely declining," while the Fourth grade (red) or "D" neighborhoods were defined as areas "in which things taking place in C areas have already happened."

The HOLC's assumptions about urban neighborhoods were based on both an ecological conception of change and a socioeconomic one. Adopting a dynamic view of the city and assuming that change was inevitable, its appraisers accepted as given the proposition that the natural tendency of any area was to decline—in part because of the increasing age and obsolescence of the physical structures and in part because of the filtering down of the housing stock to families of lower income and different ethnicity. Thus physical deterioration was both a cause and an effect of population change, and HOLC officials made no real attempt to sort them out. They were part and parcel of the same process. Thus, black neighborhoods were invariably rated as Fourth grade, but so were any areas characterized by poor maintenance or vandalism. Similarly, those "definitely declining" sections that were marked Third grade or yellow received such a low rating in part because of age and in part because they were "within such a low price or rent range as to attract an undesirable element."

The HOLC did not initiate the idea of considering race and ethnicity in real estate appraising. As Calvin Bradford has demonstrated, models developed at the University of Chicago in the 1920s and early 1930s by Homer Hoyt and Robert Park became the dominant explanation of neighborhood change. They suggested that different groups of people "infiltrated" or "invaded" territory held by others through a process of competition. These interpretations were then adopted by prominent appraising texts, such as Frederick Babcock's *The Valuation of Real Estate* (1932) and *McMichael's Appraising Manual* (1931). Both advised appraisers to pay particular attention to "undesirable" or "least desirable" elements and suggested that the influx of certain ethnic groups was likely to precipitate price declines.

The HOLC simply applied these notions of ethnic and racial worth to real estate appraising on an unprecedented scale. With the assistance of local realtors and banks, it assigned one of its four ratings to every block in every city. The resulting information was then translated into the appropriate color and duly recorded on secret "Residential Security Maps" in local HOLC offices. The maps themselves were placed in elaborate "City Survey Files," which consisted of reports, questionnaires, and workpapers relating to current and future values of real estate.

Because the two federal agencies under analysis here did not normally report data on anything other than a county basis, the St. Louis area was selected as a case study. There, the city and country were legally separated in 1876 so that there was no alternative to individual reporting. In addition, an even older industrial city, Newark, New Jersey, was selected because of the availability of an unusual FHA study.

The residential security map for the St. Louis area in 1937 gave the highest ratings to the newer, affluent suburbs that were strung out along curvilinear streets well away from the problems of the city. Three years later, in 1940, the advantage of the periphery over the center was even more marked. In both evaluations, the top of the scale was dominated by Ladue, a largely undeveloped section of high, rolling land, heavily wooded estates, and dozens of houses in the $20,000 to $50,000 range. In 1940, HOLC appraisers noted approvingly that the area was "highly restricted" and occupied by "capitalists and other wealthy families." Reportedly not the home of "a single foreigner or Negro," Ladue received an "A" rating. Other affluent suburbs like Clayton and University City were also marked with green and blue on the 1937 and 1940 maps, indicating that they, too, were characterized by attractive homes on well-maintained plots and that the appraisers felt confident about mortgages insured there. And well they might have been; in University City almost 40 percent of the homes had been valued at more than $15,000 in 1930, while in Clayton the comparable figure was an astounding 72.3 percent (see Table 1).

At the other end of the scale in St. Louis County were the rare Fourth grade areas. A few such neighborhoods were occupied by white laborers, such as "Ridgeview" in Kirkwood, where the garagelike shacks typically cost less than $1,500. But the "D" regions in the county were usually black. One such place in 1937 was Lincoln Terrace, a small enclave of four- and five-room bungalows built about 1927. Originally intended for middle-class white families, the venture was unsuccessful, and the district quickly developed into a black neighborhood. But even though the homes were relatively new and of good quality, the HOLC gave the section (D–12 in 1937, D–8 in 1940) the lowest possible grade, asserting that the houses had "little or no value today, having suffered a tremendous decline in values due to the colored element now controlling the district."

In contrast to the gently rolling terrain and sparse settlement of St. Louis County, the city had proportionately many more Third and

TABLE I

Home Values, HOLC Ratings, and Population Growth in Selected St. Louis Area Communities.

| Community | Percentage of Homes Owner-Occupied in 1930 | Value of Owned Homes, 1930, (in thousands of dollars) | | | | Predominant HOLC Rating in 1940 | Population in 1940 | Population in 1970 |
		Below 3	3–7½	7½–15	Above 15			
St. Louis City	31.6%	11.6%	49.6%	30.1%	7.7%	C	816,048	622,236
University City	50.1	4.8	19.9	23.2	37.5	A	33,023	46,309
Webster Groves	78.5	7.3	29.5	39.2	23.2	A	18,394	27,455
Maplewood	56.3	7.0	60.9	28.2	12.0	C	12,875	12,785
Kirkwood	68.3	13.0	41.9	32.1	11.2	—	12,132	31,769
Richmond Heights	57.2	6.5	28.3	50.6	13.8	B	12,802	13,802
Clayton	49.8	2.5	7.5	17.4	72.3	A	13,069	16,222
Ferguson	72.7	9.7	52.2	29.6	7.4	B	5,724	28,759
Brentwood	66.3	14.6	70.5	13.2	1.5	C	4,383	11,248
Ladue	84.6	1.2	4.8	14.9	79.1	A	3,981	10,591

SOURCE: 1930 United States Census Tracts for St. Louis; HOLC City Survey Files in National Archives, and National Resources Committee, *Regional Planning, Part II—St. Louis Region* (Washington: Government Printing Office, 1936), p. 52.

Fourth grade neighborhoods, and more than twice as many renters as homeowners. Virtually all the residential sections along the Mississippi River or adjacent to the central business district received the lowest two ratings. This harsh judgment was in part a reflection of their badly deteriorated physical character. Just a few years earlier, the City Plan Commission of St. Louis had made a survey of 44 acres surrounding the business section. Only about 40 percent of the 8,447 living units had indoor toilets, and the tuberculosis morbidity rate was three times that of the city as a whole. As the St. Louis Regional Planning report pessimistically concluded in 1936:

> The older residential districts which are depreciating in value and in character constitute one of the most serious problems in this region. They can never be absorbed by commercial and industrial uses. Even if owners wished to build new homes within them, it would be inadvisable because of the present character of the districts.

But the HOLC appraisers marked other inner-city areas down not because of the true slum conditions but because of negative attitudes toward city living in general. The evaluation of a white, working-class neighborhood near Fairgrounds Park was typical. According to the description, "Lots are small, houses are only slightly set back from the sidewalks, and there is a general appearance of congestion." Although an urban individual might have found this collection of cottages and abundant shade trees rather charming, the HOLC thought otherwise: "Age of properties, general mixture of type, proximity to industrial section on northeast and much less desirable areas to the south make this a good fourth grade area."

As was the case in every city, any Afro-American presence was a source of substantial concern to the HOLC. In a confidential and generally pessimistic 1941 survey of the economic and real estate prospects of the St. Louis metropolitan area, the Federal Home Loan Bank Board (the parent agency of HOLC) repeatedly commented on the "rapidly increasing Negro population" and the resulting "problem in the maintenance of real estate values." The officials evinced a keen interest in the movement of black families and included maps of the density of Negro settlement with every analysis. Not surprisingly, even those neighborhoods with small proportions of black inhabitants were typically rated "D," or hazardous.

Like St. Louis, Newark has long symbolized the most extreme features of the urban crisis. In that troubled city, federal appraisers took note in the 1930s of the high tax rate, the heavy relief load, the per-capita bonded debt, and the "strong tendency for years for people of larger incomes to move their homes outside the city." The 1939 Newark area residential security map did not designate a single neighborhood in that city of more than 400,000 as worthy of an "A" rating. "High class Jewish" sections like Weequahic and Clinton Hill, as well as Gentile areas like Vailsburg and Forest Hill all received "B" or the Second grade. Typical Newark neighborhoods were rated even lower. The well-maintained and attractive working class sections of Roseville, Woodside, and East Vailsburg were given Third grade or "C" ratings; the remainder of the city, including immigrant Iron-bound and every black neighborhood, was written off as "hazardous."

Immediately adjacent to Newark is New Jersey's Hudson County, which is among the half-dozen most densely settle and ethnically diverse political jurisdictions in the United States. Predictably, HOLC appraisers had decided by 1940 that Hudson County was a lost cause. In the communities of Bayonne, Hoboken, Secaucus, Kearny, Union City, Weehawken, Harrison, and Jersey City, taken together, they designated only two very small "B" areas and no "A" sections.

The HOLC insisted that "there is no implication that good mortgages do not exist or cannot be made in Third and Fourth grade areas." And, there is some evidence to indicate that HOLC did in fact make the majority of its obligations in "definitely declining" or "hazardous" neighborhoods. This seeming liberality was actually good business because the residents of poorer sections generally maintained a better pay back record than did their more affluent cousins. As the Federal Home Loan Bank Board explained:

> The rate of foreclosure per 1000 non-farm dwellings during 1939 was greater in St. Louis County than in St. Louis City by about 2½ to 1. A partial explanation or causation of this situation is the fact that County properties consist of a greater proportion of units in the higher priced brackets.

The damage caused by the HOLC came not through its own actions, but through the influence of its appraisal system on the financial decision of other institutions. During the late 1930s, the Federal Home Loan Bank Board circulated questionnaires to banks asking about their mortgage practices. Those returned by savings and loan associations and banks in Essex County (Newark), New Jersey, indicated a clear relationship between public and private redlining practices. One specific question asked: "What are the most desirable lending areas?" The answers were often "A and B" or "Blue" or "FHA only." Similarly, to the inquiry, "Are there any areas in which loans will not be made?" the responses included, "Red and most yellow," "C and D," "Newark," "Not in red," and "D areas." Obviously, private banking institutions were privy to and influenced by the government's Residential Security Maps.

THE FEDERAL HOUSING ADMINISTRATION

Direct, large-scale Washington intervention in the American housing market dates from the adoption of the National Housing Act on June 27, 1934. Although intended "to encourage improvement in housing standards and conditions, to facilitate sound home financing on reasonable terms, and to exert a stabilizing influence on the mortgage market," the primary purpose of the legislation was the alleviation of unemployment in the construction industry. As the Federal Emergency Relief Administrator testified before the House Banking and Currency Committee on May 18, 1934:

> The building trades in America represent by all odds the largest single unit of our unemployment. Probably more than one-third of all the unemployed are identified, directly and indirectly, with the building trades.... Now, a purpose of this bill, a fundamental purpose of this bill, is an effort to get the people back to work.

Between 1934 and 1968, the FHA had a remarkable record of accomplishment. Essentially, it insured long-term mortgage loans made by private lenders for home construction and sale. To this end, it collected premiums, set up reserves for losses, and in the event of a default on a mortgage, indemnified the lender. It did not build houses or lend money. Instead, it induced leaders who had money to invest it in residential mortgages by insuring them against loss on such investments, with the full weight of the U.S. Treasury behind the contract. And it revolutionized the home finance industry in the following ways.

First, before FHA began operations, first mortgages typically were limited to one-half or two-thirds of the appraised value of the property. During the 1920s, for example, savings and loan associations held one-half of America's outstanding mortgage debt. Those mortgages averaged 58 percent of estimated property value. Thus, prospective homebuyers needed a down payment of at least 30 percent to close a deal. By contrast, the fraction of the collateral that the lender was able to lend for a FHA-secured loan about 93 percent. Thus, large down payments were unnecessary.

Second, continuing a trend begun by the HOLC, the FHA extended the repayment period for its guaranteed mortgages to 25 or 30 years and insisted that all loans be fully amortized. The effect was to reduce both the average monthly payment and the national rate of mortgage foreclosure. The latter declined from 250,000 nonfarm units in 1932 to only 18,000 in 1951.

Third, FHA established minimum standards for home construction that became almost universal in the industry. These regulations were not intended to make any particular structure fault-free, or even to assure the owner's satisfaction with the purchase. But they were designed to assure with at least statistical accuracy that the dwelling would be free of gross structural or mechanical deficiencies. Although there was nothing innovative in considering the quality of a house in relation to the debt placed against it, two features of the system were new; first, that the standards were objective, uniform, and in writing; second, that they were to be enforced by actual, on-site inspection—prior to insurance commitment in the case of an existing property and at various fixed stages in the course of construction in the case of new housing. Since World War II, the largest private contractors have built all their new houses to meet FHA standards, even though financing has often been arranged without FHA aid. This has occurred because many potential purchasers will not consider a home that cannot get FHA approval.

Fourth, in the 1920s, the interest rate for first mortgages averaged between 6 and 8 percent. If a second mortgage was necessary, as it usually was for families of moderate incomes, the purchaser could obtain one by paying a discount to the lender, a higher interest rate on the loan, and perhaps a commission to a broker. Together, these charges added about 15 percent to the purchase price. Under the FHA and Veterans Administration (VA) programs, by contrast, there was very little risk to the banker if a loan turned sour. Reflecting this government guarantee, interest rates fell by two or three percentage points.

These four changes substantially increased the number of American families who could reasonably expect to purchase homes. By the end of 1972, FHA had helped nearly 11 million families to own houses and another 22 million families to improve their properties. It had also insured 1.8 million dwellings in multiunit projects. And in those same years between 1934 and 1972, the percentage of American families living in owner-occupied dwellings rose from 44 percent to 63 percent.

Quite simply, it often became cheaper to buy than to rent. Long Island builder Martin Winter recently recalled that in the early 1950s, families living in the Kew Gardens section of Queens were paying almost $100 per month for small two-bedroom apartments. For less money they could, and often did, move to the new Levittown-type developments springing up along the highways from the city. Even the working classes could aspire to home ownership. As one person who left New York for suburban Dumont, New Jersey, remembered: "We had been paying $50 a month rent, and here we come up and live for $29 a month. That paid everything—taxes, principal, insurance on your mortgage, and interest." Not surprisingly, the middle-class suburban family with the new house and the long-term, fixed-rate FHA-insured mortgage became a symbol, and perhaps a stereotype, of "the American way of life."

Unfortunately, the corrollary to this achievement was the fact that FHA programs hastened the decay of inner-city neighborhoods by stripping them of much of the middle-class constituency. This occurred for two reasons. First, although the legislation nowhere mentioned an antiurban bias, it favored the construction of single-family and discouraged construction of multifamily projects through unpopular terms. Historically, single-family housing programs have been the heart of FHA's insured loan activities. Between 1941 and 1950, FHA-insured single-family starts exceeded FHA multifamily starts by a ratio of almost four to one (see Table 2). In the next decade, the margin exceeded seven to one. Even in 1971, when FHA insured the largest number of multifamily units in its history, single-family houses were more numerous by 27 percent.

Similarly, loans for the repair of existing structures were small and for short duration, which meant that a family could more easily purchase a new home than modernize an old one. Finally, the only part of the 1934 act relating to low-income families was the embryonic authorization for mortgage insurance with respect to rental housing in regulated projects of public bodies or limited dividend corporations. Almost nothing was insured until 1938, and even thereafter, the total insurance for rental housing exceeded $1 billion only once between 1934 and 1962.

The second and more important variety of suburban, middle-class favoritism had to do with the so-called unbiased professional estimate that was a prerequisite for any loan guarantee. This mandatory appraisal included a rating of the property itself, a rating of the mortgagor or borrower, and a rating of the neighborhood. The lower the valuation placed on properties, the less government risk and the less generous the aid to the potential buyers (and sellers). The purpose of the neighborhood evaluation was "to determine the degree of mortgage risk introduced in a mortgage insurance transaction because of the location of the property at a specific site." And unlike the HOLC, which used an essentially similar procedure, the FHA allowed personal and agency bias in favor of all-white subdivisions in the suburbs to affect the kinds of loans it guaranteed—or, equally important, refused to guarantee. In this way the bureaucracy influenced the character of housing at least as much as the 1934 enabling legislation did.

The FHA was quite precise in teaching its underwriters how to measure the quality of residential area. Eight criteria were established (the numbers in parentheses reflect the percentage weight given to each):

(1) relative economic stability (40 percent)
(2) protection from adverse influences (20 percent)
(3) freedom from special hazards (5 percent)
(4) adequacy of civic, social, and commercial centers (5 percent)

TABLE 2

New Housing Starts in the United States, 1935–1968
(in thousands)

Year	Total Starts	FHA Starts	VA Starts	Public Housing
1935	216	14	0	5
1936	304	49	0	15
1937	332	60	0	4
1938	399	119	0	7
1939	458	158	0	57
1940	530	180	0	73
1941	619	220	0	87
1942	301	166	0	55
1943	184	146	0	7
1944	139	93	NA	3
1945	325	41	9	1
1946	1015	69	92	8
1947	1265	229	160	3
1948	1344	294	71	18
1949	1430	364	91	36
1950	1408	487	191	44
1951	1420	264	149	71
1952	1446	280	141	59
1953	1402	252	157	36
1954	1532	276	307	19
1955	1627	277	393	20
1956	1325	192	271	24
1957	1175	168	128	49
1958	1314	295	102	68
1959	1495	332	109	37
1960	1230	261	75	44
1961	1285	244	83	52
1962	1439	259	78	30
1963	1582	221	71	32
1964	1502	205	59	32
1965	1451	196	49	37
1966	1142	158	37	31
1967	1268	180	52	30
1968	1484	220	56	38

SOURCE: U.S. Bureau of the Census, *Housing Construction Statistics, 1889–1964* (Washington: GPO, 1966), TABLE A-2; and U.S. Department of Housing and Urban Development, *HUD Trends: Annual Summary* (Washington: HUD, 1970).

    (5) adequacy of transportation (10 percent)
    (6) sufficiency of utilities and conveniences (5 percent)
    (7) level of taxes and special assessments (5 percent)
    (8) appeal (10 percent).

Although FHA directives insisted that no project should be insured that involved a high degree of risk with regard to any of the eight categories, "economic stability" and "protection from adverse influences" together counted for more than the other six combined. Both were interpreted in ways that were prejudicial against heterogeneous environments. The 1939 *Underwriting Manual* taught that "crowded neighborhoods lessen desirability" and "older properties in a neighborhood have a tendency to accelerate the transition to lower class occupancy." Smoke and odor were considered "adverse influences," and appraisers were told to look carefully for any "inferior and non-productive characteristics of the areas surrounding the site."

Obviously, prospective buyers could avoid many of these so-called undesirable features by locating in peripheral sections. In 1939, the Washington headquarters asked each of the 50-odd regional FHA offices to send in the plans for six "typical American houses." The photographs and dimensions were then used for a National Archives exhibit. An analysis of the submissions clearly indicates that the ideal home was a bungalow or a colonial on an ample lot with a driveway and a garage.

In an attempt to standardize such ideal homes, FHA set up minimum requirements for lot size, for setback from the street, for separation from adjacent structures, and even for the width of the house itself. While such requirements did provide air and light for new structures, they effectively eliminated whole sections of cities, such as the traditional 16-foot-wide row houses of Baltimore, Philadelphia, and New York from eligibility for loan guarantees. Even apartment owners were encouraged to look to suburbia: "Under the best of conditions a rental development under the FHA program is a project set in what amounts to a privately owned and privately controlled park area."

Reflecting the broad segregationist attitudes of a majority of the American people, the FHA was extraordinarily concerned with "inharmonious racial or nationality groups." Homeowners and financial institutions alike feared that an entire area could lose its investment value if rigid white-black separation was not maintained. Bluntly warning, "If a neighborhood is to retain stability, it is necessary that properties shall continue to be occupied by the same social and racial classes," the *Underwriting Manual* openly recommended "enforced zoning, subdivision regulations, and suitable restrictive covenants" that would be "superior to any mortgage." Such covenants were a common method of prohibiting black occupancy until the U.S. Supreme Court ruled in 1948 (*Shelly v. Kraemer*) that they were "unenforceable as law and contrary to public policy." Even then, it was not until late 1949 that FHA announced that as of February 15, 1950, it would not insure mortgages on real estate subject to covenants. Although the press treated the FHA announcement as a major advancement in the field of racial justice, former housing official Nathan Straus noted that "the new policy in fact served only to warn speculative builders who had not filed covenants of their rights to do so, and it gave them a convenient respite in which to file."

In addition to recommending covenants. FHA compiled detailed reports and maps charting the present and most likely future residential locations of black families. In a March 1939 map of Brooklyn, for example, the presence of a single, nonwhite family on any block was sufficient to mark that entire block as black. Similarly, very extensive maps of the District of Columbia depicted the spread of the black population and the percentage of dwelling units occupied by persons other than white. As late as November 19, 1948, Assistant FHA Commissioner W. J. Lockwood could write that FHA "has never insured a housing project of mixed occupancy" because of the expectation that "such projects would probably in a short period of time become all-Negro or all-white."

Occasionally, FHA racial decisions were particularly bizarre and capricious. In the late 1930s, for example, as Detroit grew outward, white families began to settle near a black enclave near Eight Mile Road. By 1940, the blacks were surrounded, but neither they nor the whites could get FHA insurance because of the presence of an adjacent "inharmonious" racial group. So in 1941, an enterprising white developer built a concrete wall between the white and black areas. The FHA then took another look and approved mortgages on the white properties.

One of the first persons to point a finger at FHA for discriminatory practices was Professor Charles Abrams. Writing in 1955, he said:

> A government offering such bounty to builders and lenders could have required compliance with a nondiscrimination policy. Or the agency could at least have pursued a course of evasion, or hidden behind the screen of local autonomy. Instead, FHA adopted a racial policy that could well have been culled from the Nuremberg laws. From its inception FHA set itself up as the protector of the all white neighborhood. It sent its agents into the field to keep Negroes and other minorities from buying houses in white neighborhoods.

The precise extent to which the agency discriminated against blacks and other minority groups is difficult to determine. Although the FHA has always collected reams of data regarding the price, floor area, lot size, number of bathrooms, type of roof, and structural characteristics of the single-family homes it has insured, it has been quite secretive about the spatial distribution of these loans. For the period between 1942 and 1968, the most detailed FHA statistics cannot be disaggregated below the county level.

Such data as are available indicate that neighborhood appraisals were very influential in determining for FHA "where it would be reasonably safe to insure mortgages." Indeed, the Preliminary Examiner was specifically instructed to refer to the Residential Security Maps in order "to segregate for rejection many of the applications involving locations not suitable for amortized mortgages." The result was a degree of suburban favoritism even greater than documentary analysis would have indicated. Of a sample of 241 new homes insured by FHA throughout metropolitan St. Louis between 1935 and 1939 a full 220 or 91 percent were located in the suburbs. Moreover, more than half of these home buyers (135 of 241) had lived in the city immediately prior to their new home purchase. Clearly, the FHA was helping to denude St. Louis of its middle-class residents. As might be expected, the new suburbanites were not being drawn from the slums or from rural areas, but from the "B" areas of the central city.

A detailed analysis of two individual subdivisions in St. Louis County—Normandy and Affton—confirms the same point. Located just northwest of the city limits, Normandy was made up in 1937 of new five- and six-room houses costing between $4,000 and $7,500. In 1937 and 1938, exactly 127 of these houses were sold under FHA-guaranteed mortgages. Of the purchasers, 100 (78 percent) moved out from the city, mostly from the solid, well-established blocks between West Florrissant and Easton Streets.

On the opposite, or southwest, edge of St. Louis, Affton was also the scene of considerable residential construction in 1938 and 1939. Of 62 families purchasing FHA-insured homes in Affton during these years, 55 were from the city of St. Louis. Most of them simply came out the four-lane Gravois Road from the southern part of the city to their new plots in the suburbs.

For the period since 1942, detailed analyses of FHA spatial patterns are difficult. But a reconstruction of FHA unpublished statistics for the St. Louis area over the course of a third of a century reveals the broad patterns of city-suburban activity. As Table 3 indicates, in the first 27 years of FHA operation (through December 31, 1960), when tens of thousands of tract homes were built west of the city limits, the county of St. Louis was the beneficiary of more than five times as much mortgage insurance as the city of St. Louis, whether measured in number of mortgages, amount of mortgage insurance, or per capita assistance.

One possible explanation for the city-county disparities in these figures is that the city had very little room for development, that the populace wanted to move to the suburbs, and that the periphery was where new housing could be most easily built. But in the 1930s, many more single-family homes were constructed in the city than in the county. Moreover, more than half of the FHA policies traditionally went to *existing* rather than *new* homes, and the city of course had a much larger inventory of existing housing than did the county in the period before 1960. Even in terms of home improvement loans, a category in which the aging city was obviously more needy, only $43,844,500 went to the city, while about three times that much, or $112,315,798, went to the county through 1960. In the late 1960s and early 1970s, when the federal government attempted to redirect moneys to the central cities, the previous imbalance was not corrected. Figures available through 1976 show a total of well over $1.1 billion for the county and only $314 million for the city. Thus, the suburbs have continued their dominance.

TABLE 3

Cumulative Total of FHA Home Mortgage Activities and Per Capita
Figures for Ten Selected United States Counties, 1934–1960

Jurisdiction	Cumulative Number of Home Mortgages, 1934–1960	Cumulative Amount of Home Mortgages, 1934–1960	Per Capita Amount of Home Mortgages, as of January 1961
St. Louis County, Mo.	62,772	$558,913,633	$794
Fairfax County, Va.	14,687	190,718,799	730
Nassau County, N.Y.	87,183	781,378,559	601
Montgomery County, Md.	14,702	159,246,550	467
Prince Georges County, Md.	15,043	144,481,817	404
St. Louis City	12,166	94,173,422	126
District of Columbia	8,038	66,144,612	87
Kings County (Brooklyn), N.Y.	15,438	140,330,137	53
Hudson County, N.J.	1,056	7,263,320	12
Bronx County, N.Y.	1,641	14,279,243	10

SOURCE: These calculations are based upon unpublished statistics available in the
Single Family Insured Branch of the Management Information Systems Division of
the Federal Housing Administration.
a. The per capita amount was derived by dividing the cumulative amount of home
mortgages by the 1960 population.

Although St. Louis County apparently has done very well in terms
of per capita mortgage insurance in comparison with other areas of
the nation, the Mississippi River was not an isolated case of FHA
suburban favoritism. In Essex County, New Jersey, FHA commitments
went in overwhelming proportion to Newark's suburbs. And in neighboring Hudson County, residents received only $12 of mortgage in-
surance per capita through 1960, the second lowest county total in the
nation after the Bronx (Table 3).

The New Jersey data reveal that the most favored areas for FHA
mortgage insurance were not the wealthiest towns. Rather, the most
likely areas for FHA activity were those rated "B" on the Residential
Security Maps. In 1936, 65 percent of new housing units in suburban
Livingston were accepted for insurance; for Caldwell and Irvington,
also solidly middle-class, the percentages were 59 and 42, respectively.

In elite districts like South Orange, Glen Ridge, Milburn, and Maple-wood, however, the FHA assistance rates were about as low as they were for Newark, or less than 25 percent. Presumably this occurred because the housing available in the so-called "Best" sections was beyond the allowable price limits for FHA mortgage insurance, and also because persons who could afford to live in such posh neighborhoods did not require government financing.

Even in the nation's capital, the outlying areas were considered more appropriate for federal assistance than older neighborhoods. FHA commitments at the beginning of 1937 in the District of Columbia were heavily concentrated in two peripheral areas: (1) between the U.S. Soldiers Home and Walter Reed Hospital in white and prosperous Northwest Washington and (2) between Rock Creek Park and Connecticut Avenue, also in Northwest Washington. Very few mortgage guarantees were issued in the predominantly black central and southeastern sections of the district. More important, at least two-thirds of the FHA commitments in the metropolitan area were located in the suburbs—especially in Arlington and Alexandria in Virginia and in Silver Spring, Takoma Park, Bethesda, Chevy Chase, University Park, Westmoreland Hills, and West Haven in Maryland. Perhaps this was but a reflection of the 1939 FHA prediction that:

> It should be noted in this connection that the "filtering-up" process, and the tendency of Negroes to congregate in the District, taken together, logically point to a situation where eventually the District will be populated by Negroes and the suburban areas in Maryland and Virginia by white families.

Following a segregationist policy for at least the next 20 years, the FHA did its part to see that the prophecy came true; through the end of 1960, as Table 3 indicates, the suburban counties had received more than seven times as much mortgage insurance as the District of Columbia.

For its part, the FHA usually responded that it was not created to help cities, but to revive homebuilding and to stimulate homeownership. And it concentrated on convincing both Congress and the public that it was, as its first Administrator, James Moffett, remarked, "a conservative business operation." The agency emphasized its concern over sound loans, no higher than the value of the assets and the repayment ability of the borrower would support, and its ability to make a small profit for the federal government.

But FHA also helped to turn the building industry against the minority and inner-city housing market, and its policies supported the income and racial segregation of most suburbs. Whole areas of cities were declared ineligible for loan guarantees; as late as 1966, for example, FHA did not have a mortgage on a single home in Camden, New Jersey, a declining industrial city.

Despite the fact that the government's leading housing agency was openly exhorting segregation, throughout the first 30 years of its operation, very few voices were raised against FHA's redlining practices. Between 1943 and 1945, Harland Bartholomew and Associates prepared a series of reports as a master plan for Dallas. The firm criticized FHA for building "nearly all housing" in the suburbs and argued that "this policy has hastened the process of urban decentralization immeasurably." And Columbia Professor Charles Abrams wrote in 1955 against FHA policies that had "succeeded in modifying legal practice so that the common form of deed included the racial covenant."

Not until the civil rights movement of the 1960s did community groups and scholars become convinced that redlining and disinvestment were a major cause of neighborhood decline and that home improvement loans were the "lifeblood of housing." In 1967, Martin Nolan summed up the indictment against FHA by asserting, "The imbalance against poor people and in favor of middle-income homeowners is so staggering that it makes all inquiries into the pathology of slums seem redundant." In the following year, Senator Paul Douglas of Illinois reported for the National Commission on Urban Problems on the role of the federal government in home finance:

> The poor and those on the fringes of poverty have been almost completely excluded. These and the lower middle class, together constituting the 40 per cent of the population whose housing needs are greatest, received only 11 per cent of the FHA mortgages. . . . Even middle-class residential districts in the central cities were suspect, since there was always the prospect that they, too, might turn as Negroes and poor whites continued to pour into the cities, and as middle and upper-middle-income whites continued to move out.

Moreover, as Jane Jacobs has said, "Credit blacklisting maps are accurate prophecies because they are self-fulfilling prophecies."

The main beneficiary of the $119 billion in FHA mortgage insurance issued in the first four decades of FHA operation was suburbia, where approximately half of all housing could claim FHA or VA financing in the 1950s and 1960s. In the process, the American suburb was transformed from a rich person's preserve into the normal expectation of the middle class.

CONCLUSION

The HOLC was created in the midst of the Great Depression to refinance mortgages in danger of default or foreclosure. In the course of accomplishing its mission, the HOLC developed real estate appraisal systems that discriminated against racial and ethnic minorities and against older, industrial cities. But HOLC apparently extended aid without regard for its own ratings and evaluations and met the needs of a variety of families and neighborhoods.

The FHA cooperated with HOLC and followed HOLC appraisal practices. But unlike the HOLC, the FHA acted on the information in its files and clearly favored suburban areas over industrial cities. It is conceivable that the heavy disparity demonstrated in this article was the result not of prejudicial intent, but of other factors, such as family size, attitudes toward child rearing, or stages in the life cycle. In my judgment, however, the evidence is clear; both FHA guidelines and actual FHA assistance favored new construction over existing dwellings, open land over developed areas, businessmen over blue-collar workers, whites over blacks, and native-born Americans over immigrants.

14

Creating G.I. Jane: The Regulation of Sexuality and Sexual Behavior in the Women's Army Corps During World War II

LEISA D. MEYER

● *War has a way of sweeping aside old prejudices and habits of thought. Traditionally women were seen as the weaker sex, and soldiering had as its presumed purpose the protection of wives, mothers, and children at home. During World War II, however, the stakes were so high, the enemies so formidable, and the manpower demands so huge that no nation could afford for half of its able-bodied population to remain on the sidelines. As armaments factories, munitions plants, and ship-yards shifted to round-the-clock production schedules, American women entered the workforce in unprecedented numbers. In Muncie, Indiana, for example, the population increased by only 2,500 during the war, but employment jumped by 20,000. "Rosie the Riveter" was not just a slogan; women could and did equal or better the performance of men.*

Even military service itself ceased to be an all-male preserve, as both the the Army and the Navy prepared to train and equip female personnel. Eventually, more than 200,000 women wore the uniform of their country between 1941 and 1945. Most of them served in unglamorous and circumscribed tasks, usually far behind the lines. But their very presence was challenging to the prewar status quo, and military leaders were determined that the WACs and the WAVES remain respectable havens for "the best class of women." Sexuality was a major concern, and homosexuality was a major fear, as the following essay by Professor Leisa D. Meyer indicates.

This article is reprinted from *Feminist Studies*, volume 18, number 3 (Fall 1993): 581–596, by permission of the publisher, Feminist Studies, Inc., c/o Women's Studies Program, University of Maryland, College Park, MD 20742.

Several years after World War II ended, a journalist summed up the difficulties the Women's Army Corps encountered in recruiting women by observing:

> Of the problems that the WAC has, the greatest one is the problem of morals . . . of convincing mothers, fathers, brothers, Congressmen, servicemen and junior officers that women really can be military without being camp followers or without being converted into rough, tough gals who can cuss out the chow as well as any dogface. . . .

The sexual stereotypes of servicewomen as "camp followers" or "mannish women," prostitutes or lesbians, had a long history both in the construction of notions of femaleness in general and in the relationship of "woman" and "soldier" in particular. Historically, women had been most visibly associated with the military as prostitutes and cross-dressers. The challenge before women and men who wanted to promote "women" as "soldiers" during World War II was how to create a new category which proclaimed female soldiers as both sexually respectable and feminine. The response of Oveta Culp Hobby, the Women's Army Corps director, to this challenge was to characterize female soldiers as chaste and asexual; such a presentation would not threaten conventional sexual norms. Clashing public perceptions of servicewomen and internal struggles within the U.S. Army over the proper portrayal and treatment of military women were the crucibles in which this new category was created. Such struggles profoundly shaped the daily lives of women in the Women's Army Auxiliary Corps (WAAC) and the Women's Army Corps (WAC) and framed the notorious lesbian witchhunts of the mid- to late-forties.

This article focuses on the regulation and expression of women's sexuality within the army during World War II. I will examine the debates between female and male military leaders over the most appropriate methods of controlling female soldiers' sexual behavior and the actions and responses of army women themselves to the varied and often conflicting rulings emanating from WAAC/WAC Headquarters and the War Department. Framed by public concern with the possibilities of both the sexual independence and sexual victimization of servicewomen, the interactions between and among these groups illuminate the ongoing tension between the mutually exclusive, gendered categories "woman" and "soldier."

The entrance of some women into the army paralleled the movement of other women into nontraditional jobs in the civilian labor force as the need for full utilization of all resources during World War II brought large numbers of white, married women into the labor force for the first time and created opportunities for many women and people of color in jobs historically denied them. Women's service in the armed forces was especially threatening, however, because of the military's function as the ultimate test of "masculinity."

The definition of the military as a masculine institution and the definition of a soldier as a "man with a gun who engages in combat" both excluded women. Moreover, military service had historically been the obligation of men during wartime, and the presence of female soldiers in the army suggested that women were abdicating their responsibilities within the home to usurp men's duty of protecting and defending their homes and country. Thus, the establishment of the WAAC in May 1942, marking women's formal entrance into this preeminently masculine domain, generated heated public debate. It heightened the fears already generated by the entry of massive numbers of women in the civilian labor force and by the less restrictive sexual mores of a wartime environment.

Public fears of the possible consequences of women's economic independence were often manifested in concerns with women's economic independence as the war accelerated the shift to city living and provided millions of young people with increased opportunities for economic autonomy and social freedom. Such changes had historically triggered fears of declining standards of morality and disintegrating gender and racial boundaries. Historian Elaine Tyler May has argued that in the forties the anxieties generated by these changes focused on female sexuality as a "dangerous force ... on the loose" and featured calls for women, especially those engaged in more "masculine" pursuits, to maintain their "femininity" in order to offset this danger. In particular, May has demonstrated that public concerns over the potential increase in heterosexual promiscuity among women were generated by the belief that women's right to "behave like a man" by joining the work force or the military meant also their "right to misbehave as he does," especially sexually.

The dangers inherent in women's loss of "femininity" were inscribed not only in public fears of increasing promiscuity but also in the specter of female homosexuality. As John D'Emilio has observed, the theories of Freud, Ellis, and Kraft-Ebbing all linked "proper sexual development" to conventional definitions of "femininity" and "masculinity" and described women's deviations from prescribed "feminine" gender norms as one possible sign of female homosexuality. In addition, although contemporary psychiatric wisdom was moving away from connections between "mannishness" in women and homosexuality, prevailing popular attitudes still linked the two.

In a culture increasingly anxious about women's sexuality in general, and homosexuality in particular, the formation of the WAAC, a women-only environment within an otherwise wholly male institution, sparked a storm of public speculation as to the potential breakdown of heterosexual norms and sexual morality which might result. Not surprisingly, these concerns focused on the potentially "masculinizing" effect the army might have on women and especially on the disruptive influence the WAAC would have on sexual standards. Public fears were articulated in numerous editorials and stories in newspapers and journals, as well as in thousands of letters to the War Department and the newly formed WAAC Headquarters in Washington, D.C. These anxieties were expressed in accusations of heterosexual promiscuity and lesbianism and concerns over women's lack of protection within the military. Among other allegations, the public expressed fear that, in forming the WAAC, the military was trying to create an organized cadre of prostitutes to service male GI's.

The potentially "masculinizing" effect of the military on women was not only in women's taking on male characteristics, appearance, and power but also in women adopting a more aggressive, independent, and "masculine" sexuality. Many civilians as well as some elements of the mainstream media characterized Waacs as sexual actors who engaged in the same type of promiscuity, drunkenness, and sexual adventure condoned in male GI's. Although explicit references to female homosexuality in the WAAC were seldom made in the mainstream press, reports of rumors submitted to WAAC Headquarters by recruiting officers in the field demonstrated that public concern with lesbianism was also pervasive. As WAC historian Mattie Treadwell notes, there was a "public impression that a women's corps would be the

ideal breeding ground for [homosexuality]." She attributes this view
to the "mistaken" popular belief that "any woman who was masculine
in appearance or dress" was a homosexual. In a postwar interview
Colonel Oveta Culp Hobby, WAAC/WAC director from 1942 to 1945,
elaborated on this, remarking: "Just as a startled public was once sure
that women's suffrage would make women unwomanly, so the thought
of 'women soldiers' caused some people to assume that WAC units
would inevitably be hotbeds of perversion." Thus, "masculinization"
implied both women's potential power over men and their sexual independence from them, a threat to gender and sexual norms. "Promiscuous" heterosexual women were presumably independent from and
uncontrolled by particular men, and "mannish" women were presumably independent of all men.

The sexual stereotypes of the female soldier as "loose" or "mannish"
were seen both as inherent in women's military service *and* as a product
of the particular kinds of women believed to be most likely to enter
the WAAC. In other words, the army either attracted women who were
already "sexually deviant," or the experience of military life would
make them that way. In addition, the corollary to concerns with wom-
en's sexual agency were discussions of army women as potential sexual
victims. Integral to this contention were questions of who would protect
women inside the military. Removed from the control of their families,
what would the state's control of servicewomen mean?

The army's response to this negative publicity was orchestrated by
Colonel Hobby. She organized this response around the need to assure
an anxious public that servicewomen had not lost their "femininity."
Hobby's definition of "femininity" was rooted in the Victorian linkage
between sexual respectability and female passionlessness. As a result
she characterized the woman soldier as chaste, asexual, and essentially
middle class. For example, in cooperation with the War Department
she arranged public statements by a number of religious leaders who
assured all concerned that the army was a safe and moral environment
for young women, and further, that women who joined the WAAC/
WAC were of the highest moral character and from "good family
backgrounds." She characterized the WAAC/WAC as acting *in loco
parentis,* as a guardian of young women's welfare and morals. And to
demonstrate that the WAAC/WAC attracted "better-quality" women,
Hobby emphasized the greater educational requirements mandated for

women compared with their male counterparts, illustrated by the high ratio of women with college degrees. Thus, in countering allegations that to join the WAAC/WAC meant to "lower one's self," army propaganda reflected and supported contemporary definitions of respectability which explicitly connected class status and sexual morality.

These pronouncements on sexual respectability coincided with other army public relations campaigns aimed at defusing public concerns with homosexuality. In these efforts, attempts to limit the visibility of lesbians in the women's corps were linked with the implicit encouragement of heterosexuality. In responding to fears that the military would make women "mannish" or would provide a haven for women who were "naturally" that way, for instance, some army propaganda highlighted the femininity of WAAC/WAC recruits and stressed their sexual attractiveness to men. These articles assured an anxious public that "soldiering hasn't transformed these Wacs into Amazons—far from it. They have retained their femininity." Presenting women in civilian life in the period as sexually attractive to men did not necessarily imply that they were sexually available. However, public hostility toward women's entrance into the military and conjecture over the army's "real need" for Waacs/Wacs frequently focused on the potential for women's sexual exploitation and/or agency within the army. The army's policy of portraying servicewomen as feminine and sexually attractive to men worked both to contest the image of the female soldier as a "mannish" woman, or lesbian, *and* to reinforce the public characterizations of Waacs/Wacs as heterosexually available. Hobby's efforts to control the effects of these campaigns was to emphasize that Waacs/Wacs remained passionless and chaste while in the military and that their sexual behavior in the military was, and should be, profoundly different from that of men in the same institution.

The framework created by Hobby and disseminated in military propaganda efforts was occasionally undercut by the conflicting responses to the question of whether Waacs/Wacs should be treated and utilized as "soldiers" or as "women." On several occasions the male army hierarchy, much to Hobby's dismay, attempted to treat the regulation and control of women's sexuality and sexual behavior in the same manner as that of male soldiers. The army's approach to the issue of sexual regulation and control for men stressed health and combat readiness among troops, not morality. In fact, the army expected and encouraged heterosexual activity among male soldiers and controlled male sexuality with regulations prohibiting sodomy and addressing the prevention and treatment of venereal disease, as well as more informal mechanisms upholding prohibitions on interracial relationships. The male military hierarchy's desire for uniformity collided with the female WAAC director's firm belief in different moral standards for women and her insistence that this difference be reflected in army regulations. This struggle was clearly represented in the army's battle to fight the spread of venereal disease within its ranks.

Hobby believed the army's venereal disease program for men, premised on the assumption of heterosexual activity, would seriously damage the reputation of the corps if applied to women and would undermine her efforts to present Waacs as sexless, not sexual. Her strategy of moral suasion clashed with the U.S. surgeon general's efforts to institute a system of chemical prophylaxis in the women's corps. The surgeon general's plan for control of venereal disease in the WAAC included a full course of instruction in sex education and the distribution of condoms in slot machines placed in latrines so that even "modest" servicewomen might have access to them. This program was completely rejected by Hobby. She argued that even proposing such measures placed civilian and military acceptance of the WAAC in jeopardy. She pointed to public fears of women's military service and accusations of immorality already present as evidence that the course proposed by the surgeon general would result in catastrophic damage to the reputation of the WAAC and seriously hamper her efforts to recruit women to the corps.

Her concern was not with venereal disease per se, but rather with creating an aura of respectability around the WAAC. Her victory in this struggle resulted in the development of a social hygiene pamphlet and course which stressed the "high standards" of moral conduct (i.e., chastity) necessary for members of the corps and the potential damage one woman could do through her misbehavior or immoral conduct. The pamphlet, distributed to all WAAC officers, discussed venereal disease only in reference to the "frightful effects" of the disease on women and children, the difficulties in detection and treatment, and the ineffectiveness of all prophylactic methods for women. Hobby supported combining this policy with the maintenance of strict enlistment standards. She believed that if the corps accepted only "high types of women," no control measures would be necessary.

In stressing the class status of enrollees and the high standards of sexual morality expected of servicewomen, Hobby's response to the issue of venereal disease control in the WAAC was an attempt to place military women back within the bounds of propriety and respectability that had historically afforded a certain kind of protection for white middle-class and upper-class women. Although her goals were to build and repair the reputation of the WAAC, as well as to protect individual women from potential sexual exploitation, her methods—withholding information and highlighting the dangers of heterosexual activity for women—served to institutionalize differential expectations and consequences for the behavior of female and male GI's. Waacs, for example, could be discharged for "illicit sexual activity," but such behavior was expected and often encouraged in male soldiers. Thus, Hobby's policies firmly reinforced the sexual double standard.

Hobby's fears of the adverse public reaction that might result from the distribution of prophylactics information and equipment to Waacs were confirmed by the slander campaign against the WAAC/WAC which started in mid-1943 and continued through early 1944. This "whispering campaign" began with the publication of a nationally syndicated article which reported that in a secret agreement between the War Department and the WAAC, contraceptives would be issued to all women in the army. This piece provoked a storm of public outcry and marked the resurgence of accusations of widespread sexual immorality in the women's corps.

Subsequent army investigations showed that most rumors about the WAAC/WAC originated with male servicemen and officers. Telling "slanderous" stories about the WAAC/WAC was one expression of the resentment men felt at women's entrance into a previously male-only preserve. These attitudes also indicated the confusion present on the command level and among rank-and-file enlisted personnel as to the purpose and function of a women's corps. Was the mission of the women's corps a military one or was the WAAC created to help "improve male morale"? Was a servicewoman's primary function as a soldier, supporting her comrades in arms, or as a woman boosting sagging male spirits and providing feminine companionship for the lonely? A number of servicemen answered these questions by writing home advising girlfriends and family members against joining the women's corps, both because of the "bad reputation" of its members and the belief of some GI's that the WAAC was created solely to "serve" male soldiers sexually.

Public fears that the only "real uses" the army had for women were sexual were exacerbated by male officers who claimed that the most important function of the WAAC/WAC was not the soldierly duties it performed but the positive impact the women had on the "morale" of male soldiers. Although "morale boosting" did not necessarily imply prostitution or sexual service, the two were often linked in the public consciousness. For example, one army investigator reported that in Kansas City, Kansas, it was believed that "Waacs were issued condoms and enrolled solely for the soldier's entertainment, serving as 'morale builders' for the men and nothing more." Hobby worked to eliminate all references to Waacs/Wacs being used for "morale purposes," believing that these bolstered public concerns with heterosexual immorality in the corps.

In addition, the occasional use of WAAC/WAC units to control male sexuality seemed to confirm suspicions that the role the army envisioned for women was sexual. For example, African American WAAC/WAC units were in general stationed only at posts where there were Black male soldiers present. In part this was a product of the army's policy of segregating its troops by race. However, white officers, particularly at southern posts, also explicitly referred to the "beneficial" presence of African American WAAC/WAC units as a way to ensure that Black male troops would not form liaisons with white women in the surrounding communities. Thus, in this instance, African American WAAC/WAC units were used by the army as a means of upholding and supporting prohibitions on interracial relationships. Similarly, in December 1944, Field Marshall Sir Bernard L. Montgomery proposed using white, American WAC and British Auxiliary Territorial Service units in the Allied occupation of Germany to curb the fraternization of male GI's in the U.S. and British armies with enemy (German) women, especially prostitutes. Field Marshall Montgomery's proposal was made public in a number of articles and editorials and harshly criticized by WAC Headquarters, as well as by Wacs stationed overseas in the European theater of operations. It is clear from these examples that military policy and practice were sometimes contradictory.

This situation was made more complicated by the fact that Waacs/ Wacs and male soldiers regularly dated and socialized. This was particularly true in overseas theaters of war where military women were often the only U.S. women in the area. The only army regulations dealing with the social interaction of female and male military personnel were long-standing rules against fraternization between officers and enlisted personnel. Again the question arose of whether Waacs/Wacs should be treated like all other soldiers or if allowances should be made for female/male interactions across the caste lines established by the military. No clear answer to this query developed during World War II. In practice, the regulations concerning the socializing of male officers and female enlisted personnel and vice-versa varied from post to post and over different theaters. Many Waacs/Wacs were extremely vocal in their resentment of what they perceived as army policies dictating whom they should not date. When fraternization policies were enforced between women and men, it was usually the Waac/Wac who was punished, not the male soldier or officer, if discovered in violation of these regulations. This practice made it clear that it was women's responsibility to say "no" to these encounters and reinforced the sexual double standard which excused men's heterosexual activity and punished that of women.

Informal policies addressing issues of whether male soldiers and officers should be allowed in WAAC/WAC barracks and dayrooms (recreational and reading rooms) were usually set by the ranking WAAC/ WAC officer or the theater commander in overseas areas and varied enormously. The emphasis was on keeping such interactions local and controlled; thus, although no formal regulations were present, WAAC/ WAC Headquarters recommended that women bring their soldier dates to the dayrooms and recreational facilities provided on army posts. Hobby believed that this would allow for informal supervision and chaperonage, as well as decrease the opportunities for sexual relations between female and male GI's.

The army's negotiation between anxieties about assertive female sexuality, whether heterosexual or homosexual, and the realities of servicewomen's sexual vulnerability to abuse by male GI's and officers can be seen by examining the army's efforts to control the sexuality of servicewomen in the Southwest Pacific Area. Upon arrival in Port Moresby, New Guinea, in May 1944, Wacs found their lives unexpectedly restricted. The theater headquarters directed that in view of the great number of white male troops in the area, "some of whom allegedly had not seen a nurse or other white woman in 18 months," Wacs should be locked within their barbed wire compound at all times except when escorted by armed guards to work or to approved group recreation. No leaves, passes, or one-couple dates were allowed at any time. Many Wacs found these restrictions unbearable and patronizing and complained that they were being treated as criminals and children. The mounting complaints from women at WAC Headquarters and rumors of plummeting morale moved Hobby to protest to the War Department and ask for a discontinuation of what many Wacs referred to as the "concentration camp system." The War Department responded that it was in no position to protest command policies, especially because the theater authorities insisted that the system was required "to prevent rape of Wacs by Negro troops in New Guinea." Societal stereotypes of African American men, in particular, as rapists, and of male sexuality, in general, as dangerous for women, were used to defend the extremely restrictive policies of the military toward Wacs in the Southwest Pacific Area. In this situation the army stepped in as the surrogate male protector defending white military women's honor and virtue by creating a repressive environment designed to ensure a maximum of "protection" and supervision.

One consequence of the controls placed on women's heterosexual activities in the Southwest Pacific Area was a series of rumors in late 1944 claiming widespread homosexuality among Wacs in New Guinea. The concerns originated in letters of complaint from several Wacs stationed there who asserted that restrictive theater policies created an ideal habitat for some women to express and explore their "abnormal sexual tendencies." The War Department and Hobby sent a WAC officer to the theater to investigate the rumors. The report issued by Lieutenant Colonel Mary Agnes Brown, the WAC staff director, noted that although homosexuality was certainly not widespread, several incidences of such behavior had occurred. Lieutenant Colonel Brown felt that the situation was accentuated by the rigid camp security system to which Wacs were subjected. She suggested increasing Wacs' oppor-

tunities for recreation "with a view of maintaining the normal relationships between men and women that exist at home and avoid the
creation of abnormal conditions which otherwise are bound to arise."
When faced with a choice of protecting women from men or "protecting" them from lesbian relationships which might occur in a sex-
segregated and restricted compound, Lieutenant Colonel Brown's recommendation was to protect servicewomen from the possibility of
homosexuality.

The more repressive framework created by Hobby to control wom-
en's sexuality in the face of public antagonism was also challenged by
women, both heterosexual and lesbian, who asserted their autonomy
and right to find their own means of sexual expression within the
authoritarian structure of the army. Indeed, heterosexual women sometimes manipulated fears of homosexuality in the women's corps to
expand their own opportunities for heterosexual activity. They accused
female officers who enforced army regulations against fraternization
of male and female officers and enlisted personnel of being "antimale"
and discouraging "normal" heterosexual interactions. For example, in
February 1944, Captain Delores Smith was ordered to report for duty
as the commanding officer of the Army-Air Forces WAC Detachment
at Fort Worth, Texas. As a new commanding officer, Captain Smith
sought the help and advice of her officer staff in familiarizing herself
with the company and environment. Receiving little support from her
officers, she turned for advice to the ranking enlisted woman, Sargeant
Norma Crandall. Shortly after her arrival, Smith reprimanded several
of her company officers for allowing enlisted men to frequent the WAC
barracks and mess hall. In addition, she cautioned these officers on
their fraternization with male enlisted personnel. Two weeks later these
officers brought charges of homosexuality against Captain Smith. They
cited her restrictions on female/male interactions on post, her "dislike"
of socializing with servicemen, and her "close association" with the
enlisted woman, Sergeant Crandall, as evidence of her "abnormal tendencies." Despite the lack of concrete documentation to support these
accusations, Hobby and the Board of Inquiry felt that to allow Captain
Smith to continue as a WAC officer would only damage the reputation
of the corps, and she was forced to resign from service.

The WAC officers at Fort Worth were angered by what they perceived
as the imposition of unfair restrictions on their social lives by Captain

Smith. They responded by invoking homophobic anxieties. In doing so they simultaneously defended their right to choose how and with whom they would socialize and reinforced social taboos and army proscriptions against lesbianism. The "lesbian threat" thus became a language of protest to force authorities to broaden their heterosexual privilege.

Lesbian servicewomen, like their heterosexual counterparts, also tried to create their own space within the WAC. In these efforts army lesbians were affected by the contradiction between official proscriptions of homosexuality and the WAC's informal policies on female homosexuality, which were quite lenient. For example, in literature distributed to WAC officer candidates, potential corps leaders were instructed to expect some degree of homosexuality within their commands. They were cautioned:

> Homosexuality is of interest to you as WAC officers, only so far as its manifestations undermine the efficiency of the individuals concerned and the stability of the group. You, as officers, will find it necessary to keep the problem in the back of your mind, not indulging in witch hunting or speculating, and yet not overlooking the problem because it is a difficult one to handle. Above all, you must approach the problem with an attitude of fairness and tolerance to assure that no one is accused unjustly. If there is any likelihood of doubt, it is better to be generous in your outlook, and to assume that everyone is innocent until definitely proved otherwise....

Army regulations providing for the undesirable discharge of homosexuals were rarely used against lesbians in the WAC, and WAC officers were warned to consider this action only in the most extreme of situations. Hobby felt that such proceedings would only result in more intensive public scrutiny and disapproval of the women's corps. Instead, it was suggested that WAC officers use more informal methods of control. These included shifting personnel and room assignments, transferring individuals to different posts, and as was exemplified in New Guinea, ensuring that corps members were provided with "opportunities for wholesome and natural companionship with men." Another recommended method for dealing with homosexuality was to encourage a woman with "homosexual tendencies" to substitute "hero worship" of a WAC officer for active participation in homosexual relations. WAC policies stated:

If she is deserving of the admiration of those under her command, the officer may be enabled, by the strength of her influence, to bring out in the woman who had previously exhibited homosexual tendencies, a definite type of leadership which can then be guided into normal fields of expression, making her a valued member of the Corps....

In addition, on several posts informal WAC policy prohibited women from dancing in couples in public and cautioned against the adoption of "mannish" hairstyles. WAC leaders were concerned primarily with the image of the corps, and Hobby felt that the adverse publicity generated by intense screening procedures, investigations, and court-martials of lesbians within the WAC could only hurt the corps. Thus, as historian Allan Bérubé has noted in his work on gay GI's during World War II, the expanding antihomosexual apparatus of the military was focused much more closely on regulating and screening for male homosexuals than for their female counterparts.

Within these parameters, lesbians within the WAC developed their own culture and methods of identifying one another, although the risks of discovery and exposure remained. The court-martial of Technical Sergeant Julie Farrell, stationed at an army school in Richmond, Kentucky, provides an interesting example of this developing culture and its limits. Although she was given an undesirable discharge because of "unsuitability for military service," Technical Sergeant Farrell's court-martial focused on her alleged homosexuality. According to the testimony of Lieutenant Rosemary O'Riley, Farrell approached her one evening, depressed at what she felt were the army's efforts to make her "suppress her individuality," including criticisms and reprimands for her "mannish hairstyle" and "masculine behavior." Receiving a sympathetic response, Farrell went on to ask the lieutenant if she understood "double talk" and if she had ever been to San Francisco. It is clear that these questions were used by Farrell to determine if it was safe to discuss issues of homosexuality with O'Riley. When the lieutenant answered in the affirmative to her queries, Farrell went on to speak more explicitly of the "natural desires" of women which the military attempted to suppress. She ended with what Lieutenant O'Riley later termed as a "humiliating suggestion." Farrell was surprised by O'Riley's insistence that she had "no interest in such things" and remarked, "Well, when you first came on this campus we thought that maybe you were one of us in the way you walked."

As this example illustrates, mannerisms and coded language were a few of the ways in which lesbians identified one another. It is also clear from O'Riley's testimony that Farrell, a woman exhibiting more "masculine" mannerisms and traits, was more visible as a lesbian. In part, this seems to confirm Bérubé's arguments that "butch" servicewomen, because of their greater fit with popular lesbian stereotypes, were more likely to be targeted as female homosexuals in discharge proceedings. However, lesbians, unlike their gay male counterparts, violated prescribed gender norms simply as women entering the male military. The presence of "butch" women in the WAC subverted Hobby's efforts to frame the women's corps as a "feminine" entity. Thus, "butch" women, because they refused to work at proving their femininity, were suspect.

Lieutenant O'Riley's reports of Farrell's comments and behavior resulted in a court-martial proceeding against Technical Sergeant Farrell. In the course of this proceeding it was argued that in addition to this latest breach of military regulations, Farrell had already been the subject of "malicious gossip and rumor." Most damaging, however, were love letters between Farrell and a WAAC officer, Lieutenant Pines, that were entered as evidence. The tender and explicit discussions of the women's relationship contained within these letters were crucial to the decision of the board to dismiss Farrell from service. Lieutenant Pines avoided prosecution by claiming that the interactions described in the letters occurred only in the imagination of Farrell. Pines covered herself by asserting that she had kept the letters because of her own suspicions of Farrell. Thus, in saving herself, Pines sealed the fate of her lover.

Despite the opportunities for creating and sustaining a lesbian identity or relationship within the WAAC/WAC, the process was also fraught with danger and uncertainty. Army policies provided a space in which female homosexuals could exist, recognize one another, and develop their own culture. Yet this existence was an extremely precarious one, framed by army regulations which also provided for the undesirable discharge of homosexuals, female and male. These regulations could be invoked at any time and were widely used in purges of lesbians from the military in the immediate postwar years, purges that were in part the result of the army's decreasing need for women's labor. In these efforts the army utilized the techniques illustrated in

Julie Farrell's court-martial, enabling some women to protect themselves by accusing others of lesbianism. In addition, some lesbians used heterosexual privilege and respectability to obscure their sexual identity by getting married or becoming pregnant in order to leave the army and protect themselves and their lovers. Pat Bond, a lesbian ex-Wac who married a gay GI to avoid prosecution, described one of these purges at a base in Japan: "Every day you came up for a court-martial against one of your friends. They turned us against each other. . . . The only way I could figure out to save my lover was to get out. If I had been there, they could have gotten us both because other women would have testified against us."

The tensions between agency and victimization illustrated here are characteristic of women's participation within the U.S. Army during World War II. Hobby's attempts to portray Wacs as sexless and protected in response to accusations of heterosexual promiscuity were undercut by the need also to present Wacs as feminine and sexually attractive to men to ease fears that the military would attract or produce "mannish women" and lesbians. In addition, the army's occasional utilization of WAC units to control male sexuality seemed to confirm the belief that women's role within the military was sexual. Within this confusing and fluctuating environment, and in negotiation with army regulations and public opinion, Wacs tried to define their own sexuality and make their own sexual choices. Their actions sometimes challenged and at other times reinforced entrenched gender and sexual ideologies and were crucial to the development of a role for women within the military. The process of creating a category of "female soldier" was defined by these interactions between Wacs, the army hierarchy (which was often divided along gender lines), and public opinion. The reformulation and reconstruction of gender and sexual norms involved in this process did not end with the war but is still going on today. Women's service continues to be circumscribed by debates over the contradictory concepts of "woman" and "soldier," and servicewomen continue to grapple with the sexual images of dyke and whore framing their participation.

15

The Atomic Bomb and the Origins of the Cold War

MARTIN J. SHERWIN

• *In early August 1945, Japan was prostrate before the economic and military power of the United States. Its once proud Imperial Fleet and great battleships were at the bottom of the Pacific, its best-trained pilots were dead, its army was decimated by hopeless defenses of isolated islands, its skies were violated with impunity by the bombers of the American army and navy, and its population was practically starving. If that were not enough, the Soviet Union was already shifting its armies from Germany and Europe to the Far East, where they would attack Japanese forces on the Asian mainland.*

In such circumstances, was the United States justified in dropping atomic bombs on Hiroshima and Nagasaki? Would the Japanese have realized the hopelessness of their position even without the introduction of nuclear weapons? Could the bombs have had an equivalent psychological impact if they had been dropped in rural areas rather than in the midst of crowded cities? Was the atomic bomb the last shot of World War II or the first shot of the Cold War?

Although such questions have inspired a large and diversified literature, perhaps no one has approached the subject with more care and clarity than Martin J. Sherwin of Dartmouth College. As you read his article, and especially as you reflect upon the statement by University of Chicago scientists in the final paragraph, you might attempt to imagine yourself as the diplomatic representative of another nation—perhaps France or Russia or Japan. What reasons would they have had for assuming that the ultimate weapon was anything more or less than an instrument for advancing American foreign policy? Do you think that the United States was then, or is now, willing to share its military secrets for the benefit of mankind?

From the *American Historical Review*, 78 (October 1973). Reprinted by permission of the author.

During the second World War the atomic bomb was seen and valued as a potential rather than an actual instrument of policy. Responsible officials believed that its impact on diplomacy had to await its development and, perhaps, even a demonstration of its power. As Henry L. Stimson, the secretary of war, observed in his memoirs: "The bomb as a merely probable weapon had seemed a weak reed on which to rely, but the bomb as a colossal reality was very different." That policymakers considered this difference before Hiroshima has been well documented, but whether they based wartime diplomatic policies upon an anticipated successful demonstration of the bomb's power remains a source of controversy. Two questions delineate the issues in this debate. First, did the development of the atomic bomb affect the way American policymakers conducted diplomacy with the Soviet Union? Second, did diplomatic considerations related to the Soviet Union influence the decision to use the atomic bomb against Japan?

These important questions relating the atomic bomb to American diplomacy, and ultimately to the origins of the cold war, have been addressed almost exclusively to the formulation of policy during the early months of the Truman administration. As a result, two anterior questions of equal importance, questions with implications for those already posed, have been overlooked. Did diplomatic considerations related to Soviet postwar behavior influence the formulation of Roosevelt's atomic-energy policies? What effect did the atomic legacy Truman inherited have on the diplomatic and atomic-energy policies of his administration?

To comprehend the nature of the relationship between atomic-energy and diplomatic policies that developed during the war, the bomb must be seen as policymakers saw it before Hiroshima, as a weapon that might be used to control postwar diplomacy. For this task our present view is conceptually inadequate. After more than a quarter century of experience we understand, as wartime policy makers did not, the bomb's limitations as a diplomatic instrument. To appreciate the profound influence of the unchallenged wartime assumption about the bomb's impact on diplomacy we must recognize the postwar purposes for which policymakers and their advisers believed the bomb could be used. In this effort Churchill's expectations must be scrutinized as carefully as Roosevelt's, and scientists' ideas must be considered along with those of politicians. Truman's decision to use the atomic bomb against

Japan must be evaluated in the light of Roosevelt's atomic legacy, and the problems of impending peace must be considered along with the exigencies of war. To isolate the basic atomic-energy policy alternatives that emerged during the war requires that we first ask whether alternatives were, in fact, recognized.

What emerges most clearly from a close examination of wartime formulation of atomic-energy policy is the conclusion that policy makers never seriously questioned the assumption that the atomic bomb should be used against Germany or Japan. From October 9, 1941, the time of the first meeting to organize the atomic-energy project, Stimson, Roosevelt, and other members of the "top policy group" conceived of the development of the atomic bomb as an essential part of the total war effort. Though the suggestion to build the bomb was initially made by scientists who feared that Germany might develop the weapon first, those with political responsibility for prosecuting the war accepted the circumstances of the bomb's creation as sufficient justification for its use against any enemy.

Having nurtured this point of view during the war, Stimson charged those who later criticized the use of the bomb with two errors. First, these critics asked the wrong question: it was not whether surrender could have been obtained without using the bomb, but whether a different diplomatic and military course from that followed by the Truman administration would have achieved an earlier surrender. Second, the basic assumption of these critics was false: the idea that American policy should have been based primarily on a desire not to employ the bomb seemed as "irresponsible" as a policy controlled by a positive desire to use it. The war, not the bomb, Stimson argued, had been the primary focus of his attention; as secretary of war his responsibilities permitted no alternative.

Stimson's own wartime diary nevertheless indicates that from 1941 on, the problems associated with the atomic bomb moved steadily closer to the center of his own and Roosevelt's concerns. As the war progressed, the implications of the weapon's development became diplomatic as well as military, postwar as well as wartime. Recognizing that a monopoly of the atomic bomb gave the United States a powerful new military advantage, Roosevelt and Stimson became increasingly anxious to convert it to diplomatic advantage. In December 1944 they spoke of using the "secret" of the atomic bomb as a means of obtaining a *quid pro quo* from the Soviet Union. But viewing the bomb as a potential instrument of diplomacy, they were not moved to formulate a concrete plan for carrying out this exchange before the bomb was used. The bomb had "this unique peculiarity," Stimson noted several months later in his diary; "Success is 99% assured, yet only by the first actual war trial of the weapon can the actual certainty be fixed." Whether or not the specter of postwar Soviet ambitions created "a positive desire" to ascertain the bomb's power, until that decision was executed "atomic diplomacy" remained an idea that never crystallized into policy.

Although Roosevelt left no definitive statement assigning a postwar role to the atomic bomb, his expectations for its potential diplomatic value can be recalled from the existing record. An analysis of the policies he chose from among the alternatives he faced suggests that the potential diplomatic value of the bomb began to shape his atomic-energy policies as early as 1943. He may have been cautious about counting on the bomb as a reality during the war, but he nevertheless consistently chose policy alternatives that would promote the postwar diplomatic potential of the bomb if the predictions of scientists proved true. These policies were based on the assumption that the bomb could be used effectively to secure postwar diplomatic aims; and this assumption was carried over from the Roosevelt to the Truman administration.

Despite general agreement that the bomb would be an extraordinarily important diplomatic factor after the war, those closely associated with its development did not agree on how to use it most effectively as an instrument of diplomacy. Convinced that wartime atomic-energy policies would have postwar diplomatic consequences, several scientists advised Roosevelt to adopt policies aimed at achieving a postwar international control system. Churchill, on the other hand, urged the president to maintain the Anglo-American atomic monopoly as a diplomatic counter against the postwar ambitions of other nations—particularly against the Soviet Union. Roosevelt fashioned his atomic-energy policies from the choices he made between these conflicting recommendations. In 1943 he rejected the counsel of his science advisers and began to consider the diplomatic component of atomic-energy policy in consultation with Churchill alone. This decision-making procedure and Roosevelt's untimely death have left his motives ambiguous. Nevertheless it is clear that he pursued policies consistent with Churchill's monopolistic, anti-Soviet views.

The findings of this study thus raise serious questions concerning generalizations historians have commonly made about Roosevelt's diplomacy: that it was consistent with his public reputation for cooperation and conciliation; that he was naive with respect to postwar Soviet behavior; that, like Wilson, he believed in collective security as an effective guarantor of national safety; and that he made every possible effort to assure that the Soviet Union and its allies would continue to function as postwar partners. Although this article does not dispute the view that Roosevelt desired amicable postwar relations with the Soviet Union, or even that he worked hard to achieve them, it does suggest that historians have exaggerated his confidence in (and perhaps his commitment to) such an outcome. His most secret and among his most important long-range decisions—those responsible for prescribing a diplomatic role for the atomic bomb—reflected his lack of confidence. Finally, in light of this study's conclusions, the widely held assumption that Truman's attitude toward the atomic bomb was substantially different from Roosevelt's must also be revised.

Like the grand alliance itself, the Anglo-American atomic-energy partnership was forged by the war and its exigencies. The threat of a German atomic bomb precipitated a hasty marriage of convenience between British research and American resources. When scientists in Britain proposed a theory that explained how an atomic bomb might quickly be built, policy makers had to assume that German scientists were building one. "If such an explosive were made," Vannevar Bush, the director of the Office of Scientific Research and Development, told Roosevelt in July 1941, "it would be thousands of times more powerful than existing explosives, and its use might be determining." Roosevelt assumed nothing less. Even before the atomic-energy project was fully organized he assigned it the highest priority. He wanted the program "pushed not only in regard to development, but also with due regard to time. This is very much of the essence," he told Bush in March 1942. "We both felt painfully the dangers of doing nothing," Churchill recalled, referring to an early wartime discussion with Roosevelt about the bomb.

The high stakes at issue during the war did not prevent officials in Great Britain or the United States from considering the postwar implications of their atomic-energy decisions. As early as 1941, during the debate over whether to join the United States in an atomic-energy partnership, members of the British government's atomic-energy committee argued that the matter "was so important for the future that work should proceed in Britain." Weighing the obvious difficulties of proceeding along against the possible advantages of working with the United States, Sir John Anderson, then lord president of the council and the minister responsible for atomic-energy research, advocated the partnership. As he explained to Churchill, by working closely with the Americans British scientists would be able "to take up the work again [after the war], not where we left off, but where the combined effort had by then brought it."

As early as October 1942 Roosevelt's science advisers exhibited a similar concern with the potential postwar value of atomic energy. After conducting a full-scale review of the atomic-energy project, James B. Conant, the president of Harvard University and Bush's deputy, recommended discontinuing the Anglo-American partnership "as far as development and manufacture is concerned." Conant had in mind three considerations when he suggested a more limited arrangement with the British: first, the project had been transferred from scientific to military control; second, the United States was doing almost all the developmental work; and third, security dictated "moving in a direction of holding much more closely the information about the development of this program." Under these conditions it was difficult, Conant observed, "to see how a joint British-American project could be sponsored in this country." What prompted Conant's recommendations, however, was his suspicion—soon to be shared by other senior atomic-energy administrators—that the British were rather more concerned with information for postwar industrial purposes than for wartime use. What right did the British have to the fruits of American labor? "We were doing nine-tenths of the work," Stimson told Roosevelt in October. By December 1942 there was general agreement among the president's atomic-energy advisers that the British no longer had a valid claim to all atomic-energy information.

Conant's arguments and suggestions for a more limited partnership were incorporated into a "Report to the President by the Military Policy

Committee." Roosevelt approved the recommendations on December 28. Early in January the British were officially informed that the rules governing the Anglo-American atomic-energy partnership had been altered on "orders from the top."

By approving the policy of "restricted interchange" Roosevelt undermined a major incentive for British cooperation. It is not surprising, therefore, that Churchill took up the matter directly with the president and with Harry Hopkins, "Roosevelt's own, personal Foreign Office." The prime minister's initial response to the new policy reflected his determination to have it reversed: "That we should each work separately," he threatened, "would be a sombre decision."

Conant and Bush understood the implications of Churchill's intervention and sought to counter its effect. "It is our duty," Conant wrote Bush, "to see to it that the President of the United States, in writing, is informed of what is involved in these decisions." Their memorandums no longer concentrated on tortuous discussions differentiating between the scientific research and the manufacturing stages of the bomb's development but focused on what to Conant was "the major consideration... that of *national security and postwar strategic significance.*" Information on manufacturing an atomic bomb, Conant noted, was a "military secret which is in a totally different class from anything the world has ever seen if the potentialities of this project are realized." To provide the British with detailed knowledge about the construction of a bomb "might be the equivalent to joint occupation of a fortress or strategic harbor in perpetuity." Though British and American atomic-energy policies might coincide during the war, Conant and Bush expected them to conflict afterward.

The controversy over the policy of "restricted interchange" of atomic-energy information shifted attention to postwar diplomatic considerations. As Bush wrote to Hopkins, "We can hardly give away the fruits of our developments as a part of postwar planning except on the basis of some overall agreement on that subject, which agreement does not now exist." The central issue was clearly drawn. The atomic-energy policy of the United States was related to the very fabric of Anglo-American postwar relations and, as Churchill would insist, to postwar relations between each of them and the Soviet Union. Just as the possibility of British postwar commercial competition had played a major role in shaping the U.S. policy of restricted interchange, the specter of

Soviet postwar military power played a major role in shaping the prime minister's attitude toward atomic-energy policies in 1943.

"We cannot," Sir John Anderson wrote Churchill, "afford after the war to face the future without this weapon and rely entirely on America should Russia or some other power develop it." The prime minister agreed. The atomic bomb was an instrument of postwar diplomacy that Britain had to have. He could cite numerous reasons for his determination to acquire an independent atomic arsenal after the war, but Great Britain's postwar military-diplomatic position with respect to the Soviet Union invariably led the list. When Bush and Stimson visited London in July, Churchill told them quite frankly that he was "vitally interested in the possession of all [atomic-energy] information because this will be necessary for Britain's independence in the future as well as for success during the war." Nor was Churchill evasive about his reasoning: "It would never do to have Germany or Russia win the race for something which might be used for international blackmail," he stated bluntly and then pointed out that "Russia might be in a position to accomplish this result unless we worked together." In Washington, two months earlier, Churchill's science adviser Lord Cherwell had told Bush and Hopkins virtually the same thing. The British government, Cherwell stated, was considering "the whole [atomic-energy] affair on an after-the-war military basis." It intended, he said, "to manufacture and produce the weapon." Prior to the convening of the Quebec Conference, Anderson explained his own and Churchill's view of the bomb to the Canadian prime minister, Mackenzie King. The British knew, Anderson said, "that both Germany and Russia were working on the same thing," which, he noted, "would be a terrific factor in the postwar world as giving an absolute control to whatever country possessed the secret." Convinced that the British attitude toward the bomb would undermine any possibility of postwar cooperation with the Soviet Union, Bush and Conant vigorously continued to oppose any revival of the Anglo-American atomic-energy partnership.

On July 20, however, Roosevelt chose to accept a recommendation from Hopkins to restore full partnership, and he ordered Bush to "renew, in an inclusive manner, the full exchange of information with the British." A garbled trans-Atlantic cable to Bush reading "review" rather than "renew" gave him the opportunity to continue his negotiations in London with Churchill and thereby to modify the president's order. But Bush could not alter Roosevelt's intentions. On August 19, at the Quebec Conference, the president and the prime minister agreed that the British would share the atomic bomb. Despite Bush's negotiations with Churchill, the Quebec Agreement revived the principle of an Anglo-American atomic-energy partnership, albeit the British were reinstated as junior rather than equal partners.

The president's decision was not a casual one taken in ignorance. As the official history of the Atomic Energy Commission notes: "Both Roosevelt and Churchill knew that the stake of their diplomacy was a technological breakthrough so revolutionary that it transcended in importance even the bloody work of carrying the war to the heartland of the Nazi foe." The president had been informed of Churchill's position as well as of Bush's and Conant's. But how much closer Roosevelt was to Churchill than to his own advisers at this time is suggested by a report written after the war by General Leslie R. Groves, military director of the atomic-energy project. "It is not known what if any Americans President Roosevelt consulted at Quebec," Groves wrote. "It is doubtful if there were any. All that is known is that the Quebec Agreement was signed by President Roosevelt and that, as finally signed, it agreed practically in toto with the version presented by Sir John Anderson to Dr. Bush in Washington a few weeks earlier."

The debate that preceded the Quebec Agreement is noteworthy for yet another reason: it led to a new relationship between Roosevelt and his atomic-energy advisers. After August 1943 the president did not consult with them about the diplomatic aspects of atomic-energy policy. Though he responded politely when they offered their views, he acted decisively only in consultation with Churchill. Bush and Conant appear to have lost a large measure of their influence because they had used it to oppose Churchill's position. What they did not suspect was the extent to which the president had come to share the prime minister's view.

It can be argued that Roosevelt, the political pragmatist, renewed the wartime atomic-energy partnership to keep relations with the British harmonious rather than disrupt them on the basis of a postwar issue. Indeed it seems logical that the president took this consideration into account. But it must also be recognized that he was perfectly comfortable with the concept Churchill advocated—that military power was a prerequisite to successful postwar diplomacy. As early as August 1941, during the Atlantic Conference, Roosevelt had rejected the idea that an "effective international organization" could be relied upon to keep the peace; an Anglo-American international police force would be far more effective, he told Churchill. By the spring of 1942 the concept had broadened: the two "policemen" became four, and the idea was added that every other nation would be totally disarmed. "The Four Policemen" would have "to build up a reservoir of force so powerful that no aggressor would dare to challenge it," Roosevelt told Arthur Sweetser, an ardent internationalist. Violators first would be quarantined, and, if they persisted in their disruptive activities, bombed at the rate of a city a day until they agreed to behave. The president told Molotov about this idea in May, and in November he repeated it to Clark Eichelberger, who was coordinating the activities of the American internationalists. A year later, at the Teheran Conference, Roosevelt again discussed his idea, this time with Stalin. As Robert A. Divine has noted: "Roosevelt's concept of big power domination remained the central idea in his approach to international organization throughout World War II."

Precisely how Roosevelt expected to integrate the atomic bomb into his plans for keeping the peace in the postwar world is not clear. However, against the background of his atomic-energy policy decisions of 1943 and his peace-keeping concepts, his actions in 1944 suggest that he intended to take full advantage of the bomb's potential as a postwar instrument of Anglo-American diplomacy. If Roosevelt thought the bomb could be used to create a more peaceful world order, he seems to have considered the threat of its power more effective than any opportunities it offered for international cooperation. If Roosevelt was less worried than Churchill about Soviet postwar ambitions, he was no less determined than the prime minister to avoid any commitments to the Soviets for the international control of atomic energy. There could still be four policemen, but only two of them would have the bomb.

The atomic-energy policies Roosevelt pursued during the remainder of his life reinforce this interpretation of his ideas for the postwar period. The following three questions offer a useful framework for analyzing his intentions. Did Roosevelt make any additional agreements with Churchill that would further support the view that he intended to maintain an Anglo-American monopoly after the war? Did Roosevelt demonstrate any interest in the international control of atomic energy? Was Roosevelt aware that an effort to maintain an Anglo-American monopoly of the atomic bomb might lead to a post-war atomic arms race with the Soviet Union?

An examination of the wartime activities of the eminent Danish physicist, Niels Bohr, who arrived in America early in 1944 as a consultant to the atomic-bomb project, will help answer these questions. "Officially and secretly he came to help the technical enterprise," noted J. Robert Oppenheimer, the director of the Los Alamos atomic-bomb laboratory, but "most secretly of all... he came to advance his case and his cause." Bohr was convinced that a postwar atomic armaments race with the Soviet Union was inevitable unless Roosevelt and Churchill initiated efforts during the war to establish the international control of atomic energy. Bohr's attempts to promote this idea in the United States were aided by Justice Felix Frankfurter.

Bohr and Frankfurter were old acquaintances. They had first met in 1933 at Oxford and then in 1939 on several occasions in London and the United States. At these meetings Bohr had been impressed by the breadth of Frankfurter's interests and, perhaps, overimpressed with his influence on Roosevelt. In 1944 the Danish minister to the United States brought them together, once again, at his home in Washington. Frankfurter, who appears to have suspected why Bohr had come to America and why this meeting had been arranged, had learned about the atomic-bomb project earlier in the war when, as he told the story, several troubled scientists had sought his advice on a matter of "greatest importance." He therefore invited Bohr to lunch in his chambers and, by dropping hints about his knowledge, encouraged Bohr to discuss the issue.

After listening to Bohr's analysis of the postwar alternatives—an atomic armaments race or some form of international control—Frankfurter saw Roosevelt. Bohr had persuaded him, Frankfurter reported, that disastrous consequences would result if Russia learned on her own about the atomic-bomb project. Frankfurter suggested that it was a matter of great importance that the president explore the possibility of seeking an effective arrangement with the Soviets for controlling the bomb. He also noted that Bohr, whose knowledge of Soviet science was extensive, believed that the Russians had the capability to build their own atomic weapons. If the international control of atomic energy was not discussed among the Allies during the war, an atomic arms race between the Allies would almost certainly develop after the war. It seemed imperative, therefore, that Roosevelt consider approaching Stalin with a proposal as soon as possible.

Frankfurter discussed these points with the president for an hour and a half, and he left feeling that Roosevelt was "plainly impressed by my account of the matter." When Frankfurter had suggested that the solution of this problem might be more important than all the plans for a world organization, Roosevelt had agreed. Moreover he had authorized Frankfurter to tell Bohr, who was scheduled to return to England, that he might inform "our friends in London that the President was most eager to explore the proper safeguards in relation to X [the atomic bomb]." Roosevelt also told Frankfurter that the problem of the atomic bomb "worried him to death" and that he was very eager for all the help he could have in dealing with it.

The alternatives placed before Roosevelt posed a difficult dilemma. On the one hand, he could continue to exclude the Soviet government from any official information about the development of the bomb, a policy that would probably strengthen America's postwar military-diplomatic position. But such a policy would also encourage Soviet mistrust of Anglo-American intentions and was bound to make postwar cooperation more difficult. On the other hand, Roosevelt could use the atomic-bomb project as an instrument of cooperation by informing Stalin of the American government's intention of cooperating in the development of a plan for the international control of atomic weapons, an objective that might never be achieved.

Either choice involved serious risks. Roosevelt had to balance the diplomatic advantages of being well ahead of the Soviet Union in atomic-energy production after the war against the advantages of initiating wartime negotiations for postwar cooperation. The issue here, it must be emphasized, is not whether the initiative Bohr suggested would have led to successful international control, but rather whether Roosevelt demonstrated any serious interest in laying the groundwork for such a policy.

Several considerations indicate that Roosevelt was already committed to a course of action that precluded Bohr's internationalist approach. First, Frankfurter appears to have been misled. Though

Roosevelt's response had been characteristically agreeable, he did not mention Bohr's ideas to his atomic-energy advisers until September 1944, when he told Bush that he was very disturbed that Frankfurter had learned about the project. Roosevelt knew at this time, moreover, that the Soviets were finding out on their own about the development of the atomic bomb. Security personnel had reported an active Communist cell in the Radiation Laboratory at the University of California. Their reports indicated that at least one scientist at Berkeley was selling information to Russian agents. "They [Soviet agents] are already getting information about vital secrets and sending them to Russia," Stimson told the president on September 9, 1943. If Roosevelt was indeed worried to death about the effect the atomic bomb could have on Soviet-American postwar relations, he took no action to remove the potential danger, nor did he make any effort to explore the possibility of encouraging Soviet postwar cooperation on this problem. The available evidence indicates that he never discussed the merits of the international control of atomic energy with his advisers after this first or any subsequent meeting with Frankfurter.

How is the president's policy, of neither discussing international control nor promoting the idea, to be explained if not by an intention to use the bomb as an instrument of Anglo-American postwar diplomacy? Perhaps his concern for maintaining the tightest possible secrecy against German espionage led him to oppose any discussion about the project. Or he may have concluded, after considering Bohr's analysis, that Soviet suspicion and mistrust would be further aroused if Stalin were informed of the existence of the project without receiving detailed information about the bomb's construction. The possibility also exists that Roosevelt believed that neither Congress nor the American public would approve of a policy giving the Soviet Union any measure of control over the new weapon. Finally Roosevelt might have thought that the spring of 1944 was not the proper moment for such an initiative.

Though it would be unreasonable to state categorically that these considerations did not contribute to his decision, they appear to have been secondary. Roosevelt was clearly, and properly, concerned about secrecy, but the most important secret with respect to Soviet-American relations was that the United States was developing an atomic bomb. And that secret, he was aware, already had been passed on to Moscow.

Soviet mistrust of Anglo-American postwar intentions could only be exacerbated by continuing the existing policy. Moreover an attempt to initiate planning for international control of atomic energy would not have required the revelation of technical secrets. Nor is it sufficient to cite Roosevelt's well-known sensitivity to domestic politics as an explanation for his atomic-energy policies. He was willing to take enormous political risks, as he did at Yalta, to support his diplomatic objectives.

Had Roosevelt avoided all postwar atomic-energy commitments, his lack of support for international control could have been interpreted as an attempt to reserve his opinion on the best course to follow. But he had made commitments in 1943 supporting Churchill's monopolistic, anti-Soviet position, and he continued to make others in 1944. On June 13, for example, Roosevelt and Churchill signed an Agreement and Declaration of Trust, specifying that the United States and Great Britain would cooperate in seeking to control available supplies of uranium and thorium ore both during and after the war. This commitment, taken against the background of Roosevelt's peace-keeping ideas and his other commitments, suggests that the president's attitude toward the international control of atomic energy was similar to the prime minister's.

Churchill had dismissed out of hand the concept of international control when Bohr talked with him about it in May 1944. Their meeting was not long under way before Churchill lost interest and became involved in an argument with Lord Cherwell, who was also present. Bohr, left out of the discussion, was frustrated and depressed; he was unable to return the conversation to what he considered the most important diplomatic problem of the war. When the allotted half hour elapsed, Bohr asked if he might send the prime minister a memorandum on the subject. A letter from Niels Bohr, Churchill bitingly replied, was always welcome, but he hoped it would deal with a subject other than politics. As Bohr described their meeting: "We did not even speak the same language."

Churchill rejected the assumption upon which Bohr's views were founded—that international control of atomic energy could be used as a cornerstone for constructing a peaceful world order. An atomic monopoly would be a significant diplomatic advantage in postwar diplomacy, and Churchill did not believe that anything useful could be gained by surrendering this advantage. The argument that a new weapon created a unique opportunity to refashion international affairs ignored every lesson Churchill read into history. "You can be quite sure," he would write in a memorandum less than a year later, "that any power that gets hold of the secret will try to make the article, and this touches the existence of human society. This matter is out of all relation to anything else that exists in the world, and I could not think of participating in any disclosure to third or fourth parties at the present time."

Several months after Bohr met Churchill, Frankfurter arranged a meeting between Bohr and Roosevelt. Their discussion lasted an hour and a half. Roosevelt told Bohr that contact with the Soviet Union along the lines he suggested had to be tried. The president also said he was optimistic that such an initiative would have a "good result." In his opinion Stalin was enough of a realist to understand the revolutionary importance of this development and its consequences. The president also expressed confidence that the prime minister would eventually share these views. They had disagreed in the past, he told Bohr, but they had always succeeded in resolving their differences.

Roosevelt's enthusiasm for Bohr's ideas was more apparent than real. The president did not mention them to anyone until he met with Churchill at Hyde Park on September 18, following the second wartime conference at Quebec. The decisions reached on atomic energy at Hyde Park were summarized and documented in an *aide-mémoire* signed by Roosevelt and Churchill on September 19, 1944. The agreement bears the markings of Churchill's attitude toward the atomic bomb and his poor opinion of Bohr. "Enquiries should be made," the last paragraph reads, "regarding the activities of Professor Bohr and steps taken to ensure that he is responsible for no leakage of information particularly to the Russians." If Bohr's activities prompted Roosevelt to suspect his loyalty, there can be no doubt that Churchill encouraged the president's suspicions. Atomic energy and Britain's future position as a world power had become part of a single equation for the prime minister. Bohr's ideas, like the earlier idea of restricted interchange, threatened the continuation of the Anglo-American atomic-energy partnership. With such great stakes at issue Churchill did not hesitate to discredit Bohr along with his ideas. "It seems to me," Churchill wrote to Cherwell soon after Hyde Park, "Bohr ought to be confined or at any rate made to see that he is very near the edge of mortal crimes."

The *aide-mémoire* also contained an explicit rejection of any wartime efforts toward international control: "The suggestion that the world should be informed regarding tube alloys [the atomic bomb], with a view to an international agreement regarding its control and use, is not accepted. The matter should continue to be regarded as of the utmost secrecy." But Bohr had never suggested that the world be informed about the atomic bomb. He had argued in memorandums and in person that peace was not possible unless the Soviet government—not the world—was officially notified only about the project's existence before the time when any discussion would appear coercive rather than friendly.

It was the second paragraph, however, that revealed the full extent of Roosevelt's agreement with Churchill's point of view. "Full collaboration between the United States and the British Government in developing tube alloys for military and commercial purposes," it noted, "should continue after the defeat of Japan unless and until terminated by joint agreement." Finally the *aide-mémoire* offers some insight into Roosevelt's intentions for the military use of the weapon in the war: "When a bomb is finally available, it might perhaps, after mature consideration, be used against the Japanese, who should be warned that this bombardment will be repeated until they surrender."

Within the context of the complex problem of the origins of the cold war the Hyde Park meeting is far more important than historians of the war generally have recognized. Overshadowed by the Second Quebec Conference on one side and by the drama of Yalta on the other, its significance often has been overlooked. But the agreements reached in September 1944 reflect a set of attitudes, aims, and assumptions that guided the relationship between the atomic bomb and American diplomacy during the Roosevelt administration and, through the transfer of its atomic legacy, during the Truman administration as well. Two alternatives had been recognized long before Roosevelt and Churchill met in 1944 at Hyde Park: the bomb could have been used to initiate a diplomatic effort to work out a system for its international control, or it could remain isolated during the war from any cooperative initiatives and held in reserve should cooperation fail. Roosevelt consistently favored the latter alternative. An insight into his reasoning is found in a memorandum Bush wrote following a conversation with Roosevelt several days after the Hyde Park meeting: "The President evidently thought he could join with Churchill in bringing about a US-UK postwar agreement on this subject [the atomic bomb] by which it would be held closely and presumably to control the peace of the world." By 1944 Roosevelt's earlier musings about the four policemen had faded into the background. But the idea behind it, the concept of controlling the peace of the world by amassing overwhelming military power, appears to have remained a prominent feature of his postwar plans.

In the seven months between his meeting with Churchill in September and his death the following April Roosevelt did not alter his atomic-energy policies. Nor did he reverse his earlier decision not to take his advisers into his confidence about diplomatic issues related to the new weapon. They were never told about the Hyde Park agreements, nor were they able to discuss with him their ideas for the postwar handling of atomic-energy affairs. Though officially uninformed, Bush suspected that Roosevelt had made a commitment to continue the atomic-energy partnership exclusively with the British after the war, and he, as well as Conant, opposed the idea. They believed such a policy "might well lead to extraordinary efforts on the part of Russia to establish its own position in the field secretly, and might lead to a clash, say 20 years from now." Unable to reach the president directly, they sought to influence his policies through Stimson, whose access to Roosevelt's office (though not to his thoughts on atomic energy) was better than their own.

Summarizing their views on September 30 for the secretary of war, Bush and Conant predicted that an atomic bomb equivalent to from one to ten thousand tons of high explosive could be "demonstrated" before August 1, 1945. They doubted that the present American and British monopoly could be maintained for more than three or four years, and they pointed out that any nation with good technical and scientific resources could catch up; accidents of research, moreover, might even put some other nation ahead. In addition atomic bombs were only the first step along the road of nuclear weapons technology. In the not-too-distant future loomed the awesome prospect of a weapon perhaps a thousand times more destructive—the hydrogen bomb. Every major center of population in the world would then lie at the mercy of a nation that struck first in war. Security therefore could be found neither in secrecy nor even in the control of raw materials, for the supply of heavy hydrogen was practically unlimited.

These predictions by Bush and Conant were more specific than Bohr's, but not dissimilar. They, too, believed that a nuclear arms race could be prevented only through international control. Their efforts were directed, however, toward abrogating existing agreements with the British rather than toward initiating new agreements with the Soviets. Like Bohr they based their hope for Stalin's eventual cooperation on his desire to avoid the circumstances that could lead to a nuclear war. But while Bohr urged Roosevelt to approach Stalin with the carrot of international control before the bomb became a reality, Bush and Conant were inclined to delay such an approach until the bomb was demonstrated, until it was clear that without international control the new weapon could be used as a terribly effective stick.

In their attempt to persuade Roosevelt to their point of view Bush and Conant failed. But their efforts were not in vain. By March 1945 Stimson shared their concerns, and he agreed that peace without international control was a forlorn hope. Postwar problems relating to the atomic bomb "went right down to the bottom facts of human nature, morals and government, and it is by far the most searching and important thing that I have had to do since I have been here in the office of Secretary of War," Stimson wrote on March 5. Ten days later he presented his views on postwar atomic-energy policy to Roosevelt. This was their last meeting. In less than a month a new president took the oath of office.

Harry S. Truman inherited a set of military and diplomatic atomic-energy policies that included partially formulated intentions, several commitments to Churchill, and the assumption that the bomb would be a legitimate weapon to be used against Japan. But no policy was definitely settled. According to the Quebec Agreement the president had the option of deciding the future of the commercial aspects of the atomic-energy partnership according to his own estimate of what was fair. Although the policy of "utmost secrecy" had been confirmed at Hyde Park the previous September, Roosevelt had not informed his atomic-energy advisers about the *aide-mémoire* he and Churchill signed. Although the assumption that the bomb would be used in the war was shared by those privy to its development, assumptions formulated early in the war were not necessarily valid at its conclusion.

Yet Truman was bound to the past by his own uncertain position and by the prestige of his predecessor. Since Roosevelt had refused to open negotiations with the Soviet government for the international control of atomic energy, and since he had never expressed any objection to the wartime use of the bomb, it would have required considerable political courage and confidence for Truman to alter those policies. Moreover it would have required the encouragement of his advisers, for under the circumstances the most serious constraint on the new president's choices was his dependence upon advice. So Truman's atomic legacy, while it included several options, did not necessarily entail complete freedom to choose from among all the possible alternatives.

"I think it is very important that I should have a talk with you as soon as possible on a highly secret matter," Stimson wrote to Truman on April 24. It has "such a bearing on our present foreign relations and has such an important effect upon all my thinking in this field that I think you ought to know about it without further delay." Stimson had been preparing to brief Truman on the atomic bomb for almost ten days, but in the preceding twenty-four hours he had been seized by a sense of urgency. Relations with the Soviet Union had declined precipitously during the past week, the result, he thought, of the failure of the State Department to settle the major problems between the Allies before going ahead with the San Francisco Conference on the United Nations Organization. The secretary of state, Edward R. Stettinius, Jr., along with the department's Soviet specialists, now felt "compelled to bull the thing through." To get out of the "mess" they had created, Stimson wrote in his diary, they were urging Truman to get tough with the Russians. He had. Twenty-four hours earlier the president met with the Soviet foreign minister, V.M. Molotov, and "with rather brutal frankness" accused his government of breaking the Yalta Agreement. Molotov was furious. "I have never been talked to like that in my life," he told the president before leaving.

With a memorandum on the "political aspects of the S–1 [atomic bomb's] performance" in hand and General Groves in reserve, Stimson went to the White House on April 25. The document he carried was the distillation of numerous decisions already taken, each one the product of attitudes that developed along with the new weapon. The secretary himself was not entirely aware of how various forces had shaped

these decisions: the recommendations of Bush and Conant, the policies
Roosevelt had followed, the uncertainties inherent in the wartime alliance, the oppressive concern for secrecy, and his own inclination to
consider long-range implications. It was a curious document. Though
its language revealed Stimson's sensitivity to the historic significance
of the atomic bomb, he did not question the wisdom of using it against
Japan. Nor did he suggest any concrete steps for developing a postwar
policy. His objective was to inform Truman of the salient problems:
the possibility of an atomic arms race, the danger of atomic war, and
the necessity for international control if the United Nations Organization was to work. "If the problem of the proper use of this weapon
can be solved," he wrote, "we would have the opportunity to bring
the world into a pattern in which the peace of the world and our
civilizations can be saved." To cope with this difficult challenge Stimson
suggested the "establishment of a select committee" to consider the
postwar problems inherent in the development of the bomb. If his
presentation was the "forceful statement" of the problem that historians of the Atomic Energy Commission have described it as being, its
force inhered in the problem itself, not in any bold formulations or
initiatives he offered toward a solution. If, as another historian has
claimed, this meeting led to a "strategy of delayed showdown," requiring "the delay of all disputes with Russia until the atomic bomb
had been demonstrated," there is no evidence in the extant records of
the meeting that Stimson had such a strategy in mind or that Truman
misunderstood the secretary's views.

What emerges from a careful reading of Stimson's diary, his memorandum of April 25 to Truman, a summary by Groves of the meeting,
and Truman's recollections is an argument for overall caution in American diplomatic relations with the Soviet Union: it was an argument
against any showdown. Since the atomic bomb was potentially the
most dangerous issue facing the postwar world and since the most
desirable resolution of the problem was some form of international
control, Soviet cooperation had to be secured. It was imprudent, Stimson suggested, to pursue a policy that would preclude the possibility
of international cooperation on atomic-energy matters after the war
ended. Truman's overall impression of Stimson's argument was that
the secretary of war was "at least as much concerned with the role of
the atomic bomb in the shaping of history as in its capacity to shorten

the war." These were indeed Stimson's dual concerns on April 25, and he could see no conflict between them.

Despite the profound consequences Stimson attributed to the development of the new weapon, he had not suggested that Truman reconsider its use against Japan. Nor had he thought to mention the possibility that chances of securing Soviet postwar cooperation might be diminished if Stalin did not receive a commitment to international control prior to an attack. The question of why these alternatives were overlooked naturally arises. Perhaps what Frankfurter once referred to as Stimson's habit of setting "his mind at one thing like the needle of an old victrola caught in a single groove" may help to explain his not mentioning these possibilities. Yet Bush and Conant never raised them either. Even Niels Bohr had made a clear distinction between the bomb's wartime use and its postwar impact on diplomacy. "What role it [the atomic bomb] may play in the present war," Bohr had written to Roosevelt in July 1944, was a question "quite apart" from the overriding concern: the need to avoid an atomic arms race.

The preoccupation with winning the war obviously helped to create this seeming dichotomy between the wartime use of the bomb and the potential postwar diplomatic problems with the Soviet Union raised by its development. But a closer look at how Bohr and Stimson each defined the nature of the diplomatic problem created by the bomb suggests that for the secretary of war and his advisers (and ultimately for the president they advised) there was no dichotomy at all. Bohr apprehended the meaning of the new weapon even before it was developed, and he had no doubt that scientists in the Soviet Union would also understand its profound implications for the postwar world. He was also certain that they would interpret the meaning of the development to Stalin just as scientists in the United States and Great Britain had explained it to Roosevelt and Churchill. Thus the diplomatic problem, as Bohr analyzed it, was not the need to convince Stalin that the atomic bomb was an unprecedented weapon that threatened the life of the world but the need to assure the Soviet leader that he had nothing to fear from the circumstances of its development. By informing Stalin during the war that the United States intended to cooperate with him in neutralizing the bomb through international control, Bohr reasoned that its wartime use could be considered apart from postwar problems.

Stimson approached the problem rather differently. Although he believed that the bomb "might even mean the doom of civilization or it might mean the perfection of civilization" he was less confident than Bohr that the weapon in an undeveloped state could be used as an effective instrument of diplomacy. Until its "actual certainty [was] fixed," Stimson considered any prior approach to Stalin as premature. But as the uncertainties of impending peace became more apparent and worrisome, Stimson, Truman, and the secretary of state-designate, James F. Byrnes, began to think of the bomb as something of a diplomatic panacea for their postwar problems. Byrnes had told Truman in April that the bomb "might well put us in a position to dictate our own terms at the end of the war." By June, Truman and Stimson were discussing "further *quid pro quos* which should be established in consideration for our taking them [the Soviet Union] into [atomic-energy] partnership." Assuming that the bomb's impact on diplomacy would be immediate and extraordinary, they agreed on no less than "the settlement of the Polish, Rumanian, Yugoslavian, and Manchurian problems." But they also concluded that no revelation would be made "to Russia or anyone else until the first bomb had been successfully laid on Japan." Truman and Stimson based their expectations on how they saw and valued the bomb; its use against Japan, they reasoned, would transfer this view to the Soviet Union.

Was an implicit warning to Moscow, then, the principal reason for deciding to use the atomic bomb against Japan? In light of the ambiguity of the available evidence the question defies an unequivocal answer. What can be said with certainty is that Truman, Stimson, Byrnes, and several others involved in the decision consciously considered two effects of a combat demonstration of the bomb's power: first, the impact of the atomic attack on Japan's leaders, who might be persuaded thereby to end the war; and second, the impact of that attack on the Soviet Union's leaders, who might then prove to be more cooperative. But if the assumption that the bomb might bring the war to a rapid conclusion was the principal motive for using the atomic bomb, the expectation that its use would also inhibit Soviet diplomatic ambitions clearly discouraged any inclination to question that assumption.

Policymakers were not alone in expecting a military demonstration of the bomb to have a salubrious effect on international affairs. James Conant, for example, believed that such a demonstration would further the prospects for international control. "President Conant has written me," Stimson informed the news commentator Raymond Swing in February 1947, "that one of the principal reasons he had for advising me that the bomb must be used was that that was the only way to awaken the world to the necessity of abolishing war altogether." And the director of the atomic-energy laboratory at the University of Chicago made the same point to Stimson in June 1945: "If the bomb were not used in the present war," Arthur Compton noted, "the world would have no adequate warning as to what was to be expected if war should break out again." Even Edward Teller who has publicly decried the attack on Hiroshima and declared his early opposition to it, adopted a similar position in July 1945. "Our only hope is in getting the facts of our results before the people," he wrote to his colleague, Leo Szilard, who was circulating a petition among scientists opposing the bomb's use. "This might help to convince everybody that the next war would be fatal," Teller noted. "For this purpose actual combat use might even be the best thing."

Thus by the end of the war the most influential and widely accepted attitude toward the bomb was a logical extension of how the weapon was seen and valued earlier—as a potential instrument of diplomacy. Caught between the remnants of war and the uncertainties of peace, scientists as well as policy makers were trapped by the logic of their own unquestioned assumptions. By the summer of 1945 not only the conclusion of the war but the organization of an acceptable peace seemed to depend upon the success of the atomic attacks against Japan. When news of the successful atomic test of July 16 reached the president at the Potsdam Conference, he was visibly elated. Stimson noted that Truman "was tremendously pepped up by it and spoke to me of it again and again when I saw him. He said it gave him an entirely new feeling of confidence." The day after receiving the complete report of the test Truman altered his negotiating style. According to Churchill the president "got to the meeting after having read this report [and] he was a changed man. He told the Russians just where they got on and off and generally bossed the whole meeting." After the plenary session on July 24 Truman "casually mentioned to Stalin" that the United States had "a new weapon of unusual destructive force." Truman took this step in response to a recommendation by the Interim Committee, a group of political and scientific advisers organized by Stimson in May 1945 to advise the president on atomic-energy policy. But it is an unavoidable conclusion that what the president told the premier followed the letter of the recommendation rather than its spirit, which embodied the hope that an overture to Stalin would initiate the process toward international control. In less than three weeks the new weapon's destructive potential would be demonstrated to the world. Stalin would then be forced to reconsider his diplomatic goals. It is no wonder that upon learning of the raid against Hiroshima Truman exclaimed: "This is the greatest thing in history."

As Stimson had expected, as a colossal reality the bomb was very different. But had American diplomacy been altered by it? Those who conducted diplomacy became more confident, more certain that through the accomplishments of American science, technology and industry the "new world" could be made into one better than the old. But just how the atomic bomb would be used to help accomplish this ideal remained unclear. Three months and one day after Hiroshima was bombed Bush wrote that the whole matter of international relations on atomic energy "is in a thoroughly chaotic condition." The wartime relationship between atomic-energy policy and diplomacy had been based upon the simple assumption that the Soviet government would surrender important geographical, political, and ideological objectives in exchange for the neutralization of the new weapon. As a result of policies based on this assumption American diplomacy and prestige suffered grievously: an opportunity to gauge the Soviet Union's response during the war to the international control of atomic energy was missed, and an atomic-energy policy for dealing with the Soviet government after the war was ignored. Instead of promoting American postwar aims, wartime atomic-energy policies made them more difficult to achieve. As a group of scientists at the University of Chicago's atomic-energy laboratory presciently warned the government in June 1945: "It may be difficult to persuade the world that a nation which was capable of secretly preparing and suddenly releasing a weapon as indiscriminate as the [German] rocket bomb and a million times more destructive, is to be trusted in its proclaimed desire of having such weapons abolished by international agreement." This reasoning, however, flowed from alternative assumptions formulated during the closing months of the war by scientists far removed from the wartime policymaking process. Hiroshima and Nagasaki, the culmination of that process, became the symbols of a new American barbarism, reinforcing charges, with dramatic circumstantial evidence, that the policies of the United States contributed to the origins of the cold war.

16

The Conversion of Harry Truman

WILLIAM E. LEUCHTENBURG

● *Harry S Truman became the thirty-third president of the United States at a critical moment in the nation's history. He was immediately confronted with the problems of concluding the war with Japan and with the challenge of establishing a new kind of peace in a bipolar world. Attempting to minimize the loss of American lives, he authorized the use of the atomic bomb. And within the next half dozen years, he developed the Truman Doctrine to halt Soviet expansion into Turkey and Greece and the Marshall Plan to help Western Europe get its economy moving again. Perhaps his most spectacular challenge came in 1951, when he had to fire an arrogant General Douglas MacArthur for willful insubordination to the commander in chief.*

A man with a reputation for taking responsibility and making decisions, Truman surprised many observers with several strong actions in defense of civil rights. Initially, southerners thought that one of their own had moved in to the White House. The president, after all, came from a border state and shared many racist attitudes and ideas of the South. But Truman fought for legislation that would guarantee to African Americans some of the benefits of citizenship in a nation they had helped to defend, and he issued an executive order to desegregate the armed forces of the United States. The following essay by Professor William E. Leuchtenburg, the dean of historians of twentieth-century United States, considers the career of this remarkable man and the reasons why he converted on the issue of civil rights.

Harry Truman approached national politics with divided memories and divergent loyalties. He was reared in a border-state county as

Reprinted by permission of *American Heritage* Magazine, a division of Forbes Inc., © Forbes Inc., 1991.

Southern in its sympathies as any Mississippi Delta town and by a family that shared Mississippi's racial outlook and held dear the hallowed symbol of the Stars and Bars. Yet Truman also harbored a powerful nationalist strain. He never regretted that the Civil War had ended in a Union victory, and he came to view Lincoln as a man of heroic stature. Perhaps nothing revealed so well the conflicting tugs on him as a letter he wrote in 1941 to his daughter, Margaret: "Yesterday I drove over the route that the last of the Confederate army followed before the surrender. I thought of the heartache of one of the world's great men on the occasion of that surrender. I am not sorry he did surrender, but I feel as your old country grandmother has expressed it—'What a pity a *white* man like Lee had to surrender to *old* Grant.' "

Truman's direct ancestors identified strongly with the slave South. All four of his grandparents were born in Kentucky, and when they migrated to Missouri in the 1840s, they brought their slaves with them. Truman's grandparents received slaves as a wedding present, and in Missouri one of his grandfathers owned some two dozen slaves on his five-thousand-acre plantation. His parents, Truman recalled, were "a violently unreconstructed southern family" and "Lincoln haters." His mother was an ardent admirer of William Quantrill, the Confederate guerrilla leader who, pillaging Lawrence, Kansas, in 1863, slew at least one hundred and fifty of its citizens, including women and children. One historian has called him "the bloodiest man in American history."

Truman's Jackson County, though, revered Quantrill, because he had his counterpart in James Lane, chieftain of the pro-Union Jayhawkers. Truman's grandmother never wearied of telling of the morning in 1861 when, with her husband away, Jim Lane, at the head of a scruffy band of horsemen wearing red sheepskin leggings, rode into her farmyard, ordered her to hop to it and cook for him and his men, then killed her hens, slaughtered all the livestock, including more than four hundred hogs, toted off the still-bloody hams, pocketed the family silver, and set the barns afire.

Truman's family rehearsed, too, the awful time in 1863 when a Union commander, retaliating for Quantrill's sack of Lane's hometown of Lawrence, issued the notorious General Order No. 11, which routed all the people of Jackson County, the den of Quantrill's bushwhackers, and herded them to a Federal fort, where for months they were compelled to live on handouts. As a girl of eleven Truman's mother, Martha, trudged through the dust with her mother and five other children behind an oxcart carrying all that was left of a once-proud holding. After the Trumans and their neighbors had been evicted, Union forces set the countryside ablaze for miles. In later years Martha Truman would have no compunction about saying, "I thought it was a good thing that Lincoln was shot."

The women in his family sought to imbue Truman with an intense dislike of the Union cause and its leaders. When in 1905 the twenty-one-year-old Truman, proud of his splendid new National Guard uniform, called on his grandmother, she gave him a once-over, then told him sternly, "Harry, this is the first time since 1863 that a blue uniform has been in this house. Don't bring it here again." More than four decades later, when the President's mother was invited to the White House, one of her sons said that the only unoccupied bed was in the Lincoln Room. She retorted, "You tell Harry if he tries to put me in Lincoln's bed, I'll sleep on the floor."

Truman literally learned at his mother's knee to share the South's view of the War Between the States. He grew up detesting the meddlesome abolitionists, decried the racial experimentation of Reconstruction, and sneered at Thaddeus Stevens, that "crippled moron." He also acquired an abiding belief in white supremacy. In 1911, when he was twenty-seven, he wrote Bess Wallace: "I think one man is just as good as another so long as he's honest and decent and not a nigger or a Chinaman. Uncle Will says that the Lord made a white man from dust[,] a nigger from mud, then He threw up what was left and it came down a Chinaman. He does hate Chinese and Japs. So do I. It is race prejudice I guess. But I am strongly of the opinion that negros [sic] ought to be in Africa, yellow men in Asia and white men in Europe and America."

More than a quarter of a century later, in a letter home to his daughter about dining at the White House when he was a U.S. senator, he described the waiters, who he thought were "evidently the top of the black social set in Washington," as "an army of coons," and in a letter to his wife in 1939, he referred to "nigger picnic day."

Yet if Truman absorbed his family's and his county's Southern heritage almost by osmosis, other legacies drew him toward identification not with a section but with the nation. Early in 1860 one of Truman's great-uncles in Kentucky wrote his brother—Harry's grandfather—in

Missouri: "Andy ... I am in hopes that you are not a seceder. I am for the union now and forever & so is old Ky." The next year he wrote again: "Ky. is not willing to turn traitor yet awhile. God forbid that she ever should. You see I am a union man yet and expect to live and die one.... Are you still in ... the union, or have you seceded? Oh I hope not. I hope you have not turned against this glorious union to follow Jeff Davis and Co."

Truman's forebear's fierce loyalty to the Union, though, did not carry with it admiration for Abraham Lincoln. "My old woman is distant relation of old Abe Lincoln," he explained in 1864, "but we are not Lincolnites."

Truman's capacity for perceiving a national interest transcending his family's devotion to the Lost Cause owed a great deal to the fact that the community in which he was raised, instinctively Southern though it was, turned its face, in a highly self-conscious way, toward the West. Truman was keenly aware of Independence as the entrepôt to the Santa Fe, the Mormon, and the Oregon trails. As a boy he played on the tracks of the first railroad that ran west of the Mississippi, and in the 1920s he became president of the National Old Trails Association, which required him to travel around the country to promote using the routes of the historical trails to the West for interstate highways. On one of his trips he visited Boot Hill in Dodge City and encountered a gunslinger who had faced Bat Masterson. Truman was happy, he announced on one occasion, to be "back home—once more a free and independent citizen of the gateway city of the old Great West."

If Truman's family constantly reminded him of his Confederate heritage, it also relayed to him vivid recollections of his ancestors' experiences on the frontier. His great-grandfather, the son of an adventurer allied with Daniel Boone, is said to have been the first white child born in Kentucky, and his great-grandmother wore a lace cap to conceal a scar from being scalped in an Indian raid in 1788. As a boy Truman heard these tales countless times.

But it was the saga of his grandfather Solomon Young that made the most lasting impression. He had first headed West in the "year of decision," 1846, the same year as Francis Parkman's journey on the Oregon Trail. A Conestoga wagon master who drove huge herds of cattle across the plains, he would leave one spring and not get home until the next. He was once away so long that his young daughter did not know him when he returned. He went West one year from Independence with no fewer than 1,500 head of cattle, and in the summer of 1860 he reached Salt Lake City with forty wagons and 130 yoke of oxen.

Truman took full political advantage of this frontier past. As he campaigned through the West in 1948, he claimed so many places were spots at which Solomon Young had stopped that reporters wondered how the man had ever made it to Sacramento. In that campaign, the veteran correspondent Richard L. Strout recalled, "the further west he got the more his western vernacular increased.... All the way across the West as his vernacular got thicker he told about Grandpa's covered wagon trip to Oregon and produced an historical relative or two in virtually every area where he spoke."

Truman's behavior in that campaign left observers at the time, and commentators since, bewildered about just where he located himself. If in talking to Western audiences he exploited his grandfather's feats on the Great Plains, he took pains to remind Southern audiences of his Kentucky ancestry and his fondness for Stonewall Jackson.

To add to the confusion, some perceived him to be neither Western nor Southern. A Truman follower could call him at different spots in the same book a man "from a midcontinental state," "a Midwesterner," and "coming from a border state ... neither a Northerner nor a Southerner." The last comment is closest to the mark. He was a border stater, a man from Missouri.

But rather than being "neither a Northerner nor a Southerner," he was both. He was in the position to be at the same time inside and outside the South, able to empathize with its hurts and its hopes but to surmise that its destiny lay in the finding of a place for itself within the nation.

Nonetheless, entering the United States Senate in 1935, Truman immediately gravitated toward the Southerners. They, in turn, accepted him as one of their own. Months before the 1944 campaign some Southerners had come to view Truman as a feasible vice-presidential nominee, and at the 1944 Democratic National Convention Southerners helped conspicuously in putting him across. Afterward Gov. Chauncey Sparks of Alabama said, "The South has won a substantial victory. ...In the matter of race relations Senator Truman told me he is the son of an unreconstructed rebel mother."

When Franklin Roosevelt's death, on April 12, 1945, catapulted Truman into the White House, the white South felt confident that Truman would find its racial customs congenial. On the funeral train carrying FDR's body, the Democratic senator from South Carolina Burnet Maybank assured a Southern friend, "Everything's going to be all right—the new President knows how to handle the niggers."

But on December 5, 1946, Truman demolished these comfortable assumptions by announcing the creation of a President's Committee on Civil Rights. He had been moved to act after a delegation had called on him to protest outrages against blacks. He was appalled especially by an incident in Aiken, South Carolina, where, only three hours after a black sergeant had received his separation papers from the United States Army, policemen gouged out his eyes. In Georgia, Truman heard, the only black to have voted in his area was murdered by four whites in his front yard. In another Georgia county two black men were gunned down by a white gang, and when one of their wives recognized one of the killers, both the wives were shot to death too. On being told at a meeting with the National Emergency Committee Against Mob Violence of the blinding of the black sergeant, the President, his face "pale with horror," rose and said, "My God. I had no idea it was as terrible as that. We've got to do something!"

The very next day he wrote his Attorney General, "I know you have been looking into the ...lynchings ...but I think it is going to take something more than the handling of each individual case after it happens—it is going to require the inauguration of some sort of policy to prevent such happenings." On December 5 Truman signed an order creating a President's Committee on Civil Rights, which he directed to look into not merely racial violence but the entire universe of civil rights. To carry out this huge assignment, he appointed fifteen prominent citizens under the chairmanship of the president of General Electric, Charles E. Wilson. Only two of the fifteen were from the South, and both of them were conspicuous liberals.

In October 1947 the committee issued its historic report, "To Secure These Rights." It found that a gaping disparity between the country's ideal of equality and its behavior had resulted in "a kind of moral dry rot which eats away at the emotional and rational bases of democratic beliefs." Furthermore, it said, with an eye toward the Cold War, the United States "is not so strong, the final triumph of the democratic ideal is not so inevitable, that we can ignore what the world thinks of us or our record."

The committee came forth with nearly three dozen recommendations, including expanding the civil rights section of the Justice Department, creating a permanent Commission on Civil Rights, enacting an anti-lynching statute and a law punishing police brutality, expanding the suffrage by banning the poll tax and safeguarding the right to cast ballots in primaries and general elections, and outlawing discrimination in private employment. It also favored "renewed court attack, with intervention by the Department of Justice," on racially restrictive covenants in housing and ending "immediately" discrimination in the armed services and in federal agencies. Most controversial, it opposed not only racial discrimination but segregation. In particular, it advocated denying federal money to any public or private program that persisted in Jim Crow practices and making the District of Columbia a model for the nation by integrating all its facilities, including its public schools.

The publication of "To Secure These Rights" aroused a storm of criticism. The chairman of the Democratic committee in Danville, Virginia, wired Truman, "I really believe that you have ruined the Democratic Party in the South," and a Baptist minister in Jacksonville, Florida informed him: "If that report is carried out, you won't be elected dogcatcher in 1948. The South today is the South of 1861."

In one respect the shock expressed by the South is surprising, for Truman had built a sturdy record on behalf of civil rights as early as 1937. As senator he had twice cooperated with the National Association for the Advancement of Colored People in signing petitions to break filibusters over anti-lynching legislation, and less than two months after he took office as President he had written a public letter asking the House Rules Committee to advance legislation for a permanent Fair Employment Practices Commission (FEPC).

Yet until 1947 Southern politicians had tolerated such actions because they thought them merely expedient. They assumed that since, as senator, he came from a state with 130,000 black voters, he had to make a show of going along with civil rights bills that were doomed to defeat anyway. Even while supporting such measures, Truman had made a point of announcing that he did not question Jim Crow. In 1940 he told the National Colored Democratic Association of Chicago: "I wish to make it clear that I am not appealing for social equality of the Negro. The Negro himself knows better than that."

His performance as President had also been ambivalent. He had asked for an FEPC bill, for instance, but then had run away from the fight to get it enacted.

Yet the white South had good reason to conclude that by 1947 Truman had changed. He had done so, in part, for political reasons. In World War II Southern blacks had migrated in large numbers to states, such as Michigan and California, with big blocs of electoral votes, and in the 1946 elections, dismayed by Southern racist demagogues, they had given evidence of drifting away from the Democrats. Even in the South black voters promised to be an increasing presence following a 1944 Supreme Court decision outlawing the white primary. Truman was motivated too by foreign policy concerns. Discrimination against people of color was proving an embarrassment of the government as it vied with the Soviet Union for the allegiance of Third World nations. Probably most important, though, was Truman's outrage against the mistreatment of blacks. Truman had never been willing to condone denying to citizens, black or white, their fundamental rights, and as President he was expanding his awareness of the need to use federal power to secure to all Americans the liberties guaranteed by the Constitution. What Southern politicians thought could be explained only as self-interested bids for black votes actually represented both long-held beliefs and maturing convictions.

Once Truman set out on this new course, he would not relent. When Democratic leaders asked him to back down from his strong stand on civil rights, he replied: "My forebears were Confederates. . . . Every factor and influence in my background—and in my wife's for that matter—would foster the personal belief that you are right.

"But my very stomach turned over when I learned that Negro soldiers, just back from overseas, were being dumped out of Army trucks in Mississippi and beaten.

"Whatever my inclinations as a native of Missouri might have been, as President I know this is bad. I shall fight to end evils like this."

On February 2, 1948, Truman, undaunted by Southern criticism, sent a special message to Congress asking it to enact a number of the recommendations of his committee. Never before had a President dispatched a special message on civil rights. He called for an anti-poll tax statute, a permanent FEPC, an anti-lynching law, and creation of a Commission on Civil Rights. To end intimidation at the polls, he asked for legislation banning interference by either public officials or private citizens with the free exercise of the suffrage. He did not embrace his committee's recommendation to deprive states of federal grants if they did not abandon Jim Crow, but in keeping with recent Supreme Court decisions, he did call upon Congress to forbid segregation in interstate travel. "As a Presidential paper," the historian Irwin Ross has written, "it was remarkable for its scope and audacity."

Once again the white South reacted with rage. A Georgia congressman said his section had been "kicked in the teeth" by Truman, the Nashville *Banner* denounced his proposals as "vicious," and in Florida the State Association of County Commissioners declared that "all true Democrats" found the President's program "obnoxious, repugnant, odious, detestable, loathsome, repulsive, revolting and humiliating."

No state exceeded Mississippi in the fury of its rhetoric. "Not since the first gun was fired on Fort Sumter, resulting as it did in the greatest fratricidal strife in the history of the world, has any message of any President of these glorious United States ... resulted in the driving of a schism in the ranks of our people, as did President Truman's so-called civil rights message," asserted Representative William M. Colmer. Truman, agreed Representative John Bell Williams, "has ... run a political dagger into our backs and now he is trying to drink our blood."

In a long speech on the Senate floor, Senator James Eastland charged that the President's program was an effort "to secure political favor from Red mongrels in the slums of the great cities of the East and Middle West" who planned to defile "the pure blood of the South." The President's "anti-southern measures," he maintained, would destroy the South "beyond hope of redemption." Indeed, he concluded: "This much is certain. If the present Democratic leadership is right, then Calhoun and Jefferson Davis were wrong. If the present Democratic leadership is right, then Thaddeus Stevens and Charles Sumner were right, and Lee, Forrest, and Wade Hampton were wrong. If the President's civil-rights program is right, then reconstruction was right. If this program is right, the carpetbaggers were right."

At the Jefferson-Jackson Day dinners in mid-February, Truman got rude reminders of Southern hostility to his program. In Washington at the most important dinner, a table at the May-flower Hotel reserved and paid for by Senator Olin Johnston of South Carolina was deliberately left vacant, in a conspicuous spot near the dais. Mrs. Johnston, a vice-chair of the dinner committee, decided not to attend, she explained, "because I might be seated next to a Negro."

Truman, shocked by the ferocity of the assault on him and recognizing that his re-election was in jeopardy, sought to placate his Southern critics, but he would not appease them by abandoning fundamental principles. After a meal at the White House with members of the Democratic National Committee, Alabama's national committeewoman lectured the President: "I want to take a message back to the South. Can I tell them you're not ramming miscegenation down our throats? ... That you're not for tearing up our social structure—that you're for all the people, not just the North?" Truman reached into his pocket, whipped out a copy of the Constitution, and read her the Bill of Rights. "I stand on the Constitution," he replied. "I take back nothing of what I proposed and make no excuses for it."

With Truman unrepentant, the South wrote him off. When he announced formally that he would run for re-election, John Bell Williams told his congressional colleagues that the President should "quit now while he is still just 20 million votes behind." The South and the border states were going to cast 147 electoral votes in November, said Senator Johnston, "and they won't be for Truman. They'll be for somebody else. He ain't going to be re-elected. He ain't going to be renominated." On the floor of the House, L. Mendel Rivers of South Carolina, shaking his finger, his voice trembling, cried, "Harry Truman is already a dead bird. We in the South are going to see to that."

Sectional animosity enveloped the 1948 Democratic Convention that summer, a mood no one captured so vividly as H. L. Mencken. His dispatch of July 9 began, "With the advancing Confederate Army still below the Potomac, Philadelphia was steeped tonight in the nervous calm that fell upon it in the days before Gettysburg." On the following day he wrote: "There was an air of confidence among the Yankee hordes already assembled ... that the rebels would begin falling to fragments before they crossed the Chickahominy." Though Mencken had no sympathy for Truman or his civil rights notions, his story a day later indicated that this confidence was justified. When the Southerners caucused in Philadelphia, they revealed that they had little strength outside a few Gulf states, he reported, adding: "After the count of bayonets ... Gov. Ben Laney asked if there were any copperheads present.... A lone Trumanocide from Indiana then made himself known, and was politely applauded. But there were no others, and the gathering broke up in depressed spirits."

The Southern Democrats continued to send off salvos against the President, but it did not take long for them to learn that their threat to deny him renomination was an empty one. At the Southern caucus Governor Strom Thurmond of South Carolina insisted, "We have been betrayed and the guilty shall not go unpunished." When the roll was called, however, Truman easily defeated the Southern favorite, Senator Richard B. Russell of Georgia. Russell swept almost the entire South, but that is about all he got. So mutinous was the South, though, that the convention chairman did not dare attempt to make Truman's nomination unanimous, as was traditionally done to signify party harmony.

Truman's opponents sustained an even greater setback over the platform when a determined group of liberals pushed through a strong civil rights plank cosponsored by Hubert Humphrey, the mayor of Minneapolis. "As I walked with the young mayor ... out of that hall," one liberal activist later recalled, "I actually thought he was going to be shot.... It was very tense, very tense."

Journalists and the Southern delegates alike agreed that, as *Time* recounted, "the South had been kicked in the pants, turned around and kicked in the stomach." Senator Walter George of Georgia, in what one writer has called "a splendid Catherine wheel of mixed metaphors," expostulated: "The South is not only over a barrel—it is pilloried! We are in the stocks!" Having sustained severe losses, "the defeated army," Mencken concluded, "retired ... to a prepared position on the swamps bordering the Swanee River."

After the civil rights plank was adopted, thirteen Alabama delegates (one of them was Birmingham's police commissioner, Eugene ["Bull"]

Connor) and all of the Mississippi delegation stalked out of the hall. The rebels reconvened in Birmingham to organize a States' Rights party with the intent of defeating Truman and his program by gaining enough electoral votes to throw the contest into the House of Representatives, where the South would have substantial bargaining power. To lead them in the forthcoming campaign, the States' Rights party, or Dixiecrats as they were commonly known, chose Strom Thurmond as their presidential candidate and Mississippi's governor, Fielding Wright, as his running mate. Thurmond told seven thousand cheering, stomping delegates: "There are not enough troops in the Army to force the Southern people to admit the Negroes into our theaters, swimming pools, and homes.... We have been stabbed in the back by a President who has betrayed every principle of the Democratic party in his desire to win at any cost."

The Dixiecrats constituted a serious threat to Truman's bid for re-election. He already faced a formidable challenge from the Republican nominee, Governor Thomas E. Dewey of New York, and the left wing of his party had broken away to back the Progressive nominee, Henry Wallace. Truman's chances, slim at best, seemed negligible if he could not hold the South. But in Alabama the Dixiecrats kept the name of the President of the United States off the ballot altogether. In Mississippi and South Carolina, state Democratic committees selected Thurmond as their presidential nominee. Summing up the situation in the aftermath of the Philadelphia convention, the Chattanooga *Free Press* wrote: "This should be a day of mourning for Southern Democrats. Their only consolation is the grim satisfaction that President Truman and his unfaithful cohorts are going down in ignominious defeat."

Truman, though, held firm to his commitment to bolster the constitutional rights of blacks. When an Army buddy advised him, from the perspective of a Southerner, not to press on civil rights, the President responded, "The main difficulty with the South is that they are living eighty years behind the times and the sooner they come out of it the better it will be for the country and for themselves." He added: "When the mob gangs can take four people out and shoot them in the back, and everybody in the country is acquainted with who did the shooting and nothing is done about it, that country is in a pretty bad fix from a law enforcement standpoint." Truman concluded by saying, "I can't approve of such goings on, and ... I am going to try to remedy it and if that ends up in my failure to be elected, that failure will be in a good cause."

Truman meant what he said. On July 26 he issued two Executive orders. One, drawing upon his authority as Commander in Chief, affirmed the principle of equality of treatment in the armed forces without respect to race. The other directive forbade discrimination in the federal civil service. On October 29 he became the first President ever to solicit votes in Harlem.

Well before the Harlem speech, analysts gave Truman little chance of carrying the South. It came as no surprise, then, when in November he lost four Deep South states to Governor Thurmond. Louisiana gave Thurmond more than 49 percent of its votes, Truman less than 33 percent. In some northern parishes Truman ran third—behind both Thurmond and Dewey. He fared still worse in other states. In South Carolina Thurmond got 72 percent, Truman 24 percent; in Mississippi Thurmond received 87 percent to Truman's miserable 10 percent. Alabama, of course, registered no votes at all for Truman.

Thurmond, though, gained no states beyond these four, as Truman astonished prognosticators by sweeping all the rest of the South and winning re-election. Most Southern Democrats could not bring themselves to bolt the party of their fathers to join the Dixiecrats, and they felt even less comfortable with switching to the Republicans, the party of Reconstruction.

The Truman era, however, proved to be the end of the Solid South, at least of a South solid for the Democrats. (To be sure, not until the 1960s, when Lyndon Johnson pushed through far-reaching civil rights legislation, would the most serious cleavage occur, but Truman is the one who opened the fissure that would never be mended.) In 1948 four Deep South states had broken away to the Dixiecrats; in the next election, four more Southern states defected to the Republicans. So by 1952 eight of the former Confederate states had abandoned the Democrats. As one scholar has said: "The significant fact is that a Democratic President proposed to Congress the enactment of laws to improve the status of the Negro. This was heresy; the whole logic of the South's loyalty to the Democratic party was the assumption that the party was pledged to leave race relations in the hands of the states. When the

Democratic party ceased to be the party of white supremacy, the deepest basis of Southern solidarity had been destroyed."

In one respect, his opponents in the South misperceived Truman, for he never wholly abandoned the racist view he had absorbed from his family or his sympathy for the Southern tradition of localism. Even after blacks hailed him as their champion, he continued to sprinkle his private conversation with terms such as *nigger*. He not only opposed the 1960s sit-ins but thought they might well be Communist-inspired. In 1961 he told reporters that Northerners who went south on Freedom Rides were meddling outsiders bent on stirring up mischief where they did not belong, and in 1965 he called the Selma to Montgomery march "silly" and Martin Luther King, Jr., a "troublemaker."

Yet Truman's foes had good reason for thinking him their nemesis, because if he had a Confederate lineage he also felt intense loyalty to the Constitution and the Union. He especially revered the memory of Andrew Jackson, a Southerner but a nationalist. Eventually he was even able, despite his family background, to bring himself to cherish the Great Emancipator.

Shortly after departing the White House, Truman reflected: "Old Abe Lincoln is ... a president I admire tremendously. In a way, it's surprising ... because I was born and raised in the South ... and a lot of southerners still don't feel that way about him at all. And that included the Truman family, all of whom were against him. Some of them even thought it was a fine thing that he got assassinated.

"I realized even as a child that was pretty extreme thinking or worse; let's just call it dumb thinking, or no thinking at all. But it still took me a while to realize what a good man Lincoln really was, with a great brain and even greater heart, a man who really cared about people and educated himself to the point where he knew how government should work and tried his best to make ours work that way. I felt just the opposite of the rest of the Truman family after I studied the history of the country and realized what Lincoln did to save the Union. That's when I came to my present conclusion, and that was a long, long time ago. ... Lincoln was a great and wonderful man in every way."

Truman's reading in history and in documents such as the Declaration of Independence and the Bill of Rights had led him to question the assumptions on which he was raised. He acted as he did not because he believed in the social equality of the races, not because he was "anti-South," but because he took solemnly the oath he had sworn to sustain the Constitution.

As a border-state Democrat Truman carried within him the conflicts that divided not only Missouri but the country. He had been nurtured on the valor of Robert E. Lee, the iniquity of the Union raiders, the melancholia of the Lost Cause. Only someone who understood himself to be a Southerner could have felt such empathy for the traditions of the South. Yet he also had a schoolboy's love of the history not of a section but of a nation, took pride in having been a doughboy in the Army of the United States of America, and viewed the Constitution as sacred text. That nationalist theme, a minor one when he was a child, was the one that prevailed in the end. As a consequence Truman permanently altered the character of Southern politics. For the first time since Reconstruction, he made civil rights a proper concern for the national government, and for the first time ever the Democratic party became the main protagonist for the rights of blacks. The South, and the nation, would never be the same again.

17

"Our Needs Know No Laws": The Issue of Illegal Mexican Immigration Since 1941

JUAN RAMON GARCIA

● *The United States has always had a peculiar relationship with Mexico. Since it first emerged as an independent nation in the first quarter of the nineteenth century, Mexico has had to contend with the policies and ambitions of a northern neighbor that was richer, stronger, more populous, and more advanced. Consequently, every Mexican government has had to adjust its plans and goals to the colossus of the North.*

American policies have often been ambivalent, however. In the 1920s and 1930s presidents Calvin Coolidge, Herbert Hoover, and Franklin D. Roosevelt withstood right-wing pressure and allowed Mexico to proceed with social and economic reforms. This "Good Neighbor Policy" was designed to prove that the United States would not intervene in the domestic affairs of a nearby nation even when Washington disapproved of the direction of government policy. Thus it was hoped that the traditional mistrust of a rich and powerful Uncle Sam would be alleviated.

Unfortunately, the rhetoric of American tolerance sometimes exceeded the reality of actual policy. In the early 1980s, when Mexican peasants in the northern parts of that country seized the lands on which they worked, President Luis Escheverría legalized their occupation by supporting genuine land reform. But the resulting shock waves in an American business community that was and is dependent on lucrative winter crops from Mexico were felt in Washington. Partly because of pressure from the United States, Escheverría's successor, Lopez Portillo, backed away from the previously strong governmental support for land seizures by peasants.

The inability of most Mexican peasants to achieve a decent

*living standard has had an important impact on immigration
into the United States. As Professor Juan Ramon Garcia of
the University of Arizona argues in the following essay, successive American attempts to control illegal entrants from
south of the border have failed because they deal only with
symptoms rather than with causes. Mass deportations and
contract labor programs, he writes, will not work because the
border is so long as to be virtually unpatrollable. The real
solution lies in improving the economic position of Mexican
nationals, who will otherwise try to improve their lives by
crossing over, legally or illegally, into the easily accessible
United States.*

In 1951 an undocumented worker stood before a judge during his
deportation hearing. As the weary judge examined the file, he noted
that the man had been charged several times with entering this country
illegally. Looking up at him, the judge asked testily, "Don't you respect
the laws of this country?" The worker replied, "Our necessities know
no laws." Ten years later another undocumented worker, awaiting
transportation back to Mexico in a detention center, told an inter-
viewer, "Many people condemn us for trying to make a living. They
are so busy in attacking us that they too often forget that we are human
beings." In 1978, police in the Chicago area stopped a U-Haul truck
carrying eighteen undocumented workers. The men had been locked
in the back of the truck for forty-eight hours with no food, little water,
and only two slop buckets for their personal needs. They had boarded
the truck in Phoenix, where the temperature had been one hundred
twelve degrees. It was at least twenty degrees hotter inside the truck.
Even the case-hardened cops were moved to compassion by the suffering which these men, most of them less than twenty years of age,
had endured. As one of the policemen put it, "I thought I had seen
just about everything in twenty-five years on the job. But this is about
the worst I've seen done to human beings by other human beings."

The question of illegal immigration from Mexico to this country has
been, and continues to be, both vexing and controversial. It is vexing
because it has led to abuse, exploitation, and suffering for the people
who enter illegally. It is controversial because the problem is rooted in
a quagmire of emotional, moral, social, political, economic, and inter-

national issues which at times defy description or solution. Throughout
this protracted controversy, which dates back in terms of intensity to
the early 1940s, a number of remedies have been proposed. To date
the majority have either failed to be enacted or have been too limited
to resolve a complex and worrisome problem.

The issue of illegal immigration from Mexico has once again generated national concern and interest. In part this is due to increased
coverage of the subject by the mass media and to the fact that Americans
are in the midst of an economic crisis which affects their jobs, earnings,
and livelihoods. As has been the case historically, Americans in economically hard-pressed times are usually more sensitive to those factors
which they perceive as responsible for their problems. In their eyes the
presence of large numbers of undocumented workers in this country
is part of the problem. To critics and opponents of this "uncontrolled
influx," undocumented workers deprive American citizens of jobs, ov-
ertax social service agencies, increase the tax burden, and contribute
to a myriad of social problems which affect the overall quality of life
in the United States.

There is of course another side to the argument. Those sympathetic
to the plight of undocumented workers argue that they contribute a
great deal to the American economy, while deriving few benefits from
it. According to them, a large percentage of undocumented workers
who are employed in the United States pay a variety of taxes. Yet these
people seldom take advantage of the services available to them because
of fear of detection and deportation. Moreover, the majority of "illegals" are honest, hard-working, law-abiding people who, under different circumstances, would be considered model citizens. To date
neither side in the controversy has been able to fully substantiate its
viewpoint.

Groups on both sides of the controversy have made their views clear,
and they have increasingly exerted pressure on policymakers. Yet the
steps taken by national leaders have been both halting and of necessity
limited, for they recognize the issue is explosive and emotional. They
realize that no solution will please everyone. Further complicating matters is the fact that the great majority of illegal immigrants are Mexican
citizens. In the past this was not a matter of great concern, but the
recent discovery of vast oil reserves in Mexico, when coupled with the
energy needs of this country, now requires American officials to take

greater cognizance of this fact. They cannot afford to alienate an oil-rich Mexico by mishandling a tremendously delicate issue.

The problems confronting the United States in terms of illegal immigration and most of the proposals set forth to resolve them date back to the World War II period. United States entry into the war in 1941 created a tremendous labor shortage, particularly in the agricultural sector. Growers found that they could not compete with the wages paid by industrial employers. Those who had traditionally performed farm work either joined the military or flocked to the urban centers in search of better pay. As a result of intense lobbying pressure and the importance of agriculture to the war effort, the federal government negotiated a contract labor program with Mexico in 1941. Under this treaty Mexico agreed to provide its own nationals to perform work in agriculture and a few other designated areas for specified periods. In return the United States assumed responsibility for placing these individuals on jobs and providing food, shelter, and transportation back to Mexico once the contract period had ended. Braceros, as the temporary workers were called, would be given contracts guaranteeing them fair treatment and clearly spelling out the terms of their employment. Although the bracero program was enacted as a temporary wartime measure, it was continually renewed from 1942 to 1964. During this twenty-two-year period, some 4.5 million migrant workers came to the United States.

From the outset the program was plagued by exploitation, misunderstandings, confusion, and conflicting interests. Furthermore, it did not end the growing influx of illegal entrants from Mexico, as its proponents had predicted. Instead, the bracero program acted as one more catalyst to northern migration. The promise of a contract drew thousands of hopeful applicants to border recruiting stations. As a result there were usually more applicants than there were jobs. Those who failed to obtain a contract were loath to return home empty-handed, for many of them had either borrowed money or invested what little they had to reach the border contracting stations. They therefore opted to cross the border illegally. Thus the guest worker program only served to increase the entry of undocumented workers.

The inconsistent immigration policy followed by the United States also contributed to increased illegal entry after World War II. Then, as now, the United States implemented "special" policies with regard to Mexican immigration whenever the government deemed them necessary and beneficial to groups who held vested interests in the acquisition of cheap labor. For this reason the United States has on several occasions undertaken policies which are contrary to its own immigration laws. More often than not, this special policy has been in the form of ad hoc exemptions and administrative adjustment to those laws. A case in point was the bracero program. Another example can be found in the unilateral recruitment of Mexican workers in 1948 and in 1954.

Because of the failure of the United States to institute penalties against those who hired illegals, the Mexican government decided to terminate the bracero agreement in 1948. But it did not produce the anticipated response. Instead, the United States viewed the ploy as both arbitrary and unjustified, and it threatened to open the border if Mexico did not reinstate the program immediately. When Mexico refused, United States officials ordered the border opened to any bracero seeking employment. Word spread quickly among Mexicans who had anxiously been awaiting contracts. At first only a few bold individuals risked crossing the border in full view of American immigration authorities. When the rest realized that American officials were not going to prevent their entry, a wholesale rush occurred.

As hundreds of Mexicans crossed the river into El Paso, immigration officials placed them under technical arrest and then immediately paroled them to members of the Texas Employment Commission. As a result of the El Paso Incident of October 1948, some five thousand braceros were allowed to enter the United States illegally at the behest of immigration officials, whose job it was to enforce the laws against illegal entry. Although Mexico and the United States worked out their differences shortly thereafter, the lesson of the El Paso Incident was not lost on many. It was obvious that the United States would undertake legal and extralegal measures to acquire laborers whenever the need arose.

This was again clearly demonstrated in 1954 when negotiations over the renewal of the bracero program reached an impasse. As in 1948, American officials threatened that if Mexico terminated the agreement, they would resort to the unilateral recruitment of Mexican workers. To prove its point, the United States announced that contracting would resume on January 2, 1954, in El Centro, California, with or without an international agreement. Mexican officials responded that they were not prepared to negotiate under duress. At the same time Mexico attempted through threats and pleas to deter its people from going to the California border, but to no avail. When negotiations broke off, the United States opened the border at El Centro and seven hundred Mexicans were allowed to enter illegally. Mexico responded by posting armed guards on its side of the border. The presence of troops caused a tense situation, which was exacerbated by United States officials who resorted to a process of instant legalization of anyone who managed to cross the border. The legalization process was accomplished by having Mexicans who entered illegally run back to the official border crossing-point, put one foot on Mexican soil, and then dart back so that they could be legally processed. At times this practice approached the absurd, as depicted in a photograph showing a hapless Mexican being pulled south by a Mexican border official and north by an official of the United States. The look, a combination of fear, confusion, and chagrin, on this man's face, told the whole story.

Between January 23 and February 5, 1954, a series of bloody clashes erupted between Mexican troops and desperate, hungry braceros. According to the *New York Times,* Mexican officials were dismayed and angered at the sight of thousands of their countrymen jammed like "sardines" and gasping for air in the crunch to cross the border for a handful of harvest jobs. Tulio Lopez-Lira, who was in charge of emigration at the Mexican border port, blamed the Americans for the riots. "My countrymen," he said, "have been trapped here by American lies and propaganda that the border would be open to them." Another outspoken critic of the unilateral recruitment policy which instantly accorded legal status to illegal entrants was Congressman John F. Shelley of California. In condemning the recent events in his home state, Shelley leveled a broadside at the myopic view of the federal government on the issue of illegal immigration. "Apparently the government's reasoning is that if we simply remove all restrictions on border crossing, as we have done since expiration of the bracero agreement, all crossings will be legal and we will, therefore, wipe out the wetback problem."

Shelley's observation was essentially correct. Not only had the United States violated its own immigration laws by resorting to unilateral recruitment, but it had also implemented other questionable procedures which further encouraged illegal immigration from Mexico. One such procedure involved the legalization of wetbacks, a practice which was implemented by the Immigration and Naturalization Service (INS) in 1947 in an attempt to reduce the number of illegals in this country by "regularizing" their presence. This program was undertaken with the full consent and approval of Mexican officials, who were ostensibly opposed to any measures which would further encourage illegal emigration. The legalization process was formalized through clauses in the bracero agreements of 1947, 1949, and 1950. By 1951, the program had so proved its merits in the eyes of Mexico and the United States that it was incorporated into Public Law 78 (the official title of the bracero agreement) under Section 501. Under this clause the secretary of labor was authorized "to recruit Mexican workers, including illegal entrants who had resided in the United States for the preceding five years, or who had entered originally under legal contract and remained after it expired." Those who supported the legalization program claimed that it helped reduce the number of illegals in the country by making them legalized braceros. Thus the majority of braceros contracted after 1951 were in reality legalized undocumented workers.

This practice seriously undermined the enforcement of immigration laws. One of the strongest condemnations of the policy came from the President's Commission on Migratory Labor, which was appointed in June 1950. In its final report, the commission accused the federal government of having condoned the wetback traffic during the harvest season:

> Wetbacks who were apprehended were given identification slips in the United States by the Immigration and Naturalization Service, which entitled them, within a few minutes, to step back across the border and become contract workers. There was no other way to obtain the indispensable slip of paper except to be found illegally in the United States. Thus violators of the law were rewarded by receiving legal contracts while the same opportunities were denied law-abiding citizens of Mexico. The United States, having engaged in a program giving preference in contracting to those who had broken the law, had encouraged violation of immigration laws. Our government thus had become a contributor to the growth of an illegal traffic which it has the responsibility to prevent.

While it is evident that the United States exacerbated the problem of illegal entry, Mexico must also share in the blame, for it condoned these practices because of the benefits derived from illegal emigration. For example, the money sent back by illegals to friends, family, and creditors helped Mexico's ailing economy. More importantly, the legal and illegal emigration of Mexicans served as a safety valve, drawing out potentially explosive elements who were unemployed and disgruntled. Finally, the Mexican government netted political gains on the home front by attacking the United States for its failure to end illegal entry and to protect the rights of Mexican nationals within its boundaries. Thus the United States became a convenient and easily assailable scapegoat for Mexico. It should be noted that the above views and circumstances still apply today.

In spite of the intensity and the importance of immigration from Mexico after 1941, the American people considered the wetback influx as largely a local problem confined to the border regions. This lack of concern and interest was mirrored by newspapers, weekly news magazines, and the popular pictorial magazines. But beginning in 1951, media attitudes began to change. Seemingly overnight, the public was inundated with articles and feature stories about undocumented workers. Most of the stories emphasized the ill effects which the "silent invasion" of "aliens" had on American society. These stories charged that illegals were responsible for increased disease rates, crime, narcotics traffic, and welfare costs, and that they served as a cover for subversive elements who were infiltrating the country. Thus what became embedded in the public mind was a negative view about illegal immigration, a view which was reinforced by the widespread use of terms such as "horde," "tide," "invasion," "wetback," "illegal," and "alien" to describe undocumented persons. To most Americans these terms conjured up images of faceless, shadowy, and sinister beings who skulked across the border in the dead of night in order to deprive American citizens of their jobs and livelihood.

Of course not all Americans opposed the entry of undocumented workers. The illegal was the very backbone of economic survival for a number of southwestern communities, and the widespread use and exploitation of illegal labor from Mexico had become a long-accepted norm. Many people in these communities had developed entrenched moral, ethical, and social justifications which supported the hiring and the abuse of undocumented workers. For the most part, those who employed wetbacks were scornful of interlopers who threatened to undercut their labor supply either through legislation penalizing employers or through stepped-up enforcement measures. They believed that the "handling of wetbacks" should be left to them, for they "knew and understood" these people best. Unfortunately for undocumented workers, such understanding was grounded in deeply embedded and negative stereotypes about Mexicans. This was especially true in the Rio Grande Valley of Texas, an area where most of the Mexicans hired were illegals. To employers the Mexicans were childlike, undisciplined, and lazy. Mexicans were also perceived as subhumans who were of little value except in performing hard work. As one valley resident put it, Mexicans did not really mind the hard work, the long hours, and the low pay. They were used to this. After all, he concluded, they "have behind them five hundred years of burden-bearing and animal-like living and just can't adjust to civilization in the way a white man does." Other long-time employers of illegals agreed. In their view Mexicans had enough bad attributes, and efforts to improve their way of life only added to the problem of dealing with them. To their way of thinking, they were doing illegals a favor by hiring them. After all, if things were really that bad in the United States, why did they make such determined efforts to come here?

In 1954 rising unemployment, the continued interest of the mass media, a growing public outcry against the "illegal influx," and the expression by immigration officials that they had begun to lose control of the border all forced the Eisenhower administration to deal with the problem. Attorney General Herbert Brownell adopted a two-pronged approach. The first was the implementation of a massive program to regain control of the border and reduce illegal entry. The program, code-named "Operation Wetback," began in June 1954. It was a large-scale, paramilitary program undertaken by the INS involving concentrated strike forces and raids in areas which had heavy concentrations of illegals. Focusing on the states of California, Texas, Arizona and New Mexico, the raids lasted throughout the summer and resulted in the deportation and repatriation of more than one million undocumented workers. Although recent research has found that the success of Operation Wetback was greatly exaggerated, it nonetheless represented a major effort by the federal government and the INS to enforce the immigration laws and to restore a semblance of control along the United States-Mexican border. Since 1954 the INS has sporadically

conducted similar drives. These drives have usually followed hard on
the heels of intense and protracted media attention upon the influx of
illegals, rising unemployment, a noticeable down-swing in the economy,
and public outcry fostered by these conditions. Like Operation Wetback, the ensuing roundups merely represented a stopgap measure designed to placate an aroused public. While such drives do serve limited
purposes, they do not address the major causes of illegal entry from
Mexico.

While Operation Wetback was being planned and implemented, Herbert Brownell undertook the second part of his program. This was the
introduction of legislation to impose penalties against those who
"knowingly" employed illegals or were captured in the act of smuggling
or harboring them. The legislation was introduced in Congress in 1954
by Republican Senator Arthur Watkins of Utah and Democratic Representative Louis E. Graham of Pennsylvania.

Attempts to introduce penalty legislation against employers during
President Harry Truman's tenure had met with resounding defeat, and
from the outset it was apparent that Brownell's proposals would also
face an uphill battle. Opposing the penalty legislation was a powerful
and well-organized group in Congress which was determined to protect
the interests of those whose economic survival depended upon a cheap
source of labor. As a result of this strong opposition, Brownell's proposals were never enacted. After Operation Wetback, interest in rein-
troducing penalty legislation quickly faded. The much-publicized
"success" of the deportation drives of 1954 lulled many proponents
of such legislation into believing that the influx of illegals was at last
under control, and that perhaps penalty legislation, which would always encounter tremendous opposition, was not the solution after all.

They were of course mistaken. Operation Wetback did not signal
the end of illegal immigration from Mexico although it presented that
impression to many. After 1954, agricultural employers contracted with
individual Mexicans. Thus between 1954 and 1960, there occurred a
dramatic increase in the number of braceros hired (see Table 1). During
this same period INS figures reflected a dramatic decrease in the numbers of undocumented workers apprehended. This tended to support
the claims of the INS that the problem of illegal entry was now under
control. At the same time these figures bolstered the arguments of those
who favored the continuation of a bracero program. Proponents argued

TABLE I

Number of Braceros Contracted 1951–1964		Number of Undocumented Persons 1951–1964	
Year	Contracted	Year	Contracted
1951	190,745[a]	1951	500,628
1952	197,100	1952	543,538
1953	201,380	1953	875,318
1954	309,033	1954	1,075,168
1955	398,650	1955	242,608
1956	445,197	1956	72,442
1957	436,049	1957	44,451
1958	432,857	1958	37,242
1959	437,643	1959	30,196
1960	315,846	1960	29,651
1961	291,420	1961	29,877
1962	194,978	1962	30,272
1963	186,865	1963	39,124
1964	177,736	1964	43,844
Total	4,215,499		

[a]Includes 46,076 contracted under 1948 agreement prior to July 15.
SOURCE: U.S. Department of Labor, "Summary of Migratory Station Activities."

SOURCE: U.S. Immigration and Naturalization Service.

that it served as a deterrent to illegal entry, and they warned federal officials that termination of the program would only reopen the floodgates to illegal entry. These arguments and the power of probracero groups proved effective and resulted in the continuation of the program until 1964.

As if to underscore the warnings of probracero groups, apprehension of illegals began to increase in 1963 and 1964. On the surface it seemed that the program had in fact been a deterrent to illegal entry. Yet appearances were deceiving, as other critical factors had been responsible for the apparent decline of illegal immigration from Mexico. One factor was that after 1954 the Border Patrol returned to routine operations, largely abandoning the concentrated approach as implemented in 1954. The Border Patrol also continued the legalization of apprehended wetbacks, which meant that a good proportion of the braceros contracted were in reality illegals whose presence in this country had been regularized. Another reason for the "decline" of illegal immigration was the introduction of increased labor-saving technology, which reduced needs in the unskilled agricultural labor market.

After 1959 there was a rapid decline in the number of braceros contracted, in part because of labor-saving technology and the more rigid enforcement of wage guarantees. The government also began to tighten certification requirements for establishing the need to import and hire braceros. Thus prior to the end of the bracero program in 1964, many employers had again begun to resort to an increased use of undocumented workers. Among those employed were large numbers of commuters who had entered the United States by using a border-crossing permit. The permits, which were fairly easy to acquire, permitted the holder to enter the United States for the purposes of entertainment, shopping, visiting, or business. Holders of this permit were prohibited from working while in this country or from traveling more than twenty-five miles from the border. Those holding the permit were allowed to enter the United States for periods not to exceed seventy-two hours.

Obviously, the temptation proved too great for many. Once here they mailed the cards back to Mexico to avoid having them confiscated in case of apprehension by INS authorities. As no records were kept of the number of people entering or leaving the United States on a daily basis, it proved almost impossible to determine how many had entered legally and remained illegally. The unavailability of records in this area added to the numerical illusion that illegal entry, as shown by apprehensions, had declined.

Further adding to the incentive to enter illegally was the enactment of more stringent immigration restrictions by the United States in 1965 and 1968. Under the new regulations, applicants were given preference if they were blood relatives of citizens or legal residents already in the United States. Members of preferred professions such as engineering and medicine were also given higher priority. Preference was also shown to applicants who had employers who would sponsor them. People who did not fall into any of these categories were free to apply as well, although their chances for legal admission, given the long waiting lists, were almost nil. Many were unwilling to make application upon such slim chances, especially given the high cost and the complicated procedures.

Factors in Mexico also served to spur illegal emigration. The growth in Mexico's economy between 1950 and 1960 was not sufficient to keep up with its population growth, which had more than doubled between 1940 and 1963, rising from twenty-two to forty-five million. Therefore, the lack of employment opportunities, a rapidly expanding population, and Mexico's economic overdependence on the United States, when coupled with the availability of work in the United States and a largely unpatrolled border, all served once again to attract Mexican nationals in increasing numbers.

By the late 1960s, illegal immigration had increased significantly. Labor organizations and social reform groups once again called for measures to deal with what they saw as a problem of major proportions. Yet their concern was not shared by important government officials or the general public. The boom economy of the 1960s appeared capable of absorbing and utilizing an enlarged labor force, regardless of its source. Furthermore, the hostile environment toward undocumented persons had for the moment dissipated. Americans were more concerned with the domestic and foreign issues raised by the Vietnam War.

As the war ground to an end, as some semblance of domestic tranquility returned, and as the nation began to experience the economic problems inherent in adjusting to a peacetime economy, illegal immigration once again became an issue of major public and governmental concern. Newspaper stories and government reports reflected a steady increase in the number of undocumented persons apprehended each year. According to INS estimates, the number of illegal aliens apprehended increased from about two hundred thousand in 1968 to five hundred thousand in 1972. Accompanying these reports were renewed attacks from various groups. As in the past, undocumented workers were accused of overburdening social and welfare agencies, of depriving Americans of jobs, and of driving up rates of crime and disease. Some claimed that if this large-scale influx continued unchecked, it would lead to the formation of "welfare reservations" and "wetback subcultures" which would be breeding grounds for discontent, alienation, and potential revolution. Adding to the "alien scare" were the statements of high-ranking immigration officials who sought additional funding for their programs. One of the more vociferous was Leonard Chapman, the head of the INS. In 1972 he warned that the United States was undergoing a "growing, silent invasion of illegals" and called upon Americans to demand swift action to halt it, for there "was no time to lose."

The scare tactics and warnings had their desired effects. Stepped-up INS campaigns against undocumented workers followed, studies were commissioned, various state and federal subcommittees held hearings, and some states enacted legislation against those who "knowingly" employed illegals. For the most part, the reports and the hearings stirred a great deal of interest, debate, and controversy but did little to resolve the problem. The penalty legislation enacted at the state level also did little to discourage employment of illegals because it contained vague language and numerous loopholes which made prosecution and conviction very difficult. Instead, a number of these state laws were used by unscrupulous employers to intensify their discrimination against Hispanic people. According to one observer, some employers used the laws as a pretext for refusing to hire minorities, claiming that applicants had failed to prove beyond a shadow of a doubt that they were indeed legal residents or citizens of the United States.

At the federal level, Congressman Peter Rodino and Senator Edward F. Kennedy introduced bills in 1972 and 1974 respectively designed to regularize the status of aliens already in the United States and to impose sanctions against employers who hired illegals. Neither of the proposals won wide support in Congress. Although they continued to stir interest and controversy, repeated efforts to have the bills enacted failed. By mid–1975 the question of illegal immigration from Mexico had once again become a major issue both here and in Mexico. Deadlocked over what path to follow, Congress deferred any action. It instead adopted a wait-and-see posture.

In 1977 President Jimmy Carter introduced a series of measures which he hoped would prove acceptable to a majority of people. Similar to those proposed under Truman and Eisenhower, they called for increased personnel to patrol the border, legislation to penalize those who employed illegals, and closer cooperation with those countries from which undocumented persons came. A fourth measure entailed granting "amnesty" to illegal aliens. Under this provision, undocumented persons who entered before 1970 and who had resided in the United States continually since their arrival would be permitted to remain. They could also begin the process of becoming naturalized citizens. The plan also proposed that aliens who entered between 1970 and 1977 would be permitted to remain in the United States, but only on a temporary basis. A more definite ruling on their future status would come after the federal government "had studied the matter further." Finally, under Carter's plan, those who entered illegally after 1977 would be subject to immediate deportation.

President Carter's plan was vigorously discussed and received widespread criticism from a variety of groups and organizations. Critics of the plan assailed it as either too amorphous, too lenient, or too stringent. As debate raged around the proposals, the Carter administration came under attack from other sectors. When economic conditions in the country deteriorated further, the energy problem deepened, and affairs in the Middle East worsened, Carter's proposal on illegal immigration fell by the wayside. There was little that the beleaguered president could do to gain support for any of his proposals, and thus no legislative action was taken on them.

Yet even if Carter's proposals had been enacted, it is doubtful that they would have had any significant impact on the problem of illegal immigration. For example, it is unlikely that Congress would have enacted a stringent and effective law against employers of illegals. It is also doubtful that a large number of undocumented persons would have taken advantage of the amnesty provisions. First of all, applying for amnesty would have meant exposure to INS officials. To a group of people long conditioned to remaining invisible, such a step would have been threatening and dangerous. Furthermore, the burden of proof in terms of continuous residency before 1970 would have fallen totally on those seeking citizenship status. There was always the chance that such proof would not be accepted by immigration officials, in which case applicants would be subject to deportation. To many the process involved appeared complicated, the risks great, and the benefits minimal and uncertain. For those who had entered after 1970 the assignment of a temporary resident status was not worth the risk of identifying themselves, especially since there was little or no indication of what might happen to them after the government "had studied the matter." For obvious reasons, Carter's plan was even less appealing to those who entered after 1977.

The proposal for increasing border patrol personnel also had its weaknesses. For example, increasing personnel and equipping them with sophisticated hardware would have no impact whatsoever in controlling those who entered the United States legally by using their temporary tourist or student cards, and then overstayed, thus becoming illegals. Critics also pointed out that although this proposal would make it more difficult for those without cards to enter illegally, it would not deter them. If anything, the program would only increase the profits of "coyotes" (commercial smugglers), who already operated lucrative businesses assisting undocumented persons in crossing the border. Finally, Carter's plan contained little that would have attacked the problem at its roots. His plan did not sufficiently address itself to reducing the major push factors extant in Mexico which contribute to illegal emigration.

President Ronald Reagan's proposal also fails to address the basic causes of the problem. There is little or no discussion of helping Mexico battle its economic underdevelopment, or of alleviating the large trade imbalance which exists between it and the United States. There is also little indication that Mexico will receive increased capital from the World Bank to invest in projects such as its integrated rural development program, which thus far appears to be helping its economically depressed rural sectors. Reagan's proposals place emphasis on the unilateral approach to reducing the problem—an approach which has met with little success in the past.

In addition, Reagan's plans contain serious flaws which will exacerbate the problem. Because of the "serious dimensions" of the situation, he has requested that the government be given wide-ranging emergency powers. Among them is the authority to establish detention centers for illegals without requiring environmental studies in advance. This proposal, if enacted, might not bode well for those illegals unfortunate enough to be captured and detained. Without proper safeguards, these places might lapse into pestilential and poorly maintained camps. Reagan's program also calls for stiff fines against those who employ illegals. Yet he has provided a palatable alternative in an effort to gain the support of powerful interest groups who would vehemently resist sanctions against employers. Reagan has proposed a two-year experimental guest worker program that would bring in fifty thousand braceros to the United States each year. If successful, the program would then be expanded to bring in between five hundred thousand and one million guest workers annually. Thus the program would substitute one source of cheap labor for another.

The Reagan administration claims the guest worker program would help reduce illegal entry. Yet it might serve to encourage illegal entry, much as the bracero program of 1942 to 1964 did. In essence, there are likely to be more applicants than jobs. For those who fail to obtain a contract, the tendency will be to enter illegally. Moreover, guest workers may opt to remain illegally after their contract term has expired. Finally, the program would create a class of highly exploited laborers since extensive contract guarantees might not be included in the agreement or, if included, might not be strictly enforced given Reagan's emphasis on deregulation of the private sector. It is interesting to note that the president's proposal of a guest worker program comes at a time when the United States is experiencing high employment.

In conclusion, past experience has adequately demonstrated the ineffectiveness of mass deportations, restrictive measures, contract labor programs, and a unilateral approach in providing long-term solutions to the problem of illegal immigration. Undocumented persons will continue to seek better opportunities in the United States so long as those opportunities are lacking or denied them at home. That is one of the consequences of a contiguous and negotiable border separating a rich nation from a poor one.

18

The FBI and the Politics of the Riots, 1964–1968

KENNETH O'REILLY

• *The United States witnessed both triumph and tragedy in the 1960s. During that decade its citizens enjoyed material prosperity such as no people in the world had ever known. The gross national product approached a trillion dollars a year, and American astronauts placed the flag of their country on the surface of the moon. But the 1960s will also be remembered for the Vietnam War, for the assassinations of John and Robert Kennedy and of Martin Luther King, and for the ugly violence that broke the uneasy racial calm of the 1950s. In the summer of 1965, a six-day race riot in Los Angeles left thirty-four dead and more than 850 injured; in 1967, battles between black militants and police claimed twenty-five lives in Newark and forty-three in Detroit. And disturbances in more than one hundred other cities followed the assasination of Dr. King in Memphis in April 1968.*

President Lyndon B. Johnson's National Advisory Commission on Civil Disorders (the Kerner Commission) placed the blame for the rioting on "white racism." It reported that the civil rights gains of the previous fifteen years had actually done very little to improve the quality of life in the black ghetto, where millions of youngsters continued to be denied an equal chance in American society. Indeed, the principle response to the riots was increased expenditures for police and weaponry rather than serious attempts to alleviate the causes of the distress.

The United States has, of course, always been a violent nation in comparison with other advanced industrial countries. In 1993, for example, Houston, Texas, experienced more homicides than all of Great Britain or Japan, and Houston is not the most murderous of American cities. But while

Kenneth O'Reilly, "The FBI and the Politics of the Riots, 1964–1968," *Journal of American History*, 75 (June 1988), 91–114. Reprinted by permission.

personal violence continues to increase, the incidence of large-scale American disorder has been reduced in the twentieth century from the high levels of 1919 and 1921.

The following essay by Professor Kenneth O'Reilly of the University of Alaska focuses on the response of J. Edgar Hoover and his Federal Bureau of Investigation to the rioting. Although recent scholarship has been unkind to the FBI director, it is still surprising to learn that his efforts made things harder for President Johnson and easier for President Nixon.

Lyndon B. Johnson was the thirty-sixth president of the United States; J. Edgar Hoover was merely the sixth director of the Federal Bureau of Investigation (FBI). If the two men had been prizefighters, they would have been in different weight classes and they would never have fought. But they were politicians, not prizefighters. And when they clashed during the 1960s over ways to respond to the civil disorders that swept the urban North, the director won and the president, surely one of the most adept politicians ever to occupy the Oval Office, lost.

For Hoover, a fixture in American politics since he organized Attorney General A. Mitchell Palmer's famous raids in 1919–1920, the riots offered a series of bureaucratic and political opportunities. He welcomed the law-and-order climate of opinion that developed in the wake of rioting in New York in 1964, Los Angeles in 1965, and especially Newark and Detroit in 1967. Law and order meant more agents and more money, and therefore a more powerful base from which he could advance his bureaucracy's larger political objectives. Johnson, on the other hand, was threatened by the new climate of opinion. For the president, law and order signified the efforts of his Republican party adversaries to mobilize the "white backlash" vote. He believed, White House Special Counsel Harry C. McPherson wrote, that the words "law and order" were simply the new "code words for racism."

The president turned to the FBI for help in managing the politics of the 1960s' riots, not because he thought the FBI could be trusted, but because he thought the FBI could be controlled. Johnson knew that Hoover's agenda had little in common with his own. The two men, as the historian Arthur M. Schlesinger, Jr., noted, "had been Washington neighbors and friends for many years. They understood each other." The president had no illusions about the director's anticommunist politics and his interest in accumulating derogatory information on friends and enemies alike. Washington lore has it that Johnson once said, in a crude though certainly believable way, that he would rather have Hoover "inside the tent pissing out than outside pissing in." Johnson wanted the bureau's director—the most respected policeman in the nation—out front, in the public eye, and on his side. If Hoover said Johnson was tough enough, who could criticize the administration for being soft on law and order?

Obviously, it did not work. The president knew that politics was more than a matter of imagery, but in the end he could not even manage the imagery. The Hoover-Johnson partnership with regard to riot politics was a strange, unequal, and ultimately dishonest one. Each man used the other. The president used the FBI director to cope with the political problems unleashed by the riots, and the director used the president to broaden his agency's domestic intelligence mandate. The director and the president moved from one riot to the next, at times in the same direction, at other times in conflicting directions. Johnson ended up with his family on the ranch in Texas, and Hoover ended up with a surveillance empire expanding at what seemed to be a geometric rate. President Johnson's decision not to seek his party's nomination in 1968 can be best understood by reference to the Tet Offensive and a failing policy in Vietnam. But that decision cannot be fully explained without understanding the riot politics of the 1960s and the degree to which Hoover ultimately influenced those politics against Johnson's interests.

The riots themselves came as a surprise. Few people in the White House, the Department of Justice, or the FBI expected the "racial problem" to move North. It was less a matter of ignorance than a reflection of the administration's obsession with the Jim Crow South. "How distant Rochester and Harlem and the other major disturbances seemed to the Department of Justice," Ramsey Clark, an assistant attorney general when the riots first flamed, remembered. "When we thought of the North we didn't think of civil rights." Things changed on July 18, 1964, sixteen days after President Johnson signed the Civil Rights Act of 1964. The riots began in New York following the shooting of a fifteen-year-old Negro boy, James Powell, by an off-duty police officer. The Congress of Racial Equality (CORE) organized a rally, the crowd marched on a police station to demand the officer's ouster, and the violence had started. Rioting broke out in Brooklyn the next day and upstate in Rochester five days later. In August more riots followed in New Jersey, Illinois, and Pennsylvania.

Johnson knew the riots posed a threat to his Great Society programs, to his administration's attempt to promote consensus and achieve racial and economic justice. The threat was political, and it took the form of Barry Goldwater, the Republican party's presidential candidate in 1964. Aware of (perhaps encouraged by) the strong showing of an unabashed racist, Gov. George Wallace of Alabama, in Democratic presidential primaries in Wisconsin and Indiana, Goldwater conservatives argued that liberal reform, particularly LBJ's War on Poverty and civil rights legislation, would lead to a new permissiveness. In their view black Americans, perhaps the largest group of citizens who stood to gain from the Great Society, would not earn anything. They would simply be granted things—money, food, jobs, scholarships, affirmative action promises—with predictable results. The work ethic would die. Disrespect for law, laziness, and criminality would emerge as the new values.

The Republican right pointed to the riots ("Goldwater rallies," as they were sometimes called in Democratic circles) as proof of their predictions. And they sometimes did so in the crudest manner imaginable. "Goldwater himself," as the newspaper columnist and historian Garry Wills noted, cancelled one inflammatory television ad made by a California politico, "a glimpse of America sinking into a pit of sex and violence under the patronage of Lyndon Johnson."

At the very least the Goldwater Republican attempt to capitalize on the apparent breakdown of law and order threatened to cost President Johnson votes in the November elections. And, as Roy Wilkins of the National Association for the Advancement of Colored People (NAACP) wrote, Johnson "not only wanted to beat Goldwater, he wanted to crush him." Goldwater's "southern strategy" was a cause of real concern. By 1960, as the epic chronicler of the presidential campaign trail, Theodore H. White, pointed out, millions of white southerners had begun to recognize Republicans as "natural allies in preserving state sovereignty in race relations." By 1963 Andrew Young of the Southern Christian Leadership Conference interpreted federal recalcitrance on civil rights issues by reference to the attempt of President John F.

Kennedy and Attorney General Robert F. Kennedy to undercut the GOP's embryonic southern strategy. The Kennedys, Young felt, were trying "to assure the nation that they are still 'white.'" Less than a year later—and two months before the riots began—in an appearance on "Face the Nation," Martin Luther King, Jr., said the Republican party might become a "white man's party."

In a meeting with FBI Assistant Director Cartha D. DeLoach after the summer rioting had run its course, White House aide Walter Jenkins described the political impact of the riots as "the 'Achilles' heel' of the Johnson Administration." It was no coincidence that Jenkins directed the remark to DeLoach. DeLoach was Hoover's liaison with the Johnson White House, and the president called for assistance so often and on so many fronts that he had a direct-line telephone installed in the FBI assistant director's bedroom. Johnson was "toying with many possibilities," DeLoach told Hoover on this occasion, "which will give him favorable publicity inasmuch as he considers the various riots to have lost him many votes."

The most ambitious plan involved an FBI report on the riots that was intended to defuse Goldwater's law-and-order politicking and to recapture those lost votes. It was a perfect example of a master politician at work. According to Hoover, Lyndon Johnson coaxed from the very conservative J. Edgar Hoover a plug of sorts for the War on Poverty and brought in a prominent, if decidedly anti-Goldwater, Republican, Thomas E. Dewey, to put the FBI memos on the riots into a final draft. The bureau sent to the White House an incredible volume of intelligence on all the riots, including two "white kids" riots that had occurred over the Labor Day weekend in Seaside, Oregon, and Hampton, New Hampshire. "The President felt free to move in strongly," Dewey reasoned, "only because he had a couple of white riots to deal with and he thought that if they were omitted, the President would say we were putting him in the position of being anti-Negro."

In late September 1964 the media received a report surveying nine cities where rioting had occurred. The report had Hoover's name on it, but it was written by the man who ran for president on the Republican party ticket in 1944 and 1948. LBJ held the fact of Dewey's authorship in reserve; in the Washington world of government by leak, Dewey's name would surely have slipped out had Hoover's name alone failed to do the job.

Dewey's selection was logical. He had impeccable law-and-order credentials as a result of his work back in the 1930s as district attorney in New York. His name surfaced when he spoke to Max Kampelman, a lawyer, businessman, sometime diplomat, and former legislative counsel to Democratic Sen. Hubert H. Humphrey of Minnesota. Kampelman relayed the substance of his conversation to a member of the White House staff. Dewey would not "bolt with fanfare," but he was "fed up with the GOP." "Should the President call him after the convention, Max is certain that Dewey will promise his support and quiet help during the campaign." With Dewey's offer in mind, Johnson met with Hoover on July 22 to discuss the Goldwater candidacy and how the president might counter any attempts to exploit the riots for political purposes. The president wanted the FBI "to get in there and see about the communist groups and the right wingers." Hoover said he "would dig into it at once." When Dewey was finally contacted a few weeks later, he agreed to help with this FBI project.

Hoover preferred to work with Republicans. His relationship with Dewey was on the whole warm, though the two men had a sometimes-rocky history dating back to the New York rackets investigations. The minor feuding between them had resulted from bureaucratic and jurisdictional jealousies, not ideological incompatibility. Over time Dewey had been a favorite of the FBI. During the 1948 presidential campaign the bureau had compiled campaign literature on the red menace for Dewey's use and sent it by airplane to the governor's mansion in Albany. The material was released under Dewey's name and the name of the Republican National Committee.

Dewey came to the riot project with experience in political ghost writing and with the desire to find a middle ground between Johnson's welfare state and Goldwater's warfare state. He shared many of Hoover's concerns about the new permissiveness, bleeding heart judges, and the civil rights groups—from "the responsible Negro organizations, such as NAACP," to "the more violent people, like CORE." When speculating with Hoover on the new permissiveness, Dewey asked about the salacious novel *Fanny Hill*. The director sent over a memo and a copy of the paperback edition. Dewey and Hoover also agreed on the culpability of "the responsible Negro organizations." The "more violent" actions (as Dewey designated the *nonviolent* "sit-ins, et cetera") of the past three years, they agreed, had led to the current breakdown of law and order.

Johnson expected Dewey to be the more moderate half of the Dewey-

Hoover partnership. He expected Dewey to control Hoover, to keep the director's crusty anticommunism out of the report. As it turned out, Hoover was the more moderate. Understanding his role and his limited options better than Dewey, the director counseled caution. "All of those actions" by the civil rights groups had contributed "to a breakdown of law and order and respect for the administration of justice," he agreed, but it might be best to avoid any such statement in the report. "It was a delicate situation...because Roy Wilkins of the NAACP and [Whitney Young of] the Urban League are trying to be the restraining influence." When Dewey said "they started it and now want to put out the fire," Hoover pointed out that "they are being called by the younger generation 'Uncle Toms' and are being disregarded and people of more violent disposition are taking over and that is the thing I would hesitate about and think over very carefully about attaching blame to them." In the meantime, the director sent Dewey memos on the involvement of any member of any civil rights group in the riots.

Hoover and Dewey agreed on the big question—whether the riots were sparked by Communist conspirators or other organized radicals. Once again, the director staked out a cautious and fairly accurate position. Because the riots "caught" them "by surprise," Communist party members "moved in" only "after the riots started." The violence that followed was "not communist inspired but communist encouraged." That was as much as the nation's preeminent anticommunist was willing to say. However, neither Hoover nor Dewey intended to ignore radicals, whether they were card-carrying reds or something else. In the case of the New York riots, the director stressed the activities of a former Communist party organizer, the involvement of the Progressive Labor movement, and the rhetoric of Malcolm X. A typical memo from Hoover, delivered to Dewey with a copy to Jenkins at the White House, read: "By agitating through inflammatory propaganda and rallies, and stepping into explosive situations to fan the flames of disorder, these culprits [Communists, Maoists, Black Muslims] play an important role in racial violence."

When Dewey finished the report on September 21, DeLoach delivered it to Johnson and met with the president's aide William Moyers to review the statement LBJ intended to issue when releasing the report. Hoover had instructed DeLoach to head for the center. The FBI assistant director argued for the removal of "one specific paragraph with respect to the non-precipitation of riots by subversive and extremist organizations," and the deletion of another sentence that read, in part, "the riots were not related to the legitimate demands of the Negro citizens."

Johnson, Moyers, and Jenkins all read the report and raised a few minor objections with the FBI. Hoover said they were "nit-picking." "They took exception particularly," he complained to his senior staff, "to page four of the report wherein the word 'Negro' is used three times and they felt that was overdoing it." On September 26 Johnson asked Hoover to release the report to the press. The director gave the report to the Justice Department and told the department to release it.

Many conservatives were concerned about Hoover's apparent defection from right-wing orthodoxy. The report emphasized social and economic factors, not subversive conspirators, and "cleared the civil rights movement completely," as Roy Wilkins noted. "After the F.B.I. report there was no excuse for race to be drawn into the campaign." Because poverty and discrimination were identified as the principal causes of unrest, the FBI implied that the Johnson administration programs designed to address those problems represented the best possible response. When William F. Buckley, Jr., noted the director's conclusions, the liberal Catholic magazine *Commonweal* conceded an ironic "twinge of sympathy for Mr. Buckley.... There is nothing wrong with coming out in favor of the Johnson war on poverty, but it is not for Mr. Hoover to do so in a report on civil rights disturbances. We wouldn't have believed it six months ago, but acting on Mr. Buckley's tip, we had better keep an eye out for liberal propaganda in future F.B.I. reports."

Lyndon Johnson's accomplishment should not be minimized. He covertly maneuvered a prominent Republican and overtly maneuvered his anticommunist FBI director into issuing a report that endorsed the War on Poverty and helped blunt the Goldwater Republican challenge. The FBI report played down every sort of conspiracy theory. There was no evidence that the riots were organized on a national basis or that any of the disturbances were a "direct outgrowth of conventional civil rights protest." And there was no black-white violence whatsoever—the only interracial clash of note involved blacks and Puerto Ricans in Brooklyn. In the Hoover-Dewey view, the incidents in New

York, Pennsylvania, and elsewhere were not even "race riots." That was a comforting thought, exactly the sort of message Johnson had hoped to propagate when he first called on his FBI director and a disaffected Republican.

Hoover and Dewey raised the radical specter, but there were no Bolsheviks-are-coming rhetoric and no red menace theatrics. They explained the government's interest in the politics and everyday doings of the people who inhabited America's ghettoes in the language of federalism *and* of federal surveillance: "Keeping the peace in this country is essentially the responsibility of the state government. Where lawless conditions arise, however, with similar characteristics from coast to coast, the matter is one of national concern even though there is no direct connection between the events and even though no federal law is violated."

The report was never intended to serve as a basis for policy. Its value was therapeutic; its usefulness confined to the world of public relations, not direct or continuing political action. Only Hoover had it both ways. He managed to tell the president what he wanted to hear, much to Buckley's chagrin, and also to expand his bureaucracy's surveillance responsibilities. And he did so, not by promoting the red menace, but by downplaying it. "In certain instances," a headquarters directive of August 20 reminded all bureau field offices, the evidence "clearly indicated that such [racial] disturbances were sustained and nurtured, if not actually initiated, by subversive elements and/or other organizations." The FBI could not even define who it wanted to spy on. The "subversive, criminal or other elements" bureau officials were interested in were not believed to be connected in any way with "so-called civil rights groups." They were simply people who "may initiate and fan such smoldering racial resentments into violence solely to serve their own purposes." By the end of 1964 FBI policy required "a vigorous investigation to determine the causes and forces behind . . . threatened or actual mob violence or rioting." The field was urged to use "informants . . . to determine the underlying cause" and "whether there is an organized pattern emanating from subversive or radical groups or other outside sources."

The riots also encouraged the growth of other FBI activities. Five days after the report was released President Johnson asked Hoover to expand the riot control curriculum for state and local police officers at the FBI National Academy. Four months later, in February 1965, the bureau published a brief manual on urban violence, *Prevention and Control of Riots*, with the assistance of the United States Army. The booklet included instructions for state and local police in baton techniques. All strokes, including the "smash," should be "short and snappy," the FBI said.

Johnson's decision to expand FBI riot control responsibilities after the summer's violence cut across the grain of his political instincts. Although he hedged his bet, he did not really expect the riots to continue. When they did, he sounded at times a bit like former president Herbert Hoover, who implied that blacks had no reason to riot because "our 19 million Negroes probably own more automobiles than all the 220 million Russians and the 200 million African Negroes put together." "How is it possible," LBJ asked, "after all we've accomplished? How could it be? Is the world topsy-turvy?" Johnson had matured politically under the patronage of the New Deal, and in his world the disadvantaged were not supposed to respond to federal largess in such a manner. Joseph A. Califano, Jr., who moved to the White House staff in July 1965, remembered the impact Watts had on the president: "He just wouldn't accept it. He refused to look at the cables from Los Angeles.... I tried to reach him a dozen times. We needed decisions from him. But he simply wouldn't respond."

Only the FBI director expected the riots to continue, and continue they did; but not a single one of the policemen trained by Hoover's riot control instructors was on hand in Los Angeles in August 1965 when the Watts ghetto exploded. The chief of the Los Angeles Police Department (LAPD), William H. Parker, a fiercely independent man, often incurred Hoover's wrath, and as punishment members of Parker's department were denied entry to the FBI National Academy. In any event, Los Angeles police were familiar enough with "the smash." Roger Wilkins, then an assistant director of the Community Relations Service in the Department of Justice and a member of a federal team sent by President Johnson to the scene of the riot, identified police brutality as a fundamental cause of the Watts riot. "The [LAPD]... was not fond of Negroes," Wilkins concluded, with considerable understatement. "Its members had killed about thirty looters and many of them called their nightsticks 'nigger sticks.'" Few federal officials listened to Wilkins. Although police brutality could not be ignored (it was too obvious to ignore), the Johnson administration seemed more concerned with subversives wandering around Los Angeles than with brutal police officers or Director Hoover's feud with Chief Parker.

The president's assumptions about ghetto rioting began to change after Watts. In 1964 he had simply wanted the FBI to see what the radicals were doing so there would not be any surprises later. His primary interest was in interpreting the riots in terms of environment rather than subversion. He wanted to emphasize the economic inequality crushing black culture more than the revolutionary rhetoric hammering on black minds. With the law-and-order issue building all over again, the president—unable to comprehend the visible rage of Watts—turned to the FBI once more. This time he was less interested in using the bureau's agents as amateur sociologists and more interested in using them as the professional countersubversives they were.

On August 17, 1965, when things began to settle down, Hoover submitted a long memo on the Watts disturbances to the Justice Department. Attorney General Nicholas DeB. Katzenbach sent it on to the president. If there was little "in the way of evidence as to subversive involvement," Katzenbach advised, the FBI would keep looking and investigate "this aspect" more "directly." But there would be no "general investigation through the FBI of other aspects of the riot." That remained the responsibility of local law enforcement agencies. After reading the FBI memo and Katzenbach's proposals, Johnson approved a "limited investigation."

The FBI did not limit its investigation. Even in regard to subversive involvement Hoover did not confine the bureau to intelligence gathering. The director moved his bureaucracy into the realm of counterintelligence, reminding the Los Angeles field office of the need "to expose any communist influence or attempt to capitalize for propaganda purposes upon the recent racial riot."

Hoover also entered the riot prediction business after Watts, partly as a result of the proddings of an increasingly isolated president. Johnson asked the FBI for briefings whenever he planned to visit an area where there might be "Negro agitation." After more summer rioting in 1966, the FBI began preparing semimonthly summaries of possible racial violence in major urban areas. Intelligence collected by "racial, criminal, and security informants" and any other "established logical sources" was processed at headquarters and organized under such topics as "General Racial Conditions." All organizations involved in "local racial situations," from mainstream civil rights groups to the Ku Klux Klan, were identified. The names of leaders were run through the files in search of "affiliation or association with Klan-type, communist or related subversive organizations."

The director had anticipated a long hot summer in 1967, but his prediction of "trouble" in "8 or 9 cities" turned out to be overly optimistic. Black neighborhoods in nearly 150 cities experienced disorders—from minor disturbances to widespread looting, arson, and sniping in Newark and Detroit.

The political problems the violence posed for the Johnson administration were more predictable. Many Republicans and a few conservative Democrats blamed the permissiveness of the Great Society once more. There seemed to be a "vacuum of Leadership" in the Congress, as Chalmers Roberts of the *Washington Post* described it to White House aide Douglass Cater. Roberts said "the Leadership doesn't seem to have any policy." Conservative critics of the administration favored an inquiry of some kind, but they had no idea "how to handle [it]." It looked like Sen. James O. Eastland, a Mississippi Democrat and an ardent segregationist, was "getting ready to carry the ball," and Sen. Everett Dirksen, an Illinois Republican, was "out to make hay on the issue." Outside of Washington, the FBI described the riots and the decision to commit paratroopers in Detroit as "a political football between the President and the [Republican] Governor of Michigan," George Romney. In Maryland, another Republican governor, Spiro T. Agnew, claimed the riots had been "thoroughly planned beforehand." Even Dwight D. Eisenhower suggested there was "a pattern" to the riots. Implying that Johnson had Hoover on a short leash, the former president called on Congress to pass whatever legislation was necessary to "empower the FBI to move into the situation."

The administration controlled the damage as best it could, with Johnson asking Hoover to confront Agnew and Eisenhower. In the former case, when two FBI agents buttonholed the governor, he admitted "he had no firsthand information." "He is now backwatering completely," as the director put it. In the latter case, Johnson told Hoover to contact Gen. Andrew Goodpaster, Eisenhower's aide, and to let him know the FBI had "full authority to spend anything to get the facts." LBJ's hill country ramblings lose a bit of their flavor in the

stream-of-consciousness memos the director habitually wrote after
speaking with the president on the phone, but the gist of what the
president told Hoover comes through clearly enough:

> Tell Eisenhower we don't want to put it on full page headlines
> the FBI is going to 'eat you up' and scare everybody and put
> them on notice what we are doing, but I have the authority and
> the President is on top of it and called me weeks ago when
> in Newark and insisted I get anybody, including their wife if
> she contributed. The President then stated he noticed this
> Rap (Brown) outfit said he was going to get a gun and shoot
> Lady Bird.

Before hanging up, Johnson told Hoover once again to "call General
Goodpaster and say I have all the approval and authority and money
and if I don't he, the President, will go to Texas and get it, and to tell
Goodpaster to get Eisenhower fully briefed." Hoover's response: "I
told the President I would do this." Goodpaster was just as businesslike.
He said "he would talk to General Eisenhower and straighten him
out."

Concerned about the continuing implications of the Detroit riots,
Johnson called upon Hoover once again on July 25, 1967, summoning
him to a White House meeting with Attorney General Clark, Secretary
of Defense Robert S. McNamara, Supreme Court Justice Abe Fortas,
Secretary of the Army Stanley R. Resor, and Army Chief of Staff Harold
K. Johnson. Cyrus Vance, Johnson's representative on the scene in
Detroit, called in every half hour with a status report. The president,
according to Hoover's account of the meeting, was obsessed with "intelligence." He was "of the opinion that there was a . . . pattern about
all of these riots" and "that members of the Poverty Corps had been
participants." He told the director to keep his "men busy to find a
central character to it, to watch and see and we will find some central
theme." Hoover agreed, up to a point. He said he "would dig into that
thoroughly," but he advised Johnson not to expect too much. "Outsiders" did not initiate any of the riots, though "carloads of individuals," including Communists, arrived "after" the riots were "in full
force." With regard to the poverty workers, Hoover mentioned Julius
Hobson, then an economist at the Department of Health, Education,
and Welfare and local chairman of ACT who was "making militant

speeches throughout [the District of Columbia]," and Marion Barry, the Student Nonviolent Coordinating Committee's (SNCC's) first chairman and then director of that group's Washington office and a fifty-dollar-a-day consultant for a community relations program that received federal funds. Johnson asked for memos on both men and a general summary of subversive influences in the riots.

Hoover submitted everything the next day, in the form of a report that summarized "major riot situations" in twenty-nine cities and included a section on the linkage between the anti—Vietnam War movement and the civil rights movement. The basic conclusion was restrained. Most of the riots were "sparked by a single incident generally following an arrest of a Negro by local police for some minor infraction." But there were exceptions. In Atlanta, Georgia; Nashville, Tennessee; and Cambridge, Maryland; the FBI credited "the exhortations of 'Black Power' advocates Stokely Carmichael and H. Rap Brown" with triggering "volatile situations . . . into violent outbreaks." Most of the other "racial disturbances, even if they were spontaneous outbursts of mob violence," the FBI executives who wrote the report added, were made much worse "by the involvement of other violent, criminal, subversive and extremist elements as the disorder grew and spread."

Bureau officials linked the moderates with the radicals. The civil rights movement itself, not just violence-prone demagogues, was to blame. "Certain individuals who have been prominent in civil rights activities," the FBI reasoned, "must bear a major burden of the guilt and responsibility for the turmoil created by the riots." Such "hypocritical individuals," movement people "who have openly professed abhorrence for violence," were credited with setting "the stage." They were "false prophets," working "the civil rights field" and sowing "seeds of confusion and disorder. . . . The Nation is [now] reaping the harvest of their handiworks."

Now fully committed to smearing the civil rights movement, LBJ relied on the FBI to provide the evidence to make his case. Throughout August 1967 the bureau flooded the White House with intelligence on the radicals and the moderates, and the volume of information overwhelmed Johnson's staff. When the White House asked the bureau to hold the "more or less minor" stuff and send over "the major information" only, Hoover refused. "If they don't want to use it after they get it, it is their responsibility." The administration, in any event, was scarcely more pleased with the quality of the intelligence submitted. With regard to the subversive connection and the business of assigning blame to the civil rights movement, the FBI's reports were short on facts and long on rhetoric.

Johnson administration officials had been concerned about the civil rights movement's move to the left and increasing involvement in antiwar activities for some time. When watching televised hearings before the House Committee on Un-American Activities (HUAC) in August 1966, the president himself had ordered one of his aides, Marvin Watson, to arrange an appearance by Hoover "before this group." Johnson wanted his FBI director to name "rioting participants as members of various subversive organizations" and thereby discredit the more radical civil rights groups by linking them to these unnamed "subversive organizations." He told Watson to call Cartha DeLoach and set it up. Both men were incredulous, and Watson told DeLoach not to do anything unless he called back. He never did. Nearly a year later, in July 1967, a few days before the Newark riot began, Johnson and Watson met with DeLoach and the president told the FBI assistant director he wanted the bureau to organize HUAC hearings on SNCC's Carmichael and CORE's Floyd McKissick. DeLoach declined.

The secretary to the cabinet, Robert Kintner, proposed something a bit more sophisticated during the spring of 1967 in anticipation of riots and a new round of protests against the Vietnam War. If the attorney general could develop "correct information" showing that the riots were "well-planned" and "in very many cases" organized by "the same people," Kintner told the president, a report could be "authentically prepared" and disseminated in "a speech by someone who cannot be criticized as a McCarthyite." Johnson approved the recommendation, and Kintner contacted Attorney General Clark. When the FBI failed to develop "correct information" about the riots, the administration not only asked Hoover to dig deeper but also solicited assistance from other sources. By the end of July 1967 the president's principal foreign policy advisor, Walt W. Rostow, was coordinating an effort to collect "such evidence as there is on external involvement in the violent radical fringe of the Negro community in the U.S." Rostow mobilized the entire intelligence community, but his people realized that "the hard evidence will have to come from inside the U.S. via the FBI" on such topics as "Cuban involvement in the civil rights and 'Black Power' movements." Hoover's agents, however, could not get the job done. They "came up with a blank." The Central Intelligence Agency was no more helpful, although its director, Richard Helms, did send over a compendium on world press coverage of Carmichael's visit to Cuba.

In some ways the FBI's response to the administration's demands was ambivalent. In mid-September 1967 the Justice Department received a tip from Walter Sheridan, a onetime troubleshooter within the department, that NBC news had interviewed a number of black citizens in Newark and Detroit who claimed the riots were thoroughly organized. The network planned to use those interviews during a special television program on urban violence. Clark responded by ordering the FBI to "use the maximum available resources, investigative and intelligence, to collect and report all facts bearing upon the question as to whether there has been or is a scheme or conspiracy by any group of whatever size, effectiveness or affiliation, to plan, promote or aggravate riot activity." The FBI nearly balked at Clark's order and at the attempts of John Doar, the assistant attorney general in charge of the Civil Rights Division, to follow up. At least one agent tried to make the point that such investigations posed a threat to the bureau's autonomy. "Up to now," he wrote, "we have run out any logical leads indicating [the] possibility of a conspiracy.... The attached [memo] appears to be an attempt on the part of John Doar to involve the Bureau in a fishing expedition of the rankest type."

Hoover responded otherwise, rejecting the good-manager approach and demanding a larger budget to handle the new responsibilities that were being thrust upon him. But the director was never interested merely in bureaucratic empire building, in trading autonomy for a larger taxpayer subsidy. If the FBI was to move into "community surveillance," Hoover would do so on his own terms.

An FBI inspector with a great deal of field experience in "racial matters," Joseph A. Sullivan, questioned the desirability of a greatly expanded domestic intelligence mission in a slightly different way. "Where do we go from here?" he asked. "The primary troublemakers throughout the riots were not organized groups in the sense that they represented some subversive forces in some civil rights or racist collectives. They were, rather, the street-corner hoodlum gangs." "Do we now program ourselves into coverage, into the development of sources, in these teen-age, street-corner gangs?" The bureau must define its "interests" before committing major resources to this "whole new field of racial operations," Sullivan advised Hoover. At best, it would be "a rather difficult and time-consuming program." When Sullivan proposed a conference of field agents to discuss the possibilities, Hoover said no. If the senior staff at headquarters had not quite made up their minds yet and did not have "the answer," the director wrote, "certainly no field group would be of aid."

In the interim the field was advised of the facts of life. "There exists in high Government circles a tremendous interest in all information regarding the racial situation throughout the United States." In Chicago, that meant a leak to Mayor Richard J. Daley regarding Martin Luther King, Jr.'s assessment of the riots: "They don't plan to burn down the west side. They are planning to get the loop." On the national level, it meant the dissemination of a bureau monograph on SNCC to fifty-one government officials and agencies. The Immigration and Naturalization Service received fifty copies and the marines thirty-one. Hoover sent a more modest number of copies (two) to West Point.

The "tremendous interest in . . . the racial situation" also led to an escalation of the FBI's investigation of Office of Economic Opportunity (OEO) personnel who might have been involved in the riots. The reform state looked vulnerable, and the White House was interested in damage control. The administration had more confidence in an FBI probe than in OEO director Sargent Shriver's ongoing in-house investigation, but the bureau was once again less than enthusiastic. No matter how interested in the sayings and doings of OEO personnel, the bureau was uninterested in helping the administration contain political fallout. On August 1, after Johnson's aide Watson requested an escalated investigation, Hoover informed the White House that the FBI had already given the National Commission on Civil Disorders (the Kerner Commission) everything in the files.

The Kerner Commission itself settled nothing for either the president or the FBI director. Johnson had appointed the commission to investigate the origins of the riots and to make recommendations "to prevent or contain such disorders in the future." The exercise was similar to the more modest effort to use Hoover and Dewey in 1964. Prominent people were brought in, including Gov. Otto Kerner of Illinois as chairman and Mayor John Lindsay of New York as vice-chairman, and the

FBI director was ordered to cooperate. Armed with a brief and "a summary of available information concerning each Commission member," Hoover supplemented his testimony on OEO before the commission with a general discussion of the causes of the riots and his bureaucracy's responsibilities.

The director's law-and-order posturing—the call for stronger antiriot legislation, improved police training, and even gun control—was qualified. FBI agents photographed rioters and took notes, he testified, but they did not arrest snipers or fire bombers because looting and arson were local crimes outside the bureau's jurisdiction. On the intelligence side, Hoover described for the commission the "catalytic effect of extremists." He focused on Brown and Carmichael of SNCC but found time to mention the Communist party, the pro-Chicom (Chinese Communist) Progressive Labor party, Students for a Democratic Society, and various teenage gangs.

On the whole, the Kerner Commission rejected Hoover's conclusions. Its final report, submitted in February 1968, dealt less with the "catalytic effect" of the Rap Browns and Stokely Carmichaels than with the social problems facing the United States. America was "moving toward two societies, one black, one white—separate and unequal." To reverse the "deepening racial trend," the commission called for "a commitment to national action," recommending sweeping reforms in the areas of employment, education, welfare, housing reform, news reporting, and law enforcement. "Discrimination and segregation have long permeated much of American life," the report concluded. "They now threaten the future of every American."

The Johnson administration rejected most of the Kerner Commission's proposals on budgetary grounds. "That was the problem," LBJ later wrote, "—money." Because the money simply was not there, the commission, as Johnson's special counsel Harry McPherson noted in his memoirs, created more problems for the administration than it solved. "It intensified arguments about the war, raised impossible demands, and implicitly diminished the significance of what was already being done."

Hoping to break the conservative monopoly of the law-and-order issue, the administration did seize upon one of the Kerner Commission's less costly recommendations, which seemingly implied acceptance of the surveillance mission that Hoover had advocated. A minor recom-

mendation, buried in the appendix, called for the creation of police
intelligence units "staffed with full-time personnel," including "under-
cover police personnel and informants." Commission members had in
mind social intelligence (for example, data on unemployment, teenage
pregnancies, and high school dropout rates), not political intelligence,
and had flatly rejected the FBI director's "countersubversive dogmas."
But the Kerner Commission report "was promptly converted by intelligence apologists into support for the very thesis it had rejected."
President Johnson himself did not wait for the publication of the report.
He immediately encouraged local police departments to establish intelligence units and to funnel any information collected to the Justice
Department through the FBI.

The department was concerned, as the former assistant attorney
general Fred Vinson recalled, because local police did not have "any
useful intelligence or knowledge about ghettos, about black communities in the big cities." As a result, the domestic intelligence apparatus
became bigger, harder to control, more intrusive, more incompetent.
A Cook County grand jury investigation of the Chicago Police Department's Security Section concluded that its "inherently inaccurate
and distortive" data, accepted without question by the FBI, contami-
nated federal intelligence. One police officer told the grand jury that
the name of "any person" who attended two "public meetings" of any
group under surveillance was forwarded to the FBI. The bureau then
passed the "*fact*" of membership in a subversive organization along
when conducting background checks on persons seeking federal employment or grants. "Since federal agencies accepted data from the
Security Section without questioning the procedures followed, or methods used to gain information," the grand jury noted, "the federal government cannot escape responsibility for the harm done to untold
numbers of innocent persons."

J. Edgar Hoover felt the Kerner Commission had paid too much
attention to the sociological side of urban violence and not enough to
the law-and-order side. When President Johnson appointed yet another
study group later in 1968, the National Commission on the Causes
and Prevention of Violence, and selected President Eisenhower's
brother Milton to chair it, the director told Clark what he thought:
There was too much "emphasis today in the press that society is sick.
... I said I hoped the new Commission ... will keep a balanced view—

point as to that because the other Commission went far astray in regard to white racism. I said there is racism but not as predominantly as the Kerner Commission found it to be....I hope the Eisenhower Commission when they get around to their finding view it with an unemotional attitude." The director tried to educate the Eisenhower Commission, but he was hardly a disinterested observer.

When Hoover testified before the commission in September 1968 he fed the very "white racism" he had complained about by stressing the "Mau Mau-type tactics" of SNCC and other militant black groups. The FBI could not decide whether SNCC was a Mau Mau-type New Left group or "a Ku Klux Klan in reverse—a black Klan." On the issue of police brutality in the ghetto, the director linked Moscow-directed revolutionaries with "vicious, hate-filled...black extremists." The "communist policy to charge and protest 'police brutality'...in racial situations" was part of an "immensely successful" and "continuing smear campaign," he said. "The net effect...is to provoke and encourage mob action and violence by developing contempt for constituted authority."

Neither the Kerner Commission nor the Eisenhower Commission had any discernible impact on the FBI. In fact, one bureau field office responded to the Kerner Commission's tendency "to absolve the Negro rioters from any large blame" by suggesting that the bureau's public relations division, Crime Records, publish a public opinion poll, "either a true poll or a false poll," that would indicate the public's tendency to place all blame on "the Negro rioters." Although Hoover rejected the proposal, surveillance and counterintelligence remained the preferred mode of governance. The director did not sit and wait and hope the commissions would issue reports he could stomach. He moved quickly to support the conservative alternative to the presidential commissions by working with Democratic Sen. John L. McClellan of Arkansas, the chairman of the Permanent Subcommittee on Investigations.

McClellan's subcommittee, the same subcommittee that Sen. Joseph R. McCarthy had once chaired, was actually the third and last of the old Cold War-era investigating committees to launch hearings on the riots. The Senate Internal Security Subcommittee had begun such hearings, but HUAC chairman Edwin Willis, a Louisiana Democrat, told DeLoach "the Senate hearings would amount to only a lot of 'socialistic crap,'" in that the Senate would later demand better housing, better jobs, et cetera." Willis wanted the FBI to provide "guidance" for his own committee's hearings. DeLoach refused. The FBI preferred to work with Senator McClellan. He was far more powerful than any HUAC member, and his staff were far more reliable (and therefore less likely to compromise their relationships with bureau agents) than the HUAC people. In their political responses to the riots there was little difference between Willis and McClellan. Before the Senate had even voted to fund his proposed inquiry, McClellan said he would emphasize "law enforcement rather than the social causes underlying the disorders." When the authorization came through in August 1967 the McClellan Committee began work on a twenty-five-part, three-year investigation into the causes of the urban riots.

The McClellan Committee wasted no time in explaining the origins of the riots with the sort of logic favored by the late Senator McCarthy. In September 1967, following a state police raid on the home of two poverty workers in Pike County, Kentucky, Margaret and Alan Mc-Surely, one of the committee's investigators made arrangements with a local prosecutor to obtain the papers and documents seized in the raid. The McSurelys, organizers for the Southern Conference Educational Fund (SCEF), were charged with violating a state sedition statute. They had attracted the committee's interest, McClellan said, because Carmichael had addressed a SCEF staff meeting and had spoken at Vanderbilt University a few days before the Nashville riots. There was a thread connecting everything. The riots were traced back to SCEF; and since that organization was widely believed by Hoover, McClellan, and even some civil rights activists to be "communist controlled," the Nashville riots could be blamed on the party. And since the McSurelys were poverty workers, the circle could be squared, brought back, as it were, to the Great Society. Obviously, things were not quite that simple. Logic and ideology aside, the Pike County prosecutor had political ambitions and economic interests. As a candidate for lieutenant governor and the owner of property leased to coal mine operators, he intended to drive poverty workers out of Kentucky.

None of those facts slowed the McClellan committee. A federal judge in Kentucky ordered the McSurelys' papers sequestered, but Mc-Clellan's man took them to Washington anyway. The senator himself seemed most interested in love letters that newspaper columnist Drew Pearson had sent Margaret McSurely. A persistent critic of McClellan,

Pearson had most recently discussed the senator in a column dated August 10, 1967, the day before the Pike County raid. It was indeed a small world. Ultimately, the McSurelys were summoned by the McClellan committee and indicted for contempt of Congress. They filed suit against the committee and the bluegrass prosecutor and were (literally) bombed out of their Kentucky home. Meanwhile the FBI gave everything it had on the McSurelys and Joseph Mulloy, a worker with an antipoverty group (Appalachian Volunteers), who was also arrested, to the Kentucky State Police. Bureau officials admitted it was not much, and in Mulloy's case there was absolutely nothing in the files; but it was "a matter of police cooperation." A bureau agent, moreover, reviewed the records seized in the raid, and a memo was sent to the White House.

The whole thing was part of what one of the president's aides described as a "nationwide investigation of the OEO involvement in the riots," an effort that confirmed Johnson's concern about the vulnerability of the Office of Economic Opportunity and the whole War on Poverty. FBI officials tried to keep a reasonable distance from the McSurelys' civil suit and the "political fight" down in Kentucky. At the same time, they provided much direct, if covert, assistance to other aspects of the McClellan committee's nationwide campaign. When McClellan asked Hoover for "the cooperation of the FBI in checking names," the director assured the senator "we would give...every assistance we could." Crime Records chief Thomas Bishop was ordered to handle all requests from the committee's chief counsel, Donald O'Donnell, "promptly."

The typical McClellan committee request called for the FBI to list all "the militant organizations or groups" in a given area and to provide brief identifications "of the individual members." That was done in dozens of cities. In Boston, the FBI provided dossiers on such groups as Mothers for Adequate Welfare and such individuals as a Roxbury housewife and veteran of the civil rights sit-ins. The woman, "a Negress ...married to...a white male," the bureau said, was an antiwar activist to boot. On other occasions, the FBI spied on the McClellan committee's rival, the Kerner Commission. Whenever something interesting turned up the director issued the appropriate order: "Let our contact on McClellan's Com. know."

Hoover and McClellan enjoyed a symbiotic relationship. The senator

was always asking for help. A week after the two men worked out the
terms of the FBI's assistance for the riot hearings, DeLoach and
McClellan discussed another appendage to the Senate Government Operations Committee, the Subcommittee on Criminal Laws and Procedures. Their conversation focused on a provision in "the pending
legislation involving the Crime Control Act" authorizing an expansion
of the FBI National Academy. McClellan asked DeLoach to write a
speech for him on law and order and to provide backup information
on the bureau's desires in the area of police training. "Senator Mc-
Clellan," as DeLoach later advised FBI Associate Director Clyde Tolson, "apparently was not aware of the tremendous amount of
information we had already furnished his Staff Director, James
Calloway."

McClellan also offered the bureau help. He gave DeLoach a copy of
his omnibus crime control bill and "asked that the FBI study this bill
very carefully and actually prepare language which could be inserted
into the bill." "This would be done," DeLoach said, "on a confidential
basis." When Calloway finished work on a new version of the bill, he
handed a copy of another bill, the law enforcement assistance bill
(which would be added to the omnibus bill) to Bishop and requested,
"on an informal basis," the FBI's "views with regard to it. This would
include not only the portions dealing with the FBI, but all other portions
of the Bill."

Less than a month later, in November 1967, Deputy Attorney General Warren Christopher phoned DeLoach to discuss an amendment
to one of the pending crime control bills that concerned law enforcement training. "Our conversation," as DeLoach summarized it for
Tolson and Hoover, "was not a pleasant one." "[The Deputy Attorney
General] and the Attorney General both felt that perhaps the FBI did
not want to be saddled with the tremendous responsibilities it was
being given." DeLoach told Christopher that was not the case. "To
the contrary, we insisted upon such responsibilities." The bureau was
fully supported by Senators McClellan and Eastland, DeLoach told
Christopher. Christopher was aware that "we had some powerful allies
in this matter," but he said the attorney general thought "another
agency"—"a national office on law enforcement . . . over in the Department"—should at least *share* the responsibilities with the FBI."
The director favored McClellan's version. "We will not agree to *sharing*

any part of this." If Christopher tried to do something about it, "he would meet considerable resistance on the Hill."

The skirmish here was part of a larger battle, a fundamental conflict between the Justice Department belief that urban violence would disappear if poverty disappeared and the FBI belief that crime would disappear if the permissivists in the department (Ramsey Clark) and on the Supreme Court (Earl Warren) disappeared. The Johnson administration experienced some fleeting success, as the historian Hugh Davis Graham observed, in attaining a "consensus between hard-line demands for crack-down and constitutional solicitude for civil liberties and due process." When the Omnibus Crime Control and Safe Streets Act became the law of the land in 1968, it included a provision creating the in-house bureaucracy Clark and Christopher wanted, the Law Enforcement Assistance Administration, and another provision increasing the number of police officers authorized to attend the FBI National Academy from two hundred to two thousand. Title I appropriated $5,110,000 to the FBI in fiscal year 1969 for its training programs.

McClellan was the principal author of the legislation. Or perhaps Hoover and DeLoach were. The instruction of local police in the "fundamentals" (DeLoach's word) of riot control was a serious business. It provided a way for the FBI to expand in size and to spread its ideology about racial matters and subversives. Riot training for policemen, the covert assistance provided to Senator McClellan's committee, and the FBI's role in drafting the Omnibus Crime Control and Safe Streets Act provided a law-and-order alternative to the social, cultural, and economic prescriptions of the Kerner Commission. It was no coincidence that John McClellan turned to the FBI for help with the hearings and the legislation.

Hoover knew the Kerner Commission and McClellan's projects were symptomatic of a cleavage in the nation. With the war (especially the war) and the riots, the United States was coming apart. You could see it just by looking at LBJ's face. And Richard M. Nixon, with his bring-us-together-again slogan, updated version of Goldwater's southern strategy, and politics of resentment, understood it best of all. "The whole secret of politics," said Kevin Phillips, aide to John Mitchell and the Nixon campaign's expert on ethnic voting patterns, "[is] knowing who hates who."

Alone in the White House, with his three-screen television console, Lyndon Johnson watched his own tragedy unfold each evening on the network news. He knew what was happening but did not know what to do about it. He never really made the choice, never really decided on a political strategy, never really gave up his dream of consensus for a more cold-blooded politics of "positive polarization" (Spiro Agnew's words). Perhaps he was too decent a man, after all. He kept drifting back and forth, from the world of the Great Society and the Kerner Commission's sociology to the segmented world of McClellan and Hoover and the methods of the Nixon campaign. "It is time to rip away the rhetoric and to divide on authentic lines," Agnew said without apology after the election. "When the President said 'bring us together' he meant the functioning, contributing portions of the American citizenry." The FBI director agreed. "To Hoover," as his biographer noted, the "protestors" of every stripe, whether ghetto rioters or college students marching against the Vietnam War, "were not part of the real America, 'the hard-working, tax-paying, law-abiding people of this country.'"

Johnson never gave up completely on the citizens the new vice-president and the old FBI director held in contempt. If he could explain the riots by reference to "a few hoodlums sparked by outside agitators who moved around from city to city making trouble. Spoiling all the progress I've made in these last few years," in the next breath he could say, "God knows how little we've really moved on this issue despite all the fanfare. As I see it, I've moved the Negro from D+ to C−. He's still nowhere. He knows it. And that's why he's out in the streets. Hell, I'd be there too."

President Johnson never quite realized, as Clark and Christopher had, that Hoover had been working for the McClellans, Agnews, and Nixons all along. In the end, Hoover made things harder for Johnson and the social reformers of the Great Society, and he made things easier for Nixon and Nixon's heirs. He helped make the Republican party the white man's party King had feared it might become, back in the spring of 1964, a few months before the fires started burning.

The FBI director's maneuverings during the riots in the 1960s suggest that he was not a shrill anticommunist ideologue or a practitioner of what Richard Hofstadter called the "paranoid style" of American politics. Rather, he was a sophisticated politician who understood power and public opinion. Hoover ingratiated himself with Lyndon Johnson and with Johnson's domestic political adversaries while pursuing his own bureaucratic and larger political interests. Johnson thought he could use Hoover to help him manage the politics of the riots, but he had no more success in controlling the director than had any of his predecessors in the Oval Office dating back to Franklin D. Roosevelt. The president used the FBI to help him manage particular problems. He used the FBI to help him govern. Hoover damaged Johnson's interests on both fronts, and in the end the director's bureaucracy, the FBI, and the director's mode of operation, federal surveillance, became further entrenched in the governing process.

One of Hoover's own aides described the director as "an absolute, totally consummate, skilled politician. . . . He handled the presidents as well or better than any bureaucrat in the city of Washington ever has." It would be hard to argue with that assessment.

19

Vietnam and the Constitution: The War Power Under Lyndon Johnson and Richard Nixon

MICHAL R. BELKNAP

• *During the 1960 presidential campaign, John F. Kennedy repeatedly criticized the Eisenhower administration for too great a reliance on nuclear weapons. After his election, the new president implemented a policy of flexible response to so-called wars of national liberation. When guerilla conflict began in Vietnam, President Kennedy sent airplanes, artillery, and 16,000 "advisers" to bolster President Diem's regime.*

The conflict continued to widen, and in 1963 Lyndon B. Johnson inherited a shaky Saigon regime dependent on American support. Rather than face charges of appeasement in world affairs, President Johnson increased the Southeast Asian involvement. In August 1964, in response to an alleged attack on an American destroyer, President Johnson ordered the bombing of North Vietnam. This prompted the Senate to pass—with only two dissenting votes—the Gulf of Tonkin Resolution, which granted the chief executive extraordinary powers to protect the national interest. By 1967, more than a half-million United States servicemen were trying to prevent a Communist takeover, "contain" China, and convince other governments of America's resolve to protect its friends.

As most people now realize, the attack in the Gulf of Tonkin never happened, and the Chinese and the Vietnamese people were contemptuous of each other. Moreover, the American military effort was unsuccessful, and the cost in the lives of young men and in more than a decade of inflation was enormous. There has been little agreement as to why the rich and powerful United States, with its technologically sophisticated weaponry and its absolute command of the air and the sea, could not bring to heel a small, poor, and backward nation

Reprinted from *This Constitution*, No. 10, Spring, 1986.

that was divided against itself. An equally important question is how the American republic got itself into such a protracted conflict without a declaration of war. This constitutional question is the subject of the following essay by Michal R. Belknap.

During the national agony known as the Vietnam War, Presidents Lyndon Johnson and Richard Nixon came under fire almost as intense as that directed at American military units in Southeast Asia. Among the charges leveled against them were allegations of unconstitutional conduct. In fact, Johnson and Nixon were guilty neither of massively misemploying their authority as commander in chief nor of abusing presidential war powers. Although often condemned for failing to obtain a congressional declaration of war, they had the support of twentieth-century practice and opinion in contending that it was for the president to decide when and against whom the United States should commit its armed forces to battle. Furthermore, neither Johnson nor Nixon claimed, as had some of their predecessors, that the war powers of their office gave them the authority to subject large aspects of American domestic life to executive control. These much-villified presidents may deserve censure for fighting the wrong war in the wrong place at the wrong time, but they were not guilty of fighting that war unconstitutionally.

PRECEDENT

It had never been quite clear what the framers of the Constitution meant when they provided in Article I, section 8, "The Congress shall have Power ... to declare war...." The declaration of war was a medieval custom associated with chivalry, which required one belligerent to notify another formally before commencing hostilities against it. By the time of the Constitutional Convention in 1787, this practice had fallen into disuse, and of the approximately 140 wars fought in the world between 1700 and 1907 (when the Hague Conference adopted a convention providing that hostilities might not be commenced without a formal warning), only a handful were declared. The draft of the Constitution prepared by the Committee on Detail gave Congress the power to "make" war, but the full Convention changed that word to "declare." It seems unlikely that the Convention intended thereby to restrict Congress only to giving formal notification of America's intention to fight or to initiating the minority of wars in which a declaration was employed. Probably, it made the change to allow the president to respond immediately if the nation were attacked. Unfortunately, debate on this issue was brief and opaque. By employing a word whose meaning was at best ambiguous, the Convention made it possible for presidents to argue later that it was constitutional for them to commence, on their own initiative, all wars which were not "declared."

In any event, by making the president the "Commander in Chief of the Army and Navy...," the Convention conceded to the executive the real power to decide when and against whom the United States would fight whether or not the war is "declared." Congress declared war on Mexico in 1846, but only after being informed by President James K. Polk that Mexico already had initiated hostilities by attacking American troops. In fact, Polk, who was seeking a pretext for war, had provoked the Mexican attack by ordering the Army into disputed territory to which Mexico's claim was considerably stronger than that of the United States.

Other presidents have used their authority as commander in chief to deploy American military forces in ways which, although not causing a declared war, have resulted in fighting and even loss of life. In 1801, for example, Thomas Jefferson started a naval conflict with the Barbary pirates by spurning their demands for increased "protection money" and ordering the Navy and Marines to North Africa.

PRESIDENTIAL WAR-MAKING

Six decades later, the Supreme Court gave backhanded legal recognition to such presidentially-initiated "wars." In 1861, Abraham Lincoln launched the fighting between the North and South by dispatching a relief expedition to Fort Sumter. He made the resulting conflict a war under international law by ordering the Navy to blockade Southern ports. In upholding the legality of that action, the Supreme Court employed language useful to later champions of presidential warmaking. Whether a congressional declaration was necessary to make a noncivil war legal as a matter of domestic constitutional law was not really an issue in the *Prize Cases* (1863), which involved a dispute over international law. In its opinion, though, the Court proclaimed that a president was bound "to resist force by force," and to do so "without waiting for any special legislative authority." He could wage war without waiting "for Congress to baptize it with a name."

During the twentieth century, presidents advanced toward the sort of executive takeover of the war-initiating function that this language seemed to sanction. McKinley moved only a little way in that direction, and he did so with the explicit permission of Congress. On April 20, 1898, the House and Senate adopted a resolution recognizing the independence of the Spanish colony of Cuba and demanding that Spain relinquish its authority over that island and withdraw its military and naval forces. At the same time, Congress directed the president to use the Army and Navy to carry its resolution into effect. In other words, Congress issued an ultimatum, then left it to the president to decide what action the United States should take if its demands were not met. Spain responded to the resolution by breaking diplomatic relations. On April 22, McKinley proclaimed a naval blockade of Cuba, and that same day an American warship fired across the bow of a Spanish steamer. On April 24, Spain declared war on the United States, and the following day Congress adopted a second resolution, which announced that a state of war had existed between the two countries since the twenty-first.

Like the Spanish-American War, World War I had explicit congressional sanction. In April 1917, Woodrow Wilson, an admirer of the British parliamentary system who believed a president should govern by leading Congress, asked for and obtained a declaration of war against Germany. Had the House and Senate refused his request, Americans might still have found themselves fighting Germans. Earlier, a Senate filibuster had prevented Wilson from obtaining congressional authorization to put guns, and Navy men to fire them, on merchant vessels. In March he took that step on his own. It was a move likely to result in American ships shooting it out with German submarines, whether or not Congress declared war.

During the period 1939–1941, Franklin Roosevelt went much further than Wilson had, reducing congressional declaration to little more than a formality. Congress voted for war against Japan only after the Japanese bombed Pearl Harbor on December 7, 1941 and for hostilities against Germany and Italy only after those countries announced they would join their Axis ally in its fight against the United States. Long before December 1941, however, this country had ceased to be neutral in the military conflicts already raging in Asia and Europe. Roosevelt had assisted China in its fight with Japan by subjecting the Japanese to escalating economic pressure and had made America into a virtual arsenal for Britain in her war against Nazi Germany. On his own authority, he transferred fifty destroyers to the British in exchange for some Western Hemisphere bases and with congressional authorization lent and leased American war materiel to Britain. Besides taking actions likely to provoke the Axis powers into attacking the United States, Roosevelt initiated combat against Germany. He ordered the Navy to convoy supplies bound for the British Isles and to fire on German submarines that tried to interfere. Several months before Pearl Harbor, the United States was already engaged in a shooting war with Germany in the North Atlantic. Of the two-year period which preceded December 7, 1941, political scientist Edward S. Corwin said in *Total War and the Constitution* (1947), "The initiative throughout was unremittingly with the President."

In June 1950, a president dispensed entirely with the declaration of war, leading the United States into a major military conflict without even consulting Congress. When North Korea attacked South Korea, Harry Truman simply ordered American air, naval, and ground forces into combat against the Communist aggressors. Explaining to legislative leaders why he had proceeded in this way, Truman declared, "I just had to act as Commander in Chief, and I did." When the tide of battle began to run strongly against the United States, Representative Frederic R. Coudert, Jr., introduced a resolution against sending additional military forces abroad without the prior approval of Congress. Conservative Republican Senator Robert Taft endorsed his position, but a host of other prominent senators from both parties, among them Paul Douglas, Arthur Vandenberg, Wayne Morse, and J. William Fulbright, defended Truman's right to send American forces anywhere he felt the security of the United States required.

By 1950 it was obvious to perceptive legislators that, whatever the members of the Constitutional Convention may have intended, the real power to determine whether or not this country went to war lay with the president. Lawyers and scholars had grasped this reality too. In 1941 University of California law professor Harry Willmer Jones observed: "Champions of the authority of Congress have long been aware that bold presidential exercise of the power of command over the armed forces may make somewhat unreal the constitutional power of Congress to declare war."

By the early 1960s, this state of affairs was widely regarded as a good thing. Victory in World War II had vindicated Roosevelt's pre-Pearl Harbor initiatives and discredited the isolationists who had criticized him for bypassing Congress. In the wake of that conflict, prominent international and constitutional lawyers took the position that the congressional power to declare war was really little more than the authority to announce to the rest of the world that the United States was engaged in hostilities. The development of atomic weapons, and of planes and rockets capable of delivering them from one continent to another, seemed to make essential vesting war-making power in a single individual, who could act quickly and decisively to meet an enemy challenge. Historians, such as Arthur Schlesinger, Jr., and political scientists, such as Richard Neustadt, praised the emergence of the "strong" presidency. Meanwhile, international law authority Pittman B. Potter, unaware of how naive and even ridiculous his views would appear by the 1980s, observed in 1954 that while the president did have a large measure of discretion, it was after all "subject to the obligation to use a large measure of prudence . . . and not to involve us in another World War without more than ample justification."

It was in this climate of opinion that Lyndon Johnson went to Congress after the Tonkin Gulf incident in August 1964 seeking a resolution expressing congressional approval and support for "the determination of the President, as commander in chief to take all necessary measures to repel any armed attack against the forces of the United States and to prevent further aggression." Johnson did not believe the Constitution required him to obtain authorization from Congress before taking military action in Vietnam, but he thought such a resolution would be politically useful. It would show the Communists that America was united behind its commander in chief and enable him to avoid the sort of partisan criticism Truman had received for his unilateral action in Korea. Although Dwight Eisenhower had sought similar expressions of congressional support during the Formosa and Middle East crises of the 1950's, several prominent senators maintained that the president already had sufficient authority to use force in Vietnam. The commander in chief needed no legislative endorsement, they insisted.

Among the proponents of this thesis was Senator Fulbright, by now chairman of the Foreign Relations Committee and later one of the sharpest critics of Johnson's Southeast Asian policies.

Such critics often faulted LBJ for failing to obtain a declaration of war from Congress before sending hundreds of thousands of troops to South Vietnam and launching a massive bombing campaign against North Vietnam, but this objection was seldom heard until after the futility of the war revealed itself late in the Johnson administration. As Professor Graham T. Allison has pointed out, had the War Powers Resolution, passed by Congress in 1973 to prevent "any more Vietnams," been in force a decade earlier, it would not have kept America from becoming militarily involved in Southeast Asia; Johnson's actions were initially popular, and he could easily have obtained the congressional authorization required for the troops he sent to Vietnam in 1965 to remain there. Furthermore, the president's conduct was in line with pre–1964 thinking and presidential practice.

So for the most part were the actions of Richard Nixon, which included expanding the war by invading neutral Cambodia in 1970.[1] In justifying the Cambodian incursion as an exercise of the powers of the commander in chief, then-assistant Attorney General William Rehnquist took a position actually more restrained than Truman's. As Rehnquist argued, Nixon's invasion was, at least in part, a tactical move designed to protect American forces already fighting in Vietnam from attacks launched by the enemy out of sanctuaries across the border in Cambodia. Truman, on the other hand, had started a brand new war when he sent U.S. troops off to engage the North Koreans in 1950. Nixon did break new and dubious ground, but only when he continued to fight in Southeast Asia despite clear expressions of congressional opposition to the war, such as the 1971 repeal of the Tonkin Gulf Resolution.

Arthur Schlesinger, Jr. is hardly warranted in asserting in the *The Imperial Presidency* (1973): "Both Johnson and Nixon ... indulged in presidential warmaking beyond the wildest dreams of their predecessors." What bothers Schlesinger is the character of the conflict which

---

1. Like thousands of college students of my generation, I participated in protests against the Cambodian incursion. I do not mean here to endorse it (or the Vietnam War as a whole) as either morally justified or politically wise.

one of these presidents escalated[2] and the other prolonged and expanded. He finds their conduct distinguishable from that of Lincoln, Roosevelt, and Truman primarily because, unlike Nixon and Johnson, those men involved the nation in just wars. That distinction may be a valid one, but it is not a constitutional one.

WAR POWERS "AT HOME"

Although Johnson was a domineering individual and Nixon's efforts to enhance the prerogatives of the presidency sometimes suggested dictatorial ambitions, neither Vietnam president was as "imperial" in his use of presidential war power on the domestic front as predecessors who have fared far better at the hands of historians such as Schlesinger. Lincoln, for example, used the war power to justify spending money never appropriated by Congress, locking up disloyal civilians, and even freeing the slaves. Indeed, the domestic presidential "war power" was largely his creation. Lincoln manufactured it by linking the commander-in-chief clause, apparently intended by those who wrote the Constitution only to make the president the head of the Army and Navy, to the provision in Article II, section 3 directing the chief executive to "take care that the laws be faithfully executed." Together, Lincoln insisted, these clauses gave him sufficient authority not only to fight the Civil War but also to deal effectively with all of the domestic problems it created. In his hands, the commander-in-chief clause became a constitutional grant to the president of almost unlimited emergency powers.

Lincoln, was, of course, fighting a unique internal war in which the very survival of the nation was at stake. The extraordinary circumstances which he confronted justified the extraordinary measures which he took. By the end of the nineteenth century, though, commentators were pointing to his actions as examples of what any wartime president

---

2. President Truman sent the first American military personnel to Vietnam. The number of U.S. advisors in that country, which stood at less than 700 at the end of the Eisenhower administration, was raised to more than 16,000 by John F. Kennedy. Besides increasing the number of American men in Vietnam from that level to about 550,000, Johnson also changed the U.S. role there in two significant ways: he introduced American ground combat units into the fighting in the South and he initiated the bombing of the North.

could do. They generalized Lincoln's conduct into a broad domestic presidential war power, available during foreign as well as civil wars.

This concept went largely untested during the Spanish-American War. That conflict, which ended victoriously only a few months after it began, was too brief and required too little in the way of economic and manpower mobilization to provide much occasion for assertions of presidential prerogative on the home front.

World War I was different. It was a cataclysmic world conflict in which several nations (although certainly not the United States) were battling for survival. Hence, it seemed to require extraordinary measures to ensure victory. Furthermore, national war efforts in an industrial age had become so heavily dependent on the economic base supporting them that a dozen workers had to labor at home to keep a single soldier fighting at the front. Under such circumstances, the use of unprecedented methods could not be restricted to the battlefield. Wilson responded to the challenge of World War I with a more sweeping domestic exercise of presidential power than anything seen since Lincoln's day. In a speech accepting the 1920 Republican nomination, Warren G. Harding complained that due to anxieties inspired by the war emergency, "every safeguard was swept away. In the name of democracy we established autocracy."

Harding's partisan recollections were not entirely fair to his Democratic predecessor. Rather than relying largely on the inherent powers of the commander in chief, as Lincoln had done, Wilson went to the legislative branch and got it to delegate sweeping authority to the chief executive. Congress gave him the power not only to draft men into the Army and Navy, but also to regulate food production, set fuel prices, license businesses, seize railroad, telegraph, and telephone lines, take over factories, censor the mails, and even imprison critics of the government and opponents of the war.

Although the scope of the authority which Congress delegated to Wilson was breathtaking, he sometimes found it inadequate, or at least too slow in coming. Consequently, the president took a number of actions for which statutory authorization was lacking, justifying them as exercises of his own war powers. The most important of these was the establishment of the powerful War Industries Board, which extended a large measure of supervision over much of American business.

During World War II, Roosevelt relied even more than had Wilson on the war powers of the presidency itself. Congress was again generous in delegating authority to the executive, but FDR did many things, even during the period September 1939 to December 1941, for which he lacked statutory authority. These ranged from creating a host of new federal agencies to lengthening the work week to 48 hours. The president insisted he had the inherent power to seize defense plants in danger of being idled by strikes and took over several before Congress got around to enacting legislation clearly giving him the authority to do this. The Justice Department argued moreover that Roosevelt's war powers provided a legal basis for Army seizure of Montgomery Ward, despite the tenuous connection between a consumer mail order house and the national military effort.

The war powers Roosevelt claimed were even greater than those he actually exercised. On September 7, 1942, he declared that if Congress did not repeal a statutory provision which was undermining the government's efforts to combat inflation, the "responsibilities of the president in war time to protect the nation" would justify him in refusing to carry out the offensive law. Corwin sharply criticized this message, lambasting Roosevelt for claiming he had the right to suspend the Constitution. Other commentators reacted differently, insisting that the nation's involvement in a "total war" justified, even required, such extreme examples of executive leadership. Neither Congress nor the judiciary, they believed, should sit in judgment of the commander in chief. The Supreme Court probably agreed, for it tended to treat many domestic actions of the President—like excluding Japanese-Americans from the West Coast and closing the civilian courts to captured enemy saboteurs—as part of his military conduct of the war, and consequently as matters in which judges should not interfere.

Like Roosevelt before him, Truman relied on extra-statutory authority to establish new agencies and give additional powers to old ones during the Korean conflict. In April 1952, when a nationwide strike threatened to shut down the steel industry and restrict the flow of war materiel to Korea, he ordered the Secretary of Commerce to seize the steel mills. In doing this, Truman relied upon what he insisted were the inherent powers of the president in a "defense emergency" (a rationale, however, with which the Supreme Court did not agree).

Johnson and Nixon managed the home front quite differently. In July 1967, when a railroad strike interfered with the movement of ammunition and military equipment to ports of embarkation to Vietnam, LBJ asked Congress for legislation to end the work stoppage and resolve the underlying labor-management dispute. When Nixon called out military reservists to deliver the mail during a 1970 postal strike, he cited as his authority for taking this action not the commander-in-chief clause but a statute. In imposing a ninety-day wage-price freeze the following year, he relied not on presidential war power but on stand-by authority which Congress had bestowed upon the president in 1970. It is true that when trying to justify some of the more dubious conduct of his administration, Nixon liked to refer frequently to the demands of "national security," but in managing the home front, neither he nor Johnson relied on the war power. As a matter of fact, the Vietnam presidents seldom even mentioned it in a domestic context.

There are probably three reasons for their failure to make greater use of the war power. One is the Supreme Court's decision in *Youngstown Sheet and Tube Co.* v. *Sawyer* (1952). In that case, the Court held that Truman lacked the authority to seize the steel mills. Since every member of the six-man majority wrote a separate opinion, it is difficult to say precisely why, but clearly only the three dissenters accepted Truman's contention that the inherent powers of the presidency provided sufficient support for his action. Two other justices might have agreed with them, had Congress not already provided a remedy for such strikes in the Taft-Hartley Act. They and two additional colleagues insisted, however, that a president had no right to ignore a statute. After 1952 the prudent course for a cautious chief executive was to cite statutory authority for any action likely to be challenged.

The growing unpopularity of the war in Vietnam also gave Johnson and Nixon plenty of reason for caution. In February 1968, LBJ chose to deal with the inflation which the war had ignited by setting up a cabinet committee to study the problem. His staff already had made a detailed analysis of the wage and price controls imposed by Truman during the Korean conflict, and many months earlier the White House Office of Emergency Preparedness had drafted the executive orders and legislation necessary to impose a variety of constraints on an overheating economy. Like the head of that agency, Johnson seems to have feared how the public might react to the idea of economic controls. Consequently, he opted for another study of inflation rather than for meaningful action to halt it. Even Nixon had to be prodded toward wage and price controls by a Congress dominated by the Democratic opposition.

Although both the *Youngstown* decision and fear of negative public reaction help to explain why Nixon and Johnson seldom resorted to presidential war power, there is another more important reason for their failure to make it their main reliance: absence of any real need to do so. By the 1960s, the statute books contained hundreds of laws which delegated often quite broad powers to the executive during a national emergency. To lawyers and judges of the era prior to 1939, only a military emergency would have justified the redistribution of power for which these statutes provided. Roosevelt erased almost completely the "bright line" between war and peace fundamental to their constitutional thought. By the time Pearl Harbor was attacked, he already had proclaimed both a limited state of national emergency (in September 1939) and an unlimited one (in May 1941). The precise legal significance of either proclamation was never entirely clear. The states of emergency which they created did not end with the fighting in September 1945. It was years before the victorious Allies managed to sign a peace treaty with Japan, and they were never able to conclude one with a divided Germany. Rather than terminating decisively, World War II dissolved imperceptibly into the developing Cold War between the United States and the Soviet Union. Neither psychologically nor legally did the country ever completely return to a state of peace. Roosevelt's proclamations remained in effect until 1952. By then Truman had declared a new state of emergency. That one did not end with the Korean conflict which had inspired it, but remained in effect at least until 1978.[3] By the time Johnson escalated the Vietnam War in 1965, emergency government had become for the United States, as Senators Frank Church and Charles McC. Mathias would note a few years later, the norm. Neither Johnson nor Nixon had any real need to resort to special constitutional powers, arguably available only during a declared war. They could instead rely upon the vast and ill-defined

---

3. In the National Emergencies Act of 1976, Congress provided for the termination, two years after the enactment of that law, of all powers possessed by the President as a result of the existence of any declaration of emergency. This law does not purport, however, to withdraw or repeal such declarations themselves. Consequently, one can argue that the national emergency which Truman declared in 1950 is technically still in existence.

statutory emergency power which Congress had bestowed upon the executive in bits and pieces, which by 1974 (as the staff of a Senate committee headed by Church and Mathias discovered), numbered at least 470 separate laws.

Unlike Lincoln, the Vietnam presidents had no need to make the war power their main reliance on the home front. They did point to their constitutional authority as commander in chief to justify plunging the country into military engagement not previously authorized by Congress, but in doing so Johnson and Nixon were merely following in the footsteps of Lincoln, Roosevelt, and Truman. They were implementing concepts accepted, and even applauded, by most lawyers, scholars, and politicians before the Vietnam debacle itself called them into question. Thus, condemning Johnson and Nixon for unconstitutional conduct is scapegoating—it personalizes responsibility for a national mistake. Had Nixon and Johnson defeated Hitler or freed four million black slaves, few would charge them with abusing the war powers of the presidency. They behaved no more unconstitutionally than their predecessors. They were just less successful.

20

Up From Segregation: The American South and the Promise of Racial Justice

JOHN SHELTON REED

● *No history of the United States since World War II could possibly be complete without an account of the black struggle for equality. In 1954, the United States Supreme Court ruled unconstitutional the "separate but equal" schools that had typified the nation officially since 1898 and in fact throughout its history. In 1956, the Montgomery bus boycott in Alabama brought national attention to segregated facilities in public conveyances, and soon thereafter sit-ins and "freedom rides" kept up a constant pressure for integration in the South. And in 1963, at the giant March on Washington, Dr. Martin Luther King, Jr., spoke from the steps of the Lincoln Memorial to proclaim the goal: "Free at Last."*

The March on Washington was followed by the Civil Rights Act of 1964, the Voting Registration Act of 1965, the explosive riots in Los Angeles, Detroit, and Newark in the mid–1960s, and the rise of a militant black nationalist movement that signaled political and social changes between blacks and whites in the United States. Southern blacks, protected by federal marshals, registered to vote and in succeeding years put into office hundreds of black officials and whites responsive to their African-American constituents.

In the following essay, John Shelton Reed argues that the momentous changes in the South in the last quarter-century have made that section the most promising in terms of the ultimate goal of racial justice. After so much pain and violence, there is at last the hope that the old Confederacy will "give the world its first grand example of two races living together in equality and with mutual respect."

Around 1970, a number of Southerners began to say something rather odd. Independently, they had concluded that the South might be coming out of a tense and turbulent era in black-white relations in better condition than the rest of the country. Some even ventured to hope that the South could show other Americans, and the world, what an equitable biracial society looks like. The then-governor of Virginia, Linwood Holton, for instance, told a Rotary convention in St. Augustine that "we in the South have a better opportunity than any area of America to resolve the American dilemma, to become a model for race relations." Other observers—journalists and scholars as well as politicians—were starting to express similar opinions. It was about that time that I wrote an article with the self-explanatory title, "Can the South Show the Way?"

As the seventies began, black Southerners were worse off than non-Southern blacks by nearly every measure one might examine—the standard of living they were able to achieve, their influence in politics, the white attitudes they confronted. But, I argued, their circumstances were improving faster in all of these respects. This had two important implications. In the first place, it helped to explain the otherwise puzzling fact that one opinion poll after another, throughout the 1960s, had shown "that Southern blacks [were] less resentful, more hopeful, and less alienated than other black Americans." People evaluate their situation not only in terms of how good or bad it is, but in light of how it is changing, and how rapidly. Things were clearly getting better for Southern blacks, and the polls showed that they recognized this. In consequence, they showed a degree of satisfaction to which many non-Southern blacks (for whom things were not improving as fast, if at all) were not disposed. This translated into a degree of patience, I wrote, that gave Southern whites the chance to make change "gracefully, in an atmosphere relatively free of urgency and acrimony."

The other implication, by simple arithmetic, was that the condition of black Southerners would soon be better than that of non-Southern blacks *in absolute terms*. I hedged: "The question is what the limits of these changes are to be. Straightforward extrapolation suggests that Southern blacks will soon be better off . . . than Northern black people; cynicism suggests that this is too much to hope for, and that [white Southerners] should be content with a pattern of race relations and racial inequalities no worse than that found elsewhere."

I don't know what Governor Holton's audience made of his speech, but the response to my article was ... mixed. Some conservatives liked its insistence that the North was far from perfection in racial matters, because it supported their view that Northerners ought to leave the South alone and put their own house in order. But others didn't care for the assumption that white supremacy was doomed; they were not hog-wild about biracial societies in the first place and equitable ones least of all. A few liberals seemed to like the article because it could be used to shame Northerners ("If even the South can have good race relations, surely we can do better"), but others disliked what they saw as my complacence; they pointed out that the trends I was so cold-bloodedly examining didn't just *happen* but were the product of human struggle and sacrifice. Other liberals apparently didn't feel the South *deserved* good race relations. And still others were damned if they were going to agree with any article published in *National Review,* as mine was.

All in all, however, the world little noted nor long remembered that article. I am still fond of it, though, not just because it was my first effort at political journalism but because its predictions increasingly look to be right.

Even at the time, although nobody knew it, black Americans were beginning to vote with their feet. In the early seventies, for the first time since the end of the slave trade, more blacks moved to the South than left it—a pattern that continues. As an expanding economy and the death of Jim Crow have created a black middle class in the South alongside the old segregated triad of preacher, teacher, and undertaker, black managers and professionals have been moving to the South's cities and suburbs. The in-gathering has been taking place at the bottom of the economic ladder, too, although there it is often not a matter of Southern promise but of crushed hopes in the North: poverty in rural Mississippi is at least safer and warmer than poverty in a Northern ghetto.

The pattern I noted of greater satisfaction and less impatience among Southern blacks has continued. A University of Michigan survey in 1978, for instance, found blacks in the South more likely than those elsewhere to say they were "completely satisfied with life": one non-Southern black in five said that, but one out of every three black Southerners did. In part this simply indicates that Southern blacks are good Southerners, since the same regional difference exists among whites. But the difference was greater among blacks than among whites; Southern blacks were more likely to express satisfaction than whites from any region; and the difference between Southern and non-Southern blacks was greater in 1978 than it had been seven years earlier. Those data suggest that conditions were still improving faster for Southern blacks than for non-Southern blacks, or at least that black Southerners were more likely to believe their conditions were improving.

If that is what they thought, they were correct. We can look in more detail at three ways that their situation was changing, corresponding roughly to what Max Weber identified as the three ways someone's situation *can* improve or deteriorate: one can have more or less *money, power,* and *respect.*

Money is the easiest to deal with, since it lends itself best to counting. In 1970 Southern blacks were (as they always had been) poorer, on the average, than blacks in any other part of the country. Black Southern families were nearly twice as likely to be poor as black families in every other region of the U.S. The gap was closing, but one could not expect it to close immediately. Part of the problem had to do with the South's economy: white incomes were lower in the South, too. And black Southerners of the older generation carried the burden of *past* discrimination: they had, on the average, poorer education and less of it than blacks elsewhere in the country; they were already in worse-paying jobs, with little likelihood that would change anytime soon.

Despite all of the built-in inertia, though, the gap has been closing, and in 1982, for the first time, the poverty rate for black families in the South was no longer the highest in the country. It was still higher than that for black families in the Northeast or the West, but it was lower than in the North Central states, and that is something truly unprecedented. Figures for family income show the same convergence. In 1982, black family income in the South averaged about $13,000— some 5 percent higher than the figure for the North Central states.

Obviously many Southern blacks still have economic problems, but their problems are now no worse than those of black families everywhere else in the nation. In part, unfortunately, this is because the situation of blacks elsewhere has been deteriorating. During the 12 years from 1970 to 1982 the percentage of black families living in poverty decreased by five points in the South, while it was increasing everywhere else: by 14 points in the North Central states, by 12 points in the Northeast, and by two and a half points in the West. Currently 38 percent of black families in the South are poor—a disgraceful figure, but that percentage is decreasing and is already lower than the figure for one other major American region. Black poverty is a serious problem, but my point here is that it is no longer a peculiarly *Southern* problem.

Moreover, the South may be better-equipped than some other parts of the country to deal with that problem; if so, the trend of the past 15 years or so should continue. The "Sunbelt" is not wholly a fiction, and the economic prospects for the South are certainly rosier than those for the cities of the Northeast and North Central states, where most blacks outside the South live. It has often been observed that a no-growth economy means one group can improve its condition only at the expense of another, which quite naturally resents and resists that improvement; in an expanding economy, though, one group can improve faster than another without anyone's particularly noticing. If the South's economy continues to generate new jobs, some at least will go to black Southerners, and some benefits will trickle down (probably an accurate phrase) to those who are now the poorest—the economically marginal rural black population of the Deep South. Finally, it is ironic that the weakness of labor unions in the South, which some see as an unmistakable mark of Southern backwardness, may work to at least the short-run advantage of Southern blacks. Elsewhere, unions may have kept up the wages of those who had jobs, but it seems likely that they have reduced the total number of jobs available and they have often operated, one way or another, to exclude blacks from employment.

When we turn from economics to politics, we see the same pattern, but even more dramatic: faster improvement, and in some respects a better situation, for blacks in the South. Here one finds an especially striking discontinuity, and it can be dated precisely: 1965. The Voting Rights Act of that year is arguably the single most important accomplishment of the entire civil rights movement.

Only 25 years ago, a mere quarter of the eligible black voters in the eleven formerly Confederate states were registered to vote. The poll taxes, literacy tests, and other devices that kept that figure low are a matter of public record; the economic and sometimes physical intimidation used for the same purpose usually operated less conspicuously. In 1964, well into the era of the civil rights movement, that figure had increased from 25 percent or so to only 38 percent, and in some states, of course, it was much lower. In Mississippi only 6 percent of eligible blacks were registered in 1965. By 1968, three years after the passage of the Voting Rights Act, the black registration percentage had increased from 38 percent to 62 percent in the South as a whole, and from 6 percent to nearly 60 percent in Mississippi. That percentage has not changed greatly since—it went up a little more by 1970 and subsequently decreased a bit—but it is almost as high as the percentage of whites registered to vote; it is about the same as the figure for black registration in the rest of the country; and it is high enough to have transformed Southern politics.

The most conspicuous change has probably been the election of blacks to public office in the South. There are tens of thousands of elected officials in the South, serving in the U.S. Congress and state legislatures, in city and county offices and in law enforcement, on state and local school boards. Of these tens of thousands, in 1965, precisely 78 were black. By 1970, when Governor Holton made his speech and I wrote that article, there had been a ninefold increase, to 711. By 1981, *that* figure had more than trebled: more than 2,500 blacks held elective office in the eleven ex-Confederate states, and Mississippi had more black elected officials than any other state in the Union.

Between 1970 and the presidential campaign of Jesse Jackson, there was no increase in the percentage of Southern blacks registered to vote, so the growing number of black politicians in the South clearly indicates the growing political sophistication of the region's black voters. (Still, registration does no good without voter turnout. Here, too, though, there are encouraging portents for those who believe that black political participation indicates a healthy body politic. In the Democratic primaries on "Super Tuesday," March 13, 1984, black Southern Democrats were half again as likely as white ones to vote; and their votes delivered Georgia and Alabama to Walter Mondale and kept Jesse Jackson's candidacy alive.)

While the number and percentage of black elected officials in the South continues to grow, there remains a disparity between the percentage of black population and the percentage of black elected officials. Although blacks are about 19 percent of the South's population, only 3 percent or so of the South's elected officials are black. But in the Northeast only ½ of 1 percent of elected officials are black; in the North Central states and in the West, ⁴/₁₀ of 1 percent. Put another way: 22 of every hundred thousand black Southerners are elected public officials. In the North Central states, the figure is 19 per hundred thousand; in the West, 15; in the Northeast, 12.

Here again, there is little cause for Southern self-congratulation. Whites are much more likely than blacks to hold public office in the South, and the number and variety of ingenious schemes to keep it that way may well merit the attention of the Justice Department. But blacks are now less underrepresented in the South than in other parts of the country; that is a remarkable change; and that is my point.

This is not because Southern whites are more willing than non-Southern whites to vote for black politicians. Public opinion polls and election results reveal no such difference. In the South, like everywhere else in the country, most elected black politicians represent constituencies with black majorities or close to it. But there are many more such constituencies in the South. The same concentration of black voting strength has drastically affected the behavior of white elected officials, even when it has not produced black office-holders. Southern white politicians are much more likely now to respond to the interests of their black constituents. Black enfranchisement has produced new faces: Jimmy Carter is probably the epitome, but there are many others. In other cases, the new faces have been affixed to old heads. Think only of George Wallace's last gubernatorial race or Strom Thurmond's recent sponsorship of National Historically Black Colleges Week. (It is probably unkind to point out that the senator has always been in favor of black colleges.)

Political predictions are even riskier than economic ones, but there are some reasons to expect these trends to continue. In the Every-Cloud-Has-a-Silver-Lining Department, the increasing segregation of the South's cities means that more and more of them, like more and more cities elsewhere, will find themselves with black mayors and city councils (although a variety of redistricting and municipal reorganization schemes—all under intense judicial scrutiny—could affect this one way or the other). Less troublesome is what may be the increasing willing-

ness of *some* white voters to support *some* black candidates. Charlotte
is only the latest in a long string of Southern communities where black
officeholders have been elected by biracial majorities. For the time
being, at least, these majorities seem to result from the so-called "Atlanta coalition" between blacks and middle-class whites, rather than
the populist coalition of have-nots that Chandler Davidson claims in
his book, *Bi-racial Politics,* to have spied once in Houston.

When we turn from considerations of money and power to matters of
respect, the problem of measuring well-being gets even trickier, but
what we are talking about here is essentially the attitudes of white
Southerners toward their black fellow citizens, and we can turn to
attitude surveys, with all their problems, for at least a first approxi-
mation. Here again, there is the familiar pattern of faster change in the
South than elsewhere, leading to regional convergence.

Consider where we started. In 1942, public opinion polls showed
that 98 percent of white Southerners favored absolute segregation of
the public schools. *Ninety-eight percent.* That's everybody. (Two percent probably misunderstood the question.) By 1956, two years after
the *Brown* decision, there had been only a little change in white Southern opinion: 14 percent of whites from the Southern and border states
thought black and white children should attend the same schools. But
by 1970, only 16 percent of white Southern parents—one in six—
objected to having their children in school with "a few" black children,
and this trend, too, has continued. By 1980, only 5 percent of white
Southern parents said they didn't want their children in school with
any black children. Again, that's practically unanimous, but it's on the
other side, and that number—5 percent—is no different from the figure
for the country as a whole.

Imagine: a regional difference of great—indeed, calamitous—importance 30 years ago has simply evaporated, or so it appears. Of
course, some of these people are lying: it is not entirely respectable in
the 1980s to express segregationist views to a stranger who turns up
on your doorstep. But in 1942, and 1956, it was not respectable *not*
to express such views. And that, too, is a change of great importance.

There are still some regional differences in other measures of racial
attitudes. White Southern parents are more likely than white parents
elsewhere to say they don't want their children in schools with a black

majority, for instance. But the regional difference is small, and most white parents everywhere say they would object to that. White Southerners are somewhat less likely than other whites to say they would vote for a qualified black presidential candidate, but most say they would. Most white Southerners say they do not approve of racial intermarriage, but almost as large a majority of non-Southern whites say that. All in all, the differences in racial attitudes between white Southerners and other white Americans are now differences only of degree, and of relatively small degree at that. Those differences are smaller than they have been at any time in the recent past, and they are getting smaller still with each year.

In practice I doubt that these remaining differences mean much. In the first place, what matters to non-Southern black people, day to day, is less the attitudes of all non-Southern whites than those of whites in the large cities of the Northeast and Midwest, where most blacks outside the South actually live. What whites in Vermont or Oregon think about race relations is of some academic interest, and occasionally of political importance, but it has little to do with the everyday experience of black Americans. I have not seen the attitudes of whites in Chicago, say, or Boston broken out separately in attitude surveys, but surely few would care to argue that they are good examples for white Southerners to emulate.

In the second place, and more important, the attitudes someone expresses to a survey researcher are only part of the story and often not the most important part. The norms, the customs, that govern interaction can be as important as your attitudes in determining how you treat somebody. We saw how this worked under Jim Crow: how a white person felt about black people (or vice versa) had little to do with how they interacted. That was prescribed in detail by an "etiquette of race relations" (to borrow the title of Bertram Doyle's 1937 book on the subject); individuals could only embroider the basic pattern a bit to suit their attitudes.

Perhaps I should say that *some* of us saw how it worked under Jim Crow. It bears emphasizing that upward of 60 percent of Southerners, black and white, are too young to remember *Brown v. Board of Education*. Those Southerners who did not live through the last 30 years—my students, for example, who have a way of being born a bit later each year—find it hard to believe what most of us took for granted as

just *the way things were* in the 1940s and 50s. My students find it
hilarious when I tell them that the *Brown* decision apparently produced
a measurable deflection in the white Southern birthrate, or when they
read in Howard Odum's *Race and Rumors of Race* about the "Eleanor
[Roosevelt] Clubs" that many Southern whites believed their black
maids belonged to. The splendid anthropological studies of the Jim
Crow South have about as much immediacy for them, I would guess,
as Malinowsky on the Trobrianders. When I describe the segregated
bathrooms and water fountains and dry cleaners and basketball teams
of my youth, they appear to believe me—just as one would believe a
Martian's description of his home planet. I gather that their parents,
as a rule, don't talk about it.

It gives me some sympathy for immigrant parents who have to deal
with American children. Southerners in their forties and older have
"immigrated," in effect, just by staying put. The South we grew up in
is as different from our children's as the Polish shtetl from Manhattan's
Lower East Side, or Naples from Boston's North End.

Even those who remember sometimes find it hard to believe. At least
I do. Last year I saw a couple of etched glass doors in a small South
Carolina town: one said WHITE, the other COLORED. I was almost
literally stunned—stunned to realize that signs like that had once been
an ordinary part of my life and stunned to realize that it had been
nearly 20 years since I had last seen any. Like so much that was once
thought to be terribly important, they had disappeared, largely without
my noticing. It is a nice touch, I think, that these doors last year were
in an antique shop—and if the dealer hadn't wanted 50 dollars for the
pair I would have bought them. God only knows what for—maybe I'd
have used them in my teaching and taken an income-tax deduction.

Obviously things have changed. Laws have changed, and attitudes
have changed, and (to return to the point) *etiquette* has changed. Not
long ago, I had to do business in the courthouse of one of the poorest
and blackest of North Carolina's counties. Ahead of me in line for the
tax clerk was an elderly black man. Thirty years ago, he would have
automatically effaced himself and I would just as automatically have
gone ahead of him. I cannot say what he would have been thinking,
but I probably would not have noticed. When his turn came, the young
white woman at the counter would have addressed him as "James"
or maybe, in that part of North Carolina, as "Uncle." She would not

have meant to demean him, and, like me, she would not have been thinking about the implications of her behavior. Indeed, she would probably have denied that her behavior *had* any implications. She and I—and he, for that matter—would just have been doing what we were supposed to do, and our attitudes would have been neither here nor there.

That is not, obviously, what happened in 1984. I dare say that if Gallup ever came to that county, he would not find it a hotbed of racial liberalism. If he interviewed the young woman at the counter, I doubt that her attitudes would satisfy the members of the old Civil Rights Commission. But in 1984 she waited on the man in his turn, exchanged some routine pleasantries with him about the unpleasant weather, called him "sir" at first and "Mr. Jones" after that—she treated him, in other words, like any other presumptively decent citizen of that county. And she was just doing what she was supposed to do.

Argument from anecdote is bad form in my trade, and I won't let my students do it, but I do believe that episode is increasingly typical. Manners *have* changed. More and more, in places like courthouses and stores and schools, Southern whites seem disposed to treat black Southerners as sort of honorary white folks—and by and large, whatever their private opinions of one another, white Southerners treat each other with courtesy and at least the appearance of good-natured respect. Southern blacks, for their part, seem willing to return the favor. The upshot is that on a day to-day basis (which is how most of us lead our lives, after all) black-white relations in the South seem more cordial, less prickly, than black-white relations in the cities of the North. There is even some survey evidence to support this (again, from the University of Michigan): overall, 44 percent of non-Southerners described their lives as "very friendly"; 54 percent of all Southerners—and 58 percent of black Southerners—did so.

There is an irony here. William Chafe, in his study of the civil rights movement in Greensboro, *Civilities and Civil Rights,* argues that the value Southerners place on civility worked against the movement to oversimplify his point, that even blacks' potential allies in the white community saw sit-ins and other forms of black protest and self-assertion as a violation of the norms of civility, as *bad manners.* If I am right, those same norms may contribute to amicable race relations today and in the future. Walker Percy has written somewhere that

Southerners know the point of manners: they exist so no one will not know what to do. A great many Southerners are apparently willing to do what they are supposed to do—whatever that may be—and that can contribute to good race relations as easily as to bad.

No doubt some would argue that the value of civility still keeps many unresolved issues from being addressed squarely, and they may be right. One should recognize, though, that it is not just *white* Southerners who value civility. That black Southerners for a time were not willing to do what they were "supposed to do" does not indicate that they do not share that value: instead, their actions were dramatic evidence of the extent of their frustration and exasperation.

One more story: After Chicago disgraced itself [in 1983] with a bitter black-against-white mayoralty campaign, Harvey Gantt, who was running for mayor of Charlotte, said that race would not be the same sort of issue there. "We're much politer here," he told the *North Carolina Independent.* "We're not going to see that kind of down-in-the-gutter fight." He was right: Charlotte didn't, and he is now Charlotte's first black mayor.

Gantt's choice of pronouns points to another change that anyone who wishes the South well must welcome. Notice who is more polite: it is *we* (Southerners), not *they* (whites). When William Ferris, director of the Center for the Study of Southern Culture, was on William Buckley's "Firing Line" a couple of years ago, he said something fascinating: "In the decade of the 80s what we're seeing is an interesting kind of evolution from the 60s and 70s to a sense of Southerners as Southerners as opposed to black versus white." Well, some days I am more ready to believe that than others, but there are signs of the growth of a sense of regional identification that transcends racial differences, if one wants to look for them, and that would be something new, and wholly delightful, in my view.

There have always been similarities of style and culture between black and white Southerners. How could it be otherwise? One frivolous example: On television [in 1983] I saw the Mighty Reverend Al Greene lead the Soul Train Dancers in a remarkable rendition of "Amazing Grace." The very next day (I swear it), on the radio, I heard Jerry Lee Lewis swing directly from "Great Balls of Fire" to "If We Could Spend Our Vacation in Heaven." Which better illustrates W. J. Cash's observation about the mixture of hedonism and piety in the Southern mind?

The great cultural similarity between black and white Southerners seems especially evident to those who have come to know one another outside the South. That experience is increasingly common, and it may have something to do with what Bill Ferris told Bill Buckley: Ferris came back to Mississippi from the Ivy League. Anyone who needs convincing really should read Albert Murray's *South to a Very Old Place*, a remarkable book with the bad luck to be published at least ten years before its time. It is certainly no accident that Murray was returning to Alabama from New York.

Despite the cultural similarity, though, Southern blacks have not generally been inclined or encouraged in the past to think of themselves as black *Southerners*, and there is survey evidence to show that as late as the 1960s most probably did not. As Merle Black and I showed in an article in the *Journal of Politics*, though, that has changed dramatically since then. (Unfortunately we had no data on how Southern whites construe the word *Southerner* and whether that has changed.) We will know the process of identification is complete when more black Southerners, like Harvey Gantt, talk, of the South's superiority—and when they habitually complain that non-Southerners do not understand the South, that they are tired of hearing the South put down, and so forth. Examples are still rare enough to be collectible, but they are starting to turn up here and there. When Robert Botsch, a political scientist, asked a black North Carolina furniture worker why he was planning to vote for Jimmy Carter, for instance, the man told him he was getting "tired of listening to all these slick Yankees who think they know everything and have all the answers." It is hard to sound more Southern than *that*.

To repeat the question some of us were asking *circa* 1970: Can the South show the way? Can the South, I wondered then, "do more than catch up with the Northern pattern of race relations?" Can it "break through to an accommodation qualitatively different from and superior to that displayed in, say, Philadelphia or Cicero?" Well, perhaps it is beginning to. It is not really for me or for any other white Southerner to say whether the South has already become a better place than the Northeast or Midwest for black Americans to live, but it is certainly a better place now than it was 30 years ago, or 15—and that may not be true of other parts of the United States. The South has not shown the way yet. Black Southerners still have many legitimate grievances. They still do not have their share of money, power, and respect. But at least there is no reason for Southerners to apologize to *Yankees* anymore.

There is, to repeat, no reason to be smug about it. Catching up with the rest of the country is not an especially impressive achievement, and only a few white Southerners can take much credit even for that. But *black* Southerners can be proud of their accomplishment, and they have served their region—our region—well. The South is now more worthy than ever of Southerners' affection for it.

Those of us who predicted that 12 or 15 years ago have no reason to be smug either. A remarkable article in *The Virginia Quarterly Review* predicted the same thing a decade earlier, in 1961, at a time when it sounded not just unlikely but downright *crazy*. Leslie W. Dunbar, then executive director of the Southern Regional Council (the South's oldest biracial organization), had no illusions about his fellow white Southerners. He knew that white supremacy would not be given up without a fight, less because white profited from it than because many Southern whites would feel it a duty to defend their past and their society. But Dunbar wrote:

> Once the fight is decisively lost (the verdict has to be decisive), once the Negro has secured the right to vote, has gained admittance to the public library, has fought his way into a desegrated public school, has been permitted to sup at a lunch counter, the typical white Southerner will shrug his shoulder, resume his stride, and go on. He has, after all, shared a land with his black neighbors for a long while; he can manage well enough even if the patterns change. There is now one fewer fight which history requires of him. He has done his ancestral duty. He . . . can relax a bit more.

And so, surprisingly enough, it has come to pass. The South has taken on a new character, as Dunbar said it would. Despite the conflict and turmoil since he wrote—indeed, largely because of it—the South still has the opportunity he saw a generation ago, one "it can fulfill better than any place or people anywhere." The South may yet "give the world its first grand example of two races of men living together in equality and with mutual respect."

21

Sam Walton and Wal-Mart Stores:
The Remaking of Modern America

SANDRA S. VANCE AND ROY V. SCOTT

• *Sam Walton was an American hero. Born on a farm in 1918, he worked briefly for the J. C. Penney Company in Iowa and then, after service in World War II, went into business for himself as a small town merchant. Copying a formula that had been developed in 1846 in New York City by A. T. Stewart, Walton kept administrative and managerial costs to a minimum, and he delivered quality goods "at low, everyday discount prices" with a money-back guarantee. His success was phenomenal, and by 1993 his Wal-Mart Stores Inc. had surpassed K mart and Sears to become the largest retailer in the United States.*

Ironically, even as Walton served the small towns and the rural areas that he loved, he was destroying the once-bustling Main Streets that gave them their soul and their spirit. This was because he located his Wal-Marts not near the courthouses or the town squares, but near highways, parking lots, and expressway interchanges far from the village centers. Soon Main Street merchants began to close up shop, and vacant storefronts became the norm rather than the exception. The Wal-Marting of America became a pejorative term, and a movement spread, especially in New England, to keep the big discount retailer far away. For example, in 1993 voters in Greenfield, Massachusetts refused to allow Wal-Mart to build a store a few miles from their downtown shopping district.

The contest between price and community is one that affects virtually every American. Sandra S. Vance and Roy V. Scott

Sandra S. Vance and Roy V. Scott, "Sam Walton and Wal-Mart Stores, Inc.: A Study in Modern Southern Entrepreneurship," *Journal of Southern History,* 58 (May 1992), 231–252. Reprinted, without footnotes, by permission of the Managing Editor.

put the issue in perspective and explain how a visionary en-
trepreneur transformed a nation.

In his presidential address before the Southern Historical Association in 1988, Professor Bennett H. Wall of the University of Georgia argued that "historians of the recent South have largely neglected many aspects of southern economic life." Wall's assessment seems accurate. In a span of three years in the 1980s, four historians produced superb books that dealt wholly or in part with twentieth-century southern agriculture, but other sectors of the economy have inspired no such interest. Business and corporate activities, especially, have generally been ignored except by authors who have noted exploitation of labor or the environment. This imbalance in historical writing is ironic, given the sharp decline in the relative importance of farming in the South in recent decades and the almost feverish concern of political, educational, and community leaders of all kinds with nonagricultural development in the region.

Yet the New New South, as Jack Temple Kirby has labeled the post-1945 South, has produced entrepreneurs—H. Ross Perot of Texas and Robert Edward ("Ted") Turner and Robert H. Woodruff of Georgia, to name only a few—whose firms have played major roles not only in the region but also throughout the nation and beyond. The significance of southerners in the business world has increased markedly from earlier periods when the South could boast of few major business leaders except North Carolina's Duke family and Florida's Henry M. Flagler, the latter a Yankee transplant. Another southern entrepreneur, comparable in some ways to Perot, Turner, and Woodruff, is Sam Walton, whose firm, Wal-Mart Stores, Inc., grew from a single variety store in Newport, Arkansas in 1945 to be the third largest retailer in the United States in January 1990, with 1,525 outlets in twenty-nine states.

Samuel Moore Walton, whose father was a farmer and farm mortgage appraiser, was born March 29, 1918, near Kingfisher, Oklahoma. He grew up in Missouri, attended high school in Columbia, where he was an outstanding athlete, and graduated from the University of Missouri at Columbia in 1940 with a degree in economics. Walton was a busy undergraduate who had to work to pay for his college education. A fraternity paper referred to him as a "hustler" and praised him for his friendliness, energy, and involvement in a variety of clubs and church activities. Perhaps most important, in light of his later accomplishments, were Walton's leadership abilities and his talent for spotting similar abilities in others.

After graduation, Walton accepted an offer of a management trainee position with the J. C. Penney Company in Des Moines, Iowa. The salary was eighty-five dollars a month. Walton spent only eighteen months with that company, but years later he recalled being favorably impressed with the firm's emphasis on employee participation in decision-making and with the manager of the Des Moines store, whom he described as a great "people person." Military service from 1942 to 1945 interrupted Walton's nascent retailing career. After being discharged from the army, Walton resolved to go into business for himself, and franchise retailing seemed to offer opportunity to an ambitious young man with limited experience.

Franchising, the mechanism that would allow Walton to go into retailing as an independent businessman, originated soon after the Civil War, but its popularity grew markedly in the twentieth century. One of the four forms of franchising was the voluntary wholesaler-retailer type, in which a wholesaler joined with independent retailers in a cooperative relationship beneficial to both parties. Among the firms functioning in this manner in the 1940s were the Western Auto Supply Company and Butler Brothers, a Chicago wholesaler. The latter firm had sold products to small general merchandise and variety stores since the 1880s and at one time was the single most important source of goods for such outlets. In 1927, with many of these customers threatened by chain stores, Butler Brothers went into franchising, establishing the Ben Franklin chain of independently owned variety stores.

The Ben Franklin stores of the post-World War II years were typical variety outlets, comparable to and often competitive with the stores of the F. W. Woolworth and S. S. Kresge companies and those of other national chains. There were 1,590 Ben Franklin stores throughout the United States in 1950, but they were most common in the Midwest, generally in small and medium-sized towns. A typical Ben Franklin variety store was small, with perhaps seven thousand square feet of space, and it generated about seventy-five thousand dollars worth of business annually.

Franchisees of Butler Brothers operated their stores in accordance with guidelines established by the franchiser. Relationships were spelled out in formal contracts. The franchiser charged an annual franchise fee that was a percentage of sales, decreasing as volume increased but averaging about 1 percent. Franchisees were expected to purchase the bulk of their merchandise from the company. The franchiser established standards for store arrangement and appearance and stipulated that a sufficient level of inventory be maintained.

In return, Butler Brothers provided its franchisees with a great deal of guidance and assistance. The goal was to give the independent merchant "a professional merchandising and promotional service, comparable in quality with that which his chain competitors receive from their headquarters." The training program was "so complete that retail experience is not necessary to successfully operate a Ben Franklin Store." Operating manuals and monthly newsletters covered most aspects of store operation. To provide more aid to storekeepers, Butler Brothers maintained at its headquarters a staff of retailing specialists and in the field a force of zone managers who regularly called on the stores in their districts.

In the fall of 1945, with borrowed funds and savings from his military service, Walton bought an existing Ben Franklin variety store in Newport, Arkansas, a town of about five thousand people located approximately eighty miles northeast of Little Rock. Walton's younger brother, James L. ("Bud") Walton, joined him in a partnership. In April 1947 Bud Walton opened a Ben Franklin store in Versailles, Missouri, thus taking the first step toward the establishment of a chain of franchised variety stores.

Located in a leased facility that was the best retail site in town, Sam Walton's Newport store turned out to be a flourishing enterprise. The store's sales volume soared from $80,000 to $225,000 in three years. While Walton was demonstrating that he could be a successful small-town merchant, he was also displaying some of those personal characteristics that would be evident later in his career. According to a longtime acquaintance, Walton "had a way of making people feel they were a part of a team. He was not such an articulate speaker, but he made sense when he did talk, and people responded to him." He also took an active role in the town's civic life, serving as president of the Chamber of Commerce and of the Rotary Club. Unfortunately, Walton's retailing success was also his undoing. When Walton's lease expired, his landlord, impressed with the improved sales performance of the business, declined to renew it because he preferred to reclaim possession of the store's location himself.

Rather than relocate his Newport business, Walton decided to start anew in another town. He selected Bentonville, Arkansas, a town of three thousand in the northwest corner of the state. There, in May 1950, he opened "Walton's 5 and 10¢ Store." Located on the town square, the store had about four thousand square feet of space, was poorly lighted, and featured an 8-by-8-foot office in the loft, which was accessible by ladder. The previous owner had done only about thirty-two thousand dollars a year in business.

Walton modernized the Bentonville store and staged a grand opening in March 1951. The next year, he established a variety store in nearby Fayetteville; soon after that he opened a third one in Rogers, a few miles east of Bentonville, the town that had become, and would remain, Walton's home base. From these beginnings, the Walton brothers went on to build a chain of sixteen Ben Franklin variety stores in Arkansas, Missouri, and Kansas. By the early 1960s the Waltons had the largest chain of independently owned variety stores in the country.

While Sam Walton and his brother were building their chain of variety stores, retailing was being changed by discount merchandising. In the early 1960s *Discount Merchandiser,* a leading trade journal, described a discount store as "a departmentalized retail establishment utilizing many self-service techniques to sell hard goods, health and beauty aids, apparel and other soft goods, and other general merchandise. It operates at uniquely low margins" that were substantially below the 40 percent markup that was near standard in department stores and other traditional outlets.

Discount merchandising grew from many sources: the self-service innovation of the Piggly-Wiggly Corporation food stores by Clarence Saunders, the company's founder; the invention of the shopping cart by Ellis D. Turnham; and the opening of cut-rate drugstores and grocery supermarkets in the 1930s. Also related was the appearance in that decade, especially in New York City, of second-story catalog stores that offered a variety of brand name hard goods at little more than wholesale prices. In the years immediately after World War II, many discount houses sprang up, mainly in the larger cities. At the outset, they handled chiefly hard goods, but soon some of the leading new establishments, such as Master's, Inc. and E. J. Korvette, Inc., branched into soft goods and for all practical purposes were department stores, lacking only their services and amenities.

Spokesmen for traditional stores and their allies blasted the discount merchants as "pirates" who constituted a grave threat to "legitimate" retailers, but such efforts achieved little. In fact, the explosive growth of discount merchandising reflected forces that could not be restrained: the growing productivity of American manufacturing, the failure of the fair trade laws, and the changes in consumer tastes and attitudes that were brought on by the increasing affluence and suburbanization of the American people. In the context of the controversial "wheel of retailing" theory, the rise of discount merchandising would be viewed as simply another revolution in a progression that since the Civil War era had brought forth in turn department stores, mail-order houses, chain stores, supermarkets, and other marketing innovations.

By 1960 discounting had its own trade association and publications and was growing rapidly. The number of discount stores rose from 1,329 in 1960 to 3,503 in 1966, while the size of the average discount outlet increased from 38,400 to 64,585 square feet. Perhaps the best indication that discounting had come of age was the entry into the field in the early 1960s of the F. W. Woolworth and the S. S. Kresge companies with their Woolco and K mart stores. By 1966 the S. S. Kresge Company was the nation's leading discounter with 273 K mart and Jupiter stores. Among the other leaders at the time were Gibson Products Company, Spartans Industries, Zayre Corporation, and Gamble-Skogmo.

Walton and his brother watched these developments from afar with great interest. Their chain of Ben Franklin stores was flourishing, but the Waltons understood clearly that variety stores were losing market share to supermarkets on the one hand and to expanded drugstores on the other and that retailing as a whole was being changed markedly by discount merchandising. Visits to discount outlets in the East and the Midwest permitted Sam Walton to learn what seemed to work and what was likely to fail. In time, Walton convinced himself that discounting could succeed in country towns, which the early discounters had studiously avoided.

In 1962 Walton asked that his franchiser permit him to establish discount stores under the Ben Franklin umbrella. For his proposed discount stores to succeed, he explained, the franchiser would have to cut its margins by about 50 percent. Greater volume and faster turnover would compensate for the reduced margins and ensure the profitability of the venture. The company, however, was not ready for discounting. An officer of City Products Corporation, the successor to Butler Brothers as the franchiser of the Ben Franklin variety stores, said that discounting was not a field the firm wanted to be in.

Thus rebuffed, Walton resolved to forge ahead on his own. He opened his first Wal-Mart Discount City store in November 1962 in Rogers, Arkansas, a town with a population of fifty-seven hundred. Like Walton's variety store in Bentonville, the new sixteen-thousand-square-foot discount outlet proudly proclaimed, "We Sell for Less." Two years later, the second Wal-Mart discount store, a twelve-thousand-square-foot unit, opened in Harrison, Arkansas, a town of sixty-five hundred people some fifty miles east of Rogers.

Not quite eight years after the first Wal-Mart discount store opened, by January 31, 1970, the Waltons had thirty-two retail outlets. Of that number, eighteen were Wal-Mart discount stores and the remainder were Ben Franklin variety stores. The variety stores were generally located on a town's main street, while the Discount City outlets were more likely to be near the edge of town where more space and parking were available. The total enterprise was profitable, generating a pretax income of $2.2 million in fiscal 1970.

As the Waltons' retail enterprise grew in the late 1960s, Sam Walton decided the time was appropriate to prepare for even greater growth in the future. Walton needed additional capital for the expansion he envisaged, so Wal-Mart Stores was incorporated in October 1969, and in March 1970 the new company offered for public sale three hundred thousand shares of stock. The securities went for $16.50 a share, and in October 1970 Wal-Mart Stores became a publicly owned firm. Its stock was traded over the counter until August 25, 1972, when it was listed on the New York Stock Exchange.

In the decade following incorporation, Wal-Mart Stores, Inc., grew dramatically. In 1970 the firm was a small, unknown concern referred to by some sophisticates as the "counturier to the hillbillies." A decade later, Wal-Mart had become a leading regional discounter with growth rates that amazed observers. The number of stores rose to 78 in January 1974, to 153 three years later, and to 276 in January 1980. Meanwhile, the number of states in which the firm operated grew from three in the late 1960s to ten a decade later. Tennessee and Louisiana were entered in 1973, Mississippi and Kentucky the next year, and Texas in 1975. In addition to these states and Arkansas, Missouri, and Oklahoma, the company had stores in Illinois and Kansas.

As Wal-Mart grew in the 1970s, Walton gradually shifted his interest from the old Ben Franklin variety stores to the new discount outlets. In January 1968, sixteen of the firm's twenty-four outlets were Ben Franklin stores. Five years later, there were only nine such stores, and by January 1976 there were none. After thirty years, Walton had severed relations with the company that had helped launch him into a career in retailing.

By the mid-1970s Wal-Mart stores were fairly uniform in size, layout, and stock. The one-story structures, which averaged forty-two thousand square feet, were open from 9 A.M. to 9 P.M. six days a week and on Sunday afternoon where permitted. All Wal-Mart stores accepted bank credit cards. Sales were almost all self-service, but store personnel prided themselves on their availability and helpfulness. An average store carried about thirty-five thousand different items distributed among thirty-six departments. All stores of the same size had about the same merchandise mix, although local demand required some variations. Major categories of goods included wearing apparel for men, women, and children, shoes, handbags, curtains and draperies, housewares and home furnishings, hardware and paint, small appliances, auto accessories, garden equipment and supplies, toys and sporting goods, photographic equipment, health and beauty aids, and jewelry. Hard goods constituted about two-thirds of all sales. Most goods other than wearing apparel were nationally advertised, brand name items. Only a few lines carried the house name. At first, outside firms operated a few departments, such as shoes, jewelry, and the pharmacy, but Wal-Mart took over such departments as the decade progressed.

In the mid-1970s Walton began to upgrade the stores. A capital improvement program replaced the harsh blue interiors with softer, more attractive colors, eliminated the last of the old pipe-rack fixtures, and installed carpets in selected areas of the stores. Meanwhile, the quality of wearing apparel offered to customers improved markedly. Cheaper private-label lines generally disappeared, and higher quality brand names replaced them.

Each store was run by a manager, at least two assistants, and perhaps one or more management trainees. This staff supervised the approximately thirty-six department heads. Store managers reported to district managers, who were responsible for about a dozen stores. District managers in turn reported to regional vice presidents, who oversaw the work of three or four district managers. Regional vice presidents, who were based in the headquarters in Bentonville, reported to the vice president of operations. District managers and regional vice presidents spent from Monday to Thursday of each week visiting stores where they worked with the entire staff, partly to suggest and partly to learn, and above all, to establish the free and open communication that characterized Wal-Mart's managerial style.

In the early 1970s Sam Walton spelled out four major strategies that guided the company in that decade and the 1980s. First, Walton proposed that the company expand steadily by placing full-line discount department stores in towns and small cities within a radius of three hundred miles of the headquarters in Bentonville. Second, Walton pledged to maintain true discount prices and one of the lowest gross margins of any chain in the United States. Third, he emphasized that the firm must make every effort to cut costs of both inventory and operations. Finally, and most important, according to Walton, was the continued development of loyalty, morale, and enthusiasm in the work force.

The company adhered to these strategies, which were enhanced in the early years by economic change in Wal-Mart's territory. Northern Arkansas, southern Missouri, and eastern Oklahoma and Kansas experienced substantial growth in the 1960s and 1970s, both in population and in per capita income. These developments were fueled by tourism, the establishment of retirement communities in the area, considerable industrial development, and, for a few years, generally satisfactory conditions in agriculture.

A major policy of Wal-Mart was to put its stores in towns and small cities that other discounters, except Gibson's and TG & Y, generally shunned. "Since its beginning," Walton wrote in the 1978 *Annual Report,* "the Wal-Mart concept was based on the theory that a quality discount store could operate profitably ... in a small community." Most of the company's stores were located in towns of five thousand to twenty-five thousand people. County seats were special targets. By 1978 the largest towns with Wal-Mart stores were Little Rock and Springfield, Missouri, but the company also had outlets near Memphis, Tulsa, and St. Louis.

This location strategy afforded certain obvious advantages. Costs of land and buildings were lower, the quality of the work force was perhaps higher, and there was less competition. In most instances, Wal-Mart was "the biggest thing around," making it the dominant nonfood retailer drawing customers not only from the town but also from a sizable surrounding area as well.

Expansion of the Wal-Mart chain of stores was carried forward systematically. Company policy dictated that the firm grow from inside an expanding circle around Bentonville. "We are always pushing from the inside out," said one company officer. "We never jump and then backfill." Since Wal-Mart saturated an area before expanding farther, it discouraged competition and ensured that name recognition in new markets would be high. By placing stores within a day's drive of Bentonville, the company was able to resupply stores quickly and to avoid both empty shelves and excess inventory.

In its pricing policy, Wal-Mart's pledge, reiterated repeatedly, was to provide "top quality merchandise at low, everyday discount prices." Prices were uniform throughout the chain unless it was necessary to lower them to meet local competition. The company maintained that it did not take advantage of its dominant retailing position in the towns it served. "Just because we were in west Arkansas we didn't charge the highest price we could get," said Walton. "We charged them the same prices as in Little Rock or Springfield. . . . "

Customer satisfaction ranked high among company goals. Wal-Mart offered customers an "unconditional money-back guarantee" and pledged to provide "quality service." In practical terms, the money-back guarantee meant that any item could be returned for any reason, and the pledge of high-quality service meant that the customer was always right. "Customer goodwill is our best investment for future successful growth," Walton believed.

Economy of operation was almost a fetish, and Wal-Mart became known for driving hard bargains with vendors. The firm's growing buying power gave it a strength not enjoyed by smaller firms, and company buyers were grimly determined to get the best bargains possible. Said an officer of one firm that did business with Wal-Mart, "These people [Wal-Mart buyers] are as folksy and down-to-earth as home-grown tomatoes. But when you start dealing with them—when you get past that 'down home in Bentonville' business—they're as hard as nails and every bit as sharp. They'll drive as hard a deal as anyone anywhere." It was a company rule, moreover, that Wal-Mart buyers did not accept gifts from vendor representatives, thus eliminating a source of conflict of interest.

One of Walton's cost-cutting innovations, which he adapted from the Ben Franklin variety stores, was the use of distribution centers. Wal-Mart's vendors shipped goods to the centers rather than directly to individual stores. The first distribution center was built in Bentonville in the late 1960s. It was enlarged more than once, another center was built beside it, and a third one went up in Searcy, Arkansas. Late in the 1970s, another was constructed in Palestine, Texas. By 1978 some 80 percent of all Wal-Mart merchandise flowed through these centers. They permitted savings on inventory and operation costs because of large orders and cheap transportation, expedited deliveries to stores, and allowed the company to exercise careful control over the quality of merchandise, especially wearables and other soft goods. Individual stores were assured of resupply from a central, company-owned facility, which allowed Wal-Mart to control its inventory. Large shipments generally arrived at the distribution centers by rail, and the merchandise was moved to the stores by truck. Within the distribution centers, huge conveyor belts and a high degree of automation reduced costs and allocated goods properly.

Wal-Mart spent less than 2 percent of sales on advertising, a smaller percentage than most retailers. The patterns of company expansion and the resulting ready recognition among customers permitted this economy. Most advertising was by company circulars and local newspapers, although radio was employed in some local promotions. The use of television increased in the late 1970s. The company's advertis-ing department and printing plant produced circulars, newspaper inserts, and formats for local advertising as well as materials for in-store promotions.

The use of advanced electronic technology also helped to minimize costs and to facilitate management. By the mid-1970s the company leased an IBM 370/135 computer system for inventory control, payroll and other financial records, and statistical data for analysis of store and department performance. Increasingly, stores were equipped with electronic cash registers that provided point-of-sale data for different managerial purposes. Later, the firm completed installation of a company-wide computer terminal network that improved communications and store operation.

An obvious strength of Wal-Mart Stores, and one related directly to costs of operation, was the dedication and loyalty of its work force, which rose from 1,500 in 1970 to 21,000 in 1979 and to 223,000 in 1989. In fact, company officers maintained that the existence of a distinctive Wal-Mart culture, more than any other one factor, explained Wal-Mart's success and made the company unique among American retail firms.

According to the *Annual Report* of 1978, the Wal-Mart culture was "nothing more than the bringing together of men and women who are completely dedicated to their jobs, their Company, and their communities. Our organization has become a team that acts with one purpose, deriving its strength from the many individuals who constitute our Board of Directors, our management, and our associates throughout our Wal-Mart organization." In the terminology of the company, employees of Wal-Mart were not employees but associates. They were treated as equals, kept fully informed of company developments, both good and bad, and were invited to make suggestions or other comments on company policy and practices. All associates were made to feel that their contributions to the proper functioning of the company were important and that their voices could be heard by anyone in the organization. As an example of the spirit of equality that prevailed at Wal-Mart, no one, including Walton himself, had a reserved space in the parking lot at the headquarters office building.

The development of team spirit was promoted in a variety of ways, some obvious, others less so. The company had a monthly employees' magazine, the *Wal-Mart World*, which performed the usual functions of such periodicals. A handbook spelled out company policies and associate responsibilities and benefits. The first annual picnic for company personnel in Bentonville was held in 1975, and, according to the firm, the event helped to create a feeling of "one big family" and engendered "much enthusiasm and dedication." Orientation meetings conducted monthly at the company's headquarters and periodically in the stores afforded opportunities for associates to ask questions to which they were assured of getting "intelligent" answers.

In more concrete ways, too, the company sought to win and keep the loyalty and dedication of its associates. Wal-Mart recognized no unions and some employees were paid only the minimum wage or very little more; but department heads, assistant managers, and managers were well remunerated. The company provided a generous benefits package, including a liberal profit-sharing plan and a voluntary investment program that permitted many workers to amass sizable holdings. Wal-Mart also maintained comprehensive training programs so that associates who wished to do so could advance in the organization. The company promoted from within whenever possible. Finally, there were financial incentives to perform well. For example, in a war against shrinkage, the retail term for the loss of merchandise due to inaccurate record keeping, damage, shoplifting, or internal theft, the company agreed to share savings equally with the work force.

Most important in the remarkable growth of Wal-Mart Stores were the abilities and personality of Sam Walton. Walton was the classic entrepreneur, the manager, the risktaker, who mixed the economic elements of distribution and marketing to create a dramatically successful firm. But to Wal-Mart Stores, Walton was more than an entrepreneur and manager. He was the inspiration and personification of the company who made the firm what it was and in a large measure what it would be in the next decades.

Walton was chairman, president, and chief executive officer of the company throughout the 1970s, except from November 1974 to June 1976 when Ronald G. Mayer held those offices. Walton was chairman of the executive committee during that interlude. When Mayer resigned, Walton announced simply that "I wasn't able to assume a passive role" in the company's affairs.

Walton disliked publicity and seemed little interested in the wealth that Wal-Mart Stores generated for him and his family. He attributed his success to circumstances and luck and especially to the support of the firm's associates. Moreover, Walton stated that he had not set out to establish a chain of discount stores, but when the first Wal-Marts prospered, he saw a challenge to establish others, a challenge that the merchant in him could not ignore.

According to Walton, the primary task of the business manager was "simply to get the right people in the right places to do a job, and then encourage them to use their own inventiveness to accomplish the job at hand." From the earliest days, when Walton selected potential managers, he looked "for a person who has energy, who's determined to succeed, willing to work and who's loyal" to the firm. He preferred to hire men with families, believing them to be more stable and motivated, and those with a strong church affiliation, since such affiliation showed that they could "identify with something outside of themselves" and "work for a common good."

Walton possessed both charisma and remarkable social skills that he used to good advantage in creating Wal-Mart Stores and its culture. An observer reported that Walton "meets people very well" and that he had the ability to make "people feel he really cares." In fact, Walton did care, and when he "gets out, interacts, and asks questions," he was simply doing what was central to his personality and management style.

Walton believed firmly that it was essential that he and the other executives spend several days a week visiting the stores. "We like to let folks know that we're interested in them and that they are vital to us. 'Cause they are. Those department heads are the ones who *really* know what's going on out there in the field, and we've got to get them to tell us," he reported. Many of the best ideas originated at that level, were later discussed at a Saturday morning executives' meeting in Bentonville, and perhaps were adopted as company policy.

In the 1970s Walton himself spent two or three days a week visiting stores. He tried to visit each store at least twice during a year. In those visits Walton's practice was to examine a store carefully and then meet with the staff. In these meetings he rarely criticized. Instead, he complimented the associates on what they were doing well and challenged them to do better. As the firm grew, it was no longer possible for Walton to know the associates and their families personally as he once had, but the personal touch remained very much in evidence. When Ol' Roy, Walton's favorite bird dog who frequently accompanied him on trips to the stores, died in 1981, Walton announced his loss in the *Wal-Mart World* much as one would write to a friend.

As the 1970s drew to a close, Wal-Mart Stores could look back on ten years of remarkable retail success. In fiscal 1970 the company's eighteen Wal-Mart and fourteen Ben Franklin stores recorded $31 million in sales and generated $1.2 million in net income. Ten years later, the old variety stores were gone, and there were 276 Wal-Mart outlets. Sales had soared to $1.2 billion, making Wal-Mart the youngest retail firm in the United States to exceed $1 billion in sales and the only regional retailer to reach that volume. Net income was $41 million. During the decade, sales and earnings had increased at an annual compound rate of over 40 percent, a record that inspired admiration and pride among stockholders and associates and amazement among competitors and in the nation's financial centers. The 1970s were but a prelude to the 1980s, when Wal-Mart Stores continued its rapid growth, approached the status of a national discounter, adopted new formats that would place it in the forefront of mass merchandising, and challenged both K mart and Sears, Roebuck for the leading position among retailers in the United States.

Moving rapidly as the new decade opened, Wal-Mart in 1981 launched an expansion drive that confirmed its place as the fastest growing major retailer in the United States. In that year in a rare departure, Wal-Mart bought ninety-two Kuhn's Big K stores, which were headquartered in Nashville. Over the next two years, the company opened new stores, expanded existing ones, and brought the total number of outlets to 551 by January 1983. The firm's territory now stretched from Florida to Nebraska. Meanwhile, to insure an uninterrupted flow of goods to the stores, Wal-Mart expanded the number of distribution centers to six. This expansion early in the decade swelled Wal-Mart's net sales in fiscal 1983 to $3.4 billion and net income to $124 million. These figures would be dwarfed by later results.

The explanation of Wal-Mart's growth during the 1980s was simply the application on a broader scale of Sam Walton's approach to retailing, the double-edged sword of careful and efficient operation and shrewd location strategy. His demand for tight-as-a-tick efficiency permeated every aspect of the firm's operations. The firm's location strategy continued to rest upon towns and smaller cities that other major retailers ignored. As Walton wryly observed, "There's a lot more business in those communities than people thought."

While in the early 1980s Wal-Mart accelerated its expansion, it also embarked upon an ambitious diversification program involving three new retail concepts: dot Discount Drugs, Helen's Arts and Crafts, and Sam's Wholesale Clubs. The first two of these new ventures would ultimately fail to reach Wal-Mart's return-on-investment expectations, but the third new departure would prove to be remarkably successful.

Wholesale clubs were part of a new, rapidly growing retail category known as superstores. Designed to be one-stop shopping magnets, superstores were very large outlets that housed both traditional supermarket items and general merchandise under one roof. Wholesale clubs generally sold to members only. Their leading customers were small businesses, such as restaurants and convenience stores, which willingly paid some amount, usually twenty-five dollars annually, for the privilege of making small wholesale purchases more cheaply than they normally could from conventional wholesalers. Clubs also solicited memberships among select consumer groups such as employees of state and federal governments, schools, and hospitals.

Deep discounting, the basis of the wholesale club business, demanded the highest degree of efficiency of operation. Wholesale clubs bought directly from manufacturers and, by routinely ordering great quantities of merchandise, demanded and received huge volume discounts. Moreover, since clubs were often able to sell their merchandise before payment was due (usually within thirty days of receipt), they were able to operate with relatively little investment in inventory. Wherever possible, the handling of merchandise was mechanized.

The first Sam's Wholesale Club opened in Oklahoma City in April 1983. The outlets were patterned after the concept's originator, Price Club of San Diego, which established its first store in 1976. Sam's was strictly a no-frills operation that lacked such amenities as credit, sales clerks, eye-catching merchandise displays, and delivery. There was no advertising and a much smaller variety of goods than conventional discount stores carried. Sam's stores were located on sites that no conventional retailer would consider, but they boasted one undeniable appeal: quality, brand name products at rock bottom prices. One caveat, however, generally prevailed—customers had to purchase merchandise in large quantities.

Wal-Mart was pleased from the outset with its new format and promptly began its expansion. Launched in metropolitan centers in the South and the Southwest, by 1986 Sam's had moved into the Midwest and by 1989 was edging the company into new territory—the Northeast. The number of stores grew from 3 in 1983 to 129 in 1990, giving the firm more outlets than any of its competitors. They were located in twenty-six states. Sales in fiscal 1990 were $6.5 billion. By that year Sam's was threatening to overtake Price Club as the national leader in sales.

Wal-Mart's success and dominance in the small cities and towns of the rapidly growing Sun Belt convinced the company's executives that expansion into the remainder of the nation was not beyond the firm's capabilities if it continued to rely upon the proven formula of opening stores within an enlarged, four-hundred-mile radius of existing distribution centers. In its first step outside its regional base, in 1985 Wal-Mart built a distribution center in Mount Pleasant, Iowa, to serve stores in Illinois, Iowa, and Indiana. Location of distribution centers, in fact, had become the clearest indication of the company's plans for future expansion.

As its field of operations became more national in scope, Wal-Mart gave greater attention to major urban areas. The company's growing interest in more densely populated areas was manifest in the expanded size of its stores from an average of forty-seven thousand square feet in 1980 to sixty-three thousand in 1985. This increase reflected Wal-Mart's commitment to developing even larger stores in the eighty-five-thousand-square-foot range in order to enter urban markets.

Wal-Mart's rapid growth in urban areas was built solidly upon America's shifting demographic patterns. In order to achieve market saturation, Wal-Mart tackled larger cities by surrounding them with several suburban stores. Wal-Mart's president and chief operating officer, David D. Glass, put this strategy in perspective, explaining, "In our areas there is still flight from the inner cities to the suburbs. The suburbs have been and continue to be growth areas. For that reason, we have always surrounded cities."

Perhaps inspired by the success of Sam's Wholesale Clubs, Wal-Mart's appetite for experimentation was whetted by another form of superstore retailing—hypermarkets. Originated in 1962 by the French retail firm Carrefour, the concept took root in France and spread to a number of other European countries. Hypermarkets were significantly larger than wholesale clubs and combined full-scale supermarket offerings with a wide range of general merchandise categories, all of which were sold to the general public. In order to succeed, hypermarkets, strictly an urban concept, required within driving range a huge number of households earning an annual average income of twenty-five thousand to fifty-five thousand dollars. Several attempts at operating hypermarkets in the United States failed in the 1970s, and the idea lay virtually dormant until the nation's two leading discount chains, K mart and Wal-Mart, decided to give it a try in the late 1980s.

From 1987 through 1990 Wal-Mart opened four Hypermart USA

units, two in the Dallas suburbs of Garland and Arlington and one each in Topeka, Kansas, and Kansas City, Missouri. Wal-Mart hoped to attract customers to what would be the ultimate in one-stop shopping, especially with bargain-priced food. Despite the undeniable appeal to customers of prices as much as 40 percent below prevailing retail levels, the alarmingly high sales volume (estimated at eighty million to one hundred million dollars annually) required to break even placed the venture in jeopardy from the outset.

The concept foundered, moreover, because the 220,000-square-foot stores were, in the eyes of some customers, just too big. The experience of one fatigued customer at the Garland outlet was instructive. After roaming through the behemoth store, as big as five football fields, in search of Canada Dry Club Soda, which he could not find, and after waiting forty minutes to pay for his other groceries, he exclaimed, "I won't go back unless it shrinks."

Shrink it did, to nearly one-half its former size. And its name was the Wal-Mart Supercenter. Although Wal-Mart continued to operate its existing Hypermart USAs, by 1990 it had no plans to open any more. The firm was enthusiastic, however, about its third superstore venture, the Wal-Mart Supercenter, which appeared at roughly the same time. Like the Hypermart USA, the supercenter was a one-stop, combination grocery-and-discount-merchandise concept. Learning from its experiences with the unwieldy hypermarkets, Wal-Mart created a more practical and profitable format by scaling down the size of its supercenters.

The company opened its first supercenter in 1988 in Washington, Missouri, a town of ninety-two hundred some forty miles west of St. Louis. Though still officially in the experimental stage two years later, when there were three units in operation, Wal-Mart executives saw almost unlimited potential in the new format. The versatile supercenters, which were essentially complete Wal-Mart discount stores with full-fledged supermarkets under one roof, quickly proved themselves capable of fitting into the kinds of smaller communities where Wal-Mart already had an established presence. In fact, the company envisioned replacing some existing Wal-Mart stores with supercenters.

In addition to moving into new marketing formats, Wal-Mart took the lead during the 1980s in technological innovations that further enhanced the company's already legendary efficiency. In 1987 Wal-

Mart inaugurated a twenty-million-dollar satellite network for interstore data communication. Over this six-channel system Wal-Mart executives could broadcast rapidly changing inventory and other merchandise information as well as directives on store management on television from Bentonville to all stores. The system also gathered data for the company's master computer, handled credit card approvals, and tracked items in the company's complex distribution system.

One of the company's most interesting innovations was its so-called Buy American program, designed to replace foreign goods with domestic products. Realizing the stigma that imports had among rural Americans in general and southerners in particular, Sam Walton in 1985 sent an open letter to three thousand manufacturers in the United States inviting them to take part in a Buy American program and offering to work with them to produce goods that were competitive in price and quality with imports. While the program was based in part upon a strain of old-fashioned patriotism that was much in evidence at Wal-Mart, it was not simply a sentimental undertaking. The firm was interested in creating jobs in the United States, but the hard-bargaining company was not willing to subsidize inefficient American suppliers. Indeed, at times Wal-Mart shifted to foreign purchases when it became clear that American manufacturers could not compete.

Wal-Mart was quick to capitalize also on the growing sensitivity of American consumers to environmental issues. In 1989 the company took out full-page advertisements in the *Wall Street Journal* and *USA Today* that proclaimed, "We're looking for quality products that are guaranteed not to last." The advertisements went on to say that the company would feature in its stores the environmental improvements made by manufacturers with special signage alongside the products. Wal-Mart believed that the information would give shoppers a choice of purchasing environmentally improved products over those that were not.

Although admired by investors, customers, and employees, Wal-Mart in the 1980s had its share of detractors. The company was criticized for being too slow to promote women, which it denied; for employing too many part-time workers; and for yielding too quickly to the fulminations of televangelist Jimmy Swaggart against *Rolling Stone* magazine by banning the periodical from its store racks in 1986. Two other groups of outspoken critics were independent manufacturers sale representatives, who claimed that the firm's effort to deal directly with suppliers virtually eliminated their livelihood, and the owners of small stores, who complained that they were being driven out of business by Wal-Mart's "Everyday Low Prices."

In a broader context, the impact of Wal-Mart upon the small-town South was a matter of some dispute. Many southerners were grateful to Sam Walton for his willingness to serve the small, rural markets of the South that other major retailers had disdained. To these people Wal-Mart was more than a store; it was a symbol of progress and hope. Its founder was a genuine hero—a retail Elvis Presley—a southerner who had made it to the top while remaining faithful to his roots. "We've got a Wal-Mart, you know," town fathers across the South proudly proclaimed, as though its very presence suggested better days to come.

Yet there lurked in the minds of some the suspicion that Wal-Mart's impact on the small towns it inhabited was not as salutary as many believed. One thing is certain—when Wal-Mart arrived, it made its presence felt. Some local merchants went out of business; while the focal point of many communities, their once-bustling main streets, withered away, and with them a way of life. For example, in Leland, Mississippi, a sleepy Delta town of sixty-five hundred people, the local newspaper editor complained early in 1990 that after Wal-Mart arrived in two neighboring towns, the last department store in Leland vanished; and as a consequence, he could not buy a decent pair of socks in his hometown. On a more serious note, he argued that the old mom-and-pop stores were best for the rural South, since they kept more profits and salaries in the community, thus providing a larger tax base.

As Wal-Mart expanded outside its southern base, seemingly more and more towns became alarmed over its potentially negative impact. This growing concern made the "Wal-Marting of America" something of a cottage industry. Academicians at Iowa State University and the University of Missouri at Columbia studied the impact of Wal-Mart, and an owner of two clothing outlets in Nebraska towns near a Wal-Mart store became a popular speaker in the firm's new western territory, lecturing on how he survived the Wal-Mart juggernaut. That commentator maintained that the basic problems were Wal-Mart's buying power and its adverse impact on local business. "They do such a tremendous sales volume and their money leaves town almost immediately. That's money that may have circulated among several businesses in town, but now, once it's gone, it's gone." Another critic asserted that when Wal-Mart entered a small town, it invariably took a "big hunk out of the retail pie," and since, according to that individual, the size of the retail pie was virtually fixed, "somebody loses."

These and other spokesmen expressed valid concerns. That Wal-Mart forced some local firms out of business is undeniable, but on balance Wal-Mart no doubt serves the greater good. Country towns had been dying for decades before the huge discounter appeared on the scene. Its stores attracted customers in droves, and local enterprises that did not compete directly with Wal-Mart benefited significantly. Sales tax revenues invariably increased when Wal-Mart arrived in a town. From the outset, Sam Walton had insisted that his stores be good citizens in the communities they served, and Wal-Mart personnel did participate in community affairs. Most important, of course, was the firm's role as a discount retailer. In that role, it made accessible in several hundred communities a wide variety of reasonably priced goods that otherwise would not have been available. In fact, had conventional stores offered such goods at acceptable prices, firms like Wal-Mart would not have appeared.

Wal-Mart spokesmen proclaimed the 1980s the "most explosive decade of growth" in the company's history. Their evaluation was certainly accurate. By January 1990, the firm had 1,402 Wal-Mart discount stores, hypermarkets, and supercenters as well as 123 Sam's Wholesale Clubs. These outlets registered fiscal 1990 sales of $25.8 billion and net income of $1.1 billion. Ten years earlier, comparable figures were $1.2 billion and $41.2 million. The company's stores stretched from New Jersey to Wisconsin to Arizona, a total of twenty-nine states, and it was an open secret that Wal-Mart would soon be in New England and California. All observers expected Wal-Mart Stores to surge past K mart and Sears, Roebuck in the near future to become the nation's largest retailer.

Presiding over the firm in its decade of greatest growth was its founder, Sam Walton. He was no longer president and chief executive officer in 1990, having given up those positions earlier, but he continued as chairman of the board of directors, and there was little doubt that he remained the dominant figure in the company. During the decade, Walton and his company garnered a variety of industry and other awards for performance and excellence, and Walton, who along with his family owned about two-fifths of Wal-Mart Stores, Inc., became one of the wealthiest men in the United States. But Walton's significance lies not in his wealth but in what he built. Like the great entrepreneurs of the late nineteenth century who did so much to build modern America, this southern entrepreneur from the Arkansas Ozarks created a firm that would surely shape life in the United States far into the twenty-first century.